IMPERIAL FAULT LINES

IMPERIAL FAULT LINES

Christianity and Colonial Power in India,
1818–1940

Jeffrey Cox

STANFORD UNIVERSITY PRESS
STANFORD, CALIFORNIA

Stanford University Press
Stanford, California
© 2002 by the Board of Trustees of the
Leland Stanford Junior University
Printed in the United States of America

Library of Congress Cataloging-in-Publication Data

Cox, Jeffrey
   Imperial fault lines : Christianity and colonial power in India, 1818–
1940 / Jeffrey Cox.
     p.   cm.
   Includes bibliographical references and index.
   ISBN 0-8047-4318-5 (alk. paper).
    1. Missions—India—Punjab—History. 2. Punjab (India)—Church
history. 3. Missions—Pakistan—Punjab—History. 4. Punjab
(Pakistan)—Church history. I. Title.

BV3280.P8C69   2002
266'.00954'09034—dc21   2001057654

This book is printed on acid-free, archival quality paper.

Original printing 2002
Last figure below indicates year of this printing:
11   10   09   08   07   06   05   04   03   02

Typeset in 9.5/12.5 Trump Medieval

For My Parents

Acknowledgments

I have accumulated so many debts in the course of writing this book that I hesitate to mention anyone for fear of leaving out someone else equally important. My colleagues in the History Department at the University of Iowa have created a wonderful environment for a historian. They encouraged the launching of a new project, in a new field requiring language study and research trips to three continents, even with the knowledge that it would take a very long time. In the preface to his dictionary, Dr. Johnson lamented, "I have protracted my work till most of those whom I wished to please have sunk into the grave." That is the case, I am afraid, for two generous mentors: my undergraduate teacher at Rice, Charles Garside, and my graduate supervisor at Harvard, John Clive.

The University of Iowa central administration provided crucial financial support with a University of Iowa Faculty Scholarship. I also received generous financial assistance from an American Institute for Indian Studies travel grant, a National Endowment for the Humanities Travel to Collections Grant, and the Research Enablement Program, a grant program for mission scholarship supported by the Pew Charitable Trusts, Philadelphia, Pennsylvania, U.S.A., and administered by the Overseas Ministries Study Center, New Haven, Connecticut, U.S.A.

Rosemary Keen of the Church Missionary Society helped me learn about missionary archives, and was the first of several archivists and librarians who have provided valuable assistance along the way, including Father James Stewart, librarian of the Brotherhood of the Ascended Christ in Delhi, Major Jenty Fairbanks of the Salvation Army Archives in London, and Frederick J. Heuser of the Presbyterian Historical Society in Philadelphia. Philip Lutgendorf, Geeta Patel, and Latika Bhatnagar took on the herculean task of teaching me Hindi, and Scott Levi provided assistance in translating Urdu pamphlets and hymnbooks. During five research trips to South Asia I was treated to extraordinary displays of hospitality, particularly from Vinod Khiyalie and W. V. Roberts in Delhi, Itty Benjamin of Baring College in Batala, Yousaf G. Saroia of Narowal, K. N. Thakur Das of Srinigar, the staff of the Guest House of the Diocese of Lahore, and staff at the offices and hostels of the American Institute for Indian Studies in Calcutta and New Delhi.

I had many informative conversations in Pakistan and India, and would like to thank in particular the Rev. Frank Kair Ullah, the Rev. Ernest Tak, Brigadier Barkat Masih (ret.) of the Salvation Army, and Vivienne Stacey of Lahore; the Rev. Alexander J. Malik, bishop of Lahore; the Rev. Khair-ud-Din, bishop of Peshawar; the Rev. Peter Magal Das and Sardar Masih of Gujranwala; Bob and Ellen Alter and the Rev. I. B. Dass of Mussoorie; Mrs. Kamlesh Jacob, James Massey, and the Rev. Samuel Sundar Singh of Delhi; Principal Nazir Masih, secretary of the Christian Society for Health and Education of Shahpur, nr. Dhariwal; and Clarence McMullen, Rajiv McMullen, and Principal R. M. Chawdhry of Baring College, Batala. In Iowa, I had the good fortune to meet Veeda Javaid, executive director, Presbyterian Education Board, Presbyterian Church of Pakistan, and Wilbur Thoburn, former professor of physics at Forman Christian College in Lahore. Mary Beth Dewey of Iowa City provided me with much useful information about the history of the United Presbyterian Church of North America; Bishop Michael Nazir Ali among others helped my understanding of Punjabi hymnody.

Andrew Porter provided a forum for my evolving views over the years at the Imperial and Commonwealth History Seminar at the Institute for Historical Research in London, and Alan Argent invited me to speak to sessions of the 1662 Society. R. K. Webb, R. E. Frykenberg, Hugh McLeod, and Susan Pedersen each took a sympathetic and encouraging interest in this project, and Janaka Nair, Antoinette Burton, and Jane Giscombe provided particularly helpful comments after hearing seminar or conference presentations. I have had many stimulating conversations about the role of religion in modern history with Roger Draper. Geeta Patel, Daud Ali, Saurubh Dube, Philip Lutgendorf, and Rosemary Fitzgerald read and commented on parts of the manuscript, and Kate Luongo and Susan Thorne read and commented on all of it

Some parts of this book appeared earlier in "Independent English Women in Delhi and Lahore," *Religion and Irreligion in Victorian Society: Essays in Honor of R. K. Webb*, edited by R. W. Davis and R. J. Helmstadter (London: Routledge, 1992); "Audience and Exclusion at the Margins of Imperial History," *Women's History Review* 3, no. 4 (1994): 501–14; and "George Alfred Lefroy: Anglicans, Untouchables, and Imperial Institutions," in *After the Victorians: Essays in Honor of John Clive*, edited by Susan Pedersen and Peter Mandler (London: Routledge, 1994). The entire book was written with a wonderful software program for scholars, Nota Bene.

My greatest debt is to my family. My parents, Jack and Lillian Cox of Teague, Texas, have been bastions of support and encouragement throughout my life, and this book is dedicated to them. Neither of my children, Flossie and David, was born when I began my research on this project; both are now teenagers. I owe a special debt of gratitude to Marilyn Adam and the staff of Small World Day Care Center, who so capably looked after my children before they started school. My wife, Lois, has put up with the large inconveniences imposed on our family by my research trips. Without her partnership, the book would never have been completed.

Jeffrey Cox

Contents

Tables

IMPERIAL FAULT LINES

1

Master Narratives of Religion and Empire

This is a book about missionaries and the people they encountered in colonial India. When I embarked upon this research project, I intended to study the workings of the missionary movement in Britain, an important but at that time neglected topic.[1] In the course of my reading, however, I became more interested in the relationships that missionaries entered into upon leaving Britain. When I wandered into the Church Missionary Society (CMS) headquarters in South London and innocently inquired about information on missionaries, perhaps in India, their helpful and efficient archivist, Rosemary Keen, directed me to their well-organized records of the CMS mission in Punjab. Those records were so absorbing and illuminating that six months later I was still reading them.

The CMS was the largest and in many ways the most influential of several important missionary societies. For several decades in the late nineteenth century the Rev. Robert Clark, head of the CMS Punjab mission, sent regular monthly reports to the CMS home office (the "Parent Committee"). Wrapped inside each letter was a packet containing anything he thought might be of interest to his employers: blueprints for new missionary bungalows, anti-missionary letters from the *Lahore Civil and Military Gazette,* nationalist attacks on the missionary movement, notes of praise from officials of the Indian Civil Service, Urdu evangelistic pamphlets in Latin script. Clark was at the center of a large group of missionary institutions not only in Amritsar but also throughout Punjab; his papers provided insight into multiple points of view. Hoping to write a book quickly, and heedless of Sir Lewis Namier's warning that the young are deficient in a sense of time,[2] little did I know that this was only the beginning of a research project that would lead me into trips to Delhi, Lahore, Srinigar, and Peshawar, undergraduate classes in Hindi at the University of Iowa, and a lengthy engagement with historians, literary critics, and anthropologists who were rethinking issues of race, class, and gender in a colonial setting. Nor did I foresee that the project would require an in-

TABLE I

Mission Societies with Abbreviations

AP	Presbyterian Church in the U.S.A.	MLI	Mission to Lepers in India
ARPM	Associate Reformed Presbyterian Mission	MOR	Moravians
		NMS	National Missionary Society (Indian)
BFBS	British and Foreign Bible Society	NZPM	New Zealand Presbyterian Mission
BMS	Baptist Missionary Society	PRBS	Punjab Religious Book Society
BZMS	Baptist Zenana Missionary Society		
		RC	Roman Catholic
CAM	Central Asian Mission	SA	Salvation Army
CECMS	Church of England in Canada Missionary Society	SDA	Seventh Day Adventists
		SPCK	Society for the Promotion of Christian Knowledge (Anglican)
CEZMS	Church of England Zenana Missionary Society		
CMD	Cambridge Mission to Delhi	SPG	Society for the Propagation of the Gospel (Anglican)
CMML	Christian Missions in Many Lands ("Open" Brethren)	UFM	Unevangelized Fields Mission
CMS	Church Missionary Society (Anglican)	UP	United Presbyterian Church of North America
CS	Church of Scotland	WEC	World Evangelization Crusade
DPM	Danish Pathan Mission		
ESPBI	Evangelical Society of the Pittsburgh Bible Institute	YMCA	The Young Men's Christian Association
FES	Female Education Society		
IFNS	Indian Female Normal School	YWCA	The Young Women's Christians Association
INWN	India North West Mission	ZBMM	Zenana Bible and Medical Mission
ME	Methodist Episcopal Church North		

quiry into the now largely forgotten history of the United Presbyterian Church, which once flourished in the American Midwest but now survives only in Pakistan.[3]

In the late nineteenth century, Punjab encompassed much of what is now northern Pakistan and northwest India (including Delhi). Although subject to Christian influences at various times, including well-documented Jesuit attempts to influence the Mughal court,[4] this part of the world contained as a practical matter no Christians at all at the beginning of the nineteenth century. By the beginning of the twentieth century, however, the Punjab and its Himalayan hinterlands had been the scene of major efforts by missionary societies representing the principal Protestant denominations of both Great Britain and the United States: evangelical and high church Anglicans; the established church of Scotland; two competing groups of American Presbyterians; American Methodists; British Baptists; and the Salvation Army—as well as Roman Catholics (mostly Flemish speaking). Smaller missions followed in their train, and in the early twentieth century (the heyday of foreign mission work in India) more than thirty societies were at work alongside innumerable private individuals and small groups of locally based philanthropists and missionaries (see Table 1).

Historians respect documentation, and each missionary society left a paper trail of bureaucratic and personal evidence running (in some cases) into millions of words. Although historians of empire and South Asia think naturally of a "missionary movement" in India, the documentation is heavily denominational, reflecting the proliferation of distinct and often inward-looking voluntary societies and denominations as the characteristic form of nineteenth-century Protestant church expansion. The inaugural narratives of missionary activity in India are equally denominational, created as they were simultaneously with the archival and documentary evidence. As a pioneer missionary in Punjab, Robert Clark of the CMS had control over not only the administration of a large mission but also the documentary material that provides the basis for its history. In his stories of western religion abroad, and in the stories of other pioneer missionaries as well, ordained male missionaries appear to be operating in a kind of vacuum, interacting with each other but not with other people—many of them female Europeans and female and male Indians—who were known to be on the scene.

Clark was obviously more interested in issues of boundary demarcation with other missionary societies than in exploring issues of race, class, and gender (although, as we shall see, those issues of necessity became central concerns of his mission). For instance, his account of a serious conflict in the 1880s with missionaries of United Presbyterian of North America (UP) contains a refutation of a contrasting contemporary narrative of missions in Punjab. Both missionary societies had been at work in the Punjab heartland since the early 1850s with very meager results, if results are defined by the number of Indian Christians. But in the 1880s thousands of Indian men, and some Indian women, began to demand baptism from missionaries in central Punjab. One UP missionary, the Rev. Samuel Martin, attributed this development, not to Indian initiative, but to the Holy Spirit, and began a series of emotion-laden tours of the countryside near Narowal, baptizing thousands of people a year.[5]

The CMS missionary in Narowal, the Rev. Rowland Bateman, had a university degree, a passion for souls, and a willingness to do what was necessary to win them. Leaving his wife in Britain, he attempted to adopt an Indian lifestyle, or at least his version of one. He extended his

influence over young, unmarried men of the district through a combination of Indian dress, a cricket league, and tactful encouragement of
conversion. Over the anguished objections of some members of their
families, a group of young Indian men, some of them Christian, would
accompany him as he donned Indian dress, mounted his camel, and
conducted village itineration.[6]

Although unorthodox by the standards of English clerical missionaries, most of whom would regard it as inappropriate to wear a turban
and attempt to alienate young men from their families in such a direct
way, Bateman shared with his Church of England colleagues a strong
belief in church order. Virtually all Anglican missionaries believed
that the key to Christianizing India lay in the creation of an educated,
upper-class Christian elite that would use its paternalistic influence to
Christianize and moralize subordinate classes. Consequently, Bateman
objected strenuously when an American evangelical fanatic began baptizing thousands of village laborers in "his" territory, and he objected
even more bitterly when the UP missionaries claimed that the Holy
Spirit had instructed them to evangelize the members of stigmatized
communities who had been purposefully neglected by the CMS.[7] Bateman persuaded the CMS Parent Committee in London to complain to
the United Presbyterian Mission in Philadelphia, who in turn instructed Martin to hand over "his" converts to Bateman. Martin com-
plied, fully confident that the CMS was, in spiritual terms, too cold to
do anything with them and that the Holy Spirit would be vindicated
before long.

Bateman and Clark presented this story as one of proper standards
of professional behavior for a missionary. Bateman scribbled in the
margins of one UP resolution a note expressing his view that the Holy
Spirit never instructed anyone to violate a gentleman's agreement.[8]
Anglican clergymen did not evangelize England from the bottom up,
and Anglican missionaries had no intention of evangelizing India that
way. Bateman took his new and largely illiterate following in hand, firing schoolmasters and catechists who could not repeat the Apostle's
Creed, excommunicating and expelling ordinary believers who could
not repeat the Lord's Prayer. But even these tactics could not prevent
the villagers from identifying themselves as Christians. Later, when
the CMS discovered that these "mass movements" could be discussed
to their rhetorical advantage, and after Bateman came to terms with
his ongoing pastoral responsibilities for a low-status Christian community, the growth of Christianity around Narowal was attributed in
CMS narratives to Bateman's initiative. This is the familiar (and an-

noying) trope of mission history: missionary initiative and indigenous response. United Presbyterian narratives, however, although always giving pride of place to the Holy Spirit, admitted Indian initiative on an equal basis with American agency. An Indian dealer in hides named Ditt was identified in the earliest narratives as the coinitiator of this revival, along with Samuel Martin, and in later narratives as the sole initiator. Unlike many Indian Christians who appear in missionary narratives, Ditt was at least named, but it is very difficult to find out anything about him from missionary records. Even in the initial UP narrative (which unlike early CMS accounts never treated untouchables as an embarrassment), Ditt's agency is displaced onto the Holy Spirit.[9]

It is not only Indian Christians who are marginalized in many of these stories; European and Indian women often do not appear at all. Feminist scholars, and historians of missionary women, have done particularly good work in calling attention to the multiple levels of inclusion and exclusion to be found in historical narratives and master narratives.[10] Pioneer missionaries like Clark and Bateman lived apart from their wives and families for long periods, but as travel became easier with the advent of steamships, Protestant missionaries in Punjab began to live as married missionary couples. Missionary wives were missionaries too, but there was little record of their activities until the late nineteenth century.[11] With the advent of large numbers of unmarried missionary women in the 1880s and 1890s, the mission societies began counting all women, including married women, as missionaries. Even then, the "adjunct" role assigned to women, married or unmarried, continued to be reproduced in missionary narratives. By the turn of the century the missionary contingent in Punjab was 60 percent female, but "women's work" was often tacked on at the end of the published histories of the various missions.[12]

Interpreting missionary records requires constant attention to the multiple levels of exclusion in the narratives, including the narratives constituted by statistics. Even recent scholarship on missionaries often fails to emphasize a central point in mission history: a solid majority of all missionaries in the late nineteenth century were female. Male clerical missionaries lived in constant and close daily contact with their missionary wives and daughters who played central roles in the mission enterprise. From the 1880s and 1890s, married male and female missionaries lived in close daily contact with unmarried women missionaries who came in large numbers, and transformed almost every mission in the Punjab into a predominantly female organization.

A second major point is often ignored: in the institutions created by missionaries, Europeans were heavily outnumbered by Indians—Christian and non-Christian. Women missionaries interacted daily with Indian women, either Christian converts or the objects of zenana visitation, or, later, students and patients in mission institutions. Male missionaries lived in regular daily contact with Indian Christians, first small groups of urban professionals who began to tell their own version of the Christian history of Punjab, and then large numbers of mostly rural converts whose point of view must be reconstructed, respectfully and with great caution, by reading between the lines. The early missionary narratives tell stories of ordained missionaries living in isolation, creating institutions where nameless women arrived to assist, calling into existence Indian churches peopled by nameless Indian coreligionists who then proved unsatisfactory or recalcitrant, or surprisingly spiritual. These stories are for the most part unpersuasive and in many cases unintelligible, unless analyzed with an eye on the assumptions that pioneer male missionaries brought with them, and their rhetorical purposes and intended audience in Great Britain and the United States.

This is not a comprehensive history of missionary work in Punjab. It is a study of how missionaries in the most important mission societies, and those with whom they associated, Indian Christians and non-Christians, struggled with the conflict between universalist Christian religious values and the imperial context of those values. One audience might describe this relationship as a conflict between faith and power; another as the relationship between universal egalitarian ideals and an exploitative imperial presence.

When presenting papers on missions in India, I have received some comments and criticism that reflect an understandable desire to see this story told from an Indian point of view, either as a social history of the Indian Christian community or as an accounting of the missionary impact on Indian society. This book contributes to both of those. I have learned enough of South Asian languages to gain an appreciation of Hindi hymnody and Urdu psalmody,[13] to carry on elementary conversations during research trips to South Asia, and to decipher vernacular missionary tracts. I have also been fortunate to have at my disposal the extremely valuable work on the missionary impact on north Indian Islamic communities by Avril Powell and Gail Minault, on Sikh communities by J. S. Grewal, and on sections of Punjabi Hinduism by Ken Jones.[14] These scholars make it clear that the missionary impact went far beyond the new ideas they brought with them, interesting as those ideas were to Muslim controversialists in particular. It was the presence of mission institutions that set off the most profound Indian reaction to the mission presence.

It is impossible to tell the story of missionaries without paying constant attention to the point of view of other players: British imperial administrators, non-Christian Indians who come into the orbit of missionary institutions or react to them from the outside, and (especially) Indian Christians. Recent works by Gauri Viswanathan and Saurubh Dube have greatly strengthened our understanding of the diversity of Indian Christianity, as has the recent biography of Bishop Azariah by Susan Billington Harper.[15] Reacting with good reason against the old missionary history trope of agency/response, these authors are not primarily interested in missionary motives and deal only with certain aspects of their impact. The missionary presence in India is in some ways taken for granted. Any history of the impact of Christianity in India depends on a scholarly, critical understanding of the history of missionaries, just as a history of modern India or Pakistan depends on a clear understanding of the missionary role in creating institutions under colonial rule.

Missionaries have played important but little understood roles in the histories of imperialism and of South Asia, not to mention the western imperialist nations. Several recent and valuable books have been devoted to the views of missionaries in India on Islam, Hinduism, and the Indian national movement.[16] Just as missionaries were far more than itinerant evangelists, they were also far more than comparative religionists or political analysts. The missionary encounter occurred first of all as part of the inner life of mission institutions.

IMPERIAL HISTORY AND THE
PRESUMPTION OF MARGINALITY

The telling of a scholarly story about missionaries presents some daunting intellectual difficulties, not merely of documentary and textual interpretation but also of defining a point of view from which to tell the story, and finding ways to persuade diverse audiences to challenge their own presuppositions about missionaries. The image of an itinerant evangelist in a pith helmet, often portrayed in a comic mode, is deeply ingrained in popular culture, and very misleading. The overwhelming majority of missionaries were not wandering preachers in search of converts but institution-builders presiding over churches, schools, and hospitals. A typical missionary in the late nineteenth century, not only in Punjab but everywhere, was not a male itinerant preacher but a female schoolteacher or administrator. The encounter of missionaries with Indians occurred, not in the open air, but mainly in an institutional setting. It is worthwhile also to examine closely the missionary encounters that occurred where missionaries interacted with Indians daily.

The comic mode is only one manifestation of a larger obstacle to understanding missionaries: the presumption of marginality found in mainstream imperial history and literature. One need only think of the portrayal of missionaries in Kipling's *Kim*, or in Rider Haggard's *She*, to see the centrality of explorers, scholars, military officers, merchants, and imperial administrators, and the marginality of missionaries, in narratives of the imperial enterprise. Lamin Sanneh, Susan Billington Harper, and other explicitly Christian scholars have attributed the hostility to, or marginalization of, Christianity in historical scholarship to the secular bias of the western academy. Anyone who has dealt with religious issues in scholarly circles will recognize the force of that argument, but the issue is far more complicated than simple political or religious bias.[17] The presumption of marginality is difficult to circumvent, and often resistant to simple assertions that "missionaries were important," in part because it is imbedded in a master narrative of imperial and western expansion that leaves little room for religion, much less for missionaries. I am using the phrase "master narrative" in a straightforward and pragmatic sense to classify the scale of a narrative. A master narrative is a big story that makes smaller stories intelligible. Because it is a master narrative it is often partly hidden, lying in the background to be deployed selectively by the historian, and brought into play to explain things that can not be dealt with explicitly.

Writing in the *Edinburgh Review* in 1807, Sydney Smith described the Baptist missionaries in Bengal as "little detachments of maniacs."[18] He was defining an attitude toward missionaries that persisted throughout the colonial period in the imperial establishment, among the explorers, scholars, military officers, merchants, and imperial administrators who regarded their mission as central. On the whole, the presumption of marginality, if not of insanity, has been carried over from the imperial establishment into the imperial history that they fostered, a history that is undergoing an interesting resurgence.[19]

In the large body of scholarly writing on missionaries, every historian has had to grapple in one way or another with the presumption of marginality in the master narratives of mainstream imperial history.

Andrew Porter, for instance, has reminded us in more than one article and chapter that missionaries have a history, and that there is little point in generalizing about them on the assumption that they are agents of a timeless, monolithic structure with a fixed relationship to western culture and other cultures.[20] Historians have analyzed the role of women in the history of American and Canadian missions, and new work is being done on British missions.[21] But the presumption of marginality is so deeply rooted in the prevailing master narrative of imperial history that it is still common to come upon major monographs in imperial history, on subjects where one would assume that missionaries might be important, only to find them marginalized or ignored altogether. Recent books by Mark Harrison and David Arnold on public health in India, for instance, deal obsessively with state and secular bureaucracies. Although acknowledging that missionaries were there, and must have been important, they leave them off the stage, and along with them the large number of Indians who encountered some form of western medicine in a missionary setting.[22]

Nationalist writers upon occasion turned their attention to missionaries in order to expose them as imperial functionaries.[23] The presumption of marginality has been carried over into nationalist history, which as Partha Chatterjee has argued was often constructed on the terms of the imperial history it rejected, creating an imperialist/nationalist master narrative of western intrusion and heroic nationalist response.[24] Not only nationalist history but also subaltern history,[25] and postcolonial imperial history,[26] often share with imperial history the presumption of marginality. The new and important emphasis on the state, and on state power, has the effect of further marginalizing missionaries in voluntary societies. Imran Ali's highly illuminating *The Punjab under Imperialism, 1885–1947* acknowledges the importance of missionaries in the story of Punjab's famous canal colonies, but the focus remains on those judged central to imperialism, the imperial administrators, jurists, and engineers.[27]

THE SAIDIAN MASTER NARRATIVE

Overlapping with and inextricable from the traditions of imperial history and its successors is a long tradition of anti-imperialist unmasking of the supposedly neutral and universal western forms of scholarship, science, and religion, designed to expose their imperial complicity. Looming over recent work in this tradition, whether acknowledged or not, is that of Edward Said,[28] who has accomplished a sustained and persuasive analysis of the imperial complicity of western scholarship about the nonwestern world that has been very difficult for critics to dislodge.[29] The Saidian approach to imperialism is sufficiently powerful to constitute an alternative master narrative in its approach to imperialism, a master narrative of unmasking. But what is it possible to say about missionaries within the Saidian framework? In the rhetoric of unmasking that characterizes the Saidian master narratives, missionaries are often regarded as hardly worth exposing. In his study of the Boxer Rebellion, for instance, Joseph Esherick takes missionary complicity so completely for granted that he uses statistics of conversion to Christianity as an index of imperial aggression.[30] Added to the presumption of marginality is the presumption of imperial complicity, but it is a complicity often assumed rather than analyzed, interpreted, or explained. Missionaries are, as Ranajit Guha put it in *Subaltern Studies*, one of the "dominant foreign groups" such as "British officials of the colonial state and foreign industrialists, merchants, financiers, planters, landlords and missionaries."[31] The missionary role is predetermined.

The best sustained, recent unmaskings of missionaries deal with Africa, and may be found in the work of T. O. Beidelman and Jean and John L. Comaroff.[32] Beidelman tells the story of evangelical Anglican missionaries in East Africa, arguing that their activity was simply imperialism by other means. He states that "Christian missions represent the most naive and ethnocentric, and therefore the most thoroughgoing facet of colonial life. . . . Missionaries invariably aimed at overall changes in the beliefs and actions of native peoples, at colonization of heart and mind as well as body. Pursuing this sustained policy of change, missionaries demonstrated a more radical and morally intense commitment to rule than political administrators or business men."[33] The Comaroffs' masterful volumes on the appropriation of Christianity in South Africa remain caught in the binarisms of collaboration and resistance. When Africans collaborate with missionaries, their minds are being colonized by the west. They can be Africans only when using Christianity to resist missionary imperialism.

Stories such as Beidelman's and the Comaroffs' define clearly the presuppositions of a Saidian master narrative of unmasking: missionaries were, simply, imperialists; if different from other imperialists, it is because they were marginal, or because they were worse. If missionaries are to be interpreted, it is through the rhetoric of unmasking. This point is made explicitly by the Comaroffs, who invoke a rhetoric of unmasking as a defense against a postmodernist critique of the colonialist character of all western scholarship: "If the discipline can unmask anything unique about the nature of the human condition—of colonialism and consciousness, of domination and resistance, of oppression and liberation—it is both possible and worthwhile."[34] Such presuppositions provide a rhetorical challenge for anyone interested in taking missionaries seriously; they also provide a political challenge. Edward Said's assertion that "one cannot be neutral about imperialism: one is either for it or against it" is a comment on the politics of scholarship that raises serious questions for historians of religion in an imperial setting, and for my own study of missions in Punjab.[35]

To put the Saidian challenge in a more straightforward way: is it possible to address the complicated story of the relationship of western religion and imperialism without becoming entangled in the celebratory categories that have defined the problem in the past, or catering to nostalgia for imperialist gratification? Are scholars of imperialism not merely unwitting celebrators of westernization but (as Jean and John Comaroff ask) an integral part of the imperialist project by virtue of being scholars?[36]

THE PROVIDENTIALIST MASTER NARRATIVE

How have scholars with sympathy for the missionary enterprise addressed these moral and political dilemmas? The field of mission studies is notable for the very large scale of the enterprise,[37] the very high quality of much of its work,[38] and its near invisibility to scholars in other fields such as imperial history, the nationalist histories of many formerly colonized nations, and western postcolonial studies. This invisibility persists despite the fact that mission studies has gone well beyond the essentially celebratory framework established in the multivolume works published in the 1940s and 1950s by Kenneth Scott Latourette.[39] Within mission studies there is a tradition of criticism of missionaries in order to improve them, or in order to teach a new generation of missionaries to avoid past mistakes (usually of racism or ethnocentrism or paternalism), or to chastise missionaries for their abundantly evident sins, usually of pride. The field is open to a diversity of critical voices; mission studies scholars are committed to high standards of fairness, documentation, and scholarly distance; there has been in mission studies a heavy emphasis upon nonwestern agency and a sustained attempt to promote history from a nonwestern point of view.[40]

Despite these achievements, mission studies scholars continue to rely on a providentialist master narrative of progress toward a multiracial Christian community, and have some difficulty in addressing head-on the Saidian presumption of imperial complicity.[41] Two evangelical Protestant scholars, Brian Stanley and Lamin O. Sanneh, have in recent books confronted directly the issue of missions and imperialism.[42] In *The Bible and the Flag*, Stanley provides an engaged overview of missionary history, and a valuable account of the history of the anti-imperial critique of the missionary movement. But his attempt to absolve missionaries from imperial complicity rests on the straightforward assertion that their motives were fundamentally distinct from those who were at the heart of the imperial enterprise: military officers, government officials, merchants, and scholars. The argument is put in an even more straightforward form by R. E. Frykenberg, who argues that, in India, "[at] no time were the majority of missionaries . . . predisposed in favor of colonialism."[43]

Both Stanley and Frykenberg are correct to draw attention to the distinction between missionary motives and those of others in the imperial enterprise. Andrew Porter, in his study of the relationship between missionaries and imperial governments, has identified a variety of different relationships determined by particular circumstances, but notes that "the original missionary sense of self-sufficiency, their disdain or suspicion of imperial politics and government, constantly resurfaced."[44] Furthermore, the majority of missionaries did not see their primary task, as missionaries, either as the spreading of western civilization throughout the world or as the maintenance of western domination and control of nonwesterners. Those might be necessary tasks for a missionary as a good citizen, but not as a Christian missionary. But Stanley's argument only begins to address the complexity of this question. Missionaries, as Beidelman and the Comaroffs have demonstrated beyond any doubt, were often deeply implicated in systems of imperial coercion and control. Far from being merely entangled with imperialism, they were active participants in the enterprise.

Lamin Sanneh's *Encountering the West* has received considerable attention in the field of missionary studies, dealing with the issue of imperialism in another way. Sanneh argues that Christianity is translatable into other cultures, indeed uniquely translatable among the universal world religions, because of the mutable and much-translated character of the Christian Bible. Resting his argument on the legitimacy of indigenous African Christianity, Sanneh implies that missionaries were a small part of a much larger expansion of Christianity that was at heart indigenous and nonwestern. The field of African church history has become sufficiently broad and sophisticated to make it clear to anyone that the old model of missionary agency and nonwestern response is entirely inadequate. Missionaries were obviously part of a much larger process of religious change that in many cases was entirely beyond the control, or even the knowledge, of western Christian agents.

Sanneh's extensive emphasis upon nonwestern agency leaves us with a muddled picture of the role of missionaries. At times Sanneh treats them as bearers of a western culture that is then translated; at times they are treated as cotranslators with African Christians. One of the consequences of a strong distinction between illegitimate western religion and legitimate nonwestern religion, as Norman Etherington has pointed out, is to further marginalize missionaries in the field of church history itself.[45] African Christians are, in effect, subalterns. Their role is to bring in an inauthentic western religion, which is then taken over by nonwesterners and made authentic.[46] Some African church history, for intelligible reasons, replicates the presumption of marginality and the presumption of imperial complicity in its treatment of foreign missionaries, ignoring the inconvenient presence of missionaries who were extremely important to the communities of nonwestern people "naturalizing" western religion.

IMPERIALISM AS A RELIGIOUS PROBLEM

Both Stanley and Sanneh are wrestling with a central issue—that is, the essential contradiction between the realities of western imperialism and the missionary aspiration to create what Jean and John Comaroff refer to as "the multiracial Christian commonwealth of missionary fantasy."[47] There is a curious parallel in Edward Said's sketchy but interesting two pages on the missionary legacy in *Culture and Imperialism*, where he discusses one aspect of the historical situation of his own community, Arab Protestantism. This community he describes as resulting from "imperial competition for converts and constituents," which created a community that "acquired their own identities and traditions, their own institutions, all of which without exception played an honorable role during the period of the Arab Renaissance."[48] Said describes the "aggrieved sensibilities" of this community as they now, having been created as separate denominations, find themselves under pressure from western denominations to merge into one ecumenical denomination, erasing the separate and presumably authentic identities that had emerged over the course of a century.

What is interesting is Said's fleeting recognition of the contradictory nature of the missionary relationship to imperialism: "One should note that this touching story concerns an experience of imperialism that is essentially one of sympathy and congruence, not of antagonism, resentment, or resistance. The appeal by one of the parties was to the value of a *mutual experience*. True, there had once been a principal and a subordinate, but there had also been dialogue and communication."[49] Before reaching the end of the paragraph, however, Said reverts to his analysis of the structural impermeability of imperialism: "The implicit argument made by the western missionary authorities was that the Arabs had gotten something valuable out of what had been given them, but in this relationship of historical dependence and subordination, all the giving went one way, the value was mainly on one side. Mutuality was considered to be basically impossible."[50] Before completing this discussion, Said refers to the need to "get beyond the reified polarities of East versus West," but it appears that he has glimpsed that possibility in his discussion of Arab Protestantism, only to pull back decisively from the brink. We are allowed only glimpses of interpretive categories that will allow us to focus on "mutual experience" or "dialogue and communication" in the imperial relationship. Instead we are left with missionaries trapped in a structure in which, in Said's words, "[it] is therefore correct [to state that] every [nineteenth-century] European, in what he could say about the Orient, was consequently a racist, an imperialist, and almost totally ethnocentric."[51]

We appear to be left with three points of view on missionaries embedded in distinct if overlapping master narratives: the imperialist/nationalist with its presumption of marginality, the Saidian with its unmasking of imperial complicity, and the providentialist with its difficulties in confronting the imperial character of the missionary enterprise. Some scholars sprawl across all three; others succeed in working successfully within one; still others (including Said) have argued for categories that transcend the rigid polarities of both imperialist and postcolonial scholarship through a redefinition of the boundaries between empire and nonempire. One attempt to conceptualize alternative forms of interpretation is Homi Bhabha's intriguing study of an early encounter in North India that has the virtue of focusing on western religion.[52] Bhabha invoked the concept of "hybridity" in order to focus on authentic, if ambiguous, nonwestern encounters with imperialism. Also concerned with authenticity in her study of western science with some obvious implications for the study of western religion,

Mary Louise Pratt unmasks its universalist narratives of anticonquest and focuses on the need to sidestep standards of authenticity in interpreting nonwestern responses to western culture.[53]

Pratt refers to what she called contact zones: "social spaces where disparate cultures meet, clash and grapple with each other, often in highly asymmetrical relations of domination and subordination—like colonialism, slavery or their aftermaths as they are lived out across the globe today."[54] She is interested in "transculturation," a "term to describe how subordinated or marginal groups select and invent from materials transmitted to them by a dominant or metropolitan culture."[55] But the interpretive schemes of both Bhabha and Pratt remain within the Saidian bipolar framework where the role of missionaries is preordained. They are the others from which nonwesterners "select and invent." Pratt concedes that expressions of sympathy, respect, love, and concern for nonwestern people can be encompassed in western imperial literature, but only in the form of a "concessionary narrative," one that "goes some way towards recognizing a native point of view and offering a critique of European behavior, but can only do this by not addressing the central issue."[56] Ditt can be freed from the taint of imperial collaboration and appropriate Christianity in an act of hybridity, but Bateman and Clark cannot escape the stigma of imperial manipulation, the desire to carry out Macaulay's famous aspiration enunciated in his minute on Indian education of 1835 to create "a class of persons Indian in blood and colour, but English in taste, in opinions, in morals, and in intellect."[57] A missionary in this master narrative can be many things, but never a subaltern.

Looked at from the inside, from the world built by missionaries, Christian Indians, and non-Christian Indians, there are multiple stories, some of them encompassing Said's mutual experience of dialogue and communication. Not only do Indians select and invent from an "other"; they also cooperate with the others (as Said briefly recognizes) in selecting and inventing together. Missionaries and Indian Christians were in many respects engaged in a common enterprise, creating something new that was neither European nor Indian but simultaneously indigenous, foreign, and hybrid. Furthermore, missionaries in India were important to Indians, and in some circumstances were, and remain, respected and admired figures in the Indian Christian community and in the collective memory of educational and medical institutions that they helped to build. Missionaries also found themselves in a zone of "transculturation."

It takes very little acquaintance with the records of missionary encounters with non-Europeans in Punjab to see the force of Edward Said's (implied) argument that every missionary, like every other European, was a racist, an imperialist, and almost totally ethnocentric. Side by side with those attitudes are touching expressions of sympathy, respect, and an often surprisingly vigorous opposition to racism as they understood it. Many missionaries managed to be racist and anti-racist simultaneously. But even more important than the *quantity* of liberal attitudes was the desire to build a common community, one that went even beyond the question asked in *A Passage to India*: "Why can't we be friends now?"[58] The question was, from a missionary and Indian Christian point of view, even more momentous: can we participate in a shared faith, on the basis of spiritual equality, in an imperial setting? The master narratives of unmasking and providence both presuppose an answer to that question. I hope to tell this story without assuming that there was a natural path to either success or failure.

I have no key to all master narratives that will unlock the secrets of missionary encounters in Punjab, and I am deeply indebted to those scholars who have wrestled with these issues from different points of view. The books of Billie Melman and Kumari Jayawardena, setting missionaries in the context of other imperial women in the Middle East and South Asia, respectively, have provided models of ways to grapple with binary thinking about imperial history.[59] Furthermore, the question of imperialism, and the related struggles with issues of race, class, and gender, are not anachronistic concerns imposed on nineteenth-century people by later scholars. Indian Christians and missionaries alike recognized the dilemma of reconciling a universal faith with the realities of cultural imperialism. At the 1898 yearly meeting of the Punjab Church Council, a body established as a forum for CMS Indian Christians to speak to each other and to foreign missionaries, the Rev. Wadhawa Mall observed: "Not only the Gospel but English ways and wealth have come with them into this country. Thus we have two gospels here; that of our Lord Jesus Christ, and that of English customs. Now we are between two stones of a grinding mill. Christ's gospel and His Spirit in us press us on one side; on the other English civilization. Which shall we choose?"[60] The Rev. Wadhawa Mall was not speaking, as it might appear, about an indigenous Indian Christianity independent of missionaries. He spent his entire life working with missionaries to create an indigenous Indian Christianity. His dilemma was all the greater for being an Indian rather than a foreigner, but the task he identified was a common task for foreign missionaries and Indian Christians.

Imperialism was not a timeless structure, but a relationship that people recognized, although not necessarily in the way that we recognize it. Many missionaries thought of their own trip to India as "by love compelled,"[61] only to find that their presence was regarded in a very different light, not only by outside critics but also by Indian Christian critics. Indian Christians continued to hope for mutuality and dialog in the face of what appeared to be hypocritical missionary assertions of power and thoughtless rudeness and insensitivity. When the Indian Christian clergyman Samuel Azariah (later to become the first Indian Protestant bishop) traveled to Edinburgh in 1910 for the World Missionary Conference, he delivered a celebrated appeal: "We also ask for Love. Give us Friends!"[62]

Although missionaries did not view the issues in the same way that most scholars would view them a century later, it was impossible to be a missionary in Punjab without confronting problems created by the nature of imperial power, the relationship between those with power and those without it, the nature of sheer material inequality and its implications, the consequences of attempting to promote universal values in a historically contingent setting, the relationship of state power and religion, the ever-present and much discussed problem of gender, and the nature of voluntary consent in spiritual matters. When looking beyond the narratives of missionary heroism, one finds extensive debate over issues of race, class, gender, and caste alongside issues of ecclesiastical authority, the nature of salvation, the status of non-Christian religions, and the definitions of religious sincerity and spiritual purity. How should white Europeans and nonwhite Indians relate to each other when they shared a commitment to spiritual equality in a church that transcends the British Empire, not only geographically but also temporally? How do Europeans relate to Indian women in an imperial context? How do European assumptions of social hierarchy apply, or not apply, to a society that is perceived through increasingly rigid categories of caste and tribe promulgated by the Census of India?[63]

Although missionaries were deeply involved in and affected by the large political events that mark the narratives of imperial and Indian national history, the history of the missionary enterprise in Punjab has its own internal patterns and rhythms. After an introduction, I have divided the story into three broad chronological sections. Part I, "The Ecclesiastical Invasion of Punjab, 1818–1890," is marked at one end by the arrival of the first missionary in Delhi in 1818, and at the other by the completion of a broad mission institutional presence. By that time the pioneer period was over, the first narratives of white male heroism in place, and the institutional focus of the missions well established.

In Part II, "Nonwhite, Nonmale, and Untouchable: Contradictions of the Mission Presence during the High Imperial Period, 1870–1930," I tell the story of large-scale (and largely female) institutional expansion, and the emergence of an Indian Christian community, heavily stratified along lines of caste and class, that was simultaneously Indian, foreign, hybrid, and historically unique. If there was ever a time when male foreign missionaries outnumbered women, it lasted only a few years. By 1900 the missionary presence was more than 60 percent female. By the 1920s the missionary enterprise reached its greatest size in Northwest India. There had been eighty foreign agents in Punjab and Kashmir in the 1870s; by the 1920s there were more than six hundred in Delhi, Punjab, the Northwest Frontier Provinces, and Kashmir (see Tables 2 and 9). Seventy percent of foreigners were women, but the foreign work force was heavily outnumbered in mission institutions by Indian mission agents.

The history of the missionary enterprise was to a considerable extent a story of mutual negotiations over the many contradictions created by its extraordinary diversity of interests. In the twentieth century, however, the missions operated in a new and challenging political and social environment with the advent of the national movement and vigorous competition from institutions created by Muslims, Sikhs, Arya Samajists, and Theosophists. Part III, "Confronting Imperialism/Decolonizing the Churches, 1900–1940," is the story of the varied ways that missionaries, Indian Christians, and non-Christians who were involved in mission institutions negotiated those challenges. The Indian Christian community was particularly vulnerable to the political changes introduced by anti-imperialist nationalism. While confronting those conflicts, they had created by the 1930s a remarkably durable set of social institutions that later survived the traumas of partition and independence intact.

I have made no attempt to write a comprehensive history of mission work in Punjab, but instead to examine those aspects of the story that I think are important, and will be important to others in a variety of disciplines. One of the paradoxes of studying missionaries is that, despite the presumption of marginality, very strong opinions appear once the subject is brought into focus, falling predictably into celebratory and unmasking categories. The producers of the BBC series *Missionaries* report that "Even among those who know very little about them, missionaries are a highly emotive subject. Those with a positive view of mission enthused about our project and reeled off the names of their particular missionary heroes and heroines. . . . Those with a less positive view, and there have been many, enjoined us to be sure to stress all the harm that missionaries have done. . . . We have been urged to expose missionaries as cultural imperialists, iconoclasts, paternalists, and even as agents of the CIA."[64]

In the history of the missionary enterprise, it is important, as Gyan Prakash has asserted for the history of colonialism, "not only to document its record of domination but also to track the failures, silences, displacements, and transformations produced by its function."[65] These stories are too complex to be encompassed within the master narratives of providence, or unmasking, or imperial complicity, but too rooted in history to escape them. As Said himself acknowledges, the theological and ecclesiastical issues that were important in Punjab cannot be fully incorporated into Said's own "imperialism for or against" binary. They cannot be incorporated easily into a utilitarian balance sheet in which individuals are judged by the net good or bad that they did in Punjab, in part because almost all of the people involved rejected utilitarian moral standards. Furthermore, a utilitarian balance sheet, however unavoidable for some purposes, is ultimately of limited use in making moral and political judgments about imperialism and its consequences. All of these methods of judgment will come into play. But first I will make some attempt to re-create the standards that missionaries set for themselves and others, following Bancroft's advice to historians: present your subject in his own terms, judge him in yours.[66]

PART I

The Ecclesiastical Invasion of Punjab, 1818–1890

2

The Empire of Christ and the Empire of Britain

In 1836 the bishop of Calcutta, Daniel Wilson, claimed the Punjab for Christ. In a boat on the Sutlej River, which then divided the territory of British India from that of the Sikh ruler Ranjit Singh, Wilson rose to his feet, stretched out his hand toward the foreign soil, and intoned: "I take possession of this land in the name of my Lord and master Jesus Christ."[1] The scene would make a perfect illustration for an introductory account of the relationship between the Bible and the flag, carried side by side in a march of triumphant imperial progress. In subsequent narratives of missionary heroism, the pretentious theatricality of this act was combined with portentous illusions to past grandeur drawn both from classical and ecclesiastical history.[2] The official historian of the CMS pointed out that the Sutlej was the very river that Alexander's Macedonian army refused to cross, and "the limit of his victorious march eastward was now the limit of British conquest westward."[3]

Missionaries entered the Punjab on the heels of a series of brutal military invasions, and British rule over the province was always dominated first of all by military and strategic considerations. The final conquest of Ranjit Singh's Punjabi territories was followed closely by the military uprisings of 1857, after which the security of Punjab became a central goal of British rule. In D. A. Washbrook's succinct summary: "Punjab, in particular, became the Raj's favourite recruiting ground and was commanded to remain changeless, a society of peasants and feudatories, to serve the armies purposes. Maintaining the 'martial races' of Punjabi society unaltered, by expending vast sums of money on irrigation projects aimed at preserving their 'traditional village communities,' was to drain the Government of India's development budget for decades to come."[4]

The analogies between military and ecclesiastical conquest, between the Empire of Britain and the Empire of Christ, gave rise to a kind of geo-religious triumphalism in some missionary circles. The new aggressiveness of nineteenth-century Protestant Christianity, which had independent origins in the evangelical revivals of the eighteenth and nineteenth centuries, coincided with relentless imperial, commercial, and technological expansion to spawn a rhetoric of global advance. The Punjab was regarded as a particular religious challenge and a particular religious opportunity. Throughout the missionary literature on the "other" in Punjab, there is a tone of respect for the military and political achievements of the Mughals and the Sikhs, and even of awe at the cultural achievements of the other great world religions.

Missionaries were particularly impressed with the architectural witness of the other religions of Punjab. In the former imperial city of Delhi, George Alfred Lefroy recalled his early days as a missionary in what he called the Babylon of Modern Times: "our quiet walks home, late on Sunday night, from Daryaganj to our own house ... along a road often bathed in the glorious Indian moonlight, and running between the Old Mogul fort of Delhi on our right hand and the solemn and beautiful Jama Musjid on the left, while further on we passed through the historic Kashmir Gate, with its undying Mutiny associations."[5] The CMS chose Amritsar as a mission station in hopes that from the Holy City of the Sikhs, with its commanding Golden Temple, the "new religion proclaimed from Amritsar would command prestige all over the land; within its walls the doctrine of Christ would be brought into immediate contact with the scholarship and whatsoever was best in the religions in possession."[6]

In interpreting India, missionaries drew upon three major rhetorical traditions, the orientalist, the utilitarian, and the evangelical.[7] Each of these traditions was, in the early nineteenth century, defamatory in its treatment of Indian culture, and in some respects the evangelical tradition of Charles Grant and Alexander Duff was the most defamatory of all. Missionaries brought with them attitudes toward Hinduism in particular that were extremely hostile. For evangelicals like Charles Grant and William Wilberforce in England, and William Ward and Alexander Duff in Bengal, something was very wrong with India, and the source of the evil was crystal clear: it was religion. Hinduism was obscene and cruel and bloody and lascivious, and so forth, and because of Hinduism, Indians were liars, thieves, widow-burners, murderers of infants, and so forth. This is painful reading, transparently awful in its ethnocentric bigotry, that has over the decades given great offense to many people regardless of their religious views.[8] The evangelical argument was often based on a distinction between religion on the one hand and culture on the other that was unintelligible not only to many Hindus but also to many secular-minded Europeans.

In the particular historical context of the ecclesiastical invasion of Punjab, however, it is striking to note how small a part defamation played in missionary rhetoric in general and homiletics in particular. However useful defamation might have been in the presentation of India to audiences in Britain and the United States, and in the recruitment of missionaries, as a rhetorical technique in Punjab defamation had limited utility. One of the purposes of the missionary presence was to persuade Indians to become Christians, and as a result missionary homiletics was often free of defamation. In other contexts defamatory denunciations of Hinduism were used even though counterproductive, but in some surprising ways, race was often used in a positive sense to counterbalance the negative judgments on religion. Insofar as early missionaries mentioned race in describing Punjabis, it was to praise them as a noble people with a distinguished history who would make wonderful Christians if it were not for the immorality of Hinduism and the bigotry of Islam.

Missionaries had at their disposal other rhetorical traditions: the Punjab School of tough-minded good government; the new science of comparative religion; Protestant traditions of individual liberty and the primacy of conscience in matters of religion; American notions of individual liberty and equality. The imperialist context set limits beyond which no missionary could stray, and there is little doubt that Edward Said is right in an important sense to observe that "in what they could say about the Orient, all Europeans were all ethnocentric and all racist all the time."[9] But the variety of rhetorical sources, the admiration of missionaries for the Sikhs and Mughals, and the practical demands of conversion and institution-building all contributed to a degree of unpredictability in mission rhetoric. Thomas Valpy French, later the first bishop of Lahore, referred to Punjab's "ancient and well-earned reputation for learning, which belonged to that country long before Britain emerged from Barbarism . . . a part of our mission field which has for so many years been highly esteemed and reported of for the massive intellect of its pundits, the acuteness and subtlety of its moolahs, the wide scope of its literature, the intricacy of the problems, religious and others, treated of by its sages."[10] This can be compared to the utilitarian Whig Macaulay's famous rhetorical question: "Who could deny that a single shelf of a good European library was worth the whole native literature of India and Arabia?"[11]

GEO-RELIGIOUS TRIUMPHALISM

Missionary rhetoric about the relationship between Christianity and other religions will be considered in more detail in Chapter 3, where it is placed in the context of institution-building. In their thinking about empire and politics, and their own relationship with the British imperial presence in Punjab, missionaries displayed a habit of providentialist thinking and geo-religious triumphalism that requires close attention in order to be made intelligible.[12] Convinced that the conversion of India would lead to the conversion of Asia, missionaries saw the Punjab as an ecclesiastical pathway to central Asia. At first ignoring Delhi and the adjacent areas of Punjab under British rule, the CMS made early efforts to "penetrate" the Himalayas.

The geo-political expansion of Britain awakened in missionaries a fascination for strategic advance that generated extraordinarily inefficient missionary strategies. Robert Clark, the pioneer CMS missionary in Punjab from the time of his arrival in Amritsar in 1852, spent much of the rest of the century attempting to create a frontier "chain" of missions, as if mission stations were military outposts. In 1886 he succeeded in reaching Quetta, on the Afghan frontier, perched on the top of a railway car, waxing lyrical over the engineering feats of the British government in opening up the frontier. That same year he visited the tiny Himalayan mission station at Kotgarh, which had after forty-six years of mission work only a small school of thirteen boys and two girls: "This mission is a city on a hill, to give light to the whole country between China and the plains."[13]

Behind the imagery of armies marching, territories claimed, empires rising and falling, and railroads crossing formerly uncrossable chasms—and embedded within narratives of missionary heroism in which Indians are barely named and European women mostly ignored—lay a set of stark contradictions. One such fault line lay along the issue of state power. Side by side with the narrative of imperial conquest lay another narrative peculiar to missionaries. This missionary account was delineated by William Carey, the pioneer Baptist missionary to Bengal, in his *Enquiry into the Obligations of Christians, to Use Means for the Conversion of the Heathens*. Published in 1792, when the former shoemaker was still a Baptist minister in Northamptonshire, the *Enquiry* sees the modern world, not as a site for the extension of state power, but as a site for "the spread of civil and religious liberty," which meant, for evangelical Protestants concerned with extending the Gospel, "a glorious door is opened, and is likely to be opened wider and wider."[14]

First persecuted by and then employed by the East India Company, Carey had very little concern for issues of state power except insofar as they were an impediment, or a providential help, to the spread of the Gospel. In some respects he appears in retrospect to have had a blank spot in his brain where issues of state power belong. But Carey was in principle a genuine voluntarist in matters of religion, and so to a greater or lesser extent were all Protestant missionaries in Punjab. Even those missionaries affiliated with the established churches of England and Scotland believed that religious conversion could not be coerced by the state, and that voluntary consent had to be genuinely uncoerced and more than a formality. The Portuguese and Dutch models of forced conversion or civil liabilities for non-Christians were entirely unacceptable to Punjab missionaries. Commenting on the completion of a new bridge over the Indus, and the general aggressiveness of government in pursuing its interest in Central Asia, Robert Clark of the CMS delineated the separate spheres of religion and power: "Their contentions and actions regards supremacy in Asia and ours does so also. Theirs is political and has to do with earth. Ours is spiritual in the interests of Lord Jesus Christ and His Church. The Angels and the spirits of just men in Heaven doubtless regard our work with far more interest than they do theirs. We might do so too."[15]

It is significant that Clark felt the need to remind himself of the central issue: the relationship between his universal religion and the temporal Empire of Britain. This was far more than a rhetorical conflict. The contradiction between the imperatives of the Empire of Christ and the Empire of Britain worked themselves out in multiple contradictions in the missionary movement. Missionaries were not primarily evangelists, but institution-builders—compulsive, inveterate institution-builders—not just in Punjab but everywhere in the nineteenth century. Institutions generate relationships, and it was in those relationships around and across imperial boundaries that the contradictions of the mission presence were exposed and negotiated. Missionaries had to define their roles not merely in terms of a geo-religious struggle for influence but also in relationship to the imperial functionaries who conquered and ruled Punjab. Following the first decision by an Indian voluntarily to consent to Christianity, missionaries and Indian Christians then began negotiations about the place of Indians in a universal Christian church under a particular historical form of imperial rule. To these familiar Protestant issues of state power and national identity would be added, later in the century, negotiations about caste and gender and race within the missionary movement and the Indian Christian church.

With hindsight we can see that many of these issues had to be negotiated in the missionary world from the day the first missionary set foot in Punjab, but they became defined as "problems" for public debate only after the contradictions became problems in the course of building mission institutions—that is, problems of human relationships. In the course of building institutions, missionaries were forcefully reminded that their interests and goals were not identical to those of the governments of India or Punjab, whether acting in their liberal modernizing or conservative, security-conscious phases. As soon as Indians were ordained as clergymen, some of them demanded equal rights with Europeans. The itinerant villager Ditt initiated the surprising and initially unwelcome mass conversions to Christianity in central Punjab. In the 1880s and 1890s, unmarried European and Indian women missionaries turned the missionary movement into a predominantly female cause, and Indian women doctors raised issues of racial prejudice in the missions. After the turn of the century the Indian national movement reminded missionaries of what they had always claimed to believe, that the "illusion of permanence" of British rule reflected in Kipling was theologically unacceptable.[16]

NON-EUROPEAN PIONEERS AND
MILITARY REBELLION

As the state-church Bishop Daniel Wilson claimed the Punjab for Christ, what was happening behind the ecclesiastical lines? Very little on the part of the state churches of England or Scotland, and a great deal that reflected the anarchic complexity of expanding Anglo-American Protestantism, and the multiracial nature of the mission enterprise. The first Protestant missionary to enter what would later become the province of Punjab was a Baptist, J. T. Thompson, who was not a European but a Calcutta-born Eurasian. Upon his arrival in Delhi in 1818, "he found himself the solitary Christian in that great city, and very naturally began his missionary work there with great depression of spirits which, however, he soon threw aside."[17] He preached in Delhi until his death in 1850, and assembled a small, self-governing church, which in 1826 had eleven members (including two Indians). From 1836 to 1840 Thompson was in Serampore working on his Hindi translation of the Bible, and leaving the care of the Baptist church of Delhi in the hands of Devagir, described only as his "native assistant."[18] In 1840, however, he returned to Delhi to spend the last decade of his life preaching and distributing tracts. An ordained Eurasian, Thompson would never have been described as a "native assistant," although he was deferential to the European Baptists at Serampore. Displacing his native assistant upon his return, he was establishing without openly acknowledging what amounted to a racialized hierarchy of authority in the most egalitarian and democratic of the denominations to work in Punjab.

The first CMS agent in Delhi was Anund Masih, a Brahmin who had been converted by a Baptist missionary in the Northwest Provinces. After the missionary was deported from the region under military guard for endangering public security by baptizing Indians, Anund Masih fell under Anglican influence and was taken up as a catechist and schoolteacher in Meerut by Mrs. Sherwood, an officer's wife and well-known writer of children's stories. Anund Masih was baptized in 1816, sent to Delhi to "pursue his scriptural inquiries" in 1822, and ordained a clergyman in 1825. Unlike Thompson, Anund Masih was not empowered to form an independent Indian congregation, and even after his ordination he remained subordinate to the Anglican chaplains and Mrs. Sherwood, who supervised his work as a teacher in both Meerut and Delhi. According to the official CMS history, in Delhi a "sect of Hindu ascetics called Saadhs came under his influence; but no great results followed."[19] More than a century and a half later, however, a mission text recounting Anund Masih's encounter with some Sadhus on a road near Delhi became the basis for Homi Bhabha's post-colonial analysis of hybridity.[20]

The first missionaries to advance beyond Delhi were of European descent but did not represent denominations of the imperial metropolis. They were American Presbyterians of the Western Foreign Missionary Society who entered Ludhiana in 1834 at the invitation of the British agent.[21] To the embarrassment of Anglicans, a Presbyterian missionary had even been summoned to Lahore to preach at the court of Ranjit Singh. Presbyterian missionary couples began arriving in 1836, "the John Newtons, the James Wilsons, and the James Campbells,"[22] with missionary wives from the first acting as missionaries, founding schools, teaching girls, conducting small-scale medical clinics, and visiting Indian women in their homes. In 1837 the Presbyterians baptized an Indian convert to the Presbyterian faith, Golak Nath.[23] The Punjab missionary presence was well on its way to being dominated in numbers if not in authority by nonmales and non-Europeans.

The defeat of Ranjit Singh in the Sikh Wars of the 1840s, which looms large in imperial history, is merely noted in mission history as another providential opening. With the exception of some isolated work in Himalayan hill stations, it was not until 1852 that the Church of England established a regular mission beyond the Sutlej, in Amritsar, supervised by the Rev. Robert Clark of the evangelical CMS. In the 1850s the advance lines of mission work were accounted for by the Rev. and Mrs. Andrew Gordon, missionaries of the Associate Presbyterian Church of North America, who entered Sialkot in 1854 one year ahead of the first missionary couple from the state Church of Scotland.[24] A second major Church of England society, the High Church Society for the Propagation of the Gospel (SPG), founded a mission station at Delhi in 1854, building on the work of the Anglican chaplaincy.

The new Anglican mission to Delhi was nearly wiped out in the rebellion of 1857. The Rev. A. R. Hubbard of the SPG was killed along with the Anglican chaplain and his daughter, as well as a British Baptist missionary who had succeeded J. T. Thompson, Thompson's widow and two daughters, and several others in the Indian Christian community including Chimman Lall, a surgeon, and Wilayat Ali, a Baptist catechist.[25] After 1857 the multiracial Delhi Christian community commemorated those Delhi Christians killed that year, Indian, Eurasian, and European, with brass memorials in the city's two oldest Christian churches, Central Baptist Church on Chandni Chowk, and St. James, Kashmiri Gate.

With her infant child and husband, the former Miss Jane Scott was in Sialkot in 1857. Her passion for mission work had been stimulated by several years of labor in Edinburgh as a Sabbath School teacher and district visitor.[26] She had married the Rev. Thomas Hunter of the Church of Scotland and had begun mission work at Sialkot in 1855, only to be killed there with her child and husband in 1857. Among American Presbyterians the most prominent hero was the first Indian to receive Presbyterian ordination, the Rev. Gopi Nath Nundy, who with his wife remained steadfast in his Christian faith under torture by rebellious Indian soldiers in Allahabad.[27]

The Mutiny, as it was called, had an enormous impact on British perceptions of India, and generated a literature of martyrdom and European heroism that continues today, but it had remarkably little effect on missionary narratives when taken as a whole.[28] The multiracial martyrdoms generated a multiracial martyrology that was added to the rhetorical armory of missionary publicists, with an eye on Foxe's *Book of Martyrs*, but the presence of Indian Christian martyrs, men and women, made it difficult (although not impossible) to masculinize and racialize the narrative of missionary heroism. CMS propagandists, eager for their own reasons to praise British administrators in Punjab, used the relative calm in the Punjab as a means of discrediting antimission officials such as the former governor-general, Lord Ellenborough, who blamed the rebellion on missions. Baptists made a great deal of the fact that one of the British military heroes of the rebellion, Henry Havelock, was a Baptist, a rarity among the officer class.[29] But the rebellion was generally portrayed as a kind of natural disaster, like flood or famine, which threatened the progress of the church, and the killing of missionaries and Indian Christians alike treated as a huge misunderstanding. The SPG and BMS rushed to rebuild their Delhi stations, and the Church of Scotland did the same for Sialkot.[30] The multiracial memorial brasses in Delhi have been ignored ever since; intelligible only within a providentialist master narrative, they fit into neither a master narrative of imperial triumph nor a master narrative of anti-imperial resistance.

THE PUNJAB SCHOOL AND THE
RHETORIC OF PROVIDENCE

Despite a late start, the Church Missionary Society would in time become the largest and in many ways the most important mission in Punjab, and it was within the CMS, with its implicit proimperial stance, that the contradictions between voluntarist Protestantism and the brute facts of imperial rule became most evident. The CMS was a voluntary religious society, committed to persuasion rather than coercion in matters of religion, but nonetheless made up of members of a church established by law in both England and India. It was an evangelical religious society committed to the spiritual equality of all before God, whose members were nonetheless deeply committed to an elitist view of religious influence emanating from the superior members of society to those below them in influence, rank, and status.

The Church of England responded to the competitive religious environment of nineteenth-century England with a campaign to maintain and extend its influence with elites, and a program of large-scale institution-building—schools, churches, publishing, and what we would now think of as social welfare institutions.[31] They did the same in

Delhi and Punjab, and it is difficult to understand the impact of missions on colonial India generally without recognizing that for many missionaries, the struggle for influence was more important than the struggle to recruit and enroll church members.

Early-nineteenth-century CMS leaders in England and in India were deeply frustrated at what they perceived as a brick wall of hostility to missions in British imperial rule in India, which they treated as a providential opportunity rather than as a straightforward extension of Christian influence. Sticking points were the failure of the government to carry out social reforms, the cooperation of governments in the maintenance of both Muslim and Hindu endowments, and the exclusion of Bible teaching from government schools following Sir Charles Wood's educational dispatch of 1854; that dispatch banned Bibles from the schools and decreed that government education should be exclusively secular. The despair of CMS leaders over these policies is difficult to understand unless one recognizes the great importance that Anglican clergymen placed on the power of official influence as a means of promoting Christian interests in the modern world. A government could not and should not force conversion, but it could extend religious influence and create an atmosphere in which religion could flourish.

Frustration at their lack of official influence in imperial circles explains the near hysterical hostility of the CMS to some military and civil officials of the East India Company, which could go as far as unconcealed gloating at their violent deaths. When in 1853 the commissioner for Peshawar, Colonel Mackeson, was asked for permission to begin a CMS mission, he replied, "No missionary shall cross the Indus while I am Commissioner of Peshawar: do you want us all to be killed?" The CMS official history reported the satisfying consequences: "A few months after . . . the Colonel was sitting in his verandah, when an Afghan approached and presented him with a petition. As he took the paper, the Afghan's knife was plunged into his heart."[32]

Colonel Mackeson's successor in Peshawar was Herbert Edwardes, a firebrand evangelical fanatic who was a member of the celebrated Punjab School of imperial administrators.[33] Official civil and military supporters of CMS missions in Punjab included, in addition to Edwardes, Henry and John Lawrence, Robert Montgomery, Donald McLeod, Reynell Taylor, Robert Cust, Arthur Roberts, William Martin, and C. B. Saunders. The depths of CMS gratitude to these men, and the extreme hero worship to which CMS officials were addicted, can only be explained by the depths of Anglican evangelical faith in the importance of elite influence, and their frustration at the secular face of British imperial rule.[34]

Although the men of the Punjab School gave the province a distinctive reputation for the religious tone of its government,[35] they in fact did little in their official capacity to Christianize the Punjab, except make unofficial statements asserting (in language very similar to Karl Marx's) that British rule in India was breaking down traditional allegiances and creating an open door for both science and religion. They used a rhetoric of providence as a means of reconciling what were very different interests. The administrators of the Punjab School were evangelical Protestants, unwilling to use coercion or civil liability to promote the Christian faith; nor were they prepared to use government funds to support proselytizing organizations. However sympathetic to missions, their first obligation was to govern. They were adamant, for instance, in their refusal to allow military officers to show any official support for Christianity, particularly in connection with the small number of Indian Christian soldiers. In 1857 Robert Clark's involvement with the 24th Punjab Infantry at the Peshawar Garrison, where thirty or so Mazhabi Sikhs from the Manjha tract of Punjab had converted to Christianity, led to draconian orders prohibiting any officers from discussing religion or worshipping together with Indian Christians, and prohibiting missionaries access to military lines altogether. The government was not impressed with Clark's argument that these were private acts, and that officers were "in no ways unduly using their official influence to the prejudice of the native religions." Instead the government was engaged, from Clark's point of view, in "another plot against their very existence" as missionaries.[36]

What Punjab School administrators were willing to do was publicly declare that they were not only rulers but also Christians. This compromise was eventually enshrined in the Queen's statement to the people of India following the 1857 rebellion: "Firmly relying ourselves on the truth of Christianity and acknowledging the solace of religion, we disclaim alike the right and the desire to impose our convictions on any of our subjects."[37] The Queen was no friend of foreign missions, but she had personally struck the word "neutrality" from the declaration. India after all had an established Protestant church, even if its ministrations were meant only for European Christians (a confusing category in its own right). But grateful though they were for an official statement endorsing the truth of Christianity, many mission critics of government policy in India recognized that a policy of even-handedness in matters of religion worked to the great benefit of Hinduism and eventually Islam. Even while withdrawing from direct subsidies of non-Christian religious practices, the government was reorganizing the laws governing endowments of religious sites in a way that greatly benefited certain aspects of Hinduism.[38] As Gauri Viswanathan has shown, the rule of law in British India was far from being sympathetic to converts from Hinduism to Christianity; especially if converts were women, their standing as autonomous individuals was in serious danger from laws treating Christian converts as Hindus despite their protestations.[39] Evangelicals in the CMS, and a few supporters in the government of Punjab including Herbert Edwardes, lost an extraordinarily bitter battle over attempts to provide Bible teaching in government schools, a practice that Anglican missionaries did not regard as contradicting their voluntarist principles.[40] What the CMS and other missions accepted, instead of Christian teaching in government schools, was an end to aggressive official hostility to missions, extensive private patronage of mission institutions by some officials,[41] and public appearances by officials at private conferences designed to promote the cause of missions, including a much publicized missionary conference held in Lahore in 1862–63.[42] Eventually they compromised further with a system of government grants to religious schools that initially benefited mission schools disproportionately, but opened the door ultimately for effective competition for the missions from the Hindu reformist Arya Samaj and later from Sikh and Islamic competitors.[43]

Despite the grand rhetoric in praise of the Christian sentiments of the Punjab School, in the end the CMS was left with little more than a providential open door under a voluntarist state, and the consolations of providentialist rhetoric. One of the purposes of providentialist rhetoric was the justification of British rule in Punjab, and it was regularly used to that end both by Punjab School administrators and missionaries. I will argue later in this chapter that providentialist rhetoric had multiple uses that are obscured by an exclusive focus on a convergence of interests between missions and British imperial rule. But the convergence should not be forgotten. The providentialist argument from an evangelical imperial administrator was put in its bluntest form by Herbert Edwardes, who could always be counted on to put on display the identity of religion and empire. At a CMS meeting in London's Exeter Hall, the never-modest Edwardes adopted the voice of God in a long-remembered peroration:

"I am the Lord of the World. I give Kingdoms to whom I list. I gave India into the hands of England. I did not give it solely for your benefit.

I gave it for the benefit of my millions of creatures. I gave it to you to whom I have given the best thing a man can have—the Bible, the knowledge of the only true God."[44]

Edwardes's point is clear, and when set beside the parallel providentialist arguments from nonmissionary apologists for British rule such as Macaulay or Charles Trevelyan, who believed that British rule would break down both Hinduism and Islam and open up India to a variety of beneficial western influences, including Christianity, the convergence of missions and imperialism is transparent and hardly needs to be unmasked.

Nineteenth-century Indian critics of missions grasped the point as self-evident, and it was later incorporated into a scholarly nationalist tradition in works such as B. D. Basu's five-volume *Rise of the Christian Power in India*, published by the Brahmo Samaj Press in 1923, which bases its indictment of British rule as specifically Christianizing on an exegesis of texts by Macaulayan improvers and missionary providentialists.[45] A recent reading by Arun Shourie of texts by Macaulay and Trevelyan, by the Victorian Indologists such as Max Muller and Monier Williams, and by missionary providentialist speeches comes to the same conclusion. The role of government was to create a vacuum; the role of missions to fill it. "The clear object: to perpetuate British rule into the indefinite future. The definite instrument: to instruct the natives in western learning, to inculcate in them western values so that they come to perceive their own interest in the perpetuation of British rule."[46]

Shourie concedes that there were many disagreements between British administrators, missionaries, and Indologists: "A surface reading therefore suggests a tugging and pulling in different directions."[47] Because Shourie's view is axiomatic in much scholarly work on missionaries, it is worth taking a closer look at the tugging and pulling, for providentialist rhetoric had more than one purpose. There are some peculiarities in the rhetoric of missionaries that make missionary activities in Punjab difficult to comprehend if they are simply lumped together with those of other imperialists. If the "failures, silences, displacements, and transformations" identified by Gyan Prakash as essential elements of colonialism are ignored in the case of western religion, we are left with a one-dimensional history of missionaries that is little more than an effort to "document its record of domination."[48] Providentialist rhetoric is complex, with multiple convergences of interest, and there are important countervailing, voluntarist currents among both officials and missionaries that are obscured if the transparent areas of convergence are documented and put on display as fragments of incontestable information.

Providentialist rhetoric was used not only to justify British rule but also as an answer to the influential tradition of imperial indifference to, and contempt for, the missionary enterprise. In a famous article in the *Edinburgh Review* in 1807, Sydney Smith declared missionaries "little detachments of maniacs,"[49] and that tradition continued through Lord Ellenborough to Kipling. Guari Viswanathan has unmasked the hostility to missionaries and in particular to conversion deeply imbedded in colonial jurisprudence, "[o]ften anticlerical in bias and deeply suspicious of evangelical fervor."[50] Another neglected element of official rhetoric is the politician's opportunistic appeal to an evangelical constituency. Shourie and the evangelical propagandist Eugene Stock, in a convergence of rhetorical interests, both quote Lord Palmerston: "[It] is in our own interest to promote the diffusion of Christianity as far as possible throughout the length and breadth of India," without acknowledging that Palmerston was attempting to buy off evangelical critics with praise while heading off their (in his view) lunatic demand to impose Bible teaching in government schools in India.[51]

Punjab School administrators in India often took the trouble to lecture overenthusiastic evangelicals on the rudiments of their own voluntarist principles. Sir William Mackworth Young laid out the principles of separation of government and religion in a paper read at the CMS meeting in Simla in 1892. Posted to Punjab in 1863, he served as secretary to the Punjab government from 1880 to 1887 and would later become lieutenant governor. Mackworth Young takes the conventional providential line that the "Pax Britannica" has brought in its train "the treasures of knowledge, of freedom, of authority," which are causing superstition to crumble. But he chides his evangelical audience for their impatience with the government: "It is not lawful for us as officials to employ the organisation of the State for influencing the consciences of those over whom for specific purposes we have received authority. We have an official conscience. Don't smile—I know some people cannot see it—they think such an idea is intolerable. But the matter has been thought out by wise men, and Christian men too." He then responds to those who think that Christian administrators should use their authority to promote Christianity as advocates of "unlawful means, carnal weapons, for fighting our unseen foes."[52]

Punjab School administrators not only did little to Christianize Punjab, but in addition, most of them were bound by their own principles to support non-Christian schemes of education and improvement when possible. To take only one example, the Dev Dharma Samaj (one of the Punjabi counterparts to the Brahmo Samaj of Calcutta) routinely published lists of laudatory comments from government officials, including promission officials, that are interchangeable with those made to missionary bodies: Sir James B. Lyall, lieutenant governor of Punjab, 1892: "His Honour wishes the Society all success in their laudable efforts to promote the spirit of true godliness in the country"; Sir Denzel Ibbetson, lieutenant governor in 1905: "Sir Denzil Ibbetson is in sympathy with the Samaj as far as it helps to promote morality and to extend education especially among girls"; Sir Louis Dane, late lieutenant governor of Punjab, on a visit to the Dev Samaj Girls High School: "With lofty ideals of Culture and Character and Regeneration of Women before you, you are bound to do great work."[53] The motives of these officials are reasonably clear, and their statements to this non-Christian body resemble Lord Palmerston's earlier flattery of missionary bodies in Britain.

Finally, providentialist rhetoric was used upon occasion to remind missionaries, imperial administrators, and Indian Christians that British rule in India was ephemeral. Even Herbert Edwardes, speaking as God in his memorable peroration at Exeter Hall, reminded his listeners: "You have neglected the charge I gave you. You have ruled India for yourselves."[54] The narrative of the providential open door carried within it, from the very first, an implicit and sometimes explicit recognition of the fleeting character of British rule. As early as 1791 the editor of the annual report of the Society for the Promotion of Christian Knowledge commented on a sermon by a "native priest" in South India, Sattianaden: "How long it may be in the power of the Society to maintain Missionaries; how long the fluctuations in the affairs of this world will afford duration to the Mission itself, is beyond our calculation; but if we wish to establish the Gospel in India, we ought to look beyond the casualties of war, or the revolutions of empires; we ought in time to give the native a Church of their own, independent of our support."[55]

"Beyond the revolutions of empires" is a decisive phrase. The British Empire, like the Roman Empire, was doomed to disappear, while God's work on earth would continue much longer. Anglicans had to work harder to grasp the centrality of that point, perhaps, than the American United Presbyterian missionary Robert Stewart, who conceded during the Afghan Wars that, despite a prejudice in favor of the English over the Russians, as missionaries, "it mattered comparatively little which kingdom exercised authority over us. Both are nominally Christian governments and, as Americans, we might hope for fair treatment even from Russia, which, in political matters at least, has always been a friendly power."[56] His goal was not, in Arun Shourie's phrase, to "perpetuate British rule into the indefinite future," but to prepare as soon as practical for the end of British rule. Despite his obsession with the behavior of Punjab's rulers, Robert Clark "held strongly that the presence of the foreign missionary was merely an incident in the evangelisation of the land, and that the stranger would not abide for ever."[57]

Thomas Valpy French, the first bishop of Lahore, prefigured *The Heart of Darkness* in his musing that "[o]ne has a painful sort of feeling sometimes that at no long distance of time the tables will be turned, and the native church in this land be rather the missionary church to us than we standing in that relation to them."[58] As a CMS missionary in the 1850s he was writing urgent appeals to Henry Venn, the secretary of the CMS in London, urging that more be done to put missions in the hands of Indians: "putting, if possible, the more intelligent of the new converts in *responsible* situations. For this is a point in which it appears to me we have not taken full advantage of the elements of good which the native character does possess. They seem capable of responsibility."[59]

In the historical scheme of things, the door was open but might not remain open. Furthermore, missionaries were on their own, without the aid of the secular arm that had been provided to the Dutch and Portuguese in India. God might have opened a door, but he left no precise instructions about what to do while it was open. Confronting the problem of how to build a Christian church that would survive and transcend the imperial boundaries of the Empire of Britain, missionaries first experimented with two expedients: early ordination, and the promotion of self-government in the infant Indian church (see Chapter 4).

EARLY ORDINATION

The first ordained Indian in Punjab, if Eurasians are to be considered Indian, was the Baptist J. T. Thompson, sent by Carey's mission from Bengal in 1818 to initiate Christian work as the "solitary Christian" in Delhi.[60] Next came the baptized Brahmin Anund Masih of the CMS, although he never supervised a permanent mission. In 1844 American Presbyterians ordained a Bengali working for the mission in Fatehpur, Golak Nath, who was given independent charge of a mission station in

Jullundur after its annexation by the British. The Rev. Golak Nath used his position to launch a dispute with the mission over his status and salary, making claims for racial equality with the missionaries based on Christian principles.[61]

After two years of work in Amritsar, Robert Clark of the CMS regarded the recruitment of an Indian minister as a matter of great urgency in the light of twenty-three baptisms. The danger, from his point of view, was the emergence of a Punjabi church that would remain "fettered in the trammels of Western form and fashion . . . a weak copy of men and things Western."[62] Clark settled on Daud Singh as a candidate for the ministry despite his lack of knowledge of English, Latin, Greek, or Hebrew, for "the armour of the West would have been but an incumbrance as things then stood."[63] Daud Singh was ordained by the bishop of Calcutta in 1854. In Delhi the SPG moved quickly to ordain an Indian after the rebellion of 1857. The Rev. Thomas Skelton, fellow of Jesus College, Cambridge, arrived in 1859 and baptized, among others, Tara Chand, who was ordained in 1863 and helped establish Anglican work in Delhi with the Rev. Robert Winter and Priscilla Winter, his wife, who arrived in 1860. The Rev. Tara Chand was later given independent charge of a mission on Ajmer, in Rajastan, where he retired in 1913.[64]

The rush to early ordination, which can be found in other missions as well,[65] reflected a high degree of confidence in the ability of Indians to act as ministers, and is worth stressing for two reasons. The first is to establish the contrast between the missionary point of view, and the approach to India of the modernizing cultural imperialists who wished to use education to create in British India, in Macaulay's infamous words from his *Minute on Education* of 1835, "a class who may be interpreters between us and the millions whom we govern; a class of persons, Indians in blood and colour, but English in taste, in opinions, in morals, and in intellect."[66] The missionary aspiration was to create a class of persons who were Indian in taste, in opinions, and in intellect, but Christian in religion, and therefore in morals. For some purposes this distinction does not matter, since there were multiple maneuvers with the same end, the maintenance of imperial control. Furthermore, the missionary attempt to make distinctions between culture and religion broke down in a mass of contradictions when they attempted to put it into practice. But for purposes of understanding the missionary movement, the distinction makes a great deal of difference. Robert Clark insisted, when addressing Indian Christians in 1878, that "the missionary was in no wise entitled to enforce as an essential part of the religion of Christ the fruits it had borne in the social fabric of his own or any other nation." He argued instead: "The hope of a Christian India lies in the gathering together of men who shall be ... as thoroughly Hindu as they are Christian, and more intensely national than those who are not Christian."[67]

The aspiration to see an Indian Christianity that was a synthesis of East and West, but one truly naturalized in India, had wide appeal across the missionary spectrum. An early educational missionary of the CMS, the Rev. Thomas Valpy French, arrived in India with a fixed determination to "like everything native that is not positively harmful."[68] In 1866 he read a paper to a gathering of clergy at Gloucester, where he outlined a proposal for a divinity school in India that would produce a Christian synthesis of East and West, and the proposal was adopted by the CMS in 1867. Given French's background at Rugby and Oxford, the project was elitist and literary in its aspirations. St. John's Divinity School was opened under French's direction in the pretty Maha Singh Garden in Lahore in 1871, with a curriculum heavily focused on church history, doctrine, Hebrew, and Greek, which were counterbalanced with lectures on "Hindu and Mohammedan systems."

This school was hopelessly elitist and paternalist, but there is no doubt that French intended to demonstrate the reality of his hope that "there is approaching a stage of native inquiry, at which they will appreciate the fact that the gospel of Christ has only an *accidental, not essential* connexion with the English."[69] He took on himself the task of lecturing on Hinduism and Islam, but looked forward to the day when those topics "ere long will be handed over to native professors."[70] At a time when missionaries in some parts of the world were insisting that Christians wear western dress, French rigorously attempted to demonstrate the accidental relationship between Christianity and the English by enforcing a nonwestern dress code on students.[71] Eager to enforce his code on an equal opportunity basis, he even extended the requirement to an English sergeant from Rawalpindi who was so eager to enroll that, initially, "even the restriction about native dress would not restrain him."[72]

DEPENDENCY AS AN IMPERIAL PROBLEM

The CMS would quietly close St. John's Divinity School after the turn of the century, admitting their failure to transcend imperial boundaries. But the aspirations of its founder are important to keep in mind as a contrast with modernizers who explicitly wished to westernize Indians. They also illustrate a second important point about missionaries: aspirations to overcome the barriers of race and empire were not limited to enlightened missionary administrators in Britain and the United States. The distinction between enlightened administrators and benighted missionaries is particularly evident in mission studies historiography concerning Henry Venn, who was from 1846 until his death in 1872 the secretary (that is, primary administrator) of the Church Missionary Society. He was also one of the most eminent mid-nineteenth-century missionary theorists, and twentieth-century missionary historians, looking for anti-imperialist forefathers, have found one in Venn; they stress his far-sighted struggles with missionary paternalism.[73]

Although Venn was not the only nineteenth-century missionary administrator to deal with the contradictions between imperialism and missions, he was the most systematic.[74] It is often difficult to recognize that his arguments deal with imperialism, steeped as they are in theological and administrative arguments. He frequently deployed a virulent anti-Catholicism as a means of warning Protestants of the snares of statism, and of the need for religious conversions to be genuine, uncoerced, and self-sustaining.[75] Missions dependent on state power could never be a success, because the nature of the assent to religion was corrupted. Venn went beyond a consideration of state power, however, prefiguring the recent interest among historians in dispersed and informal but nonetheless effective forms of power and coercion, in his extensive treatment of the dangers of missionary paternalism. As a missionary administrator he found himself in charge of religious institutions encompassing "a few scattered converts ... in an artificial state of dependence upon Christian Europeans."[76] Venn recognized the corrupting power of the relationship of dependency. Informal dependency, like the direct exercise of state power, was an imperial relationship that corrupted voluntary consent. Venn identified the problem, and the problem was imperialism.

In his discussion of dependency Venn never focuses on the dependency of women on men, except for some predictable propagandistic flourishes about the debased state of Indian women compared with western women. Missionary wives carried out their own partly autonomous professional responsibilities to a far greater extent than clergymen's wives at home. But the status of women as missionaries in their own right was addressed explicitly only in the thirty years after Venn's death, when the missionary movement was flooded with single women who demanded recognition of their own professional status. The status of Indian Christian women became an issue only when they were organized as mission employees. Both missionaries and Indian Christians are assumed to be men, which allows Venn to evade any consideration of gender. But in his discussion of dependency he faced squarely the issue of unequal power between western Christians and nonwestern Christians.

In searching for a formula for a nonwestern Christian church in a new world of contested religious terrain, Venn elaborated the celebrated threefold formula of "self-support, self-government, and self-extension." He was not the only advocate of that formula, but he was the most systematic in his attempt to implement it. The CMS issued the formula as a policy directive to missionaries in 1855, and the subsequent papers of 1861 and 1866, which were reissued in 1866 as a statement of official CMS policy and published again as official regulations in 1883: "The ultimate object of missions, viewed in their ecclesiastical aspect, is the settlement of Native Church, with Native Pastors, upon a self-supporting, self-governing, and self-extending system."[77] Tied with this formula was another phrase describing the role of the western mission in this development: the "euthanasia of the mission." Euthanasia was to be achieved by the creation of a nonwestern pastorate supported by the funds of the nonwestern church that would survive as an independent, non-European church beyond the revolutions of empire.[78]

These were aspirations shared by early missionaries in Punjab, acting on a narrative of conquest (or anticonquest)[79] that treated empire as ephemeral, and was the basis for experiments with early ordination. But early ordination soon proved to be entirely inadequate, and created new contradictions and crises. Clergymen required an ecclesiastical structure, but the dominant ecclesiastical structures in Punjab were the mission (which was foreign) and the Anglican Ecclesiastical Establishment, which was meant for European Christians. For the Baptists in Delhi, the issue of a native clergy was evaded until after 1850 because of the ambivalent racial status of the Rev. J. T. Thompson, who was pastor of the autonomous Baptist congregation in Delhi. Among the Presbyterians, there existed a ready-made model of presbytery and synod. As soon as they could be put in place, they were regarded as the appropriate place for Indian clergy, and the imperial tensions that plagued the Presbyterians were fought out within those structures, and in conflict between presbytery and synod on the one hand and the mission on the other. The Church of England experimented with early ordination and with training at the Lahore Divinity School. But Indian clergy had no structure of presbytery and synod, only employment under the supervision of missionary and bishop. That, from a Vennite voluntarist point of view, was a serious imperial problem.

The CMS pioneers, Venn, French, and Clark, accepted episcopacy with varying degrees of enthusiasm, but they all agreed upon the absurdity of a bishop without a church. The church should come before the bishop, and it should be an indigenous Indian church. But the episcopacy of the actually existing Indian church was transparently English and imperial, and nowhere to a greater degree than in Punjab. Macaulay declared the Church of Ireland "the most absurd ecclesiastical establishment that the world has ever seen,"[80] but surely that honor belongs to the Indian Ecclesiastical Established, created in 1813, which outlived the episcopal establishments in both Ireland and Wales. Sees of Madras and Bombay were added to that of Calcutta in 1833, but proposals for further bishoprics became enmeshed in disputes over the appropriate mechanisms for creating them, and their ultimate purposes. Sentiment for nonterritorial missionary bishoprics, which would presumably be the nucleus of an independent Indian church organized along racial lines, was strong in some CMS circles, and advocated by Henry Venn. But the ideal of the geographical and racial unity of the church was even stronger in Anglicanism.[81]

THE DIOCESE OF LAHORE, OR THE NATIVE CHURCH COUNCIL?

In the end it was the sheer administrative unwieldiness of the diocese of Calcutta that led to the establishment of new dioceses of Rangoon and Lahore in 1877. In 1876 a committee in England raised more than £20,000, with contributions of £5,000 from the Society for the Promotion of Christian Knowledge, £3,000 from the Colonial Bishoprics Fund, £2,000 from the SPG, and £1,000 from the Marquis of Salisbury. The government was prepared to supplement the income from the endowment with £800 per year, the stipend then of a senior chaplain, which provided an income of £1,600 for Thomas Valpy French, the new bishop chosen by Archbishop Tait. At the time of his appointment there were roughly twenty million Hindus, Muslims, and Sikhs in his diocese, twenty thousand Europeans (mostly military), sixty clergymen (missionary and chaplaincy), and only eleven hundred Indian Christians.[82] French was consecrated in December of 1877 in Westminster Abbey. After some discussion, Delhi with its SPG mission was included in his diocese, and he embarked on a decade of institution-building, dominated by the building of the impressive Early English–style Lahore Cathedral, "the grandest Christian place of worship in India."[83] Bishop and cathedral supplied a highly visible embodiment of the imperial dimension of the ecclesiastical invasion of Punjab.

For all his aspirations to develop an Indian church, French had become part of the imperial establishment, with responsibility for the military chaplains in a diocese with a military presence second only to Winchester. Despite his affected contempt for the grandeur expected of an imperial bishop, he moved into a house built eighteen years earlier by Sir Robert Napier. Then he headed for the frontier, wishing among other things to visit the medical mission at Tank conducted by an Indian Christian doctor, John Williams. He was driven there from Dera Ismail Khan by Major Macaulay, nephew of Lord Macaulay, forty miles in a two-horse cart with an escort of cavalry and outriders accompanying them all the way. One of his first ceremonial acts, done at his request but with the specific consent of the Viceroy, was conducting divine service at the opening of the new bridge over the Sutlej.[84] By the time of the consecration of Lahore Cathedral in 1888, the clergy of the diocese were ninety-one, including twenty-nine chaplains; forty-two CMS missionaries, including fourteen Indians; six SPG and six Cambridge Mission to Delhi missionaries (two Indian); and five other clergy (three at schools). In official statistics the personnel of the diocese were identified by ordination rather than gender. Nonclerical missionaries included eight lay CMS males (five medical); thirty-seven women of the Church of England Zenana Missionary Society (CEZMS), (thirteen honorary); two ladies of CMS; nineteen ladies of SPG/CMD; and three Sisters of St. Denys School, Murree.[85] It is only by concentrating intently on statistics, and ignoring the narratives of missionary heroism, that one realizes that by 1888 the multiracial Anglican missionary presence in Punjab was already dominated by women, with forty-eight male and sixty-one female missionaries in addition to the still uncounted missionary wives.

The Diocese of Lahore was riddled with imperial contradictions. Within the Church of England alone, there were competing visions of the church and its relationship to empire. There was the imperial vision of a united established church with a diocesan structure, which being multiracial in principle had to adopt pastoral responsibility for non-European Indian Christians. There was the Vennite ideal of an indigenous, self-supporting Indian church, which implied a racial stratification that contradicted evangelical universalism. The contradictions were reflected in Bishop French's insistence on talking in Vennite terms of two churches divided by race within his own united diocese. In a letter to B. F. Westcott, he referred to the case of Lahore, "Where two churches (native and European) are united under one bishop."[86] His aspiration was to see "our English and the native church brought into holy, loving, harmonious cooperation for the advancement of the Kingdom of their Lord and ours; but rash and precipitate measures of extreme men on both sides may disastrously dash those hopes to pieces, and throw away the golden moment. The marriage of the two churches, could it be accomplished honorably to both, would be in no sense a *mésalliance*; but the proposals and acceptance must be mutual."[87] French's biographer was sufficiently embarrassed by French's apparent confusion that he felt compelled to note that "the phrase 'two churches' is technically incorrect. Ecclesiastically they were always *one*; the difference is but in state support and social sympathies."[88]

From the CMS point of view, the creation of a diocese caused more problems than it solved. How does an imperial episcopal church generate a self-governing native church?[89] The CMS response to the creation of an imperial diocese was the establishment in 1877 of an alternative to the ecclesiastical imperialism of Lahore, the Punjab Native Church Council. The Church Council was intended to be the germ of a self-governing, independent Indian church, where Indian Christians would learn the arts of self-government, self-support, and self-extension. It was to be separate from the mission, and dominated by Indians. Both Venn and Clark recognized that mixed institutions of Europeans and Indians, such as presbytery and synod, or a diocese with English and Indian clergy involved in a diocesan synod, would inevitably be dominated by Europeans, who would retard the development of Indian Christians who were "as thoroughly Hindu as they are Christian." Clark's goal was for the missionary to "keep ourselves and our modes of thought studiously in the background. We must aim at something far greater than collecting scattered congregations around English clergy who may reflect to our eye faint and imperfect images of ourselves."[90] The Punjab Native Church Council was also meant to be a forum for Indian Christians to speak to each other, and to speak to European Christians in their own voice. Robert Clark went to great trouble to publish the proceedings of the Native Church Council in both Urdu in India and in English in London, under the ringing title of *A Native Church for the Natives of India*, so that European Christians could learn the point of view of Indian Christians.[91] Indian Christians did speak at the meetings of the church council, and missionaries (as we shall see in Chapter 4) did not like what they heard.

For the High Church Anglicans of the Society for the Propagation of the Gospel in Delhi, the contradictions of empire were met with yet another narrative of anticonquest. Unlike the evangelicals of the CMS, the SPG missionaries were unequivocal in their commitment to episcopacy. A church was defined by the presence of a bishop, and in the early nineteenth century they developed the concept of the "missionary bishop" who would precede the church and provide the nucleus for the organization of a "native" church. But even from the point of view of the SPG there were problems, since the missionary bishop was envisaged as going to a place where there were no Christians, or at least no episcopalians. The first missionary bishop in the Anglican communion was ordained in 1835 for Missouri and Indiana, and at his consecration sermon George Washington Doane, bishop of New Jersey, outlined the fields where such a person might be appropriate: "And if there be, in Indiana or Missouri, in Louisiana, Florida or Arkansas, some scattered handfuls here and there of Churchmen—or, if obedient to the Saviour's mandate, to preach the Gospel unto every creature, we send out heralds of the Cross to China, Texas, Persia, Georgia or Armenia."[92]

If Delhi and Lahore had been situated in Texas, a missionary bishop would have been appropriate, but episcopacy existed in India long before the SPG began its work in Delhi. The first bishop of Calcutta (1814), Thomas Middleton, had in his early years limited his ministry to the nominally Christian European population. Unsure if Indians were even subjects of the British crown, he refused to ordain them at first.[93] But even when that issue was settled, and episcopal authority over Indian Christians accepted, High Church Anglicans recognized the need to create institutions that would survive the revolutions of empire. It was at Cambridge that Anglicans developed for Punjab their own distinctive narrative of anticonquest, one that motivated the work of the Cambridge Mission to Delhi.

DELHI—A NEW ALEXANDRIA

In the 1870s, B. F. Westcott, the Regius professor of divinity and a well-known New Testament scholar, had delivered a series of lectures to missionary meetings at Cambridge in which he encouraged undergraduates to think in terms of a special mission to the East, modeled on the Alexandrian School of the second and third centuries.[94] Orientalist scholarship and missionary idealism blended to produce a vision of a special mission from Cambridge to the Orient. The Alexandrian school was distinguished, according to Westcott, by its acknowledgment of truth in Greek philosophy. The Alexandrian theologians, Clement and Origen, believed that the incomplete truth apprehended by Greek philosophers found its fulfillment in Christ. Thus God's revelation of truth had been partially revealed to the Greeks as well as to the Jews in preparation for the full revelation in Christ. Westcott anticipated later liberal Protestant approaches by encouraging missionaries to look for truth in Hinduism and to identify ways in which the lesser truth pointed to the greater truth in Christ. "And is it too much to hope," Westcott asked, "that we may yet see on the Indus, or on the Ganges, some new Alexandria?"[95]

T. V. French also influenced Westcott by interpreting his own Divinity School project as an example of potential synthesis, and by arguing for a search for Christian truth in Sanskrit texts: "[T]he highest ethics may, in some very scarce passages of the Vedas, and very large and full passages of the Socratic writings, be caused to lead up as corroborative witness to the morals and even some of the dogmas of the Gospel. . . . God who is the author of the "lively oracles" of our faith is the author likewise of the human conscience."[96] Working together at this new Alexandria, western and Indian theologians would incorporate the best of Indian culture into a new Christian theological statement, which in turn would provide the basis for the conversion of India and ultimately all of Asia to Christ.

Westcott was an orientalist fantasizer, but it is important to recognize the genuine liberal appeal of his ideas. While attempting to disentangle Christianity from western culture, he offered a way around the Christian triumphalism that declared Hinduism depraved and Islam fraudulent. At a time when the superiority of western culture was axiomatic in England, and when racist ideas were growing more prevalent and more virulent, Westcott encouraged potential missionaries at Cambridge to listen for things of value from people in other cultures rather than merely preaching at them.

In practice, however, Westcott knew very little about Hinduism. In the discourse of the Cambridge Mission to Delhi, Indians appeared, not as Indians, but as Egyptians—or, to be more specific, as Greek-speaking inhabitants of the Roman Empire living in second-century Alexandria. Women appeared not at all, not even as wives, since the Cambridge Mission to Delhi was committed to clerical celibacy. Even from a missionary point of view, Westcott's ideas provided no practical guidance about what to do in a mission, which not only involved Indian men and women but also in which European women soon outnumbered male clerical missionary heroes. But the impracticality of the ideas did not dissuade Cambridge recruits. Six men inaugurated the Cambridge Mission to Delhi with a breakfast at Pembroke College in 1877; two years later the same six met in Delhi "for breakfast and a truly 'common' life," not on the Indus or the Ganges, but on yet another river, the Yamuna, the chosen site for a new Alexandria.[97]

COMPETING NARRATIVES OF
CONQUEST AND ANTICONQUEST

There are several missionary counternarratives, or narratives of anticonquest, at work in Punjab: the global spread of Christianity in a context in which empires and modern technology are merely providential; the desire to create churches beyond the revolutions of empires through the ordination of Indians; the promotion of "a native church for the natives of India"; the creation of a new Christian synthesis of East and West in a new Alexandria. To these would be added in subsequent years other alternative narratives: the radical egalitarianism of the Salvation Army, the explicit identification of the Gospel with Indian nationalism in the arguments of C. F. Andrews, and the assertion of a special bond of sympathy between English women and Indian women. How these work out in practice we shall see, but even a glance at the statistics of the foreign ecclesiastical presence in Punjab indicates the complexity, and the prospect of the emergence of multiple, conflicting points of view. Indian men and women and European women outnumbered European men in the missionary enterprise, and in the 1870s conflicts over the relationship of mission and imperial state, and between the Indian church and the mission, would broaden into conflicts over both caste and gender.

In 1857, the "Indian Female Normal School and Instruction Society" (later known as the Zenana Bible and Medical Mission) decided to expand their work beyond Calcutta and send Miss Jerrom and Miss Branch to Amritsar, the first foreign lady missionaries there other than missionaries' wives. Robert Clark expansively claimed exclusive credit for the CMS for initiating independent women's work in Punjab,[98] but until 1880, when the Church of England Zenana Mission Society was founded and absorbed some of their work, the Indian Female Normal School Society was an independent organization supporting unmarried women missionaries not only in CMS stations but also in American Presbyterian (AP) stations (where they supported at least one Indian missionary, Miss Golak Nath at Jullundur).[99] By the turn of

TABLE 2
Indian and Foreign Agency in Punjab, 1871

	(1)	(2)	(3)	(4)	(5)	(6)	(7)	(8)
AP	13	5	1	4	19	28	15	115
BMS	1	0	2	3	12	6	3	5
CMS	15	3	3	5	13	25	8	98
CS	1	1	1	2	6	2	1	29
FES				2				
Other[a]	3	3	1	3	1	2	1	10
SPG	2	1	3	6	7	2	5	28
UP	3	1	1	2	8	3	2	27
ZBMM				1				2
TOTAL	38	14	12	28	66	68	37	314

SOURCE: Calcutta Missionary Conference, *Statistical Tables of Protestant Missions in India, Ceylon, and Burma for 1871* (Calcutta: Baptist Mission Press, 1873), passim.

COLUMNS: (1) ordained foreign males; (2) ordained Indian agents; (3) male lay agents, foreign; (4) foreign female agents; (5) Indian Christian preachers; (6) male Indian Christian teachers; (7) female Indian Christian agents; (8) non-Christian teachers.

NOTE: Total European, 78 (50 male, 28 female); total Indian Christian, 185 (148 male, 37 female).

[a] Other: Moravian mission, Christian Vernacular Education Society; FES = Female Education Society; ZBMM = Female Normal School).

TABLE 3
Indian and Foreign Agency in Punjab, 1890

	(1)	(2)	(3)	(4)	(5)	(6)	(7)	(8)
AP	20(15)	15	3	19(1)	32	36	21	131
BMS/ZMS	6(5)	7		11	4	26	21	2[a]
CEZMS				43(2)	3	1	112	25
CMS	37(18)	13	4	3	45	75	54	172
CS	5(3)	4	1	19(2)	15	50	7	70
FES				9			2[a]	7
MORAV	1(1)					1		
SPG/CMD	10(3)	1		20	21	22	19	43
UP	12(11)	10		14(2)	173	14	29	175
ZBMM				8			0[a]	
TOTAL	91(56)	50	8	146(7)	293	224	266	625
1871	50	14		28	66	68	37	314

SOURCE: Calcutta Missionary Conference, *Statistical Tables of Protestant Missions in India, Burma and Ceylon, Prepared on Information Collected at the Close of 1890, at the Request of the Calcutta Missionary Conference* (Calcutta: Baptist Mission Press, 1892). These tables, based on reports of the mission societies, undercount the considerable agency employed informally or locally.

COLUMNS: (1) male missionaries (= married); (2) ordained Indian agents; (3) male qualified doctors; (4) foreign female agents, mostly unmarried (qualified doctors); (5) Indian Christian preachers (unordained); (6) male Indian Christian teachers; (7) female Indian Christian agents; (8) non-Christian teachers (women included in total = 92).

[a] Obviously incomplete figures.

TABLE 4

Growth of Indian and Foreign Agency in Punjab, 1871–90

	1871	Percent of all agents	1890	Percent of all agents	Increase %
All agents	577		1,695		193
Foreign agents	78	13.5	237	14.0	204
Indian agents	499	86.5	1,458	86.0	192
Foreign male	50	8.6	91	5.4	82
Foreign female	28	4.9	146	8.6	421
Indxtn male	148	25.6	567	33.5	232
Indxtn female	37	6.4	266	15.7	619
Nonxtn male	314	54.4	533	31.4	68
Nonxtn female	?	?	92	15.7	?
Male agents	512	88.7	1,191	70.3	133
Female agents	65	11.3	504	29.7	675

SOURCE: Derived from Tables 2 and 3.

the century unmarried women, appointed as independent missionaries, would outnumber ordained males, a trend that was already evident even in official statistics as early as 1871 (see Tables 2, 3, and 4). The work of unmarried women required its own justification and its own justifying narratives (which disguised the important role played by women in the missions before the arrival of independently appointed women).[100] Their stories exploited the special qualities assigned to women in variants of nineteenth-century separate spheres ideology, extolled an alleged special bond of sisterhood between European women and Indian women, and claimed special rights of access to India based on the alleged seclusion of Indian women and the unique professional qualifications of European missionaries (see Chapter 6).[101]

The several narratives justifying the foreign ecclesiastical presence all fail to account for the material reality of the mission presence, which by 1871 was multiracial and heavily stratified by race, gender, and professional qualifications. In one sense all the mission stories became submerged in the overwhelming imperial presence in India. But mission narratives were distinct from Macaulay's civilizing, moralizing cultural imperialism, and provided a sense of justification for the missionary presence that is evident in the puzzlement missionaries expressed when they were confused with imperialists, with the government, or with other Europeans. On the eve of his death at the hands of Indian troops in 1857, Thomas Hunter of the Church of Scotland wrote from Sialkot that "our object in settling here has not been grasped by the native mind."[102] Citing a list of errors that Christians must combat, in 1871 a Presbyterian missionary, the Rev. C. B. Newton, identified the belief that we are kidnappers, that we are introducing our own national religion, that we wish to change the customs of the country, or that every European a is Christian.[103]

Missionaries confronted not merely suspicion about their motives but also puzzlement. When Rowland Bateman had his students at Dera Ismail Khan explain using words of Scripture why missionaries came from Great Britain to India, one response was: "[M]issionaries come to preach the gospel in India because a prophet is without honor in his own country."[104] Addressing a group of Indian Christians who, we can assume, were suspicious of his motives, Robert Clark argued that "it is not merely we, who are only a few teachers from a foreign country, who are seeking to interfere with the old religions of India. It is the Truth itself which commands men everywhere to repent and to believe in Christ. . . . Our great power as missionaries in India, is that we have no personal motives; that we seek nowhere for our own profit in the people's conversions."[105]

The subsequent history of Clark's relationship to Indian Christian clergy is sufficient to demonstrate the unpersuasiveness of his point of view, but it is important to keep it in mind as a starting point for understanding the missionary enterprise. However bolstered by their theological understanding of history, and however much they might claim to admire their own lack of personal motives, missionaries also understood that they lived in a particular historical context. They had little sense of entitlement to exemption from the judgment of posterity merely because they were creatures of their time. "In ages to come," T. V. French asked, "what judgment is the Church likely to pass upon our missionary agencies? . . . I have a sorrowful conviction that the Church of the future will, in some important respects at least profit rather from being warned by our mistakes than helped by the record of our wisdom, courage, abilities, and patient constancy and perseverance."[106] In the midst of conflict, and while awaiting the judgment of posterity, the missions redoubled their efforts to build Christian institutions. Within those institutions, the fault lines of the imperial enterprise took on outward and visible form.

3

Visible Institutions, Invisible Influence

For nearly thirty years after 1818, J. T. Thompson preached at public places in Delhi, addressed crowds on the banks of the Jumna, and embarked on a regular pilgrimage to preach at a major Hindu festival, Hardwar Mela.[1] His strategy represented the initial approach of almost all Protestant missionaries, even High Church Anglicans: set forth the Word of God, and allow its intrinsic power to work in India. The divinely ordained methods of propagating the Gospel, preaching and Scripture publication, were pursued without reference to utilitarian standards of success or failure.

By the late nineteenth century the heart of the Punjab missionary enterprise lay, not in the proclamation of the spoken Word, or the distribution of the printed Word, or the polemical dismantling of the other great world religions, but in a large-scale program of institution-building with the corresponding development of new European and Indian professions for both men and women. Alongside the gospel of the spoken word, and the gospel of the printed word, was the gospel of institutional presence. It was there, in mission institutions, that the fault lines of the mission enterprise lay exposed; it was there that missionaries encountered Indians as people rather than as abstract idealized or demonized images; it was there that the missionary enterprise had its greatest impact on Punjab, in the people associated with mission institutions who were, by 1891, 85 percent Indian and nearly 50 percent non-Christian. What missionaries built was in many ways more important than what they said.

In the beginning, however, was the word: language study, public preaching, and publication. When Robert Clark arrived in Amritsar in 1852, he commenced language study, opened a school, and began visiting influential people. Within a year of his arrival he preached his first vernacular sermon.[2] In the 1860s, Church of Scotland missionaries began itinerating from Sialkot, preaching human sinfulness and Christ as the only hope of salvation. The towns of Narowal, Daska, Pasrur, and Zafarwal would later become the Christian heartland of Punjab, but early preaching had little visible effect.[3] Even the High Church Cambridge Mission to Delhi emphasized public preaching. The Rev. G. A. Lefroy's Urdu was judged to be good, and he preached publicly to interested crowds gathered at open spaces near Delhi's principal mosques.[4]

Missionaries as a rule reported friendly crowds, and in villages the missionary tours were a public spectacle, involving as they did camels, tents, magic lanterns, and in some instances women preaching in public to women. In many instances the preaching would have been unintelligible, since language skills varied enormously among missionaries who often had little grasp of the language of their audience. They first learned "Hindustani," the nineteenth-century term for the semipopular Urdu spoken or at least understood widely throughout Punjab. But the vernacular Hindi of the Delhi hinterlands was distinct from the Persianized Hindustani of the towns and educated classes.[5] In central Punjab villages, Punjabi was often the only language, or the dominant one, or the language of the home. The Rev. Mian Sadiq complained that missionary Urdu could not be understood in the villages. Many villagers, he claimed, think that Urdu is English: "The preaching of the missionary was almost a riddle which the people could hardly solve."[6] Some missionaries learned Punjabi despite the absence of Scripture translations, creating further sensation. Miss E. G. Gordon of the United Presbyterian Sialkot Mission reported preaching at a village Christian funeral to non-Christian relatives of the deceased: "We take our Urdu Bible in hand, and mentally translating it as rapidly as possible, we read it off in Punjabi. We have been afraid lest some one might detect us and say that we were not reading that which was in the book."[7]

Other missionaries used Pushto for work in Peshawar. By 1890 the CMS claimed to be using nine languages in Punjab and Sindh: Urdu, Punjabi, Hindi, Persian, Pushtu, Kashmiri, Beluchi, Sindhi, and Gujarati; in 1886, American Presbyterians claimed some expertise in Persian, Urdu, Punjabi, Hindi, Kashmiri, Sindhi, Pahari, and Tibetan.[8] But for the overwhelming majority of missionaries in Punjab the important languages were Hindustani and Punjabi, and many missionaries regarded Hindustani as the appropriate (because elevated) language for a sermon even in Punjabi-speaking areas. Bishop French was known in Lahore as the "seven tongued Padri" from his knowledge of languages, but he always regarded Punjabi, the main vernacular of his diocese, as a "mongrel language" not worthy of his attention.[9] To this day Punjabi-speaking congregations in Pakistan often hear sermons in Urdu.

In Bishop French's case, elitist contempt for the vernacular was compounded by his idiosyncratic (not to mention incompetent) approach to Hindustani. Known as a linguist, French dedicated an aisle in Lahore Cathedral (modeled on the transept at the Cathedral of St. David's in Wales, dedicated to preaching in Welsh) to preaching exclusively in the vernacular. But it is unlikely that the hearers could make much of the sermon when French preached, for his own Hindustani was heavily Arabicized, extending to the introduction of Ab and Ibn for Father and Son. Furthermore, French paid little attention to gender (in the grammatical sense), which must have produced constructions that were, if intelligible at all, hilarious.[10]

The early missionaries all took language study seriously, and some of them at least recognized their own deficiencies. One of the best known CMS itinerants, Rowland Bateman, who "never was a scholar," had great difficulty with Punjabi, but "at last, largely through prayer, he became a sure master of the colloquial language."[11] But the efficacy of prayer did not extend to Urdu in Bateman's case. When nursing him through an illness, Thomas Valpy French became convinced that Bateman was delirious and called a doctor upon hearing him claim that he was finding comfort in Hindustani prayers.[12]

As language study in the missions became subject to fixed examination, new missionaries faced a gauntlet of language training lasting several years and encompassing several scripts. By the 1890s the United Presbyterians tested new missionaries yearly for five years in Urdu and Punjabi (in both Arabic and Gurmukhi script). By the fifth year they were expected to be fully conversant with forty questions of the Shorter Catechism in Urdu.[13] Various experiments were tried with centralized language schools, the most durable being the American Presbyterian foundation at Landour, Mussoorie, but language training remained for the most part informal, individualized, and humiliating. Self-mocking tales about language mistakes abound in missionary letters, especially those related to medical work and zenana visitation. Miss Hewlett reported advising some women to care for a sick woman by making a camel (*unt*) very hot and putting it in the bed against the patient's feet (she meant brick, *int*); and of telling a zenana student that she had a blind man (*andha*) for breakfast when she meant an egg (*anda*).[14] Occasionally a missionary was sent home for inability to learn the language, and one recruit to the SPG was dismissed with this ominous comment: "too old to learn the language."[15] Others soldiered on without mastering the language, or tried to wriggle out of the requirements. Missionary nurses and doctors objected that language exams were too stringent, not necessary for their work, and a danger to health; a CMS report of 1899 blamed the death of one missionary on overwork from language exams.[16]

PROCLAMATION AS DIVINE IMPERATIVE

Even among those missionaries who placed public preaching at the center of their mission, the standards of "effective" or "ineffective" were not always directly relevant. Proclamation was a divine imperative; preaching the source of intrinsic beneficial qualities. A colleague once found T. V. French reading Scripture aloud by a mosque with no apparent audience.[17] Backed by divine sanction, the most common homiletic approach was argument by assertion. H. M. Clark described his father's characteristic style of preaching: "The uncertainty of life and the certainty of death, the contrast between heaven and hell, between realities and vanities, between eternity and time, constitute the stimulating arguments which make this all-important duty imperative on all men. As messengers of God it would seem that our simple duty is to deliver our message faithfully, and even authoritatively, as a direct communication and command of God to them, and then to leave all results and consequences, of whatever kind, in the hands of Him whose work it is we are endeavouring to perform. We do not, therefore, state at once why it is so, or how it is so, but simply that it is so. Its truth rests upon the truth of the Word of God." But even Clark, who disliked disagreement, felt compelled to move from assertion to justification: "[T]he reasons why we know the Bible to be the Word of God, must then be forthcoming when we are called upon to declare them."[18]

Preaching and Scripture were alternative forms of The Word, and the printed Word was broadcast indiscriminately. J. T. Thompson brought to Delhi the supernaturalist scripturalism of Carey's Serampore mission, which attributed intrinsic persuasive power to the sheer physical presence of a copy of the Bible.[19] Missionaries hoped to see many stories such as that of Fazl-ud-din, a Muslim who read a copy of the New Testament and other Christian books in his father's library, leading to baptism and enrollment in the Lahore Divinity School.[20] Missionaries consequently made large investments in translation and publication.

In 1822 Thompson took time off from his preaching to travel to Serampore to see through some tracts in Hindustani, and again in 1835 to supervise the printing of his Hindi version of the New Testament and Psalms. With his publication in 1846 of the first Hindi-English dictionary, the elitism of missionaries in this part of the world, and their great respect for indigenous Indian cultures, did its part to contribute to the differentiation of Hindi from Urdu as a distinct literary language. Pointing out (in reference to the vernacular Hindi of the Delhi region) that the dialect "spoken by ploughmen, menial servants, or labouring mechanics, is not that, on which the learned in any country form their language," he encouraged European scholars to accept his introduction of Sanskrit terms into Hindi so that they might "adopt a style that shall shew his attainments to be on a par with those of the learned men of the country."[21] Subsequent students of Hindi had occasion to lament the paucity of words in Thompson, but his dictionary was incorporated into later Hindi-English dictionaries by Forbes and Bate (also a Baptist missionary).[22]

With the founding in 1836 of the Ludhiana Mission Press by American Presbyterians (with help from the Baptist Mission Press in Calcutta), Christian publishing got under way in Punjab. Between 1861 and 1871 the Ludhiana Press claimed publication of 31 editions of scripture (14 Urdu, 16 Hindi, 1 Punjabi) with 188,000 copies, and 286 tracts and books (183 Urdu, including Latin Urdu, 60 Hindi, 42 Punjabi, 1 English) in 1,346,675 copies.[23] Much of this flood of print consisted of portions of Scripture, or moralistic evangelical conversion pamphlets translated directly from the English. In one visit to the Hardwar Mela, Presbyterian itinerants gave away 25,000 "books," an expenditure that had to be justified by the Rev. John Newton under a paragraph headed "Waste?"[24]

Waste was a more fitting description than Newton could concede in terms of one intended function—that is, persuasion. There is little evidence that the hundreds of thousands of copies of Scripture handed out in Punjab changed the minds of more than a handful of people in matters of religion, although it is highly likely that they gave at least some people a general idea of the views that missionaries were promulgating. But missionary literary work was also intended to provide a Christian liturgical, devotional, and scriptural literature for a barely existent Indian church, and to promote language skills in general. Punjab missionaries contributed to the stock of regularly consulted Hindi, Urdu, and Punjabi grammars and dictionaries, some of which have stood the test of time. The Rev. J. D. Bate followed up the pioneering work of his Baptist predecessor Thompson in Hindi with his own *Dictionary of the Hindee Language* in 1875 (republished in 1925).[25] American Presbyterians concentrated on Punjabi. John Newton published a Punjabi grammar as early as 1851;[26] an 1898 revision continued to be cited as a standard text in the early twentieth century, along with the *Punjabi Dic-*

tionary (Lahore, 1895) compiled by CMS missionary H. M. Clark and Bhai Maya Singh.[27] Newton also collaborated with his cousin Levi Janvier in the publication of a Punjabi dictionary in 1854, although their cooperation came to an end when Janvier was clubbed to death by an offended devotee at a Hindu mela.[28] Their Presbyterian colleague Samuel Kellogg's *Hindi Grammar* (1876, 1893) is still consulted today.

Missionaries in Punjab failed to achieve the broad literary influence attributed to William Carey and other Baptist missionaries in Bengal, or to Bishop Caldwell of Madras.[29] Urdu, Hindi, and Punjabi were being transformed by powerful indigenous re-evaluations in the nineteenth century, and missionary grammars and dictionaries were more likely to be of use to the government of Punjab than to indigenous scholars of Urdu, Hindi, or Punjabi.[30] Avril Powell has shown how the missionary presence had a powerful influence among north Indian Muslims, although of a reactive sort not anticipated by missionaries, and the public debates between Muslim scholars and Christian missionaries or Indian Christian clergymen that began in the early nineteenth century continued to attract attention well into the twentieth century.[31] But the bulk of missionary literary work consisted, not of polemical or controversial works directed to the refutation of Hinduism or Islam, but of translations of portions of, and eventually all of, the Christian Bible and respective denominational liturgies and catechisms, beginning with J. T. Thompson's commentaries on and translations of the Scripture into Hindi and Urdu.[32]

CMS missionaries Robert Clark, T. R. Wade, T. J. Mayer, and Arthur Lewis published portions of Scripture in Pushto, Kashmiri, and Baluchi (the first publication in the language). *Pilgrim's Progress* was a favorite with both Anglicans and Presbyterians, being translated into Pushto by T. J. Mayer and Punjabi by Edward Guilford. In addition to compiling a Sindhi-English dictionary, George Shirt translated large portions of the Bible, and *Pilgrim's Progress*, into Sindhi.[33] Other translations reflected denominational preferences, with the evangelical Clark cooperating with the Rev. Imad-ud-din to produce biblical commentaries in Urdu on St. Matthew, St. John, and Acts. Shirt set to work translating the large number of tracts by Charlotte Tucker, a celebrated Victorian Christian pamphleteer known as A.L.O.E. (A Lady of England) who, at the age of fifty-four, transferred her moralizing activities to Batala (near Amritsar). She continued for another eighteen years her prodigious output of tales "in allegorical form, with an obtrusive moral," which sold more widely in India (in English) than any other Christian literature.[34] For High Churchmen there was an Urdu version of *The Pastoral Rule of Gregory the Great;* for Presbyterians Dr. Barr's translation of the theological works of the Princeton fundamentalist theologian Charles Hodge.[35]

CMS and Presbyterian missionaries developed cooperative committees to produce common versions of the Urdu and Punjabi Bibles, and the different branches of Anglicanism attempted by committee to produce an acceptable common version of the Book of Common Prayer.[36] As foreigners produced literature for a small Indian Christian community, which had a limited ability to produce scholars for purposes of consultation, there were numerous literary disasters. It was even difficult to agree on something as basic as the Christian word for God. Allah was of course too Muslim, and various Hindi words (such as Bhagwan) had idolatrous associations. Eventually different words were settled on for Urdu (*Khuda*) and Hindi (*Ishwar*), although Bishop French intervened with the Bible committee to promote a direct transliteration of the Divine tetragrammaton (that is, a new word wholly unintelligible to everyone).[37]

Bishop French's revision of the Urdu Book of Common Prayer was another notable literary disaster. Published in 1886, it was rejected by the congregation at St. Stephen's Church, Delhi, because a translation "so derived from the original Latin regardless of the English collect of the Prayer Book made it impossible for an ordinary congregation like that of St. Stephen's, Delhi, to appreciate or even understand it."[38] High Persian terms were substituted for words in common use, while unintelligible Arabic terms were used for elevated religious terms, generating a Prayer Book that was rejected as useless by Indian Christians generally.[39] Objections from Indian Christians at St. Stephen's were based on their appreciation for the older version of the Urdu Book of Common Prayer, which was also unintelligible from a vernacular point of view, but "some devout and educated native Christians, while admitting that the phrases were not current idiom of the day, yet said that 'they had now become almost stereotyped, that they knew what meaning was intended, and that they had got to love what they had become used to.'"[40]

The response of St. Stephens Indian congregation demonstrates that literary work in the end proved to be less a matter of outreach than of institutional and communal self-definition. The same could be said of missionary polemics, the public controversies conducted and controversial literature published on the relationship between Christianity and Islam, Hinduism, and Sikhism. Avril Powell's work has shown the deep impression made on some Muslim scholars and leaders by the missionary presence, and by the celebrated conversion in 1852 of Ram Chandra, a mathematics professor at Delhi College. Missionaries saw Ram Chandra's conversion as a portent of the success of their elitist strategy of recruiting the Indian elite to Christianity, and Powell has shown how this conversion, and the aggressive literary work of Charles Gottlieb Pfander, provoked some Muslim scholars into an open debate with missionaries in Agra in 1854.[41] Presented as if the goal were to change the minds of devotees of Indian religions, missionary polemics served more as a vehicle of Christian self-definition in a new imperial context.

Where Bishop French, despite his genuine commitment to an indigenous Indian church, was arrogant and upon occasion incompetent, Pfander was a loose cannon. A Lutheran missionary affiliated with the Basel Missionary Society, he compiled a Persian summary of Christian arguments against Islam, the *Mizan al-Haqq*. Expelled from the Persian borderlands by Russian authorities, he affiliated with the CMS, who placed him in Agra, and later with Robert Clark in Peshawar. He eventually took Anglican orders, and was sent to Constantinople where he caused trouble for the British authorities with what were judged to be ill-advised attacks on the Prophet.[42] Pfander and T. V. French conducted a celebrated two-day public debate in Agra in 1854 with Maulvia Rahmat Ullah of Delhi and Dr. Wazir Khan, a government surgeon in Agra.

What strikes one now is the sterility of the issues debated, turning as they did on the relative reliability of the Koran and the Christian Bible and based as they were on scriptural literalism. Christians were at a severe disadvantage on this terrain, given the sheer incoherence of the Christian Bible in relationship to the Koran. Muslim protagonists argued, based on a study of Christian commentaries down through the centuries, that the text of the Christian Scripture had been corrupted since its original composition, an argument met by Pfander with a point of logic: "This deduction we denied as false, because not proved."[43] The same arguments were carried into the twentieth century by learned Indian Christians, who debated the orthodox Muslim controversialist Sana Ullah Amritsari at Gujranwala as late as 1916 on the corruption of the biblical text and the canonical status of the Gospel of Barnabas.[44]

There was obviously a great deal more at stake in these debates than the formal issues of textual corruption. One notable aspect of Pfander's strategy is that it corresponded with the assumption of leading Presbyterian and Anglican missionaries that other religions should be attacked at their strongest points, intellectually and socially. With their geo-religious view of a momentous clash of the great world religions coming to a climax in the nineteenth century, they hoped that those who were most strongly committed to Islam would abandon their faith, bringing the entire edifice down very quickly. It never occurred to them that those most thoroughly committed to their faith would be the least likely to abandon it.

As Muslims proclaimed throughout North India a great rhetorical triumph, missionaries continued to seek out distinguished Muslims, preach near mosques, engage in disputations with learned Maulvis, and lavish attention on the very rare convert. The baptism in 1894 of Moulvie Hafiz Nabi Bakhsh, Head Arabic Moulvie in the Muslim High School in Amritsar, created a sensation not only in missionary circles but also in the new nationalist press.[45] In Delhi, Lefroy's only visible success was the celebrated "Blind Maulvi," who lapsed to Islam after being denied an increased stipend in 1893 and then returned to the church.[46] Lefroy could at least claim one change of heart, unlike his SPG colleague Thomas Williams of Riwari, who after years of preaching confessed: "It does not fail to admonish me that I with my elaborate preparation and formidable array of argument have not had one single case of application for baptism through conviction wrought by argument."[47] Since Williams specialized in defamatory attacks on Islam and the Hindu reformist Arya Samaj, his complete lack of success is not a surprise.

Missionaries were entirely sincere in their belief that short-term results were beside the point. They hoped to establish a diffusive influence throughout Indian society that was independent of actual recruitment, a goal that reflected the domestic as well as the foreign strategies of the established and mainstream denominations in both Europe and North America, determined as they were to maintain political influence and control over education, morals, and (later) religious broadcasting. Missionary rhetoric reverberated not only through Islamic communities in North India but also deeply influenced the Hindu revivalist Arya Samaj, which self-consciously mimicked missionary methods, institutions, and literature.[48] This was hardly the kind of influence that missionaries hoped for, although they might have expected it. But missionary preaching was also an exercise in self-definition, as Christianity was differentiated from contrasting religions.

DEFAMATION AND ITS LIMITS

In the new competitive environment of nineteenth-century Europe and North America, the established and mainstream churches found that their strongest appeal lay in asserting and reasserting their role as the guarantors of morality and social cohesion, work that found its visible form in educational and philanthropic work. The cry of "no religion, no morality" had a powerful appeal to western elites concerned with social stability, but it also appealed to families of all social classes, and in some contexts appealed especially to mothers, concerned about family stability and raising children with the proper moral values. In Punjab missionaries also asserted a unique relationship between Christianity and moral values that they regarded as universal, an argument that condemned by implication the major Indian religions to a morally inferior role in society. This point was psychologically satisfying to Christians, but in India as opposed to Europe it was rhetorically harmful to the mission enterprise, for it involved the direct condemnation of the religious convictions of most of their hearers, and generated a bitter Indian response that continues today.[49] Furthermore it undercut or obscured the "fulfillment" theme of finding the good in Indian religions that inspired the Cambridge Mission to Delhi and was explored by other pioneer missionaries, even evangelicals.

Missionaries had to tread carefully in their treatment of the moral effects of Islam, for they had to contend with Christian Islamophiles in Britain who took a positive view of Islamic morality. A United Presbyterian convert, G. L. Thakur Das, reported in 1882 on the need to write articles for Sialkot local newspapers on the beneficial effects of Christianity to counteract Bosworth Smith's *Mohammed and Mohammedanism*, which were quoted and published in a Mahommedan paper against Thakur Das's earlier article on morality, "The Koran Not Needed."[50] At the Wolverhampton Church Congress of 1887 Canon Isaac Taylor suggested that Islam might be better suited than Christianity to the lower level of civilization in Africa, a suggestion that was emphatically rejected by both the major Anglican missionary societies.[51] This argument exposed the contradictory attitudes toward the relationship between religion and civilization that were unresolved in nineteenth-century Protestantism. Even the archbishop of Canterbury, Edward White Benson, in a speech to the SPG Annual Meeting in 1892, asserted that "Muhammedanism does form high characters. . . . We must go to them acknowledging that God has brought them a long way on the road to Him." Taylor and Benson offended, on the one hand,

voluntarist evangelicals who rejected any relationship between the
level of civilization and the individual's relationship to God, and who
associated the arguments of Taylor and Benson with abusive racist
Afrophobes like Richard Burton.[52] On the other hand Taylor and Benson undercut missionary critics of Islam like the Rev. G. A. Lefroy of
Delhi, who agreed with them that the level of civilization mattered
and hoped to raise the level of civilization in India, but disagreed with
them entirely on the value of Islam in elevating moral character. Criticism of the morality of Islam could lead into even more dangerous waters if extended to the character of the Prophet, a point that western
non-Muslims appear to be unable to appreciate even today. The government of India was very unhappy with any public criticism of the
Prophet. A defamatory sketch of the life of Mohammed published by
the Rev. T. Williams of Riwari in 1892, with assertions that the Prophet was a *Dacoit* (highway robber), led to public disorder by Muslims,
government pressure on the mission backed up with a threat of legal
action, and an agreement by the SPG to withdraw the pamphlet.[53]

In was in their treatment of Hinduism, as they conceived it, that
missionaries were at their most offensive and ethnocentric. The lack
of sympathetic interest in Hinduism led to simplistic and even laugh-
able polemical accounts of its essential features, which were usually
followed by the assertion that Hindu idolatry is responsible for the
moral deterioration of India.[54] In 1903, writing as Bishop of Lahore, Lefroy described Indian morality in an article in the generally liberal *East
and West* as an "atmosphere of suspicion and mistrust on the one
hand, with their invariable correlations of deceit, falsehood, and un-
trustworthiness."[55] Missionaries shared with twentieth-century tour-
ists an exotic interpretation of Hindu worship, but the meaning of exoticism has changed entirely since the mid–nineteenth century. Where
westerners are now likely to find aspects of Hindu worship colorful,
exciting, and possibly even a source of enlightenment, missionaries
shared with most nineteenth-century Europeans a response of shock
and disgust that colored their entire attitude to Indian religions. This
response was heightened by the genuine Protestant revulsion against
idolatry, which was particularly strong in the prominent denominations in Punjab, extending even to the High Church Anglicans of the
Cambridge Mission to Delhi.

Even C. F. Andrews, who arrived after the turn of the century and
from the first made an effort, in the Cambridge mission tradition, of
seeing the good in Indian life, could report as late as 1908 his first encounter with idolatry in Benares: "For hours I stayed watching the

stream of Hindu devotees passing through, from temple to temple, performing their round of ceremonies, doing Puja with Ganges water, marigold-flowers and rice, at the different idol shrines. . . . How repulsive it was, yet how full of pathos! No other country in the world has stronger religious instincts. No other country in the world has allowed them to go so perversely astray . . . their objects of worship so hideous—Shiva as the bull, Kali with her red tongue and her necklace of skulls, cows, and monkeys—the religious, the spiritual instinct so strong, the material embodiment so gross. . . . Idolatry has ever been and ever will be the curse of any country, and the fruitful source of national deterioration."[56]

This is *in part* rhetorical exoticism directed to a home audience, but the recurrent missionary theme of attraction/repulsion, reminiscent in some ways of evangelicals contemplating Italian Roman Catholic devotional practices, implies an ambivalence that is more complex than simple rejection. Miss S. S. Hewlett, a medical missionary in Amritsar with great sympathy for Indian women, loved to retell to western audiences, with obvious enjoyment, the Hindu stories that she heard directly from women. At the end of one account she would draw back and admonish her audience: "Every story connected with Hindu worship is wicked, so that all that the little children hear is evil, and they have no good examples set before them to make them try to do right and be good."[57]

There is some evidence that some missionaries might have been afraid of Indians. Lefroy's partner in the Cambridge Mission to Delhi, S. S. Allnutt, suffered from recurrent nightmares about being murdered and could not sleep on the roof in the hot weather because of the danger that he would awaken screaming and rush toward the parapet. The Rev. W. S. Kelly was once suddenly "aroused by a terrible scream from Allnutt, and sat up to see him bursting through his mosquito curtains and making straight for the low parapet of the flat roof."[58] (It would be interesting to compare Allnutt's European scream with the scream described by Kipling in *Kim*, the "terrible, bubbling, meaningless yell of the Asiatic roused by nightmare."][59]

The imperial setting provided a license for moralists like Lefroy to defame Hinduism and Islam and with them Indian national character, but the imperial setting also set restraints on such rhetoric that were absent in Britain and the United States. Antoinette Burton has documented the ways that some British feminists used a particular image of Indian women as helpless and dependent in order to promote their own agenda in Britain.[60] Missionaries in Britain did the same for India in general, producing an image of India that C. F. Andrews complained about after having lived in India. He remembered missionaries that came to speak at Cambridge "whose picture of India and the East was uniformly dark. They were noble-minded men and they attracted me by their evident sincerity and sacrifice, but on missionary subjects they were almost one and all narrowly bigoted. . . . I hardly ever heard anything really good about the people of India from them."[61]

FULFILLMENT AND INDIAN RELIGIOUS REFORM

Whatever the undercurrents of imperialist self-congratulation on the one hand, and anxiety-laden fear on the other, missionaries in India were not in a position simply to assert their own moral superiority over their host cultures. A British supporter (and critic) of CMS missions put it this way: "What should we think in London, if the Italian mission, backed by a foreign power, who had defeated us in battle, were to come in swarms, settle down in our streets, abuse us in our periodicals, and under cover of treaties wrung from us in an hour of weakness, attack our cherished form of religion, denounce Westminster Abbey as a place of adoration of ancestors?"[62] Missionaries recognized that they were foreigners who had to persuade, or exert their influence in ways that reflected some sympathy with India, which many of them genuinely felt. Bishop Lefroy's defamatory rhetoric is an exceptional case, perhaps merely in his honesty, and it is difficult to see how Indians could associate with him if they took his strictures on Indian moral character seriously. But it is notable that Lefroy was repeatedly praised in Punjab's nationalist press, especially the *Tribune*, for his sympathetic utterances as bishop of Lahore on the Indian national movement. He was even hailed on his death as a special friend of the Indian people.[63] Like other colleagues in the Cambridge Mission, Lefroy was interested not merely in defamation but in "fulfillment."

Nineteenth-century fulfillment preaching, the argument that Christian truth is prefigured in the teachings of Indian religions, is sometimes treated as if it were itself a prefiguration of twentieth-century theological liberalism. It is true that Robert Clark of the CMS rejected proposals to affiliate with the Cambridge Mission to Delhi on the grounds that their fulfillment ideas were inconsistent with evangelical truth, and it is also the case that twentieth-century liberal Protestants have made great use of fulfillment theologies.[64] But fulfillment preaching first emerged as a homiletic alternative to defamation. In 1874, for example, Thomas Valpy French and Robert Clark preached together in

Srinigar, in the open by the river bank, on the following themes: "How Christianity meets all wants. Buddha's desire—to escape age, decay, sickness, death, desire, etc. Mohammed promises to gratify desire perpetually. Brahmin yogi—to be absorbed in God. All heightened and purified in Christianity."[65] Fulfillment preaching was an improvisation, of a piece with experiments to dress Indian or design buildings in what they imagined was an Indian style. In the 1870s the Rev. Worthington Jukes in Peshawar reported that when he appeared on a camel in "Afghan costume," "the people at once saw that we were not visiting them as one of the conquering race, but by adapting their dress they instinctively felt that we wished to approach them in a friendly way."[66] Jukes and his colleagues built a guest house where visitors could sit on pillows and smoke hookahs. In their preaching they emphasized the positive aspects of Islam, its kinship with Christianity, and its respect for Jesus as a prophet filled with the spirit of God. The Christian faith was presented as the true Islam: "[We] must not allow the word 'Islam' to be reserved solely to the Muhammedan religion as is so often the case. . . . [No] one submitted to God's will as did Jesus himself. We must therefore insist on Christianity being the true Islam."[67]

Missionaries also set Christianity in the context of other Indian reforming religions, whose fault lay in their failure to go far enough. Buddhism was frequently used to the disadvantage of Hinduism in the nineteenth century. The evangelical *Church Missionary Intelligencer* asserted: "The morality of Buddha is comprehensive of the laws of the second table, nor is it possible to conceive that it could have been derived from any other source. . . . The moral theory of the Buddhist was pure; the Brahminical involved in it a subversion of all morality."[68] Punjab missionaries could be just as defamatory about the Sikh religion as any other. Many of them were heavily influenced by a German philologist, Ernest Trumpp, who put his German philological training and Lutheran piety to the service of both the government and the missions with the first English translation (1877) of the *Guru Granth Sahib*.[69] He described the reading of the "incoherent and shallow" Holy Scripture of the Sikhs as a "most painful and almost stupefying task."[70] Other missionaries, however, ignored Trumpp and treated the founder of the Sikh religion, Guru Nanak, as another seeker after truth: "The grand doctrinal element of his system was the recognition of one God, and, in combination with this, certain inculcation to morality. But the aspect in which he presented the one was too dim and indistinct to induce obedience to the other."[71] A Church of Scotland woman missionary claimed that the Sikh religion "has so many strange lights and

foreshadowing of the Great Revelation. . . . Surely they are a chosen
people, meant to inherit the gift of eternal life, with many other nations who shall at that day be found saved, and walking in the Light of
the Lamb."[72] Fulfillment treatments of Sikhism were taken up and
elaborated by Liberal Protestant missionaries in the twentieth century.[73]

Overlapping to some extent with Sikhism was the Kebir Panth,
which also received positive commentary when encountered by missionaries. The *Bijak* was a set of poems composed for song and recital
by Kebir, a remarkable religious teacher of the fifteenth century venerated by some Punjabis.[74] Some of his works were partially incorporated
into the *Guru Granth* of the Sikhs. Bishop French treated the Kebir
Panth as another movement for the reform of Hinduism,[75] although
itinerant missionaries found that the complexity of the situation in
the villages, where Kebir was often venerated by untouchables, made
nonsense of any systematic theological analysis.[76] There was also genuine enthusiasm among some missionaries for the spread of Brahmo
Samaj, Deva Dharma Samaj, and Arya Samaj, with their programs to
reform Indian society and Hinduism. The Brahmo Samaj was active in
Lahore from at least 1873, when Shri Dev Guru Bhagwan, a drawing
master at Government College, founded a branch. The Brahmo Samaj
represented both an opportunity and a threat from the missionary
point of view, endorsing as it did "all progressive movements of the
day which aimed at the intellectual, social, moral and religious advancement of the people."[77] In 1887 Shri Dev Guru Bhagwan founded
the Dev Samaj based on personal conversion, renunciation of ten great
sins (including polygamy and polyandry), and cultivation of the higher
life, and created a set of schools that claimed to have produced broad
changes in the moral behavior of thousands of persons.

The Arya Samaj would eventually prove to be a much more extensive socioreligious movement in Punjab, and by the turn of the century
would be an effective competitor to the missions in rural Punjab, dog-
ging the missionary movement, copying its organizations one by one,
and countering its strategies at every turn.[78] But the first missionary
response was to welcome it as countering deadness and indifference,
breaking up and discrediting Hinduism, and leading to a competitive
environment in which Christianity would have a better chance to get a
hearing. Missionary polemicists felt obliged to remind their colleagues
of the shortcomings of the Arya Samaj, which was accused of picking
and choosing in the Vedas for a purified form of Hinduism, and of ignoring the elements of sacrifice in the Vedas (regarded as self-evidently

immoral).[79] The indefatigable and utterly ineffective missionary po-
lemicist T. Williams attacked the Vedas for obscenity in the *Lahore
Civil and Military Gazette,*[80] but the overall treatment by most missionaries of various Hindu reforming movements (which had little in
practice to do with each other) was to dilute the unrelenting hostility
to Hinduism found in missionary rhetoric.

Another contrast in both tone and style may be found in women's
account of their own work with Indian women. The British feminist
depiction of Indian women as helpless and dependent is found even
more densely in the much more extensive women's missionary writing on Indian women. If British feminists depended on this image,
women missionaries needed it even more to justify their intrusion into
the world of male clerical heroism. But unlike British feminists, missionaries knew Indian women directly; indeed their privileged access
to Indian women, unavailable to male missionaries, was the justification for their entry into mission work, first as zenana visitors, then as
doctors, nurses, teachers, and administrators.[81] Some women missionaries developed affectionate and sympathetic relationships with zenana students, which often reflected a sense of personal sympathy and
self-consciousness about their position or a straightforward and acute
frustration with the plight of Indian women. Frances May wrote in
1903 that "I think one gets a kind of passion for one's own sex out
here; it is so downtrodden, and so much nicer than the other, in spite
of everything."[82]

Polemical assertions, or even direct proselytization, were obviously
out of the question in a zenana visit, if only on grounds of courtesy.
What comes out of the published accounts, and even more strongly in
privates ones, is the assertion of a special bond of sympathy between
western women and Indian women. When Christian themes were introduced into teaching, some Hindu women in particular went to considerable lengths to reassure their missionary visitors that they were
Christians at heart in some sense, an assertion that missionaries were
not well equipped to interpret. Emily Pilkington reported another
woman who prayed for the conversion of India, but cannot pray "for
the sake of Jesus Christ, according to his word. 'I can't do that yet,
Miss Sahiba, not till my heart is quite sure.' I told her certainly not to
say one word that she did not believe with her whole heart and soul.
This pleased me too as a proof of sincerity, a priceless virtue, especially here. I love this woman so truly, and am so deeply interested in
her, that I could go on writing about her and her sayings, but I must
not."[83]

MULTIRACIAL INSTITUTIONS

This is a far cry from Lefroy's calumnies on Indian national character, or the uniform depiction of Indian women as nameless, helpless victims that characterized missionary reports directed to Great Britain and the United States. In Punjab the missionary enterprise was multiracial. It was difficult to issue defamatory comments on Indian national character from institutions that employed Indians. As early as 1871, a count of "agents" of the major Punjab missions showed the 78 Europeans outnumbered by 185 Indian Christians and 314 "non-Christian teachers" (see Table 2). The Calcutta Missionary Conference attempted another count twenty years later (see Tables 3 and 4), showing among other things a rapid growth in both Indian and non-Christian agency. The mission presence in 1891 was not only 85 percent Indian but more than 50 percent non-Christian. How did this happen?

We must look first to the assumptions lying behind the missionary enterprise. A missionary enterprise composed of institution-building was itself historically contingent, the result of the changing nature of religious institutions in nineteenth-century Europe and North America where the churches were blanketing their respective countries with new churches, schools, hospitals, publishing houses, and political parties. It would be tempting to attribute the heavy emphasis on institution-building in Punjab to the peculiarities of the region, notably the monolithic lack of response to Christianity from the major religious traditions. There can be little doubt that the image of Punjab as a site of advanced civilizations shaped a missionary response emphasizing institutions. Rosemary Fitzgerald's research has demonstrated that the image of the Zenana was a powerful incentive for women's medical work as a particularly appropriate method for Punjab.[84] The heavy emphasis upon institution-building was also used retrospectively as a justification for ongoing mission work in settings such as Srinigar or Peshawar that always remained resistant to Christian recruitment.

So convinced were missionaries of the efficacy of Christian ethos in an institutional setting that they genuinely believed in a Christian influence that was invisible. A missionary in Kashmir wrote to a colleague: "I do not see, humanly speaking, any greatly increased prospect of any considerable accessions to the church by baptism of either Mohammedans or Hindus. But there is an impression being made literally upon thousands; a feeling after God—dimly—a widespread knowledge of spiritual truths, and above all a widespread belief in Jesus Christ."[85]

It was a missionary saying in Punjab that "many a Christian will at the Resurrection come forth from a Mohammedan grave."[86]

It is important to remember, however, that Punjab missionaries had no idea what kind of response they would receive when they began building institutions. Many of them optimistically thought that Hinduism and Islam would crumble in the face of nothing more than a Christian presence. When Punjabis began to respond to Christianity in unexpected ways (see Chapter 5), missionaries did not change their strategy despite its massive inefficiency. Although missionaries built a notable concentration of institutions in Punjab, they also built them throughout India, and for that matter throughout the world. Missionaries from Europe and North America built institutions in many instances regardless of local conditions, producing a peculiar result noted by Henry Whitehead, bishop of Madras, in 1907: "We persist in spreading our best energies year after year in preaching the gospel to people who show no readiness to accept it."[87] They were interested in recruiting members ("converts"), but equally interested in extending a Christian penumbra of influence emanating from Christian institutions. It is only by focusing on that commitment that some of the most glaring contradictions of mission policy in Punjab can be understood. For missionaries, the proclamation of the Gospel was a threefold task: proclamation through preaching, proclamation through publication, and proclamation through the construction of Christian institutions.

Although missionaries built institutions everywhere in the world, what happened within these particular institutions can be understood only with reference to the history of Punjab. The fault lines of mission institutional policy first became apparent in their schools. Missionaries were not merely co-opted by government or local pressures, or by a lack of alternatives, into building schools where non-Christians taught non-Christians. They regarded the creation of institutions with a Christian moral ethos as an essential of the spread of Christianity. Exactly who should attend the schools, and who should teach in them, was a highly divisive issue at home as well as abroad, and these divisions took on a new urgency in a setting recognized by everyone as an imperial one. Church of Scotland missionary Thomas Hunter moved to Sialkot in 1856, taking no notice of his fellow Presbyterians from the United States who were already there.[88] Hunter promised the foreign mission committee that he would learn the language and preach but open no schools, as the government was doing that work. "Afterwards native Christians might quietly collect small schools; but never employ heathen teachers."[89]

Hunter came from a parochial religious tradition, where a clergyman was expected to exercise a Christian moral influence over parishioners whether they were Christian (in the evangelical sense) or not. His wife, Jane Hunter, had spent many years as a Sunday-school teacher and district visitor in Edinburgh, visiting the heathen and the redeemed, the churched and the unchurched, indiscriminately.[90] It is not surprising to find that Hunter's skepticism about schools soon evaporated. He began to appeal to the Foreign Missions Committee: "The greatest want now is more help, an increase of *machinery*, European and native, but both Christian." He described his "evangelistic scheme" as two small vernacular schools, one for boys and another for girls because, "after all our inquiries, we have been able to find, in or near Sialkot, no school, even heathen, for the neglected daughters of India."[91]

A SCHOOL AS A "WITNESS IN ITSELF"

Nineteenth-century church men and women were committed to "machinery," and the machinery of parochial institutions included schools. Missionaries like Hunter, who initially attempted to restrict the schools to Christians, were at a disadvantage in their work in comparison to missionaries like Robert Clark, who arrived in Peshawar in the 1850s and opened a school. "Christianity had come to take possession, and the school was to be in evidence, a witness in itself. Its place, therefore, was not to be in obscurity, however safe that might be."[92] The notion that the physical presence of a Christian institution was a "witness in itself," an alternative form of proclamation to set beside the preaching of the Word and the printing and distribution of the Word, was deeply entrenched in the mentality of nineteenth-century clergymen and church women. After the Hunters were killed in the 1857 rebellion, the Scottish machinery really began to roll in Sialkot, with the help of a sympathetic Settlement Commissioner, Mr. Prinsep, and his wife. By 1866 the mission owned £3,100 in property, including the Hunter Memorial Church in Sialkot (Gothic, still standing), a boys and a girls orphanage, two schools (one in Sialkot given by the government), fifty acres of land rent free from the government, and two extensive mission houses (another essential feature of the machinery). The mission was troubled (almost as an afterthought) by a lack of parishioners. Nine families of the Megh community were settled on the land. According to the official history: "They were not Christians, but they professed to be inquirers, which was sufficient guarantee to the sanguine missionaries."[93]

After 1864 the CMS Peshawar Mission was in the hands of the Rev. T. P. Hughes, who in addition to tending the school spent a great deal of time and money on entertainment. The CMS sponsored a guest-house operated according to missionary notions of traditional Afghan hospitality. According to an account by the chaplain of the bishop of Calcutta, Hughes reserved it for "native visitors to the city who may desire to converse with or hear, or at least have the reflected honor, of becoming guests of so great a *moulvi* as the Christian missionary."[94] Mr. Hughes was evidently willing to discuss any subject, even religion, with his visitors, one of whom in 1881 was "a very aged and very learned Wahhabi *moulvi* who owed to Mr. Hughes his reinstatement to a position from which he had been driven by the Akhund of Swat."[95] Hughes believed in "stratified diffusion": influence the upper classes and those below will follow. The Peshawar mission sponsored a hostel for the sons of distinguished Afghan chiefs who wished to attend the CMS high school, where children were identified in public procession according to their social rank, and a Christian literary society with reading rooms in the main bazaar where English lectures were given on improving subjects, including religion. Although not a university man (which might account for the tone of the bishop's chaplain), Hughes developed enough of a reputation as an authority on Islam to be elected to the Royal Asiatic Society. He published among other things a *Dictionary of Mohammedanism*; the government textbook for examinations in Pushto; and *The Roman-Urdu Quran* with an introduction for the use of missionaries.[96]

The parochial model of influence and institution-building was instituted regardless of local circumstances. Transferred to Karnal in 1891, the Rev. A. Haig reported feeling "strange and isolated in this out of the way place, after having spent 7 1/2 years in Delhi. . . . Soon after my arrival I called on the principal citizens of Karnal. . . . As at home, so here, one must expect a certain amount of reserve in one's parishioners which time alone can overcome. I don't therefore despair of getting to know the better among the people of Karnal, if I settle down among them. I have already found three or four men here whom I can respect and like and look forward to knowing better in the future."[97] The role of the nineteenth-century clergyman included simple presence, which was assumed to exert a healthful moral influence on the locality.

In 1888 Dr. Jex Blake, a former headmaster at Rugby who took an interest in the Cambridge mission, admitted: "The actual results garnered already by the Delhi Cambridge Mission are small; but it is impossible that 5 or 6 men of such high quality, so devout, so earnest, so disinterested, so intelligent, should live years there without making a deep and durable impression."[98] In order to get closer to the people, G. A. Lefroy of the Cambridge Mission took a room on Chandni Chowk, the main thoroughfare of Old Delhi: "I go there pretty often in the mornings and sit most of the day. . . . I hope that some may realize my accessibility . . . and drop in for a talk and inquiry. . . . [It] seems to bring me closer to them, even if only in my own thought, for I confess I have not so far been encumbered by the rush of visitors, inquirers, or the like. Still, they may come."[99]

In Peshawar, the crowning glory of T. P. Hughes's tenure came with the construction of a church for the eighty or so Christians who huddled around the CMS institutions. Poor Christians in England were not expected to build their own churches, and neither were the poor Christians of Peshawar. Hughes personally raised £2,000 for the church, which he hoped would be "in harmony with the tastes and feelings of the people—a purely oriental structure."[100] Opened in 1884, the church was described in CMS literature as the most beautiful in India, an adaptation of mosque architecture with Persian biblical texts on the walls, a chancel floor set with patterned Peshawar pottery, wood screens carved in native Peshawar patterns, and a screened transept set aside for women in purdah.[101]

In this parochial context, work by missionary wives for women appeared as if it were the natural order of things. After some training at King's College Hospital, London, Elizabeth Clark accompanied her husband, Robert, to postings in Peshawar and Srinigar in the 1850s, where she established the first medical mission dispensaries and entertained a daily stream of household visitors. Priscilla Winter opened a dispensary in Delhi in 1870 with a one-time-only grant of £20 from the SPG. By 1875 it was run on fees from private patients; local donations sustained a nurses class for Indian Christian women. Other women's work under her supervision included zenana visitation, normal schools, an industrial school, a girls' school, a school for English children, a class for training future zenana missionaries, and a small "refuge for fallen women."[102] Ten years later the mission report noted that women's work in Delhi "is much like that of parochial mission women at home."[103] In Lahore the new cathedral was surrounded by institutions for women and girls including the Society of St. Hilda (needlework and fine art society, diocesan secretary, Mrs. W. F. Armstrong), the Lahore Cathedral Girls School, and the Lahore Cathedral Orphanage and Day Schools.[104] St. Hilda's was later transformed into a Protestant sisterhood for missionary and other deaconesses, with an impressive deaconesses' house next to the cathedral. Miss M. V. Durell, a probationer of St. Hilda's Society in 1908, reported that she had been assigned to the Girls' Friendly Society and that "in most ways it is very like village parish work at home."[105]

Depending on local circumstances, the parochial and institutional commitments of missionaries were reinforced by both selective government encouragement and indigenous demand. After receiving a B.A. second class math in 1876 at Queen's College, Oxford, Arthur Lewis was sent by the CMS in 1878 to Dera Ghazi Khan on the Indus, where he arrived not knowing what to do. "I felt very much the necessity of some settled and systematic work. . . . Accordingly, without further delay, I resolved upon opening a school for boys." But the first schoolmaster, from Amritsar, was regarded by the local inhabitants as a foreigner, and no one would send students. Lewis sent the schoolmaster back and was "left with only bare walls to look at. . . . Some well educated natives of the city, who felt confident in their power to collect children, offered their services. I closed with them and we lived down all opposition." Responding to local demand for education on their terms, he soon had eighty scholars. "If a government grant should eventually be obtained, the school might be largely developed."[106] A missionary in Multan wrote to the CMS home committee complaining of pressure put on him to build institutions, and suggesting that the CMS should curtail work in schools rather than accept government aid. But the head of the mission, Mr. Clark, he complained, is constantly asking, "Can't you get more from the government? Can you get something from the municipality?"[107]

In 1890 the CMS had schools at Majitha, Amritsar, Batala, Peshawar, Simla, Kotegarh, Kangra, Dharmsala, Bhawalpur, Multan, Dera Ishmael Khan, Dera Ghazi Khan, and Tank. There were 2,626 scholars on the books, including 201 girls at schools in Amritsar, Kotegarh, and Kangra. Teachers included forty-seven Christians, forty-nine Hindus, forty-one Muslims, and three "other"—that is, a teaching staff only one-third Christian.[108] One of the flagship high schools was Edwardes High School in Peshawar, a city worked by the CMS since the 1850s that had a considerable Christian institutional presence and hardly any Christians. Robert Clark's school already had 45 students in 1855, and Clark could see early results: "I have been much pleased lately with the altered appearance of some of them; their whole manner and character seem changing, and not only do they seem to be laying hold of and appropriating what they learn, but also to be a different class of beings from the rough, ignorant, and wild creatures which they were before."[109] By the early 1880s the high school had 473 scholars, not one of them a Christian. Several of the non-Christian teaching staff were graduates of the school, which offered no religious teaching at all except in the upper forms. When Robert Clark revisited Peshawar in 1883 to report on the progress of Christianity, he proudly reported that the mission was now "bearing fruit." There were 473 scholars in the school, many of good family, who would one day have an influence in India. He cited as a particular evidence of success one of the school's first pupils in the 1850s, "who, although not a Christian, had evidently received many benefits to his own spirits and mind from his *contact* with Christianity, and is still in charge of the Persian and Urdu department."[110]

Among the goals of the missionary movement were converts (recruitment), an indigenous Indian church, and a self-justifying institutional presence (influence). By the turn of the century, in town after town in Punjab from Delhi to Peshawar, there was a notable, visible mission institutional presence, documented unsystematically in the Imperial Gazeteers and still evident today. In his "Remonstrance against American Methodist Episcopal Mission Occupying Amritsar" of 1887, Clark conceded that the CMS system has been worked for years, and "it has obviously led to the number of Church Members remaining small and this, we understand, has been alleged in some quarters as a mark of the inefficiency of the CMS work generally. We cannot consent to adopt this argument come what may. . . . [We] are . . . being used as God's instrument for totally disintegrating false religions and we are persuaded that the issue is not far off."[111] He cites as evidence in support of his argument the array of CMS institutional work in and around Amritsar:

> *Amritsar:* 1. A mission school and branches with 1100 pupils up to entrance standard of Calcutta and Punjab universities. 2. Female schools under the CEZMS, 18 branches, 400 pupils. 3. A medical mission with branch at Sultanwind near the city. 4. A medical mission for women with two medical/two non-medical ladies, 10 Christian assistants, 20 non-Christian assistants. 5. Zenana work. 6. A Christian congregation with two native clergy. 7. 3 Sunday schools. 8. A bookshop with colporteurs. 9. Mission lectures vs. Arya Samaj 9. The Alexandra School with 77 Christian girls/12 day students. 10. A girls' orphanage with 52 "inmates."
>
> *Jandiala,* 10 miles to the east: 3 CEZMS ladies, an itinerant catechist, a CMS medical mission outpost at Sathiala 15 miles further out, two catechists at Uddake.

Ajnala, 16 miles to north: 3 CEZMS ladies, and schools with a native pastor.

Tarn Taran, 14 miles south: 1 missionary, 2 catechists, two female assistants of the CEZMS mission, a leper asylum.

Majitha: a mission school endowed by a non-Christian native, 160 boys and an itinerant catechist.

Batala, 24 miles northeast: a Christian boys boarding school with 57 boys, 3 CEZMS missionaries including ALOE (Charlotte Tucker); an itinerant missionary, 4 sub-stations with schools.

Narowal, 32 miles north: 2 CEZMS missionaries, 1 missionary, a large mission school.

Neither the missionary reports, nor the Imperial Gazeteers, nor the government of Punjab's extensive educational reports, provide a way to quantify the entire mission institutional presence in the late nineteenth century. There can be little doubt that the sheer physical presence of mission institutions had an impact. The CMS's Alexandra School was placed outside the walls of the old city of Amritsar in the new civil lines, along with the railway station and the civil hospital.[112] Although serving a small number of mostly Christian girls, the school had an enormous and imposing building that was meant to establish the parity of Christianity with the Sikh presence centered on the Golden Temple. The modest CMS mission church near the Ram Bagh gate was easier to ignore. Seeing competition from missionaries in schools for Christians and non-Christians, and from the Arya Samaj as well, Sikhs responded with their own program of educational expansion. The foundation stone of the Sikh Khalsa College was laid in Amritsar in 1892, and the school soon became the "premier educational institution of the Sikhs" and the basis for rapid expansion in secondary education for both boys and girls.[113]

The mission institutional presence is difficult to quantify in part because much of it remained local and ad hoc. Missionaries often built institutions out of their own pockets, acting as local donors. T. P. Hughes and Rowland Bateman built out of personal funds beautiful churches at Peshawar and Narowal. Other CMS patrons included Francis Henry Baring, a son of the bishop of Durham and a CMS Punjab missionary, who personally endowed the Baring High School for boys in Batala and later the entire Batala Mission, and H. E. Perkins, a retired civil servant and honorary missionary who constructed CMS institutions at Amritsar and Asrapur.[114] Missionaries used not only personal money but also funds raised directly outside the normal bureaucratic channels. Dr. John Youngson faced repeated attempts by the

Church of Scotland Foreign Mission Committee to account for his private spending. In 1883 the home committee inquired about whether the Rs 10,000 he was spending on a church and school was unnecessary. Youngson paid the salaries of low-caste teachers and founded an agricultural settlement called "Youngsonabad" and a school at Daska for Indian catechists known as the "School of the Prophets." Similar inquiries about alleged extravagance emanated from Edinburgh again in 1907.[115] Katherine Beynon, a grand-niece of John Lawrence of the Punjab School, moved to Lahore in 1893 to organize work among the "domiciled community," mostly nominally Christian Eurasians, and built a new Deaconesses' House on the cathedral compound at her own expense.[116]

The assumption of institutional diffusion, with its rhetoric of bricks and mortar, was not limited to the established churches. In 1896 a Baptist missionary in Delhi, F. W. Hale, strongly defended the "mission station" approach against those who assert that missionaries "should concern themselves only with the preaching of the gospel." Institutions "have preached the Gospel as the tongue could never do," he asserted, and argued that every mission should have a strong district station with a medical mission, a strong central educational institution of some kind, an orphanage, an industrial home or a district school, and a boarding house for Christian boys. "Every man sent to India should be a specialist."[117]

FAMILY AND PROFESSION

Hale neglected to mention the mission bungalow, the location of a central feature of the mission station, the missionary family. The parochial assumptions of the missionaries were based on the presence of a clerical family, which would provide a wholesome model as Christian influence. But the conflict between family obligations and the requirements of mission service led to chronic, severe, and sometimes anguished and sometimes bitter conflict. Some of the pioneer missionaries of the CMS were obviously in flight from family obligations, living an almost Kim-like life of excitement on the imperial frontier (see Chapter 8). George Maxwell Gordon, who never married, was a "Fakir" missionary who dressed native and itinerated in the hottest and most desolate parts of Punjab. Unlike Gordon, Rowland Bateman of Narowal was married, but he more or less abandoned his wife in England and went to live "like an Indian" in the obscurity of the village of Narowal.[118] During his trips back to England to see his wife and children, he was struck with a sense of guilt over his neglect of the mission field. "Even now that I am coming within a year of my proposed retirement," he wrote, "I have not that comfortable assurance that I am acting honorably by my missionary vocation. . . . Another brother of the Rev. Dina Nath's, a bachelor of 32 years, a lovely character, is drawing near to the Font, already openly confessing his Saviour."[119]

After his wife's death in 1896, Bateman was back in Punjab: "I have had quite an ideal journey through the CMS part of the Bar, almost wholly on foot and without a *khansaman*, sleeping under *van* bushes, and eating *dal*, condensed milk, and biscuits—blistered my feet but had admirable wakings and sleepings—found a few of the scattered sheep." In 1900, at sixty years old, he walked 2,386 miles in 9.5 months, 62 miles a week. Until the very end, the drama of the conversion of young men was the center of his life. In 1901 he wrote: "[A] young Khoja of Narowal (aged 18) . . . has just come out clear of mother's and father's entreaties and threats and declared that he will be a Christian. I have been angling for him ever since he was two years old when his father, on old pupil, cousin of Waris, put him into my arms proudly. So off and on it has been going on with the father's knowledge all of these years."[120] Bateman retired to parochial and deputation work in England for thirteen years between 1902 and 1915, unhappy with "modern developments," in pain much of the time, singing Punjabi hymns for entertainment, and longing to return to India.

Other early male missionaries felt more anxiety over the abandonment of family than neglect of India. T. V. French's wife, over the objections of her father, accompanied her husband to India, but eventually returned to England, defeated by the task of raising children in India. French wrote to his wife: "I never so thoroughly realized the anxieties and harrowing perplexities which a family entail. . . . God knows how thankfully I should have accepted the duty and responsibility which, jointly with my beloved wife, attaches to me as the head of a family had God in His providence opened the way. . . . So far from shrinking from the load, it is one I should have loved to bear."[121] Robert Clark wrote similarly to his wife after they decided that she should return to her family home in Scotland: "It is hard for you and me to be so much parted; but the children need a mother more than a father, and we must commit each other to Him and follow as He leads us. This is for us the way of peace and blessing. If He gives us length of days to live together when the children no longer need you, then we will try and bring forth more fruit in old age, in India, I trust; for here I am 'at home.' "[122]

One solution to these contradictions was celibacy, pioneered as a principle by the Cambridge Mission to Delhi, the Brotherhood that allowed men to openly live with other men with religious sanction. CMS missionaries might be "at home" in India, but S. S. Allnutt of the Cambridge Mission could reply to suggestions that he might marry with an abrupt, "No, I'm married to India."[123] But celibacy in the end turned out to be more useful for women than men, an effective way of creating an institutional place for single women missionaries. For men the domestic ideal triumphed over both brotherhoods and itineration in "native dress," reinforced by the powerful Protestant commitment to a married clergy, and the opportunities for women provided by the role of "missionary wife." The steamship and the telegraph made family life in India less remote, and the growth of medical missions made it more secure.

Male missionaries, except in the Cambridge Mission, were meant to be married. In 1905 the United Presbyterian Mission informed the Home Board that they would accept unmarried male missionaries only as an exception.[124] One evangelical critic of missionary luxury complained that the missionary reports from India should be renamed "Matrimonial News." R. M. Cust represented an undercurrent of severe criticism directed against the evangelical practice of supporting families in the mission field, and the assumption that the presence of families abroad, as at home, had an intrinsic worthwhile effect. Cust parodied the argument this way: "In my hearing the present Bishop of Calcutta at a meeting in London stated, that the exhibition of a white baby was favorable to conversion; as a matter of surprise the exhibition of a spaniel or a ferret would have had more effect."[125]

There is a familiar element here of blaming women, or the presence of women, for imperial failures. But Cust was fighting a losing battle, not only against Protestant tradition and the Victorian cult of domesticity but also against the material realities of the mission. Missionary wives were missionaries, essential to the running of its institutions. As women's work became more professionalized, married missionary women's work changed. The early dispensary work in particular was transferred to trained professional women, both European and Indian. Dr. Andrew Jukes wrote from Dera Ghazi Khan in 1892 appealing for a trained medical woman, explaining that Mrs. Jukes can do dispensary work, but "she came out too late to make herself tolerably acquainted with Urdu, much less the district colloquial."[126] But even as unmarried specialists displaced them,[127] married missionaries continued to act as general mission workers in the overlapping spheres of home and mission. Dorothy Cuming's account of "tomorrow's duties" in twentieth-century Rawalpindi represents the missionary experience far better than Rowland Bateman's masochistic wanderings in the desert: "Getting out Jim's summer clothing; calling on two sick professor's wives; girls clubs; four Christian students to do hymn practice; temperance play practice; transpose a song from the key in which the girls were singing it up to where the boys can sing it comfortably; write English words for a college song; oversee another room being house cleaned; send flowers to a little girl; send word for some war knitting to be sent back; interview a girl about getting her sister into school and herself into the Women's Auxiliary Services."[128]

Even though criticism of missionary families was a losing battle, it was never given up, for it was related to a contradiction built into the missionary movement that surfaced as recurrent, bitter debates about missionary luxury. Maintaining missionary families was expensive, and contradicted the image of the missionary as a wandering preacher or self-denying ascetic living on the level of local people. Typical was a letter in *The Scotsman* in 1906 attacking Dr. Taylor of the Church of Scotland mission for taking the money contributed for the conversion of India and building "a nice rustic retreat" in Jalalpur.[129] Although difficult to recognize as such, this was a debate about imperialism. The missionary aspiration was based on sympathy for Indians as spiritual equals. How does one deal with people as equals from a position of decisive material advantage? Criticism of missionary luxury led to investigations that invariably found that missionaries lived very good lives, not only by Indian but also by British and North American standards.[130]

The Church of Scotland provided a particularly handsome standard of living for male married career missionaries, with an average salary of £333 in 1887, although the United Presbyterians were not far behind at £325 (Rupees 4,575 and 4,457 @ 13.73/£). There were additional allowances for outfit, passage, carriage allowance, and house accommodation. A pension was provided of £100 a year after twenty years of service, and £50–75 a year after fifteen to twenty years of service, with provision for shorter terms depending on circumstances.[131] The CMS was at first glance more spartan, with a basic allowance for a single male missionary in 1883 set at Rs 1,840/an, married 2,530/an, each child under 8 + 150/an. But there was a yearly medical and drugs allowance, conveyance allowance, confinement allowance, annual leave at six weeks with grant Rs 100–150, discretionary sick leave, furniture on arrival (Rs 500/700, property of missionary after five years), munshi/pundit allowance; additional allowance after eighteen years of service to meet costs of dependent children not at home, passage to and from England, and support in England on leave at rate of £200/yr for two months until medical board report, then full curacy with allowances arranged or deputation work at £275/year, etc.[132]

Most missionaries, it appears, like most privileged people, took their status and prerogatives for granted, and attempted to live with the contradictions they generated. Some even complained about their salaries. As head of the Punjab Mission, Robert Clark regarded it as his job to secure as much as possible for his missionaries. He disdained "going native" or living lives of visible poverty; missionaries should avoid hypocrisy and live as what they were, foreign clergymen living in a foreign land: "Robert Clark had no fear of 'luxury' before his eyes. He left that haunting terror to be the monopoly of certain subtle humorists who, amidst the comforts of their peaceful homes, are forever afraid of the superfluity of luxurious naughtiness into which the missionary abroad may launch forth."[133]

Other missionaries were deeply worried about the effects of inequality on their relationship with Indian Christians, particularly when confronting face-to-face criticism on the subject from Indian colleagues (see Chapter 4). Missionaries also worried about whether they were doing the right thing, and whether the mission strategy was producing the results that were intended. Rowland Bateman wrote in his journal in 1888: "Here I close my twentieth year as a missionary, wretched cumberer of the ground I feel. Nobody else seems to think so, and I have many proofs that the labour has not been in vain, and yet my own heart condemns me."[134] After eight years of service, Trevor Bomford wrote to Robert Clark: "The recent troubles raise the question of what good am I doing here. . . . I am not in touch with the native brethren here. They don't understand me nor I them."[135] Depression about ineffectiveness even occasionally creeps into the upbeat reports for the home audience. The death of a pioneer Church of Scotland missionary in 1868 was attributed to his being "prematurely old from hard service," not to mention parental opposition to his work and anxiety about an inability to "extend the field and fully occupy the position to which the church sent him to fill."[136] In her annual letter in the *Female Missionary Intelligencer*, Miss Reuther reported: "It is not easy to tell you about my work. I cannot point to any one thing and say that the Lord has done this through me. I long for more definite results, and often fear lest the labour should be in vain, and the strength spent for naught." (The editor inserted a footnote pointing out that she was temporarily working alone due to illness and furloughs of colleagues.)[137]

It is important to remember that missionaries did not regard themselves as living a life of luxury in an exotic locale. Despite the highly visible privileges that they enjoyed, which brought them recurrent criticism from home, many missionaries lived in periodic isolation not only from their families but also from colleagues. Even the majority of missionaries who worked in institutions and cities often regarded themselves as exiles from home. D. Emmet Alter wrote in 1935 from furlough in the United States: "India seems far more like home than America. I suppose that is because of the call of the work; for certainly as just a place to live it is one of the last we would pick out for a lifetime."[138]

Many missionaries took special delight in the company of other missionaries, especially on holiday or at the annual meetings. Emma Dean Anderson served as a UP missionary from 1881 to 1933, and then retired in India on her pension to do voluntary work. She wrote in 1936: "Communion Sabbath was the high day of the feast of good things. As you know, there is just no other Sabbath like Communion at Annual Meeting and this year the service seemed unusually fine."[139] Fellowship and worship were linked to missionary piety, in all its variety. Evangelicals in particular had a longing for the coming of God's Kingdom, and a strong sense of immortality. Robert Clark wrote to his wife: "That is, after all, the true secret of happiness, to do his will, and then the end! I always think of the coming of Jesus with more and more joy—the more so as I see more of myself or of others, as of the world generally. Long has the curse been on the ground and blighted God's creation—but then there will be no more curse. Long has there been pain and sorrow, but then there will be no more sorrow or crying, for he will wipe away all tears."[140] Following the death of his infant son, R. Maconachie received the following letter from Rowland Bateman: "[S]trange to say at the very hour you were laying your little one in the grave, I was reading the service over Harrison's child's corpse—little did I think how precious those words of hope and triumph would be to me soon, as taken for the sure pledge of my little godson's safety. How unexpected the welcome which such little ones will receive to their Saviour's bosom! We have believed in His unbounded love which comes over mountains to His beloved, and so we *expect* fullness of joy at His right hand; but how wonderful that the first intelligence which your son exercises should be in such a scene of blessedness!"[141]

Hope of immortality was a thin reed for even devout evangelicals to grasp, as their constant introspection on the subject betrays. More important as a consolation to missionaries was the sheer business of the everyday life of professionals administering institutions whose value and importance seemed self-evident. Supplanting a rhetoric of proclamation, a rhetoric of bricks and mortar was rooted in the institutional realities of the mission presence. On the fiftieth anniversary of the American Presbyterian Mission in Punjab, its official chronicler drew up a balance sheet, admitting: "The results of missionary labor in our Mission, in actual conversions, during the 50 years it has been in existence, have been so much smaller than we might fairly have expected, that it becomes us at this semicentenary stage of our work, to ponder the situation." The reasons for failure included the spiritual unfitness of many missionaries, who were "not in a state of mind to give him all the glory"; "the natural corruption of the human heart"; mistakes in strategy; unspecified external obstacles; the wicked lives of many Europeans; and "the worldliness which characterizes a large part of the church at home."[142] On the other side of the balance sheet were favorable influences, "which, in forecasting the future, ought not to be overlooked." These included the gradual undermining of Hinduism by western science and the spread of reforming sects such as Brahmo Samaj; the weakening of the bonds of caste, and the easing of the severity of treatment of converts by families; "the silent influence of the instruction given in Mission Schools, and especially the evangelization of Heathen females; the circulation of Christian books; the conciliating influence of Mission and other European Dispensaries, Hospitals, and Asylums."[143]

The rhetoric of institutional diffusion was just as strong among American Presbyterians as it was in the state churches of England and Scotland. In 1891 Dr. John Gillespie, secretary of the Presbyterian Board of Missions, U.S.A., visited the mission college (later Forman Christian College) in Lahore, and his address to the students, and an official response from the student body, reported in the *Lahore Civil and Military Gazette*, are worth citing at some length in order to lay bare the assumptions behind the missionary presence, and the response that they expected from Indian students as evidence of their success. Gillespie congratulated the students "for having the courage of their convictions to own that, though none of them could be Christians, yet no one could deny the influence of the moral teaching imparted in the university." He compared this work to "the Presbyterian ministers who used to gather together a number of boys in their log cabins to impart intellectual training side by side with the religious even in those days when the white man first found his lodgement in the U.S."

In response, an address prepared on behalf of the students was read by Mr. Pentanji, fourth year:

> Your evangelists are in no light sense the pioneers of a movement which is revolutionizing rapidly the moral status of the people, a movement which has struck deep its roots in this congenial soil. They are the active cooperators in the great moral upheaval that is going on all around us, being supported by the more charitable portion of the people of Europe and the United States. But the sphere of their work has not been confined to morals simply; it has widened into a larger circle, embracing the social and intellectual welfare of the land they love and instruct. Working for the people and identifying themselves with the people, their influence has permeated all the walks of life and all ranks of society.
>
> The amount of success which they have achieved by dint of watching and praying seems to us the more remarkable, when we reflect that they had so little to recommend themselves to a congeries of creeds by reason of their faith being domesticated opposite to all the established religion in India. . . . [T]hey have done, and are still doing, a really solid work in the cause of morality, humanity, and reason. . . . We acknowledge that as proselytizing bodies your missions have distinctly been unsuccessful in comparison with the work done by the Jesuits; but believe this as our honest conviction, that when the soul stirring blast of the Jesuits has passed away, the bright and well sustained flame of the Presbyterian is consuming slowly but surely the old prejudices and the bigotry of, perhaps, the most conservative and the most orthodox of the people of the earth. We are now in a transition stage which will have to end sooner or later in a mighty convulsion.[144]

This was obviously just what Dr. Gillespie wished to hear. The address ended with an appeal to raise the institution to the M.A. level, indicating the characteristic convergence of interests between mission institution-building and local demand for educational institutions. But the missionary view of a Christian penumbra extending from its institutions, and gradually moralizing and Christianizing India, should not be dismissed as a mere co-optation or an expedient improvisation on the barren spiritual soil of Punjab. As Gillespie indicated, the strategy was rooted in the nineteenth-century domestic strategy of mainstream and established churches in Britain and the United States. It was the linking of the utilitarian value of their institutions with their overarching sense of Christian mission that sustained missionaries in their work. In her novel *Clear Light of Day*, Anita Desai has captured a sense of this link with her depiction of the SPG missionaries of Queen Mary's School in mid-twentieth-century Delhi, seen through the eyes of the schoolgirl Tara:

> The missionary ladies who ran the grey, austere mission school ... were all elderly spinsters—had, in fact, taken the vow of celibacy although not the nun's habit—awesomely brisk, cheerful and resourceful. Having left the meadows and hedgerows, the parsonages and village greens of their homes behind in their confident and quixotic youth, they had gone through experiences of a kind others might have buckled under but they had borne and survived and overcome like boats riding the waves—wars and blitzes, riots and mutinies, famines and droughts, floods, fires and native customs—and had then retired, not to the parsonages and village greens, but to the running of a sober, disciplined mission school with all their confidence, their cheerfulness and their faith impeccably intact.[145]

PART II

Nonwhite, Nonmale, and Untouchable

Contradictions of the Mission Presence during the High Imperial Period, 1870–1930

4

An Indian Church for the Indian People

E ach Punjab mission was committed to the creation of an indigenous Indian Protestant church that would become sufficiently strong and independent to survive the eventual demise of the
British Empire. From the very first the imperial nature of the missionary entry into Punjab made this aspiration seem hopeless to some and
hypocritical to others. Shortly after arriving in Delhi in 1879, G. A. Lefroy wrote: "I believe that our position as the ruling power puts a dead
weight on the missionary enterprise which nothing but the direct
grace of God can possibly enable us to lift."[1] It is not as though missionaries were passive victims, caught in an imperial trap not of their
own making. Their convergence of interests with the government over
educational policy reinforced the popular belief that they were "closely
allied with the rulers."[2]

Among the imperial fault lines, even more important than their
ambiguous relationship with government was the scale of resources
controlled by missionaries, which set them apart not only from the
vast majority of the people of India but also from the Indian Christians
who were to sustain the indigenous church. Even the most deferential
of Indian Christians became adversaries of missionaries at one time or
another over this issue; they did not have to be hypercritical to detect
hypocrisy in missionary stewardship and missionary paternalism. The
missions for their part never entirely gave up experimenting with what
appears in hindsight to be the impossible task of devising a self-
governing, self-supporting, and self-extending Indian church within a
generation or two. Although they often threw up their hands in despair, they could not give up. The aspiration to extend their influence
beyond the revolutions of empire was an essential rationale for their
presence. The ultimately ephemeral nature of their presence made
their task universal rather than merely imperial, while their heavily
institutional strategy gave their presence an air of permanence. The
result was chronic conflict along a variety of imperial fault lines.

The history of missions in Punjab fits awkwardly into the narratives

of persistent progress toward a multiracial Christian community depicted by John Webster, or the straightforward exercise of power disguised as religion unmasked by T. O. Beidelmann, or the translation of
a universal Christian message through the medium of the vernacular
languages invoked by Lamin Sanneh.[3] It was instead a series of negotiations in an imperial framework between various groups of foreigners
and various groups of Indians that produced unanticipated (and sometimes unwelcome) results. Conflict was already evident at the Punjab
Missionary Conference of December–January 1862–63, where Punjab
School government administrators and leading missionaries assembled
in Lahore, surrounded by vivid reminders of the recent military occupation of Punjab, and possessed of vivid memories of the trauma of the
rebellion of 1857. The Punjab School administrator John Lawrence
wrote from England that in official circles, "there were people who believed that it was an unwise proceeding and productive of mischief."[4]
The mischief, however, was not directed at imperial rulers but at missionaries, and it was produced by the decision to allow Indian Christians to speak freely. Unlike the Indian feminists analyzed by Antoinette Burton, who spoke for Indians, missionaries were committed
to allowing Indians to speak.[5] It was a token of their good faith, an attempt to negotiate what Edward Said referred to as an imperialism of
"sympathy and congruence, not of antagonism, resentment, or resistance," one based on an appeal to "mutual experience."[6]

SYMPATHY AND ITS IMPERIAL LIMITS

In a conference session devoted entirely to the topic "Sympathy and
Confidence: How Can Foreign Missionaries Secure, in the Highest Degree, the Sympathy and Affectionate Confidence of Their Native
Brethren?" one missionary after another confessed to anguish over the
antagonism that existed between missionaries and Indian Christians.[7]
The Rev. D. Herron of the American Presbyterian Mission explained
that in the choice of a topic "there is an implied confession . . . that, as
a *general* thing, there do not exist, between the Native and foreign
members of our mission churches, the affectionate freedom, the warm,
confiding, brotherly feeling, and the intimate and sweet communion,
which should be found among brethren in Christ." Herron put the
blame squarely on missionaries for the imperfect attention to the pastoral role that Providence had thrust upon them, referring to the dis-
tractions created by the missions' institutional strategy that left little
time for missionaries "to visit them in their houses; and there con-

verse with them about their souls; to instruct their children; and endear ourselves to them by a kind and tender interest in all their affairs." His solution? "It is love that begets love. It is love, that will secure, in the highest degree, the sympathy and affectionate confidence of our Native brethren."[8]

The appeal for love emerges repeatedly from Indian Christians as well as missionaries, but the next speaker made it clear that an appeal for greater love had to be backed by positive steps on the part of missionaries. The Rev. Golak Nath of the American Presbyterian mission delivered to his obviously uncomfortable audience a lengthy catalog of the shortcomings of missionaries, in what amounted to an early Saidian critique of the entire enterprise:

> I have failed to discover how an European or American missionary *can* secure the *full* sympathy of Native converts: for sympathy must be considered a sort of substitution, by which we are placed in the situation of another, and are affected, in a good measure, as he is affected. . . . But the social position of a missionary, his intellectual and spiritual attainments, his highly civilized ideas, and his cultivated, refined feelings, must place him so far above his converts, generally, that there can scarcely be any fellow-feeling between them. A missionary would hardly find any *loveliness* in the character of his converts, to excite much kind feeling towards them. They are necessarily objects of his compassion and pity, but hardly worthy of his friendship, or capable of communion with him, except on religious subjects.[9]

This would appear to put an end to deliberation on the subject, for Golak Nath put missionaries in the position that Edward Said puts all nineteenth-century Europeans: "It is therefore correct [to state that] every [nineteenth-century] European, in what he could say about the Orient, was consequently a racist, an imperialist, and almost totally ethnocentric."[10] Furthermore, Golak Nath roots the dilemma in the institutional presence of the mission. "The missionary is not only to teach that which relates to their souls' eternal salvation but also to promote in them a spirit of industry, enterprise, and moral courage; to create for them a social and political standing; and to prepare them for an independent mode of life. In short, he has to conduct their temporal affairs, and polish their social manners, with the law of the Gospel."[11]

What Golak Nath and other Indian Christians at the Lahore Conference had done was identify the problem, which was, quite simply, imperialism. Golak Nath's imperialism was not the imperialism of rampaging British soldiers torturing and then hanging the rebellious troops of 1857, but the genteel imperialism of professional advantage and material inequality. His is not an analysis of state power, but of other forms of power: the power of western wealth and prestige; the power of the employer; the power of the educator; the power of the clergyman; the power of the professional. There was an imperial gulf lying between the aspiration to create a church that would survive the revolutions of empire, and the missionary commitment to building strong, attractive, durable, decently funded Christian institutions.

Consider, however, the point of view of the Rev. Golak Nath. A Christian minister, he was a missionary himself with independent charge of the American Presbyterian Mission at Jullundur. His daughter would become one of the first independent women missionaries in Punjab. Golak Nath was as committed as foreign missionaries to building up an Indian Christian community that would survive the revolutions of empire. Indian Christians too confronted imperial fault lines, and Golak Nath not only identified a set of contradictions that would persist throughout the colonial period and beyond but set out to provide prescriptions for overcoming the imperial fault lines.

Golak Nath proceeded to outline measures that, if unable to produce "sympathy" in the sweeping sense that he defines it, might at least produce a cooperative sense of mutual trust and respect within the mission. What he set out were the terms for negotiation between missionaries and Indian Christians that remained remarkably stable for the next three-quarters of a century. Not all Indian Christians were employed by the missions, but even at this embryonic stage the small Christian community was overshadowed by missionary institutional presence, and negotiating their relationship with it was their greatest single collective concern. How does one combine the sympathy of mutual respect and spiritual equality with the mission reality of dependence implicit in the employer/employee relationship? It is difficult to measure the precise degree of dependence on the missions by Indian Christians, but even those not in direct employment were in many ways in a position of dependence on the missionaries.[12] When Indian Christians spoke, they depicted a situation described succinctly by Henry Venn as "few scattered converts . . . in an artificial state of dependence upon Christian Europeans."[13]

Golak Nath and other Indian Christian speakers at the Lahore Conference complained about arbitrary treatment of Indian Christians by missionaries, and called for a uniform set of salary scales covering all the missions, British and American. Complaints of unfair behavior were linked to complaints of missionary coldness or aloofness, and of faultfinding interference with the customs of Indian Christians. The popular image of the missionary as itinerant evangelist is matched by the image of the missionary mindlessly westernizing converts, especially in matters of dress. Punjabi Christians complained instead of missionary interference with customs judged to be "European" and therefore denationalizing. Examples included Indian worshipers' desire to sit on chairs or pews instead of the floor, Indian women's desire to wear European shoes, and converts' desire to read the Bible and Prayer Book in English rather than Roman Urdu. The missionary aspiration for a truly Indian church directly contradicted the wishes of Indian Christians themselves. Mr. J. P. Raow, a writer in a government office, praised the very few missionaries who were willing to "put as much English theology, and English science, as they can into the heads of converts. And, although they anglicize them, they make them independent, and not *hangers-on* to European missionaries."[14]

The equation between Anglicization and independence underscores the complexity of the issues. The underlying issue, however, was clear enough: inequality of power between missionaries and Indian Christians. Missionary insistence on telling Indians how to run their lives was seen as an imperial intrusion unacceptable in a mission committed to an independent Indian church. Related to unequal power was unequal wealth, and both were tied up with the issue of motive. The missions were obsessed with the purity of motives of converts, wanting to avoid (for obvious reason) accusations that the Indian church was composed of "rice Christians" (a phrase used even in Punjab, although "chappati Christians" would have been more appropriate). Missionaries could not be satisfied in principle with nominal adherence, however inevitable it might be in practice. In these and other debates, Indian Christians put forward a more sophisticated analysis than did missionaries of the mixture of motives involved in religious decisions. Nothing brought a more acrimonious response from Indian speakers than the assertion of a missionary that some Indian Christians sought not only Christianity but also "position, honour, wealth." Golak Nath had already made the obvious response. Missionaries too had mixed motives, seeking power and privilege rather than sympathy and love. If missionaries "would adopt the life of a Hindoo fukeer, retire from his family and friends, and live in a Dhurmsala with his converts, sympathy could easily be secured." But instead, "Many converts look upon the missionary, merely as a paid agent of a Religious Company, sent for the purpose of converting Hindoos and Mussulmans to the faith of the Gospel; and, having collected them into colonies, to be their superintendent."[15]

Indian Christians would have been unaware of the decades of hand-wringing in the west about missionary motives. In its very first public statement, in 1799, the CMS pointed out the dilemma of missionary professionalism, and exposed their own anxiety that missionary recruits would be attempting a back-door entry into the clergy.[16] Unable to devise a means to ordain clergymen for overseas service only, and required by the demands of their mission to institute nonuniversity training schools for nongraduates, the CMS kept a vigilant eye on the motives of its recruits, especially those who were not quite gentlemen.[17]

But in India a missionary was a gentleman, rendering claims to "sacrifice" unpersuasive. Mr. J. P. Raow claimed to be unable to "understand what the gentleman means, by sacrifices made in coming to India. . . . The common saying is, that they come to enrich themselves; and because they do not find work in their own country. . . . Nor do I see that missionaries make sacrifices—when apparently they have all the needful comforts of life." Furthermore, converts make considerable sacrifices themselves: "No sooner does a Hindoo, or Mahomedan embrace Christianity, than he is lost, or dead, to his relatives:—all earthly ties are cut off; and he is considered an outcast. No European has had to suffer this."[18] If missionaries had mixed motives, they should be tolerant of the mixed motives in Indian Christians. Golak Nath pointed out that "Native Christians generally are poor and ignorant; and they do not pretend to conceal the fact, that when they cast in their lot with the people of God, they had some hope—many of them at least—of securing some of those worldly advantages, which the Gospel brings to Christian nations."[19]

MIXED MOTIVES AND SPIRITUAL STATUS

Debates about motive are notorious for their ferocity. Indian Christians in effect requested that missionaries give up their squeamishness about mixed motives of converts and inquirers, and recognize their own mixed motives. But it appeared to some missionaries that Indian Christians were requesting lower spiritual standards, which would undermine the entire goal of the missionary enterprise. This trading of charges about motive produced insoluble, chronic, and inexorably bitter conflict decade after decade. Given the imperial setting in which missionaries worked, purity of motive was almost impossible to establish on their part. Given the institutional setting into which Indian converts would come, purity of motives was very difficult to establish.

For women, it was virtually impossible. The small SPG women's hospital in Delhi had a "refuge" attached in 1877 where, "as a rule the women that take refuge here become Christians and not a few marry respectably."[20] Some women (and men) were brought into the churches through orphanages.[21] Other women converts appear in male conversion narratives as a problem to be dealt with after the conversion of the husband. Miss Wauton listed in *The Indian Female Evangelist* ten women described as *"some* of the converts from the schools" in Amritsar in 1880. Indian Christian women are almost never given the opportunity to speak directly. It is clear from missionary accounts that these women are mostly from an untouchable background (see Chapter 5) and all in some sense refugees, or would-be refugees, from their families. Presmi came with her whole family and is now in the Mazhabi Sikh Normal Class. Rupan, described only as an "old Sikh nun," came with her niece, Har De, a gentle child who was studying in the Mazhabi Normal Class and is now at Clarkabad (that is, an orphanage); Uiliali from the same class was now living in the orphanage as a teacher; Tara and Narani were two girls who escaped from their homes to be baptized. Tara, cast out by relations, was trained as an ayah (midwife), and married a Christian man but still lives in the compound. But Narani is "still a prisoner in her own home." Toti was "forced against her will into a marriage with a Mussulman," and Daku married to a Hindu husband who "is often annoyed by the neighbors on account of his keeping a Christian wife." Haro from the Mazhabi School was recently baptized, along with Chando, a teacher at the school in Tarn Taran.[22]

For women converts, the question of motive was tied to marital status. The Zenana workers who visited respectable homes denied the accusation that they attempted to prey on women who were unhappy in their marriages, but they could hardly disguise the fact that some Indian women unhappy with their husbands were interested in Christianity.[23] Women converts, or potential converts, were treated not as autonomous individuals with a point of view, but as individuals with institutional obligations that were disrupted by a change of religion. As Gauri Viswanathan has shown, women who converted without family sanction were often left at the mercy of an imperial legal system that was distinctly unfriendly to Christian converts in general and women converts in particular.[24] Missionaries in these circumstances often found themselves at war with family values. Miss Basu, a Christian doctor at Ajnala who shared with other Indian Christians a broader tolerance of mixed motives, wrote that "a Mohammedan woman of good position came to us. She had been a long-neglected wife, the husband having married another. Nearly all the winter she came regularly as an outpatient, always staying as long as she could. ... Whenever she was not satisfied with the Bible-woman's teaching she would slip into the ward and ask the head nurse to tell her about salvation." She finally escaped to the hospital. "Her friends have given us some trouble, and now and then we thought she might become un-steady and go back, but she remained steadfast, was prepared for Bap-tism, and on Easter Sunday, 1900, received the holy rite."[25]

Male conversion narratives provide their own obscurities. Those published in missionary literature for home consumption fit into fa-miliar hagiographic conventions of doubt, persecution, and eventual triumph. The CMS collected manuscript conversion narratives from Indians interested in ordination, and they show great complexity and little predictability.[26] Despite the persistent Indian Christian call for greater tolerance of mixed motives, those who wished for missionary approval were required to show some degree of purity of motive. Fur-thermore, Indian Christians themselves were concerned with high spiritual standards even if they defined them in a different way. They never accepted the accusation that they were advocating lower stan-dards or were dominated by worldly motives.

In these narratives interest in Christianity was stimulated either by Christian literature or by instruction in a Christian school. Although Buta Singh Peter could not find a missionary, and baptized himself in the Ganges, others report the intervention of an ordained missionary patron who served as a spiritual guide. There is little attention to guilt or fear of hell; only a musing on religious truth, followed by a convic-tion that Christianity is true. Family conflict is less prominent than one would expect. The Rev. Imad-ud-din wrote a biographical account of his father explaining his lack of conversion in terms of Muslim big-otry, with hopes for the eventual triumph of Christian truth (his father was later baptized). Imad-ud-din became a Christian theologian and so accounts for his conversion in theological terms, both in the context of the Muslim controversy and a conventional evangelical Pauline analy-sis of sin and salvation.[27] But anxiety about motives appears even here, since he wrote his account shortly after baptism at Amritsar in 1866 to clear up confusion about any desire on his part to improve his worldly position. He became a Christian (p. 3) "with the single object of obtain-ing salvation."[28] In 1896 the Rev. Ihsan Ullah of Narowal wrote to the CMS Parent Committee in London asking for permission to amend his account of his motives in his 1891 spiritual autobiography. There he had claimed that his motives in becoming a Christian were unmixed. He now recognizes that they were, in the first place, worldly, and asks for this correction to be added to his statement.[29] On the one hand converts felt a deep sense of spiritual mentorhood in their attitude to missionaries; on the other there was chronic conflict over issues of motives and spirituality.

RACE

Golak Nath identified the issues in 1863 with remarkable prescience: a conflicting analysis of the motives of both missionaries and Indian Christians; the desire of Indian Christians to adopt European dress and clothing, and use English; Christian agents' insistence on better pay and working conditions and protection from arbitrary treatment. Relations were repeatedly rubbed raw by the Indian Christian request for more money, since this brought to the fore the related issues of purity of motive and the missionary standard of living. Adopting the clerical elitism of the Presbyterian and Anglican traditions, Indian Christian clergy saw no reason to be embarrassed about the need for an Indian Christian clerical elite. In some cases missionaries supported the Indian Christian case to a home board skeptical of both missionaries and converts. In other cases missionaries used alleged venality, and implied unspirituality, as evidence against Indian Christians in conflicts over the distribution of resources and status.

Golak Nath did not include race in his anti-imperialist indictment of the missionary presence, but by the 1870s racial rhetoric was becoming more prevalent in mission circles. It is extraordinarily difficult to disentangle race from other distinctions, in part because the language of race in nineteenth-century India, as in nineteenth-century Europe, was extraordinarily fluid. Sweeping racial distinctions were the common currency of Victorian interpretations of both European and Indian history. Race was sometimes interchangeable with language; at other times it was an off-hand code word for what we would now refer to as "national character." There was never one dominant racial theory in the task of imperial classification of the peoples of India. Even a "scientific racist" like Herbert Risley, who was deeply impressed with the prospects of classifying the entire Indian population into groups based on the shape of the nose, drew promiscuously on multiple rhetorical sources when it suited his purposes. Scientific or biological or genetic models of racial difference were of almost no use at all to missionaries, committed as they were in principle to Christian universalism. Punjab missionaries were more influenced by the arguments of Denzil Ibbetson, whose influential Punjab census reports stressed environmental and economic factors more than innate physical difference.[30]

Patrick Brantlinger has summarized the now conventional view of the growth of racial consciousness in late-nineteenth-century imperialism: "Imperialist discourse is inseparable from racism. Both express economic, political and cultural domination (or at least wishes for domination) and both grew more virulent and dogmatic as those forms of domination, threatened by rivals for empire and nascent independence movements (the Indian National Congress for example) began gradually to crumble in the waning decades of the century. Not only do stereotypes of natives and savages degenerate toward the ignoble and the bestial in late Victorian thinking, however; so do the seemingly contrasting images of European explorers, traders, and colonizers."[31] Race consciousness in the missions was not the result of some hidden hand moving over imperial India, forcing people to think in racist ways, nor did it result in missionaries depicting their Indian coreligionists or Indians generally as bestial savages. But racialized rhetoric did become more important in the late nineteenth century, a change that was rooted in specific and identifiable changes in institutional and personal relationships: (1) the attempt to build up self-governing Indian ecclesiastical institutions, and (2) the struggle over resources between the growing number of Indian Christian religious professionals, men and women, and the missions.

Each ecclesiastical tradition in Punjab attempted in very different and complicated ways to experiment with methods of self-government for Indian Christians.[32] The most aggressive early attempt was the Punjab Native Church Council of the Church Missionary Society, which first convened in 1877. The Punjab Mission had been under pressure for some time to take positive steps to put into effect Henry Venn's prescription for a self-governing, self-sustaining, and self-propagating church, but an additional incentive came in 1877 with the creation of the new Anglican Diocese of Lahore.

The First Synod of the diocese was held in December 1878, and despite its ramshackle structure it provided one model of a multiracial church encompassing the civil and military chaplains of the Anglican ecclesiastical establishment, those missionaries who were willing to participate, and Indian Christian clergy and laity. Thirty-four clergymen, including two Indians, and twenty laymen, including three Indians, heard sermons from Bishop Thomas Valpy French on, among other topics, "A Comparison of Early Celtic Missions with Those in This Province."[33] Although a former CMS missionary, French had become increasingly diocesan in his outlook and had little interest in Henry Venn's ideas of separate churches for separate cultures. The creation of a diocese was a direct threat to missionaries of the more evangelical wing of the CMS, who had deep suspicions of episcopacy and long traditions of cooperation with Presbyterianism. The rise of Anglo-Catholicism within the Church of England caused severe anxiety among CMS missionaries, who were afraid that CMS Indian clergy would be infected with Anglo-Catholic influence if they associated in a diocesan synod with High Church chaplains, or with missionaries and Indian clergy from the High Church Cambridge Mission to Delhi. They might begin adorning the altar with candles or adopt the eastward position at Holy Communion.

Much was at stake in these trivial-sounding disagreements, including the character of the church that would be left behind after the end of British imperial rule. Bishop French's views on the use of wafer-bread, the mixed chalice, noncommunicating attendance, evening communions, and the eastward position all caused great or small storms of controversy in the CMS, which forbade its missionaries to participate in any diocesan synod that had legislative as opposed to strictly deliberative purposes.

The CMS alternative to the diocesan model, the Punjab Native Church Council, was launched in 1877 amidst effusive expressions of goodwill to Indian Christians from the head of the mission, Robert Clark, who was determined to promote multiracial harmony in the church and give Indian Christians an uncensored forum where their views could be aired. The opening service was far more Indian than anything in the explicitly imperialist Diocesan Synod, with full participation by Indian clergy and missionaries sharing all elements of the liturgy and sermons. Of the eighty-five communicants, eighteen were Europeans, a strong contrast to the diocesan synod where participating Indian clergy were entirely submerged in an imperial presence. Clark was committed to cooperation in everything between Indians and Europeans. "The European element is almost entirely discarded," he told the council. "We court your criticism on the present state of the Church: for you are our brethren and our friends, and with perfect confidence, we desire the freest discussion." Our desire, he claimed, "is to see you gradually become what you ought to be, an indigenous church of India."[34] Clark was attempting to foster what Edward Said has referred to as an experience of imperialism that is "essentially one of sympathy and congruence, not of antagonism, resentment, or resistance."[35] In the contradiction between Clark's multiracial goodwill and ecclesiastical paternalism lay the elements of the council's failure.

Clark intended to eliminate the problem of the "nameless Indian" in missionary literature. All proceedings and sermons were conducted and published in Hindustani (Urdu), and then published in India and circulated in Britain in English translation by Clark. In his preface to the report of the second meeting, he notes: "We will at any rate not allow it to be said, that we think *little* of *their* opinion, or hold too firmly to our own. Their opinion, like ours, may in some respects be open to criticism; but in no case can the opinion of the native brethren be ever said to be unimportant or trivial. Whatever they are, they contain the germs of the future Church of India, and we shall do well, very carefully to note them all."[36] The Indian speakers are so forthright in their criticism of missionaries and the western church, and their concerns so similar to those expressed elsewhere in this period, beginning with Golak Nath's unmasking of the mission in 1863, that I am persuaded that Clark made a good faith effort at transcription.

In its stated goal of providing the nucleus of an indigenous Indian church, the Native Church Council was a failure. It is more interesting, however, as a site of negotiation, a feature recognized by Indian Christians themselves. After a barrage of criticism of missionaries at the Sixth Meeting of the Punjab CMS Native Church Council held in 1881, the Rev. Mian Sadiq concluded that these papers show that the major value of the Native Church Council is that it allows Indians Christians to talk. "Formerly our mouths were closed; now they are open."[37] The members of the NCC represented a small but cohesive, largely urban, Urdu-speaking Christian community, working in Christian institutions or for the government, that was developing its own forms of social solidarity and religious piety. Papers were presented by Professor Ram Chundar, late Director of Public Instruction of Patiala State; Mr. Abdullah Athim, Extra Assistant Commissioner, Ambala; Mr. Mya Das, Tehsildar Muktsar, Ferozepore District; Mr. Chandu Lall, Government Education Department, Lahore; I. C. Singha, Headmaster of the Mission School, Amritsar; the Rev. Imad-ud-din, Lahore; Mr. Rallia Ram, pleader, Amritsar (see below); Mr. Nobin Chunder Das, Mission School, Amritsar; Mr. Sher Singh, Munshif, Shakargarh, Gurdaspur District. This was the Anglican (and Presbyterian) vision of the future Indian Church, with distinguished laity in positions of influence in society serving as lay pillars of a church, sustaining a learned clergy exerting a moral influence on society, and participating in dialogue and controversy with the leading currents of public opin-ion.[38]

Many of these converts had tales of conversion that involved the terrible hardship of separation from their own families. To cite only one example, Rallia Ram was the son of a Khatri shopkeeper. After his baptism in 1870, while attending the CMS mission school in Amritsar, "[h]is father," according to Clark, "deliberately starved himself to death. . . . His mother, although she lived only a few streets from him, would never even hear his name." Rallia Ram's wife did return to him in 1871, and was baptized, but when a younger brother, Narayan Das, was converted, yet another brother, Daulat Ram, brought a charge in court against the missionary; he attacked Rallia Ram in court, knocked off his turban, and struck him in open court.[39] These men (and they were all men on the Native Church Council) had gone through considerable hardship for their Christian faith, and the conventional forms of English-language Anglican piety had great significance for them. When Rallia Ram was ill in 1892, he asked a Christian friend to sit by him and sing "Abide with Me" in English.[40]

INDIAN, FOREIGN, AND HYBRID

The Indian Christian community was beset with suspicion from all sides, including from missionaries, who found Indian piety suspi-ciously "English" and the determination to use mission institutions for their own educational advancement "unspiritual." But to unmask urban Indian Christians as Macaulayan cultural collaborators, "Indians in blood in colour, but English in taste, in opinions, in morals, and in intellect," is to undercut their own point of view, essentialize Hindu-ism and Islam as the natural religions of South Asia, and deny Indian Christians the right to define their own religion on their own terms. The Rev. Wadhawa Mall identified the permanent tension within In-dian Christianity, and their own commitment to a religion not tied to a particular culture, in comments to the Native Church Council in 1898: "Not only the Gospel but English ways and wealth have come with them into this country. Thus we have two gospels here; that of our Lord Jesus Christ, and that of English customs. . . . [N]ow we are between two stones of a grinding mill. Christ's gospel and His Spirit in us press us on one side; on the other English civilization. Which shall we choose?"[41]

Indian Christians were not becoming English, but for their own rea-sons becoming Christian, making their own history in ways not al-

ways of their own choosing. It is not clear that their history is best described as "translating" the Christian message or engaging in some
kind of "transculturation."[42] The categories of East and West, Orient
and Occident, Resistance and Hegemony, Indian and British, leave little room for the Christian universalism adopted by the Rev. Wadhawa
Mall. It is easy at this point to have some sympathy with E. P.
Thompson, who in a consideration of his own missionary father
reached the point where he abominated "abbreviated categories which
too often close enquiry before it has commenced. Some in the West are
prisoners of vast undiscriminating categories . . . and bring those ready-
made slide-rules to measure, and often to obliterate, the complexities
of the past."[43]

Having been asked to speak, the Indians on the NCC spoke. They
asked that missionaries cease interfering with Indian Christian customs deemed "too European." They asked for better terms and conditions of employment for CMS employees, and for an expansion of employment opportunities for Indians in CMS institutions. They urged
the CMS to improve and upgrade the educational opportunities it supplied for the children of middle-class Indian Christians, especially at
the two Christian boarding schools, the Baring School for Boys at
Batala and the Alexandra School for Girls at Amritsar. They pressed
for formal equality between mission employees and missionaries, and
uniform scales of pay and rules governing dismissal and promotion for
mission employees. They suggested that the Indian clergy must be
learned and influential, and avoid any taint of low-caste associations.

Despite the real sense of sympathy that Indian Christians felt for
missionaries, sympathy was not the whole story. Many of them believed that too much was at stake for them to be silent in deference to
Clark's wishes. There was not only sympathy; there was subordination. They could see the imperial fault lines, and they could see the
gratifications of racial superiority that Clark never acknowledged.
They could see that there was a sense in which, to repeat the words of
Edward Said, "It is therefore correct [to state that] every [nineteenth-
century] European, in what he could say about the Orient, was consequently a racist, an imperialist, and almost totally ethnocentric."[44] Because of the genuine good feeling that existed between Clark and his
friends on the NCC, it is necessary to read between the lines to see the
implied criticism of missionary paternalism and privilege. But Clark's
own responses demonstrate that race was part of the issue. He attempted to calm Indian Christian impatience by referring to the history of the English church.

That the issue was in part one of race can be seen in the nature of Clark's (unpersuasive) responses to criticism from the members of the Church Council. He attempted to reassure his Indian Christian critics by pointing out that the first five archbishops of Canterbury were Italians. If we could tolerate Italians, surely you can tolerate the English. Furthermore, he argued, for one hundred years after the Norman Conquest no Saxon was appointed to a bishopric. Comparing British rule to the Norman Conquest was not a very wise analogy, but it is entirely consistent with the missionary point of view that empires come and go but the Empire of Christ is universal, transcending not only the revolutions of empire but also time itself. Clark thought in terms of the very long haul.

In a response to racially charged rhetoric, the CMS changed the name of the Native Church Council to Indian Church Council in the 1880s, in part because the word "native" was beginning to take on a new stigma, but in part "as an indication that language rather than race lay at the root of this separate organization."[45] Clark's lack of rhetorical success is demonstrated in the subsequent history of the Punjab Church Council, which was in terms of its stated goals an ongoing failure that could not be abandoned, and generated acrimonious conflict with Indians and Europeans, blaming each other for its failure.[46] At the twenty-first annual meeting in 1895, the majority of those present voted for the extinction of the council, and the Rev. Wadhawa Mall asserted, "Such Englishmen as were members seem to me to have been only spies to see how it worked. They had no responsibility."[47] Robert Clark wrote plaintive letters to London in the 1880s and 1890s complaining about the malevolent growth of racial antagonism in India generally, and appealed to Indian Christians: "We are foreigners, and are always liable to make mistakes. . . . [We] need loving help and sympathy as well as criticism."[48]

If Clark was patient with criticism, other missionaries were shocked or infuriated by accusations of paternalism or racism. Rev. Dina Nath of Narowal was appointed lecturer in Greek, Hebrew, and theology at the Lahore Divinity School, and was ordained by Bishop French in 1886. Two years later he resigned from the CMS in a protest over the CMS's "despotic principles of administration," which according to him were that English missionaries, no matter how inexperienced, should supervise natives, no matter how experienced; and that there is only nominal appeal from his decision, with little hope of redress.[49] Although Dina Nath did not openly charge the missionaries with racism in his resignation letter, it is clear from other letters that racial issues were becoming more explicit as the missions grew larger and more bureaucratized, and as racial rhetoric became more polarized in the late nineteenth century. One of the missionaries in conflict with Dina Nath wrote that Indian Christian talk of "'ruling-race, down-trodden natives' is utterly disgusting to us missionaries who have never been conscious of race distinction. . . . The Dina Naths seem to think us degraded hypocrites using religion as the tool to gain us influence."[50]

Although Indian women were neither ordained nor represented on the NCC, professional qualifications loomed over conflicts about the role of Indian women in the mission. Both European and Indian women learned quickly that educational and medical qualifications could be used as a kind of battering ram to gain status in the mission. As early as 1884 the CMS hoped to bring into its service Miss C. V. Bose, the first Indian women to receive an M.A. But Miss Bose set off a crisis in the mission with the following request: "Do you think the C. M. Society will be willing to give an Indian Lady the same privileges that it gives to English ladies, if it finds the former have the same qualifications? I have heard that there is a great deal of race distinction in your society. . . . In missions this evil should not exist, as missionaries profess to show that there is no difference between us and them."[51]

Clark forwarded her letter to the CMS Parent Committee in London with his own cover letter, a rambling and incoherent survey of the contradictions of his own position.[52] The result of CMS confusion was evident in Miss Bose's subsequent letter: "I have read Mr. Clark's letter, and from it I see this clearly that native agents cannot properly receive the same salary (or allowance as he calls it) on the ground that they do not need all that a foreigner needs. But who is to judge? Natives of our country are making progress not only mentally but in their manner of living so that, what would have sufficed at one time would not do so now. . . . [It] is but just that workers should have enough to live comfortably in their proper positions. The upper and middle classes of our country do not need less to maintain themselves than those classes do in your country."[53]

Neither the CMS nor any other mission ever developed a consistent policy on pay for Indian agents. CMS grants for Indian Christian clergy in 1892 were in the range of Rs 400–600/an, less than 10 percent of a missionary salary.[54] Fixed scales became more common in the twentieth century, but they were constantly being revised in ways that appeared to leave the maximum amount of discretion to the mission. The need for a higher standard of living was given a theological justification by the Rev. Imad-ud-din in an address to the Native Church Council. In the days of the early church Christianity progressed, it is true, through men of modest means. But those who argue that point "forget, that in former times, the preachers of Christianity possessed the power of working miracles, but we are not to expect those in every age. In the present day God no longer works by miracles, but by means, and by blessing the labours of those who work for him." Therefore we must have more Christians of influence. "The First Islamic converts were from the nobility and the faith spread from them."[55]

One of the results of these disputes was to persuade the CMS home committee that the church in Punjab was not yet ready for self-government, a position that became official at the turn of the century with the publication of Eugene Stock's definitive history of the CMS.[56] Robert Clark's son and biographer, Henry Martyn Clark, answered Stock by placing the blame squarely on missionary paternalists: "The story is distressful and humiliating. The non-success was, to put it briefly, not due in the main to the Indian Christians. Possibly the plan was premature, but the failure is to be traced to the shortcomings of the foreign workers. Instead of frank confidence, the Council met with suspicion, jealousy and opposition in quarters where it should have commanded generous support. Cramping regulations fettered its liberty of action, and the withering blight of a narrow ecclesiasticism stunted its free developments."[57]

That missionary attitudes made an important difference in the success or failure of missionary initiatives to promote indigenous churches is clear enough in the history of missions in Punjab and elsewhere. Accounts of mission failures in other parts of the world stress the bureaucratic triumph of missionary paternalism,[58] or the spread of racist ideas,[59] or the new influence of the perfectionist theology associated with the Keswick Conventions in England,[60] and all of those factors were evident in Punjab. But the fundamental problem was inequality of resources and power, which placed limits on the efficacy of sheer good will. In 1899 the CMS surveyed eighteen missions throughout India on the progress of self-government, and the results showed striking uniformity. Missionaries were in control because of their access to foreign resources. At the same time, in a bewildering array of synods, presbyteries, conferences, and hybrid missionary/ecclesiastical bodies, Indian Christians had rights of representation, and missionaries and Indian Christians were in a state of permanent negotiations over the allocation of those resources, and over the definition of a new phenomenon: a multiracial Indian Christian church.[61]

The success of Indian Christians in working their way into middle management in mission and ecclesiastical institutions would be a tedious story if it were not for the highly charged rhetoric surrounding the struggles. At stake was not merely patronage, but the future of the Christian church, the British Empire, and immortal souls. That sympathy survived these debates alongside subordination is evident in the example of Dr. Datta. In 1885 Dr. Dina Nath Pritho Datta, MB (Edinburgh), applied for a position as a medical missionary with the CMS. A protégé of Rowland Bateman's from Narowal, Datta's exciting tale of his conversion, with harrowing accounts of separation from his family, washing in sacred springs, and appearances before magistrates, featured prominently in CMS literature. Datta received a thorough British education, obtaining a gold medal for his University of Edinburgh postgraduate thesis on the plague.[62] On the basis of those qualifications, and the precedent of appointments of other Indians as CMS missionaries, Datta insisted on the same terms of employment as a British missionary. Bateman wrote to London: "I believe that he is not fighting a personal battle, but being filled with national enthusiasm, no less real because its basis is crude, he thinks it a point of honor to assert himself as a native of India. He is a very prayerful youth and so I have great confidence that you will have no real difficulty with him and that if not at once at least before long I shall have the joy of welcoming him as a fellow worker."[63] During negotiation, Datta took a position as a government surgeon, although he wrote to Bateman from Karnal (where in the absence of a chaplain he took the English services in the civil station church) that he still hoped for a CMS position.[64] Despite Robert Clark's efforts to secure an appointment, the Parent Committee took the position that a policy of appointing qualified Indians in the mission would have injurious consequences for, and prolong the dependence of, the infant Indian church. Datta remained a civil surgeon.

Far from becoming bitter over his rejection, Dr. Datta became a ubiquitous CMS lay Christian in Punjab. Addressing the Lahore Diocesan Synod in 1892 on the subject "How Can English Congregations Be Brought into Closer Touch, Social and Otherwise, with Native Christians?" he admonished European Christians to condemn anyone heard using the words "black" or "nigger."[65] He was deeply involved in the inner spiritual and bureaucratic life of the CMS mission, serving as a member of the lay and mostly European Corresponding Committee, and also as an Indian member of a joint committee of missionaries and Europeans created after the failures of the Punjab Native Church Council.[66] In 1916 he offered his services to the CMS on his retirement at age of fifty-five, and they agreed eventually to provide a house but no stipend to supplement his private practice.[67] In 1919, however, he was asking once again for a full missionary connection. The mission secretary, C. M. Gough, wrote warning that "Dr. Datta has an excellent influence, is loyal to CMS but in Committee nearly always votes for the greatest liberality to Indians in money matters."[68] The Parent Committee eventually approved an increase in stipend, persuaded in part by a letter from a missionary enclosing a letter from Dr. Datta that "breathes a spirit of affection for the CMS."[69]

BIBLE WOMEN AND CATECHISTS

A key role in the emergence of a multiracial Indian church, caught permanently between subordination and sympathy, was played by "Bible Women." Deployed in part to meet the particular needs of the Indian Christian community, Bible Women were also modeled on the armies of paid and volunteer district visitors who blanketed late Victorian cities. The problem of the "nameless Indian" is particularly irritating in the case of Bible Women. The missions recruited large numbers of women assistants of various kinds, classified under shifting categories in the statistical tables and often identified individually not by name but as "a bible woman." Their recruitment and deployment remained decentralized until the very end of the missionary period in Punjab. The Lahore branch of the Zenana Bible and Medical Mission (ZBMM) never even submitted statistics on the number of Bible Women employed, although the ZBMM throughout India in 1891 claimed 47 European missionaries, 27 "assistants" (mostly Eurasian Christians), 149 "native teachers and nurses," and 54 "bible women."[70] Accounts of Zenana visitation often assume that it was done primarily by European women, but after clearing away the tales of European female missionary heroism, it turns out that ZBMM work in Lahore was initiated by an Indian Bible Woman, named only as Martha, who began work on the ZBMM payroll in 1863 under the supervision of American Presbyterian missionaries. "All her early morning hours were given to visiting, and she had ten women under daily instruction. Her husband complained that she had so much to do that she could hardly attend to her household work. . . . She had some simple skill in medicine and nursing, which was much appreciated."[71]

Often the wives of catechists, if not unmarried or separated converts, Bible Women visited in home and village, telling Bible stories to assembled groups in public or private and providing small amounts of education or medical care. In Multan Mrs. Briggs, an Indian Christian married to a British missionary, and her daughter Janie Briggs supervised the work of one Christian teacher and two Bible Women, one named Hannah. Janie described Hannah's work in 1881: "She has been working here for rather more than a year, and in a very good neighbourhood. Several of the husbands of the women whom she visits are very respectable, and well off, some holding good offices in the Kacharie (Court). One of them is an inspector of schools." She visited regularly about twenty houses, more Hindu than Muslim. "In some the women are very anxious to read, and to do darning on net, which makes very pretty *chaddars*. At the Inspector's house they are always very eager to have the New Testament read to them. . . . All seem very fond of their teacher, and welcome her heartily."[72]

Miss M'Reddie gave an account of her visit with Rebecca to new work in the village of Ihaledra, making it clear that Bible Women provided language skills unavailable to missionaries. The wife of a local hakim had asked for someone to teach village children. On the roof of her house eighteen children assembled as prospective scholars, and forty adult women. "After the preliminaries of taking down the names of the girls who meant to sit in the prospective school, Rebecca took out a large picture of Daniel in the lions' den. Great was the astonishment and delight at the picture of the lions, they having no idea what the creatures were like. Then, amid deep silence and great attention, she told them in broad Punjabi the story of Daniel's courageous faith in his God, and of the loving, watchful care of that God, and the wonderful deliverance He granted His servant. It is very rarely that a village woman is found who can read, and those who can are always the wives of the headmen. So to sell portions of Scripture or Gospels is utterly impossible in the villages among the women. Of course, in cities, women who read are abundant now, and we always make a point of giving all those who are our pupils a neat copy of the New Testament and a single gospel."[73]

The reports of four Bible Women working in Ludhiana in 1893 are worth quoting as direct accounts, even though mediated by a missionary. They do not include the horror stories about Indian family life that characterize missionary platform rhetoric; they do include the routine Indian Christian assertion that they know many "secret Christians" who cannot come forward for social and family reasons. *Aishan*, who works with middle-class Muslims, claims that many confess Jesus Christ as Saviour privately to her. *Manglo* appends a list of fourteen Hindu and Mohammedan women "who hear the Word of God with their whole heart. . . . There are very many others in the city to which the Word is read, but those I have named hear with gladness, and my heart also is made glad. Bhagwanti is a Hindu woman who joins in singing the hymns, and so does another woman, a Granthi (i.e. one who reads the Granth, the sacred book of the Sikhs)." "Both of these have gladly bought hymn-books for the purpose of being able to join in the singing." *Ruth,* wife of village school teacher Yusuf in Banohar, visits caste Hindus: "The women often ask about Christ's second coming, when it will be, and in what manner. They call me to their houses of their own accord, and listen both gladly and thoughtfully. They also ask, 'Why has death come into the world?' and they say, 'We are all like sheep, your words are right, but we cannot do them, for we are occupied day and night in our household duties; we can only think of our work, we cannot think of God.'" *Partapi* visits Hindus of all sorts; "they also learn to read, and some to knit gloves and stockings. They also take pleasure in committing to memory hymns, texts, and prayers."[74]

The work of the Bible Women replicated the work of domestic visitation in England and Scotland, where it was directed indiscriminately to a population of churchgoers and nonchurchgoers. Unlike English nonchurchgoers, Punjabi nonchurchgoers were non-Christian, but the theory of "diffusive Christianity" allowed Bible Women to broadcast Christian values without reference to recruitment. "Influence" was regarded as a form of evangelism, whether it produced converts or not, but the pastoral work of Bible Women, and of male clergymen and catechists, was broadcast with equal vigor to the small Christian community. Their hymns, texts, and prayers became the elements of a distinctive Indian Christian piety shaped jointly by missionaries and Indian Christians.

Professional training for Bible Women remained decentralized and informal until the 1930s, as there was no high vision of clerical professionalism for missionaries to impose. For men it was a different story. T. V. French's divinity school in Lahore, opened in 1871, was designed to produce an educated Indian elite and foster the emergence of a new Alexandria in Lahore. Given French's background at Rugby and Oxford, it was thoroughly elitist and focused on literary study, but also vernacularist with a curriculum of church history, general history, Christian doctrine, Christian evidences, the liturgy, Hebrew with exegesis of the Old Testament, Greek with exegesis of the New Testament, and lectures in the Hindu and Mohammedan systems. The students were set to work on Hebrew and Greek, with lectures on "The

Being of God," "Proofs from Design in Creation," and "The Best Arguments to Be Used with Infidels." The Rev. Rowland Bateman had
some inkling of how unsuited this scheme was to the practical needs
of the Indian church. Having reached an agreement with the Rev. Mian
Sadik to embark upon a village tour, he received a summons from
French to abandon work in Narowal in order to teach in Lahore: "Our
own arrangement was that Sadik should teach me Punjabi. The new
order was that I should teach Sadik Greek. We had got a camel to carry
us both; now we were to spend our time in a class-room, mounted at
best upon chairs."[75]

Irrelevant to the pastoral needs of the Indian church, the Divinity
School was never a success. Even French, in the midst of discussions of
the Nicene Creed and the Fifth Book of Hooker and a close study of
Butler's *Analogy*, took time out to teach his students repetitive apho-
risms, with a focus on Jesus: "Masih par dekh, Masih par dekh" ("Look
to Christ").[76] The Divinity School's Annual Letter for 1891 reported
that two students were reading Greek, one Hebrew, and one Persian,
but added optimistically that Makhan Singh has developed a talent for
music and plays the American organ in chapel and a harmoniflute at
our evangelistic meetings.[77] The Divinity School was quietly closed in
the early twentieth century, and theological training continued by the
CMS on an ad hoc and localized basis for "catechists," a category from
the early church revived in an imperial setting for a new subordinate
class of clergy. By the 1930s professional training for catechists was
conducted at "pastoral institutes" directed by ordained Indian clergymen (Rev. James Williams, Feroz-ud-din Tak, E. Jawahir Masih, Bara-
kat Ullah, Jawahir Masih) at Amritsar, Ajnala, Clarkabad, Fategari, and
Lahore. The SPG had a similar institute at Karnal, with a missionary
in charge, and the UP maintained a successful theological seminary in
Gujranwala in the hands of a missionary; a missionary directed the
Church of Scotland's "School of the Prophets" in Daska.[78] The UP
maintained a curriculum in Hebrew and Greek at Gujranwala, but at
all of these institutes for training Indian clergy and catechists attention was eventually paid, not to Greek, Hebrew, and Reformation
apologetics, but instead to "hymns, texts, and prayers" with a focus on
the person of Jesus as an object of devotion.

AN INDIAN CHRISTIAN CULTURE

Under the noses of missionary theorists, administrators, and theologians, a hybrid Indian Christian culture emerged in churches, homes,

and schools, shaped jointly by missionaries, Indian Christians, and British supporters of the missionary movement. Indian Christianity was unselfconsciously hybrid and multicultural as well as multiracial. Indian urban worship services displayed a superb eclecticism with a polyglot liturgy and a mixture of foreign and indigenous Christian music. A worship service in Amritsar in 1880 was conducted by an Indian catechist (nameless in Miss Wauton's account) in the Mission House Schoolroom. Benches faced a plain table and chair with yellow cloth spread on the floor, a harmonium, and the "little band of native Christians, who form the choir, have arrived, and sit down in native fashion on the ground." Girls arrived from the various Christians schools, thirty or so at the beginning of service, swelling to fifty toward the end. The men outside in the braziers' bazaar stop work during the service. "We commence with a hymn, or rather a bhajan, sung very heartily by all who know the words, while the native instrument (something like a guitar) is played to keep the voices in time, and the Baboo, sitting by the choir, beats on his drum to add to the effect." Prayers were read first in Urdu, then in Punjabi. "After this the Psalms are read, verse by verse, the Glories chanted in Punjabi, which, with its alliterative words, 'Pita ate Putr ati Pawitar atuva di ustat howe,' has by no means an unmusical sound." Then a text from the Punjabi New Testament, followed by a hymn with harmonium instead of drums, "Awe Prablin Tera Raj," "Lord Let Thy Kingdom Come," then another bhajan, sung to a "native tune" with the band, followed by the discourse, "by no means short," by which time the number of worshipers had grown to 60.[79]

Indian Christians developed an enthusiasm for illuminated texts in Urdu and Punjabi, and biblical scenes, especially the life of Jesus. In 1876 the Rev. Mian Sadiq's house in Batala contained "clean whitewashed walls,—on one side a coloured print of our Lord sitting by the well of Samaria,—the 'Silent Comforter' in Urdu turned over at the text for the day,—and on the other, some shelves well stocked with books."[80] In the Multan FES dispensary, Mrs. Grimke's illuminated scripture texts in Urdu and Punjabi were used as dispensary tickets, and mission hospital wards in Punjab were decorated with Gurmukhi and Hindustani texts from the Daybreak Workers' Painting Union, an organization of British women dedicated to supplying the material culture of Christianity for the Indian church by illuminating text cards in unfamiliar languages. In 1886 British Baptist women from Tunbridge Wells, Edinburgh, Glasgow, Bristol, Leicester, Birkenhead, Abingdon, Kettering, Cheltenham, Wisbech, Gloucester, Hemel Hempstead, and

Clevedon shipped Christmas gift boxes to India containing dolls, scrapbooks, toys, workboxes, ready-made clothing, books, workbooks, knives, pencils, thimbles, book bags, jackets, skirts, tops and other toys, remnants of prints or flannel, coloured pictures, Scripture pictures and illuminated text cards in Hindustani, Hindi, Bengali, Tamil, or Telugu.[81]

In the Christian schools, negotiations over what language to use, what to wear, and how to sit (especially in worship services) generated a chronic if low-level state of crisis. The teachers at the Lahore Christian Girls School attempted to answer charges that they were Anglicizing their students with accounts that only put on display the deep contradictions involved in their institution. Miss Keay wrote: "Our girls all wear the native dress, that is, they do not wear hats, and we enjoin on them the propriety of having their dresses simply made. . . . At the same time I must here observe that the native dress is sometimes rather indecent . . . and I do not see that we can do better than recommend to them a simple English dress under the chaddar." To demonstrate their good faith, the teachers attempted to go native themselves: "In this I have tried to set before them an example. Miss M'Phun and I actually went to the bazaar one day with the intention of purchasing chaddars for our own wear, but failed to find the kind of material we sought. Every one cried out so against it, that we, for the time, abandoned the idea. When I told the girls what we had been meditating, they immediately and with one voice strongly objected, adding, 'Oh, then, if you wear chaddars, we will wear hats.' Of course that silenced me, for I could not deny that they had sound logic on their side."[82]

In the emergence of indigenous Christianity in Punjab, nothing was more important than the development of popular Christian hymnody. Missionaries proved in the long run to have considerable influence on but little control over Indian Christian hymns, which were from the first of enormous popularity and importance in worship services and festivals. The second meeting of the CMS Native Church Council was held at Christmas in 1878, and the celebrations associated with the meeting were more important in the long run than the deliberations about Indian self-government. Christians in Amritsar were awakened before daylight by Christmas carols sung by boys before the door of every member of the Christian Church. A Christian Mela in Ram Bagh, with badminton, a merry-go-round, and evening fireworks, followed this.[83] The embrace of Christmas (Bara Din, literally "Big Day," in Hindustani) provided along with hymnody an important link between urban and village Christians. In the 1880s Baptist Christians from Baraut walked thirty-six miles into Delhi to join urban Christians for their Christmas celebrations.[84]

Just as missionaries attempted translations of the Bible and Prayer Book, so did they translate hymnbooks. The first edition of the *Masihi Git ki Kitab*, which would become the standard hymnbook for the Anglican communion in North India, was published in Agra in 1843, and a new edition with tunes was issued in 1879.[85] Dr. Newton compiled an American Presbyterian book of psalms and hymns in Urdu, some contributed by Mr. Bowley of the CMS, a Eurasian in Lutheran orders (although in the words of Dr. Newton, "Mr. Bowley was not a born poet").[86] Newton compiled a second hymnal, with the Rev. J. F. Ullman's revisions of Bowley's contributions, and in 1872 a third AP hymnal was published with 332 hymns from Ullman's hand alone.

These official translations remained popular with some urban congregations, but they were rapidly supplemented by Hindustani hymns set to popular tunes, which fell into the categories of bhajans (Hindu) and ghazals (Muslim). How this worked can be seen in attempts by teachers to provide suitable hymns for children in schools, where hymns were sung daily. At the Christian Girls Boarding School in Lahore, a good portion of each Sunday was devoted to singing, beginning with early-morning worship at St. John's Divinity School, followed by open-air hymn-singing in the afternoon (weather permitting) and an evening service at Mr. Forman's American Mission Chapel, following which the girls would sit out in the cool of the garden, singing hymns.[87] Only about one-half of the girls spoke English; for them hymns were readily available, accompanied by a harmonium, from Ira B. Sankey's *Sacred Songs and Solos*, whose songs, despite their incompatibility with the traditions of High Church Anglican and formal Presbyterian worship, had a deep and abiding influence on North Indian hymnody.[88] The other girls were treated to Hindustani hymns, which caused more difficulty for the teachers.

At Miss Wells's Baptist Girls Boarding School in Delhi, the girls greeted their teachers on Christmas morning in 1884 by singing a hymn translated for them by a missionary, Miss I. M. Angus, who had studied Urdu for two years.[89] Designed to be sung to the tune "Mendelssohn" (best known as "Hark the Herald Angels Sing"), the text is a straightforward translation of a Victorian favorite, put into a formal Urdu style.[90] "He bore the weight of sin" is a rather difficult concept to put into metric Hindustani, but the refrain is very serviceable and foreshadows the simple praise for Jesus that characterizes much Hindi hymnody.

Even in a school setting, with a large degree of control, missionaries found the practice of writing hymns beyond them. Students wrote their own hymns, such as "The Longing for the Heavenly Home" composed by Jane Daud (described as a "little lame girl") of the Christian Girls School in Lahore.[91] Written in simple, straightforward Hindustani, it resembled in style the simple if emotional evangelical hymns of late-nineteenth-century British and American revivalism. But the missionary, Miss Henderson, did not think that the translation, written also by Jane Daud, did justice to the "sweet and simple little hymn, and she has very kindly made a fresh translation," printed alongside the Roman Urdu, into the flowery romanticism of mid-Victorian popular piety. It is hard to envisage what Ira B. Sankey would have done with this translation, but it is difficult to imagine "Deliver Me. Who Can? No Help for Me in Man" being sung at a Moody revival.

Missionaries readily conceded their helplessness in the face of a growing enthusiasm for song among Indian Christians. When G. A. Lefroy first arrived in Delhi in 1880, he was taken to a Christian service at the home of an unnamed catechist in the Daryganj neighborhood. The catechist began the service with a bhajan, an Indian hymn with Hindi lyrics, and bhajans were interspersed with the Anglican elements of the service—confession, absolution, Lord's Prayer, magnificat, creed—throughout the evening as the crowd grew from eight to twenty-five or thirty, all male, the majority of them according to Lefroy not Christians. "Of the melody I will leave you to judge, but I must confess that, though . . . now getting quite accustomed to them, I shall not easily forget the impression they made on me the first night I heard them."[92]

The use of bhajan and ghazal tunes by Christians was controversial among missionaries and Indian Christians alike. Bhajans in particular were associated with popular lyrics deemed obscene, arousing fear that the obscenity would be invoked even with new Christian lyrics. But missionaries found themselves unable to use prerogative as a means to control the growth of hymnody through translation, and were faced with a rapid expansion of a Christian hymnody that can only be described as indigenous. Even the most respectable of Indian Christians took up hymnody. At the second meeting of the Native Church Council, the Rev. Imad-ud-din was praised for his translation of a work by Archdeacon Pratt of Calcutta, in reply to the atheists in Europe. But he explained to the meetings that, as a result of the death of his wife leaving an infant child, "thus causing me a sorrow that will not be removed until I shall see her again in heaven," he hoped to compose a book containing Christian Ghazals, or native poems.[93]

By the 1880s missionaries were not only translating western hymnbooks but also transcribing Indian hymns and tunes for a missionary and western audience—a way of allowing Indians to speak in song. In 1886 Mrs. J. D. Bate, a Baptist, published the *North India Tune Book*, with a preface explaining that "in no instance have any been given that have not been taken down by the compiler from the lips of the singers, and carefully compared, when possible, with the same tunes as sung elsewhere."[94] This book records a vibrant tradition of hymnody, one shared by the different missions throughout North India: "It has been generally supposed that the same tunes are sung by Native Christians very differently in different stations. The writer has taken every opportunity of comparing the versions given by persons from different Missions and other stations, but has arrived at the conclusion that the variations are slight and unimportant."[95]

Mrs. Bate preferred ghazals to bhajans, as "tunes in the Urdu style" were well marked with "something of a martial ring." But she confessed herself "unable to obtain any clue whatever to the metrical names of the Ghazals," and as for the bhajans, "It really seems as if the ancient pundits composed their curious systems for the express purpose of throwing dust in the eyes of the unlearned." Furthermore, "singing natives do not confine themselves to the strict routine of the tune as English singers do, they consider this poor and monotonous; shakes, roulades, turns, and slight alternations to give a freshness to the tune are much admired, particularly by the singer himself." But Mrs. Bate persevered. "As to the existence of the metres there can be no doubt, and they will be found duly classified in this book, the first time, it is believed that such a classification has been attempted."[96]

Neither the tunes nor the hymns in the *North India Tune Book* are attributed to a particular person; indeed Mrs. Bate does not mention a single Indian. But despite that characteristic discourtesy, the *North Indian Tune Book* is a respectful book, deferring to an Indian Christian tradition and intended to enlighten missionaries and other foreigners about a lively tradition that was growing before their eyes. This task was made even easier with the publication of Mrs. Emma Moore Scott's *Hindustani Tune Book* in 1888, which provided harmonized tunes for singing by missionaries, and for accompanying with a harmonium the unison singing that prevailed in Indian congregations. This expanded the range of songs to include those most popular with the American Presbyterian and Methodist Episcopal missions. Neither included Hindi translations of Moody/Sankey hymns; both contained many hymns of praise to Jesus, as Yishu or Masih or both, as in tune 9 from the *North India Tune Book*, featured as tune 1 in the *Hindustani Tune Book*: "Yishu Masih mero prana bachaiya" ("Jesus My Dearly Beloved Saviour").

As ordained missionaries and Indian Christian men wrangled over issues of self-government in native church councils, synods, and conferences, Mrs. Bate and Mrs. Scott had embraced and recorded for the missionaries the songs of a self-sustaining and self-propagating Indian church centered on hymns, texts, and prayers. Missionaries showered praise on those Indian Christian clergy who wrote polemical or theological treatises, but the very fact that the authors of Christian bhajans and ghazals are difficult to identify makes it clear that their composition was out of missionary hands. When Dr. Newton's revised American Presbyterian hymnal was published in 1923, it contained sections of bhajans and ghazals, but the authors of a centenary mission history confessed: "In regard to authors . . . we were able to find very little." Eighteen bhajans were credited to the authorship of "Shuyja'at Ali," "but we have no other facts concerning him. Some of his bhajans are very popular among Christians in our villages."[97] They asserted that hymns for village work were written by catechists or Indian Christian pastors, and noted that Padre Janki Parshad of Farrukhabad is much in demand at Christian melas to sing "The Mangal Kathal, a poetical setting of the life of Christ." Padre Radha Krishan of Farrukhabad is the author of a number of bhajans popular among our village Christians. He has also written a Hindi epic poem setting forth the story of salvation as found in the Book of Romans, sung to a tune which is popular during the rainy season.[98]

The hymnal's new title, "Zabur au Git," reflected another distinctive development in Punjab, the emergence of the Psalms (Zabur) as a popular form of rural and urban hymnody. This story belongs with the large-scale growth of rural Christianity, which transformed the church as well as its hymnody (Chapter 5). In 1888, in one of his frequent laments over the failure of initiatives toward self-government in the Indian church, Mr. Rallia Ram suggested to the Indian Church council that the church had been established "contrary to the habits of the country. We ought rather to have worshipped in a hut or under a tree."[99] Convinced that the Church Council should have been, yet manifestly was not, the basis for the emergence of an indigenous church, Mr. Rallia Ram failed to appreciate the hybrid yet indigenous

Christian piety that was all around him. Furthermore, at the very time of his speaking, Punjabi Christians were already worshiping in huts and under trees in unprecedented numbers, although middle-class urban Christians and many foreign missionaries were barely aware of the unexpected development of village Christianity.

5

Village Christians / Songs of Deliverance

Missionaries and Indian Christian leaders expected the church to grow from the top down. It grew instead from the bottom up, catching them by surprise. After several decades of missionary work, there were only a few thousand Christians in Punjab by 1870 (see Table 5). The glacial progress of Christian conversion caused private soul searching, but missionary leaders placed their faith in clerical professionalism and the emanation of Christian values from Christian institutions.[1] When pressed by anxious home administrators they invariably referred to the large Christian institutional presence or the inscrutability of God's providential wisdom.[2] In 1878 the United Presbyterian Church baptized not one person; in the 1880s, however, their numbers grew from 660 to 10,165, and other missionary societies, especially the Church of Scotland and the CMS, began a pattern of rapid growth that took everyone by surprise (see Table 6) and continued in fits and starts until the 1930s, when there were nearly half a million Christians in Punjab. Although remaining a small percentage of the overall population, the Christian community was growing so rapidly that J. S. Grewal refers to the perception among other communities of "spectacular success."[3] In many parts of Punjab there was no Christian presence at all, but in the region that would become the heartland of Punjabi Christianity, the districts of Gujranwala, Sialkot, and Sheikhupura, Christians constituted more than 7 percent of the population by 1931.[4] The exodus of almost all Hindus and Sikhs from the Pakistani Punjab in 1947 resulted in the unexpected circumstance of Christianity being the second largest religion in independent Pakistan.[5]

Almost all the new Christians came from one caste or community known in the census reports as Chuhras, and usually referred to in English as "sweepers." "Chuhra" and "sweeper" are labels with a heavy stigma. Village Christians came from one of a number of Punjab communities that were treated by many of their neighbors as "untouchable," another problematic label. More recent terms, including

TABLE 5

Indian Christian Community in Punjab, 1871

	Congregations	Towns and villages containing Christians	Christians 1871	Communicants 1871	Indian Christian contributions 1871, in Rs.
AP	11	11	411	185	356
BMS	10	18	406	127	328
CMS	13	23	558	189	623
CS	2	3	80	51	32
OTHER	5	11	185	45	12
SPG	3	4	110	47	310
UP	3	8	120	63	
TOTAL	47	78	1,870	707	1,661
1861		22		1,136	358
1850		4		98	25

SOURCE: Derived from Calcutta Missionary Conference, *Statistical Tables of Protestant Missions in India, Ceylon, and Burma for 1871* (Calcutta: Baptist Mission Press, 1873).

TABLE 6

Growth of the Indian Christian Community, 1871–90

	1871	1881	Percent increase	1890	Percent increase	Percent increase 1871–90
AP	411	977	137	1,467	50	256
BMS/ZMS	406	1,010	148	2,150	112	429
CMS/ZMS	558	1,238	121	4,055	227	626
CS	80	155	93	2,191	1,314	2,638
MORAV		34		20	−41	
SPG/CMD	110	946	760	681	−10	519
UP	120	660	450	10,165	1,440	8,370
OTHER	185					
TOTAL	1,870	5,020	168	20,729	312	1,008

SOURCE: Derived from the statistics for "native Christians" in Punjab and Delhi in the Calcutta Missionary Conference, *Statistical Tables of Protestant Missions in India, Ceylon, and Burma for 1871* (Calcutta: Baptist Mission Press, 1873); Calcutta Missionary Conference, *Statistical Tables of Protestant Missions in India, Burma and Ceylon, Prepared on Information Collected at the Close of 1890, at the Request of the Calcutta Missionary Conference* (Calcutta: Baptist Mission Press, 1892).

"Harijan" (Gandhi's term), "scheduled Caste" (the official term in independent India), and "Dalit" (a term taken up by untouchables themselves in the last twenty years), are anachronistic if applied to the late nineteenth and early twentieth centuries. The statistical pattern of Punjabi rural church growth has been documented in major, programmatic twentieth-century missiological analyses designed to draw lessons from the "mass movements" for the missionary movement.[6] In the most recent of these, John Webster expresses a healthy skepticism about our ability to generalize about Dalit conversions, which were occurring throughout India both in the colonial period and after, and which we know about almost entirely through missionary sources or antimissionary polemics. What missionary sources do tell us is that conversions in Punjab set off a series of crises within the missionary movement and Indian Christianity, some still unresolved.

One of the consequences of village conversions was missionary acknowledgment of autonomous Indian agency, if only for their own rhetorical purposes. In accounting for the origins of Christian growth, missionaries identified the key agent as a man named Ditt. Almost all that is known about Ditt comes from the account of United Presbyterian Missionary Andrew Gordon, whose narrative of Ditt's conversion is treated primarily for its effect on the mission rather than its consequences for Ditt's own community, and has been repeated in almost every study of Christianity in Punjab.[7] Ditt lived in a village near Mirali in the Sialkot district, where the Chuhra community had its greatest strength of Punjab. In 1873 an Indian Christian landowner brought to the Rev. Samuel Martin "a dark little man, lame of one leg, quiet and modest in his manner, with sincerity and earnestness well expressed in his face, and at that time about thirty years of age."[8] Martin was a forceful man who had survived a bout of typhoid in a Confederate prisoner-of-war camp before embarking on a seven-month sea journey to India in 1866 to be a missionary. But he hesitated at this request for baptism. What were Ditt's motives? Martin was, after all, a Presbyterian. Could he baptize an illiterate inquirer, with no instruction, and send him on his way?[9] Martin finally baptized Ditt because he could see no scriptural ground for refusing.[10]

Although from Gordon's account we know very little about Ditt's motives, Martin's agonies were laid out in detail. Furthermore, Gordon was straightforward about Ditt's sheer usefulness to the mission: "Whilst we, with all our might and main, were grappling with the gigantic difficulty of the temporal support of native converts, God raised up this poor little illiterate cripple, of a base and despised caste, to make the 'new departure,' practically solving one of our most difficult problems."[11] As a dealer in hides, Ditt was independent of the mission. Disappearing from their view for three months, he returned with his wife, daughter, and two near neighbors, all requesting baptism. For the next six or seven years Ditt spread his views as he worked, setting off a wave of Chuhra conversions to Christianity. Although he never asked for money, he was eventually granted a monthly stipend of Rs 7 a month to act as a full-time evangelist.

Ditt's position on the mission payroll indicates that the "problem" of dependency was not solved, but only taking new forms. Missionaries and Indian Christians were now, and would remain, dependent on each other (codependency might be a better label). The "problem" of no growth whatsoever, however, was solved, in part because the UP mission missionaries decided, upon watching Ditt at work, to take the momentous step of minimizing the importance of their own judgments about a prospective Christian convert's motives. "From that time also the aim in dealing with inquirers was not so much to study their motives, as to satisfy ourselves that they know Christ and believed on him. There always have been, and always will be, some in all countries who make a profession of the Christian religion from improper motives."[12]

Why should the United Presbyterians, and not another denomination, overcome their scruples about the motives of converts? The UP mission shared with other denominations in Punjab a high view of an educated clergy spreading truth and knowledge through improving institutions. But the UP missionaries also had a sense of being outsiders that was rooted in their experience in the American Midwest, where the more prosperous small towns and cities would often support at least two Presbyterian churches, one characteristically known as the First Presbyterian Church (of the Presbyterian Church in the U.S.A.) and the other as the United Presbyterian Church. The "UP" Church was almost always smaller and less prestigious, but United Presbyterians sustained a sense of superiority over their larger mainstream brethren who were judged to be more worldly and less committed to their Presbyterian faith. Following old Scottish Presbyterian practice, United Presbyterians allowed only the Psalms to be sung in church, although they could be accompanied by instruments and set to any tune (even "Danny Boy"). Furthermore, United Presbyterians were intensely proud of their small denomination for supporting such a large body of missionaries around the world. They thought of themselves as a missionary denomination.[13]

In Punjab, as in the United States, the Presbyterian Church in the U.S.A. (AP) was the more influential of the two denominations, with prestige to lend to elite educational institutions. The AP missionaries hoped that their college in Lahore (later Forman Christian College) would be the Princeton of Punjab. They worked more closely with the Anglican evangelicals of the CMS than with their fellow countrymen in the UP mission, serving with Anglicans on the committee of the Punjab Religious Book Society and as consultants to the Government of Punjab Department of Public Instruction.[14] United Presbyterian missionary Robert Stewart reassured his readers that UP missionaries, by way of contrast with their AP brethren, shrink from "durbars, levees, dinners, and calls on the more fashionable English."[15]

The clerical and educational elitism of the American Presbyterians provided something of a contrast with the United Presbyterians, who were marked not only by their insistence on using Psalms rather than hymns in worship but also by a strain of radical spiritual egalitarianism that characterized the inner life and worship of the mission. Of Ditt, Andrew Gordon predicted that in the life to come "the low caste and humble life of the illiterate Ditt will not prevent him from eclipsing many of us who have made higher attainments, and received honors from our fellow men."[16] It is possible to imagine Dr. John Newton of the AP mission or the bishop of Lahore expressing similar sentiments in all sincerity, but they would have been less likely to imagine the implications of such a sentiment when dealing with relatively large-scale conversions in the Chuhra community. Bishop French, after all, regarded Ditt's Punjabi as a language unfit for the church.

THE CRISIS OF VILLAGE CONVERSION

John Webster contends that "it was primarily the foreign missionaries rather than the Indian Christians who responded most eagerly to the Dalit initiative."[17] It would be fairer to say that Ditt's conversion caused a series of crises among both foreign missionaries and urban Indian Christians. A number of Indian Christian clergymen provided early pastoral care for untouchable converts. Although individual missionaries in many of the missions welcomed Chuhra conversions, the response to untouchable conversions among the majority of foreign missionaries in Punjab and Delhi ranged from reluctant acceptance to sheer confusion to outright abhorrence.[18] The American Presbyterian (AP) mission was slow to embrace untouchable conversions. In 1894 one of their leading missionaries, J. C. R. Ewing, sent a letter to the Board of Foreign Missions referring to Chuhra conversions as "raking in rubbish into the church."[19]

Ewing's use of the word "rubbish" denotes a serious difficulty faced jointly by all of the Protestant missions and by the Indian Christian community. The Chuhra was, in the words of the 1881 Punjab census report, "the sweeper and scavenger *par excellence* of the Punjab."[20]

Those were the words of Denzil Ibbetson, orientalist scholar/adminis-
trator par excellence of the Punjab who directed the 1881 census and
later served (briefly) as Lieutenant Governor of Punjab.[21] Ibbetson's
massive investigation into caste in Punjab was an attempt to delineate
and explain the social structure of a conquered province in convincing
detail, but also to give the reader a sense of how Indian society appeared to Indians themselves.[22] Europeans had been aware for some
time of the category of "outcast" in India, and the very earliest missionaries were attacked for attracting only outcast converts. But in
mid-nineteenth-century Punjab untouchability had not been prominent in missionary indictments of Hinduism, which was pilloried instead for its polytheism, idolatry, lack of morality, mistreatment of
women, and superstitious reverence for the parasitic priesthood of
Brahmins. The concept of "untouchability" appeared to become more
important, and more reified, in the course of the nineteenth century,[23]
and in his early reports Ibbetson followed earlier usage by treating low-
status communities on a case-by-case basis rather than as variants of a
unified India-wide group of untouchables.

Coming from a highly stratified society, Ibbetson took social stratification for granted. But issues of social stigma as a source of hierarchy
played a large role in Ibbetson's census reports, and it is possible to see
the general category of untouchability gradually being imposed on a
variety of stigmatized communities suffering under a variety of stig-
mas.[24] Ibbetson classified the Chuhras with two other scavenger castes
as socially "the lowest of the low. As a rule [they] can hardly be said to
stand even at the foot of the social ladder. Their hereditary occupation
is scavenging, sweeping the houses and streets, working up, carrying to
the field, and distributing manure, and in cities and in village houses
where the women are strictly secluded, removing night soil. They
alone of all classes keep those impure animals, pigs and fowls; and they
and the leather-workers alone eat the flesh of animals that have died of
disease or by natural death."[25]

One might expect an imperial administration with largely secular
interests, committed to commercial progress and imperial aggran-
dizement, to focus on the economic functions of caste rather than
subjective questions of religious hierarchy and social stigma. Although
Ibbetson stressed status, he did not neglect economics. The Chuhras
were "numerically and economically one of the most important in the
Province, only exceeded in number by the Jat, Rajput, and Brahman,
while they occupy a very prominent position among the agricultural
labourers of the Panjab."[26] The phrases "agricultural labourers" and

"village menials" obscure the realities of field work throughout the north Indian plains, where various systems of servitude, sometimes referred to in the United Provinces as "jajmani," generally prevailed, and where stigmatized "village menials" labored for land-holding families and were expected to perform other kinds of forced labor.[27] In central Punjab the Chuhra head of the household might have a hereditary relationship with a group of one to four households, or serve one family full-time for a fixed term. The family was on call for the heaviest farm labor, especially spreading manure, and women cleaned houses and stables, fetched and carried, waited on visitors, and delivered messages. The family characteristically received a share of the major crops, a few chappatis a day, grazing rights, a site for a hut, branches for fuel, and gifts in return for their services at weddings and funerals.[28] Although representing a very small portion of their village duties, the removal of night soil (that is, excrement) from homes and public spaces, referred to as "sweeping," was a task characteristically associated with Chuhras only, and accounts for the highly charged allusion by Ewing to "rubbish."

Of fourteen "backward and depressed" classes identified in the 1931 census of Punjab, five constituted more than 4 percent of the population each: Chuhra, Chamar, Dhobi, Dagi/Koli, and Julaha.[29] Although defined functionally or geographically, each group belonged to the category that Ibbetson described as "village menials"—that is, agricultural laborers who performed other services in the village as well, such as sweeping or washing or weaving, depending on the circumstances. Of the five large "backward and depressed" groups, only Chuhras and Chamars reported any Christian adherents, and only Chuhras any significant numbers. By 1931 there was a scattering of Christians among caste Hindus, including Christian Brahmins, Jats, Katris, Mirasis, and Rajputs, but the majority of Christians came from Chuhra communities. Beginning in the 1870s, Chuhra conversions occurred in waves for half a century, ending in the early 1930s. The census enumeration of Chuhras in 1921 and 1931 became progressively more confused as village laborers changed their self-ascription, returning themselves as Chuhra, "Hindu" Chuhra, Musali (Muslim Chuhra), Mazhabi (Sikh Chuhra), Ad-Dharmi (see Chapter 9), Christian Chuhra, or simply Christian. It is at least possible that a plurality of Chuhras were Christian by 1931; it is certain that a large majority of the 391,270 Indian Christians enumerated in Punjab were Chuhras—that is, the most stigmatized minority in the province.[30] Those Chuhras who became Christians remained, and have remained, tenaciously devoted to their new faith. Their point of view deserves considerably more respect than it has received until very recently.

But why Chuhras, and not other "village menials"? And why some Chuhras, but not others? Confusion reigned in the official literature about distinctions between different stigmatized communities. Most Chuhra communities had small shrines to Balmiki, Balashah, or Lalbeg, about whom there were different stories depending on the region and the religious environment. The mud shrines, sites for veneration, were usually topped with a small flag, and ghee (clarified butter) or grain presented to them. It was said that the Chuhras did not believe in the transmigration of souls but believed in a heaven and a hell, the latter being temporary until the deity is pleased to allow the soul to go to heaven. Charged with classifying everyone in India according to caste, census officials struggled to sort out the difference between Balmiki and Bala Shah and Lal Beg. Their confusion was matched by ignorance and indifference in missionary literature, which treated Chuhra religion as unified.

All accounts of Chuhra religion identify stories that attribute the origins of the community to Balmiki (or Valmiki). Although the stories vary, central to each of them is the attribution of stigmatized status to Balmiki combined with the honor of composing the Ramayana.[31] Lalbeg, or Lalguru, was said to be "a corruption of Lalbhek (red attire), who was a red-coated disciple of Balmik."[32] The main difference between Balmikis and Lalbegis in some accounts was the majority religion, Hindu for Balmikis and Muslim for Lalbegis. The census enumerator argued on the one hand that "the distinction between Balmikis and Lalbegis is a purely arbitrary one," and on the other that "the two sects do not usually intermarry."[33]

Variation according to the surrounding dominant religion went much further in the districts to the east and southeast of Lahore, where the Mazhbi Sikhs claimed not to be Chuhras at all. They were classified variously as Chuhra by caste and Sikh by religion, or as "Sikh Chuhra" (Mazhabi is Punjabi for "belief"). Instead of venerating Balmiki, their guru was the Sikh martyr Teg Bahadur, whose mutilated body was retrieved from Delhi and brought to the Sikh heartland by some Chuhras who were then and there admitted to the faith as a reward for their devotion. According to Ibbetson, although Mazhabi Sikhs were "good Sikhs so far as religious observance is concerned, the taint of hereditary pollution is upon them; and Sikhs of other castes refuse to associate with them even in religious ceremonies."[34]

The census categories are arbitrary and in many ways no doubt inaccurate impositions upon a complex social reality, but there is little doubt that the issues of status and dignity were important to village laborers of Punjab and not merely to the census enumerators. Although according to Ibbetson, Mazhabi Sikhs intermarried with Lalbegis, other sources assert that "[t]he Mazbi Sikhs . . . keep themselves aloof from the Chuhras."[35] To the west of Lahore, where the majority of Chuhras had converted to Islam, they were referred to as Musalis, and were "considered distinctly a higher class than the Chuhra."[36] To a community with a history of partial camouflage in relationship to surrounding religions, the presence of missionaries itinerating throughout rural central Punjab provided yet another alternative to the broad categories of Balmiki, Lalbegi, Mazhabi Sikh, and Musali.

Missionary elitism constituted blinders that prevented them from seeing Indians who wished to become Christian. Records are scattered with accounts of groups of inquirers who took the initiative with missionaries, only to be ignored or dismissed. As a UP missionary put it: "[W]as rather they who sought us out, than we who sought them."[37] As early as 1859 a community of twenty-five Megh (weaver) families near Sialkot became Presbyterians, although the movement failed to spread further within their community.[38] In 1869 ten persons in Tapiyala village, forty-five miles southeast of Sialkot, requested baptism from Church of Scotland missionary John Youngson, who complained of little time for itineration because of schools, medical work, and orphanages.[39] Sections of the Chamar community in Delhi affiliated (separately) with the Baptist and SPG missions in the 1860s. Between 1872 and 1874, seventy-five families of weavers at Rampura, near Riwari in southern Punjab, were baptized by the Rev. Tara Chand of the SPG (one of several Indian Christian clergyman who took an active pastoral role with stigmatized communities). They maintained their new identity over several decades in the face of missionary attempts to enforce orthodoxy until the last Christian weaver was excommunicated by an SPG missionary in 1905.[40]

Neither census takers nor missionaries devoted much attention to gender divisions in the communities seeking out missionaries. But missionary women in charge of urban institutions for women found them filled with Chuhras, who upon migrating to cities were more closely identified with sweeping than they had been in the villages.[41] In 1880, while male CMS missionaries in Amritsar were obsessed with building institutions that would rival the Golden Temple, Miss Hewlett was conducting a Sunday School class for one hundred Chuhra women, including some who were attending her day school to learn needlework and reading. "Some among these are very desirous to be received into the Christian Church, and are being tested and taught, with a view to baptism. After they become Christians they must be kept and employed, as it is impossible to allow them to remain at their old work, where companions and habits would of necessity be utterly incompatible with their Christian profession."[42]

INDIGENOUS INITIATIVE

Though often nameless in mission records, the leaders in conversion movements obviously acted on their own beyond the control of the missionaries. Ditt brought "one after another of a large circle of friends and relatives for baptism."[43] A United Presbyterian report from Pathankot District in 1884 describes Sarna as a village with no Christians, but Hirá, the "head man," "reads his Bible to his people and preaches a little of his own accord." A little to the west "we found some who said they were Hirá's disciples; thus the leaven spreads." Despite missionary pressure, Hirá would not openly convert, but held back in the hopes that "by and by many others will come out with him." The same year Changhatla, an elder of the Awankha congregation, brought in for baptism eighteen of the thirty-one men from Dinanagar village.[44] The first person buried in the (CMS) Christian cemetery in Bahrwal was the "originator of all Christian work hereabouts, Vasawa Das." After his death, there was a falling away among those "who had accepted Christianity from personal love to Vasawa Das."[45] The CMS Tarn Taran report of 1925 reported the death of Isa Das, the oldest village reader who "came out with his entire village thirty years ago and has since led them unfalteringly as shepherd and guide."[46] The same year a CMS missionary at Malla reported that "I baptized the greater part of the Mazhabi Sikh community in three hours. They are a bright lot of people and decidedly above the level of the ordinary Chuhra. It was through relatives of the headman having become Christian in another part of the Punjab that these people decided to enroll themselves as catechumens."[47] In the 1920s, far away in the new canal colonies of the Jhang Bar, work was being opened for the CMS in new villages through the influence of a nameless evangelist "who goes about selling hides."[48]

In the welter of mixed motives on all sides, some village converts clearly hoped that missionaries would act as patrons or advocates in ongoing disputes over terms and conditions of labor, or perhaps even assist them in a lawsuit. This missionaries were reluctant to do, and

often refused.[49] But from the beginning of rural conversions, and continuing well into the twentieth century, there were occasional instances of missionary intervention, enough perhaps to keep hopes
alive. Given the task of setting up rules governing the relationship between village converts and the mission, the Central Punjab Village
Mission Board conceded that "whenever a true case of wanton oppression is brought to light, it will obviously be the duty of the superintendent missionary to assist the converts in their efforts to obtain redress,
either by exhorting the wrong doers or by appeal to the courts."[50] In
1925 the CMS reported from Tarn Taran that "[a] few cases of forced
labor have been settled by the good offices of the authorities, whom we
find always ready to help as far as they can."[51] In a town in Dera Baba
Nanak district, the Salvation Army supported a strike by thirty-three
Christian sweepers who were receiving only one chappati per house
swept per day plus one anna six pice each six months. The strike failed
when property owners swept their own homes.[52]

There was ambivalence on all sides in these relationships. The
adoption of the status of "Christian" did no more to transform dependency in labor relations than the adoption of the status of "Mazhabi Sikh" or "Musali," but marginal help from a missionary was better
than no help at all. Village laborers were generally ignored altogether
by British imperial rulers, although missionaries confronted understandable confusion from Christian and non-Christian Indians about
the relationship between the mission and the government. At the
same time, missionaries were willing in some cases to use their influence with the government, such as it was, fueling the very confusion
that they bemoaned. It is clear from these encounters that Indian converts, or potential converts, did not share or even understand the fine
missionary distinctions between various categories of motive.

Those missionaries sympathetic to untouchable conversions began
to develop a literature of oppression about the village Christians. UP
missionaries in particular complained in annual reports of how hard
Chuhras were worked, and of the need to preach to them at night after
they returned from hard labor. They complained even more of interference with Christian worship: "[T]heir village masters or some petty official of the government will break in among them, and drag them
away to work with blows and abuse."[53] In the 1920s and 1930s, when
the Christian communities were larger and well established, scattered
reports of missionary intervention with the authorities appear in the
records, and at least some Christians got the impression that conversion would lead to exemption from some forms of labor.[54]

Like middle-class Indian Christians, low-status converts hoped for schools and in some cases employment opportunities with the missions. The Rev. James Smith not only pioneered Chamar work for the Baptists in Delhi but also served as vice chair of the Municipal Commission; "his position enabled him to provide employment of a humble kind for the poor converts."[55] The women enrolled in the Chuhra Sunday School in Amritsar not only had the opportunity to learn needlework but later to train as midwives at St. Catherine's Hospital. Employment opportunities for rural Christians were strictly limited, but the missions naturally attempted to provide schools. The first Chuhra baptisms by CMS missionaries occurred when Rowland Bateman and H. U. Weitbrecht were camping together at Fatehgarh and the heads of a Chuhra community came to ask to be taught the Gospel and given a school.[56] The Rev. Wadhawa Mall of Bahrwal reported in 1895 that in Kathanian, one hundred Mehtars (sweepers) agreed to become catechumens if a school were opened for them, "and these all shelter themselves behind one who is their leader, saying 'when he becomes a Christian we will also.'"[57]

Missionaries and Indian Christian clergy alike were irritated and sometimes perplexed at the frank avowal of mixed motives in these requests for education. When retrenchment struck the UP mission in the early 1930s, a delegation of village Christians appeared, protesting the closing of schools in villages where the government school was unwelcoming: "We gave up untouchability to have the mission care for our boys and now you are going."[58] But early village inquirers shared missionary assumptions about the close link between religion and education, despite their lack of sophistication (or greater honesty) in expressing it. H. E. Perkins of the CMS explained, "I find that it would be easy to get hundreds of thousands of converts if only the mission will undertake to educate their children. In fact, when some of the converts of a neighboring mission were asked 'what good they expected to gain from their change of religion', this was the only advantage which they mentioned. I admit the difficulty. It is our duty to give the people so much education as will allow them to read the Bible. It is not our duty to bribe them into becoming Christians by teaching them Urdu."[59]

CONVERSION AND DIGNITY

In places where protection, employment, or education were not forthcoming, and even in places where Christian status brought disadvantages, conversions did not always cease. Conversion was not merely a question of schools, jobs, and patronage, but dignity, and dignity was worth the disadvantages that came with conversion. Caste Hindus and Muslims made fun of the pretensions of Christian converts, just as they had ridiculed Mazhabi Sikhs and Musalis before them.[60] Bapsi Sidhwa, in her novel of partition, *Ice-Candy Man*, portrays a sweeper in Lahore who has become a Christian being taunted by a Muslim mob: "O ho! He's become a black-faced gen-tle-man! Mister *sweeper* David Masih! Next he'll be sailing off to Eng-a-land and marrying a memsahib!"[61] In the villages, the abandonment of carrion eating by some converts lowered the Christian standard of living, and those Christians who abandoned the flaying of dead cattle lost the income from selling the hides. Disputes over Sunday work further disrupted relations with employers, lowered Christian wages, and often led to brutal retaliation from employers or the police.[62]

None of this deterred those Chuhras who had made the decision to become Christians. A Church of Scotland report in 1918 described Chuhras as farm laborers who "live in houses which they can never own; they have to bear the hostility of their non-Christian employers. Slavery is what they call their own condition and they would welcome an even smaller wage under Christian auspices."[63] Upon complaining that two European Catholic priests were evangelizing Protestants at Toba Tek Singh, Mr. Natha Singh observed, "[T]he people are so ignorant that they do not mind which side they follow as long as they are not called sweepers."[64] The irrelevance of Western denominational distinctions is inscribed in the 1911 Punjab census, where those who returned their denomination as "R. C. Dutt" were discovered to be Presbyterians, while the "Church of India Jesus" and the "Church of Christ Mission" adherents were determined to be Anglicans. Others described themselves as belonging to the Church of America (721 persons), Church of America Mission, Church of Africa, Church of Jesus, American Britain Church Protestant, American Brother Mission, Israeli, Jesus Army, American Army, and the Russian Mission.[65] Ignorant though they were of European theological divisions, the new Christians knew what they were doing. There was a convergence of interests among new converts, missionaries, and Indian Christians to raise the status of village Christians (an issue of no interest at all to the imperial government of India).

John Webster's unflattering contrast between missionary enthusiasm for low-status converts and the "unenthusiastic and even antagonistic" attitude of "higher status Indian Christians" is unfair to some Indian Christians. There was a spectrum of opinion, most of it negative, among missionaries and higher-status Christians. Missionaries and urban Indian Christians were divided in their opinions about what to require of village converts. Some were openly antagonistic to them, and it is no doubt fair to say that the minority enthusiastic about Chuhra conversions was larger in missionary circles than among urban Indian Christians, who had greater reason than the missionaries to be fearful of association with a stigmatized untouchable community.[66] But urban and clerical Indian Christians were consulted about, and involved in the pastoral care of, village converts from the first. In the CMS this took the form of an informal "church council" held at Narowal in February 1886, which issued a statement that no differences could be recognized in religious matters on account of caste or want of caste, but that Chuhras should give up eating unclean food (carrion), and not intermarry with non-Christians.[67]

The CMS then instituted the Central Punjab Village Mission Council of missionaries and Indian clergy, which promulgated rules for new converts,[68] but there was little consistency across denominations or regions in the conversion rituals required by missionaries. BMS missionary James Smith of Delhi required children in Christian schools who requested baptism to know some Christian hymn, a simple catechism, and the Lord's Prayer, although one of his successors decided during a wave of Chamar conversions in 1916 to require inquirers to "have the tuft of long hair on the crown of the head (by which the heathen think they will be carried to heaven) cut off."[69] Successive bishops of Lahore were supportive of the baptism of polygamists, but the First Lambeth Conference's ruling against the practice required Anglicans to enroll polygamists only as catechumens in preparation for baptism, although continuing to baptize wives.[70]

Before the advent of Christianity, the abstention from carrion or from sweeping had been markers of Chuhra conversion to Islam and Sikhism, although far from universally or even generally adopted. Those who could abstain from both formed a social elite among Musalis and Mazhabi Sikhs.[71] For Christians it was easier to abstain from carrion than from sweeping, which formed a small part of a pattern of labor obligation in the villages but was often the only form of employment open to Christians who migrated to the cities.[72] In the 1930s a Salvation Army journalist put the question directly to a (nameless) spokesman for Punjabi village Christians: "What difference has Christianity made to your lives? Christianity had brought them many benefits: cleanliness, self-respect, cessation of eating animals which died, schooling for the children, the privilege of free approach to their officers to whom they could freely tell their troubles and get helped. But what about the moral character of the People? We have learned to pray. There is now no gambling amongst us, no drink, no murder. The women sing praises to Jesus."[73] His description of a combination of self-respect, patronage, education, and the importance of hymnody rings true not only for this instance but also for the entire period of rural Christian growth.

In contrast to the pattern of Christian conversion in some other communities, Chuhra women are rarely identified as holding back from conversions, or as bastions of traditionalism in matters of family and religion. Women are almost always identified with Christian song; when cases of "heathen survivals" or syncretism are identified, they are characteristically attributed to men. Itinerating missionaries and Indian clergymen, catechists, and Bible Women encountered already existing Christian communities throughout Punjab, and it was taken for granted that women and girls were part of the community. Chak 208 of the Jhang Bar canal colony contained only five Christian households in 1911, but male and female Muslims attended their gatherings for song where "women and girls of the Christians could sing Christian hymns." It was not entirely self-serving rhetoric when the itinerant missionary concluded that non-Christians were "learning to treat the Christians with more consideration and recognition of their rights as human beings."[74]

Where Christianity brought dignity and self-respect to converts, they were willing to make sacrifices for their new faith. However, where the efforts of missionaries and urban Indian Christians to reform their ways interfered with the status of the community, village Christians resisted. A lengthy crusade to eliminate expensive weddings, and the exchanges usually labeled the "sale of brides," brought nothing but frustration to missionaries. As an "old village Christian" explained in the 1930s, "Though we are poor, yet we marry our sons and daughters in a manner that would bring credit to us. . . . After all the *izzat* (the good name) of the *biradari* (brotherhood) has some meaning—even if we cannot afford, yet we must spend."[75]

PATTERNS OF CONVERSION

Although it is difficult to explain in a straightforward way why some Punjabi Chuhras became Christians and others did not, or why so many more Chuhras converted than Chamars or others labeled "depressed classes," it is possible to identify some patterns of conversion.

Chuhras and Chamars (leather-workers) were socially and geographically complementary in Punjab, the Chamars being the characteristic "village menial," constituting around 10 percent of the total population, in the districts of Punjab stretching from Delhi north to Ambala and Ludhiana (an area encompassing the present-day Indian state of Haryana).[76] In those same districts, although in smaller numbers (less than 5 percent of the population), lived communities of Chuhras, inferior in status to Chamars, whose duties are thus described: "The Chuhra sweeps the houses and village, collects the cow dung, pats it into cakes and stacks it, works up the manure, helps with the cattle, and takes them from village to village. In the centre of the Province he adds to those functions actual hard work at the plough and in the field."[77] In the central districts of Punjab where Chuhra conversions were most numerous, and where the percentage of those returned as Chuhras ranged from 7 to 12 percent, there were very few Chamars, and (except in Delhi) few Chamars became Christians in Punjab. In the United Provinces (Uttar Pradesh) on the other hand, where Chuhras were uncommon or unknown, the Chamars became the characteristic low-status convert in the American Methodist Episcopal and American Presbyterian missions.[78]

It is possible to compile a very crude index of Christian density in relationship to Hindu Chuhras from the 1931 census figures, although it is badly skewed by the inconsistency of the census takers in counting the roughly twenty thousand European Christians in Punjab (see Table 7). Sometimes they were counted separately from Indian Christians; in other tables, the racism of the census faltered, and they were classified with low-caste Christians. Furthermore, this index only measures the relative rate of conversion from Hindu Chuhras, since Musalis and Mazhabi Sikhs are excluded. The overwhelming majority of Chuhras had become Christians in the districts of Gurdaspur, Gujranwala, and Sialkot where there were only 312 Hindu Chuhras remaining in 1931, and where the dominant missions were CMS, UP, and Church of Scotland (see Table 8). Some older rural Christians that I met in 1988 in a village near Gujranwala claimed to have no knowledge of any non-Christian Chuhras (although conceding that some Christians continued after conversion to treat Balmiki as a guru).

As one moves southeast into the Sikh heartland of Punjab,[79] and even further toward Delhi, the percentage of Chamars grows, the more elitist missions (AP and SPG) become more prominent, and the percentage of Christians falls. Chuhra conversions in Punjab occurred mainly in the central area where they were the dominant, low-status

TABLE 7

Christians and Chuhras in Central Punjab, 1931

Chuhras	H Chuh	AD Chuh	Xtian	T. Non-Xtian Chuh	Christian Density	Sikh
		LAHORE DIVISION:				
Lahore	43,038	—	57,097	76,982	.43	12,334
Amritsar	25,337	—	16,619	31,773	.34	5,027
Gurdaspur	7,729	32	43,243	10,128	.81	1,145
Sialkot	312	—	66,365	1,688	.97	—
Gujranwala	1,301	—	49,364	1,685	.96	8
Sheikhupura	6,827	2,891	49,266	10,911	.81	521
		MULTAN DIVISION:				
Montgomery	7,668	4,424	17,245	13,704	.55	547
Lyallpur	10,826	9,498	45,518	31,859	.58	6,043

SOURCE: Census of India 1931, *Punjab Part II, vol. 17*, 278–79, 281, 285, 287.
  COLUMNS: H Chuh = Hindu Chuhra; AD Chuh = Ad Dharm Chuhra (see Chapter 9); Xtian = Christians including Europeans, but excluding Eurasians; T. Chuhra = Total non-Christian Chuhra (including "Sikh Chuhra" but not Christians); Sikh = Sikh Chuhras; Christian Density = Christians as a percentage of Christians and total non-Xtian Chuhras

TABLE 8

Chamar and Chuhra Self-Ascription by Division, 1931

	(1) Hindu Chamar	(2) Ad Dharm Chamar	(3) Hindu Chuhra	(4) Ad Dharm Chuhra	(5) All Christians	(6) All Chuhras by self-ascription	5 /(5 + 6)
Ambala	345,043	3,086	134,558	1,972	17,527	149,730	.104
Jullundur	95,754	204,000	48,513	64,150	18,210	177,050	.093
Lahore	11,348	8,259	84,544	2,923	281,954	133,167	.670
Rawalpindi	3,628	1,005	5,329	—	23,639	6,900	.770
Multan	4,900	32,081	20,258	15,257	73,458	54,147	.575

SOURCE: Census of India 1931, *Punjab Part II, vol. 17*, 278–79, 281, 285, 287.

agricultural laboring community, where the landlords were primarily Muslim and Hindu rather than Sikh, where population density was the highest in the province,[80] and where the missions were willing to welcome them with some generosity.

Missionaries found one plausible explanation for the relative enthusiasm for Christianity among Chuhras in the comparative evolutionary ethnology of Ibbetson, who regarded the Chuhras as "aborigines" who preserved in their popular religion remnants of a pre-Hindu monotheism dating from before the "Aryan invasions." Some missionaries drew on elements of fulfillment rhetoric to identify elements of divine truth in Chuhra religion, to compare them to the ancient Israelites,[81] or even to argue that Chuhra religion "resembles Christianity more than nearly anything else we have in India."[82] The theory that Christianity appeals more to persons whose religion is in some way congruent with Christian theology resembles the views of Robin Horton, who identified a broadly held monotheism throughout Africa as an explanation for the rapid growth of Christianity.[83] It is difficult to evaluate these arguments, but a survey of the enormous variety of religious views to be found among those who converted to Christianity in South Asia over several centuries indicates that more than theological considerations are involved in conversion, and that the theological dimensions involve more than doctrinal convergence.[84] The religion of Punjab that most closely resembled Christianity was Islam.

Duncan Forrester has argued that Dalit conversions were the result of economic and administrative change, specifically the impact of Western disruption of the "jajmani" system. But John Webster has argued persuasively that there is little evidence of dislocation in most of the areas of relatively large scale South Asian conversion.[85] The land settlement imposed by the Punjab School caused little large-scale or fundamental disruption of the relationships of production at the level of field labor, although the system was itself in constant flux as negotiations were carried out over the particular allocation of duties within and among the "village menial" communities. Conversion did little— in most cases nothing—to interfere with the material relations of production or power in the villages. In the 1930s more than two-thirds of the Christians in Sialkot district were agricultural laborers, and another 15 percent tenant cultivators who were not allowed to own land at all, "not even the land on which their houses stand."[86] In the same period, 522 Christian families in Pasrur reported 275 instances of forced labor by the police, 122 by landlords, and 55 by agents of landlords.[87]

More important than strictly economic or strictly theological considerations was the history of Chuhra adaptation to the surrounding community, a form of religious camouflage. Unlike Chamars, they had a history of conforming to both Islam and Sikhism. Obviously Chuhras were not free and happy consumers in a marketplace of unlimited religious choice. The phenomenon that Western missionaries identified as "religion" in rural Punjab was, like Western religion itself, a subject constantly being renegotiated in a setting where the exercise of power was often transparent and unrestrained. Nonetheless, Chuhra initiative in the matter was not inconsiderable.

VILLAGE CHRISTIANITY: INDIGENOUS,

FOREIGN, AND HYBRID

Once several hundred thousand village laborers and their families began to call themselves Christians, they began a process of defining what Christianity meant in their particular social and historical context. At this point it is worth remembering the importance of skepticism about the broad categories in use when defining conversion in an imperial context. E. P. Thompson, in writing about his own missionary father, complained about the "vast undiscriminating categories" that are used as "ready-made slide-rules to measure, and often to obliterate, the complexities of the past."[88] The relevant categories in this case are "indigenous," "foreign," and "hybrid." Punjabi Christianity was all three at once. Village Christians developed their own unique indigenous forms of piety and ritual, but they did not live isolated from other people. Missionaries and village untouchables were in it together, as were urban middle-class Christians. All participated in the shaping of new forms of Christianity, as did non-Christians.

Conversion had certain self-limiting effects in some locations, as the adoption of Christian status by one community appeared to foreclose its adoption by another. In the Sialkot district there were frequent inquiries about Christianity (continuing throughout the twentieth century) from communities of Meghs (described usually as Chamars who have adopted weaving)[89] and Batwals, described as "the next caste above the Churas."[90] Attempts to follow up by both missionaries and Indian Christians came to nothing, in part because lower status Chuhras had "claimed" the label "Christian." On the other hand, there is some scattered evidence that the adoption of Christianity by one group within a generic community would lead to a strengthening of non-Christian identity among other groups within the same community. Christian conversions among Delhi Chamars occurred exclusively in one of the three main divisions in the community. Christian Chamars were not only bitterly opposed to any division of the larger Chamar community along religious lines, but were committed to continuing their normal social relationships with unbaptized Chamars who were in turn content to live on good terms with baptized Chamars.[91] When missionaries forced a division, Christians turned out to be a small minority of all Chamars. Within the Chuhra community in Pasrur, on the other hand, Christians and non-Christians coexisted within a communal structure until the turn of the century, when

Christian leaders insisted on a complete break with non-Christians, leading the remaining non-Christians to adopt Christianity.[92]

The compiler of the 1911 census made a determined effort to document the internal structures of both Chuhra and Chamar communities in Punjab, and could find no non-Christian Chuhra communal organization in the Sialkot area. In their attempt to document the hundreds of Chuhra and Chamar "sub-castes," the census takers admitted defeat "owing to the obscurity of an immense proportion of the terms used."[93] Their use of the term "panchayat" is itself suspect, for census officials, administrators, scholars, and missionaries used it indiscriminately as a label for diverse communal organizations as if they were all descended from an ancient, organic, universal social institution. But the census tables display an interesting broad contrast in Chuhra and Chamar communal organization between the areas where there were significant numbers of Christians in central Punjab on the one hand, and the "Christian desert" of southern Punjab on the other. The census identified Chuhra "panchayats" (which they classified as fixed, elective, or "democratic") in precisely those areas where Chuhras remained non-Christian (Balmikis) in significant numbers. There both Chuhras and Chamars were alleged to have strong parallel communal structures.[94]

It would be a mistake to make too much of this contrast without further information. Perhaps the absence of non-Christian Chuhra communal structures in central Punjab is no more than a predictable consequence of the disruption of the Balmiki or Lalbegi communities by conversions to Christianity, Islam, and Sikhism. Perhaps the Chuhras of southern Punjab replicated a strong Chamar communal structure that made them resistant to conversion. On the other hand, the presence of Ad Dharm Chamars and Ad Dharm Chuhras in Jullundur Division by 1931 (see Table 8) demonstrates that Chamars and Chuhras, in areas where they lived side-by-side, were not immune to the prospects of religious change. The Ad Dharm movement was an attempt to raise the status of untouchables by claiming for their religion the status of India's original or aboriginal religion.[95] Driven in part by Christian competition, and in part by the politics of the census movement, the Ad Dharm movement was only available as a method of self-ascription in the late 1920s in preparation for the 1931 census. For nearly a century before that, the American Presbyterians had been working among Chuhras and Chamars in the Jullundur district, the very people who described themselves not as Christian but as Ad

Dharm in 1931. Further south, in the Ambala (formerly Delhi) division, missionaries from the Society for the Propagation of the Gospel and the Cambridge Mission to Delhi had been working, and there Chamars and Chuhras alike remained resolute in their untouchable status, interested neither in Anglican Christianity nor the Ad Dharm movement.

The missionary role in initiating conversions was an unpredictable one. Where there was no missionary presence at all, there were few conversions, either Chuhra or Chamar. In southern Punjab and Delhi, there were periodic instances of interest in Christianity by Chamars and Meghs (and possibly by Chuhras), but an examination of the work of the Society for the Propagation of the Gospel and affiliated Cambridge Mission to Delhi (CMD) in southern Punjab and Delhi leaves some doubt about whether Chamar conversions would have been allowed even if Chamars had been breaking down the doors of the mission compounds. Missionaries of the CMD concentrated on the non-Christian Indian elite, whom the Rev. A. Haig referred to as his "parishioners."[96] The Rev. Thomas Williams of Riwari reported: "In the villages my hearers are always of the highest rank, the lower castes sitting outside my immediate circle of hearers. Special visits are not made to the quarters of the low castes as used to be done in the Deccan. This course I have taken up because it seemed to come to me more naturally."[97] The numerous Chamar and Chuhra communities in southern Punjab were invisible to these SPG missionaries. When they lowered their sights from the elite, they descended only as far as the Jats, the caste Hindus who constituted a large land-holding class and who were much admired both by missionaries and imperial administrators. Haig described them as a "simple manly people . . . easily attracted to the moral force of the gospel."[98]

These comments are testimony to the enormous power of social preconceptions to shape perceptions of reality. If there was any notable characteristic of the Jats, it was their lack of interest in Christianity. But the Rev. H. C. Carlyon began a branch of the Cambridge Mission in Rohtak in 1894 as a special mission to the Jats, one that he continued until his death in 1919.[99] In the accounts of SPG and CMD work outside of Delhi, I have found only one mention of the (to them invisible) Chamars: the Rev. B. P. W. French complained of receiving the taunt of "Chamar Padri" from some Jats.[100]

A small community of weavers in Rampura near Riwari could not be ignored by high Anglican missions, if only because they had been baptized by an Indian Christian clergyman, the Rev. Tara Chand. They then had the misfortune to fall under the pastoral care of the Rev. T. Williams, who repeatedly attempted to excommunicate them for their habit of engaging in heathen betrothals and (in his view) irregular (that is, too shallow) forms of Christian burial. He reported success at last in excluding the weavers of Rampura from Christian care, only to be forced in subsequent reports to admit that they insist on some forms of Christian observance despite his objections. "Excommunicate them? They laugh at that, as they do at baptism. Yet it will be asked, why allow them to come to service and why teach their women? My answer is: we allow heathen to come. They are really heathen. God's grace may find them at last. Exclusion, they really, now that they get no help, would not heed."[101] Williams repeated assertions that the weavers were interested only in material help was entirely undercut by his own account. The weavers of Rampura were defining Christianity in their own way, as a form of resistance to a missionary whose ministry they nonetheless insisted on attending.

The confrontation was repeated on a larger scale upon the arrival of the missionaries of the SPG and Cambridge Mission to Delhi, whose encounter with the Chamars of the Daryaganj neighborhood illuminates both the history of Indian Christianity and the nature of Victorian English Christianity. Under the influence of B. F. Westcott, the Cambridge brothers were in principle more open to Indian culture and Indian ideas than any of the other missions in Punjab.[102] Westcott was one of a number of nineteenth-century British and American missionary thinkers who tried to disentangle Christianity from Western culture.[103] His vision of a "new Alexandria" in India was based upon an attempt to promote Christian ideas in a non-Western cultural idiom, and draw on the truths to be found in non-Christian religion rather than merely declaring Hinduism depraved and Islam fraudulent. At a time when the superiority of Western culture was axiomatic in England, and when racist ideas were growing more prevalent generally, Westcott encouraged potential missionaries at Cambridge to listen for things of value from people in other cultures rather than merely preaching at them. In Delhi it is possible to see how Westcott's social Christianity took on a more malignant character in an imperial setting, and also to see the consequences of Victorian clerical professionalism.

Among the SPG's early Indian ordinands was the Rev. Tara Chand, ordained in 1863, who lived in a Chamar neighborhood in Delhi from 1866 to 1874 and baptized a number of "leather workers and day laborers." R. W. Winter and his wife, Priscilla Winter, who had arrived in Delhi in 1860, shared with the Rev. Tara Chand responsibility for their pastoral care. Further Chamar conversions were associated with a famine in 1877–79, a circumstance that discredited converts in the eyes of missionaries. But obviously more was going on than the development of "rice Christians." Winter offered a reasonably sophisticated analysis of the Delhi Chamar adoption and redefinition of Christianity. A declaration of Christian faith was consistent with their adoption of other ways of believing that did not interfere with the internal social customs of the Chamar Community:[104] "They looked on Christianity merely as what they called a *panth*, and *panth* of religion, and not as a brotherhood. They have many of these non-Christian *panths* as followers of Kabir or Ram Dass or Nanak, the founder of the Sikhs; these they can follow without bringing their women and children, they can believe in them without being outcast, and their faith in no way interferes with domestic and social customs connected with idolatry."[105]

The SPG was determined to organize the Chamar community into recognizable Christian institutions, a practice that in the long run put severe limits on their ability to expand Christian influence. In the short run, however, it encouraged even further accessions, and led to the enrollment of Chamar women in mission institutions. After 1873 a Chamar catechist, Balu Hírá Lála, acted as an effective proselytizer for Christianity, and sent converts into other parts of the Delhi Chamar community. The Winters began to organize branch schools, which led to the formation of branch parishes, and "the Chamars were very effectively brought under instruction at that time." The day schools attracted even more Chamars who thought "their boys would all grow unto Munshis and teachers on substantial monthly salaries."

This community had grown beyond the control of the missionaries without dispensing with them altogether. Christian Chamars, in cooperation with Tara Chand, Richard and Priscilla Winter, and Balu Hírá Lála, were creating their own version of Christianity, drawing on the elements of the mission presence that were useful to them. According to Richard Winter, Chamar Christians "form nearly the only portion of our people as anything approaching an independent party as distinct from the very large numbers of Christian mission agents and their families."[106] In the early 1880s they constituted eight urban parishes and several villages in Delhi and Gurgaon districts, some living as far as thirty miles down the road to Agra, others in the village of Mehrouli near the Qutb Minar south of Delhi.

One link between Chamar Christianity and the mission came through the steady round of multiracial visitation by missionary women of the SPG—European, Eurasian, and Indian. Anglican women's work was thoroughly organized in Delhi under the direction of Priscilla Winter, the wife of the SPG clergyman Richard Winter. The Winters had run the mission in Delhi very much on the lines of a large, well-funded, urban parish in England, with parochial work, schools, relief work, visitation—emphasizing the value of the personal presence of a clergyman or a female visitor as a civilizing influence on a neighborhood. The complicated negotiations about gender roles in the early missionary movement produced a Delhi mission that was predominantly female in numbers even before the advent of organized efforts to enroll unmarried European missionary women in the 1880s. SPG literature often portrayed Richard Winter as being alone in Delhi before the arrival of the Cambridge missionaries in 1878. Before that time, however, at least thirty-three women, many of them recruited directly in Delhi, helped out in one way or another as missionaries with the Winters' mission, and ten additional recruits were added in 1878 and 1879.[107]

Women missionaries provided opportunities for Chamar women and girls to make use of an array of mission institutions. Exempt from the authoritarian attitudes associated with the imposition of ecclesiastical discipline, which was a clerical affair, mission women opened schools for Chamar girls.[108] They also provided pastoral care to the women in Chamar Christian families through home visitation, where they distributed items from the material culture of the Victorian churches, taught Bible verses, and sang the extremely popular Christian bhajans. Female Chamar Christian piety appeared to be closely associated with song (see below, p. 146).

Chamar catechists supplied another crucial link with the mission. Balu Hirá Lála was identified as an evangelist, but most catechists carried out pastoral roles in the Chamar Christian community, presiding at worship in the branch parishes, translating and writing Christian bhajans, and acting as conduits for small amounts of missionary patronage. According to a Chamar proverb, the catechists lived easy lives (catechist ka kam, bohut asan). But they were useful both to the mission and the Chamar community, and played a crucial role in the setting of simple Christian hymns to bhajan tunes and composing original Hindi lyrics.[109]

In the 1880s the Cambridge Brothers hoped to find a community of Christians from whom would emerge eventually Indian theologians of the stature of the Alexandrian theologians Clement and Origen, who were judged to have forged a synthesis of Christianity and classical culture. They recognized that rapid progress was unrealistic, but they sincerely hoped to find a community of potential Clements and Origens who would provide the basis for a new Indian theological renaissance. The Delhi Christian community could hardly have provided a more striking disappointment for their hopes of a new Indian theological renaissance blending East and West. Despite their theoretically positive approach to Indian culture, the CMD's practical approach to the Christian community in Delhi was from the first authoritarian, arrogant, and elitist. The Rev. Edward Bickersteth actually proposed excluding from Holy Communion those Chamars who failed to attend worship regularly (a proposal which if imposed in England would have greatly accelerated the already noticeable decline in Anglican church attendance).[110] Of Christianity as a *panth* alongside those of Kabir and Guru Nanak, the Cambridge Brothers were entirely intolerant. Even in the midst of intolerance, however, the Cambridge Brothers were forced to negotiate, and new forms of Christianity emerged out of the relationship between Cambridge elitists and Delhi Chamars.

In the view of the Cambridge Brothers, the low social status of the Chamars threatened to discredit Christianity among the leading men of the city, and also back in the Metropole among supporters of the missions' high aspirations.[111] When visiting a rural village with a small Chamar Christian community, G. A. Lefroy first tried to talk to the caste Hindu farmers, but they "told me most bluntly that they did not want me, I had better go to my friends the Chamars. And how much such rudeness means out here—how far more than it would in England—one sees when one remembers how naturally polite even to servility all the Hindoos are to any superior."[112]

Lefroy plunged into a reorganization of the Chamar Christian Community. In 1884 he published a graphic account of his dealings with the Chamars, a pamphlet entitled *The Leather-workers of Daryaganj*, which begins with an extensive apology for adopting this work with untouchables. Why then deal with them at all? Because they are "it must be remembered in name Christians, and as such representing to the people of Delhi, high and low, rich and poor, the Church of Christ in this great city."[113] Like most nineteenth-century Protestant missionaries, Lefroy believed that the test of the truth of Christianity was its ability to transform society. The case for Christianity was not intellectual so much as moral, and the test of morality was its ability to improve both individual and social behavior. When he looked at the Chamars, he saw only degradation. If Christianity could succeed in transforming the Chamars, it would "remove a stumbling block and a scandal which could not but most grievously affect any efforts which might hereafter be made."[114] But a transformation could only come with a reorganization of their community under clerical control.

Lefroy's own account demonstrates, however inadvertently, that Chamar Christianity was both more complicated than he claimed and too sophisticated to be encompassed within a binary model of complicity and resistance. The adoption of Christianity was not merely a question of missionary stimulus and Chamar response, but part of a struggle for internal competitive advantage within the Chamar community. How a Christian Chamar was to be defined in Daryaganj was a matter still to be negotiated when Lefroy arrived on the scene, and the negotiations continued during his attempts at reorganization. What is clear is that the Christian Chamars of Daryaganj had incorporated missionary patrons, including Lefroy, into their own hierarchy of status.

The Chamar community even for a time made use of Lefroy as a broker in the complex negotiations attendant upon betrothal and marriage. Although he complained that this took considerable time, his condescending account of his duties betrays a certain relish for the job. Lefroy's predecessor had adopted a relatively relaxed set of requirements for Christian Chamars, an attitude reciprocated by those Chamars who remained non-Christian, but maintained communal ties with baptized Chamars. In order to ensure that Christian Chamars married only other Christians, Lefroy established a registry of the names of daughters aged two to twelve of Christian families. He then tried to match each of them with a Christian boy who, in his account, was with living parents or guardians, was lighter or at least no darker than the prospective partner, and was unconnected by either blood ties or friendship. His fame as a matchmaker spread after he arranged a betrothal between a boy of eight and a girl aged six perfect in all respects except for the objections of the boy's father to Christian rites. Lefroy went to the village near Delhi to meet the entire adult male population, and in a two-hour meeting "urged my case so vigorously that in a couple of hours' time a successful issue was reached, and the engagement there and then (in the absence it is true of the girl, but of what consequence was that?) formally completed."[115]

In these activities Lefroy is behaving in the way he might behave toward parishioners at home, with an ironic sense of affection for their shortcomings, which include, from his point of view, both racism and sexism. From his vantage point, Lefroy could hardly afford to be too intolerant of either, and the ironic, detached tone is continued in his account of his demise as a matchmaker:

> This piece of successful diplomacy brought my fame as a matchmaker
> ... up to a fever heat, and applications for engagements flowed in
> apace. Unfortunately amid this press of business an accident, such as
> may occur in even the best managed institution, happened, which, for
> the moment at least, caused a complete reaction, for, by the slightest
> clerical error in the entry of the names in my book, I almost succeeded
> in bringing together in the important betrothal rite two young persons
> admirably matched in almost every other respect but both, by an
> amusing coincidence, of the male sex. For a time this unfortunate in-
> cident, causing, as it somehow seemed to do, a most unfavorable im-
> pression, completely stopped the run on my office.[116]

The Chamar Christians were settling into a routine position as one of the Chamar *panths* in Daryaganj, and if Lefroy had been willing to leave them alone there might have been further conversions. But in this imperial context, Lefroy was not content to tolerate the nominal Christianity that characterized not only Chamars but English and Irish Protestant parishioners as well. The Christian Chamars he described as having only a small minority "in any real way affected by their Christianity, the rest remaining in full fellowship with their caste, sharing in its feasts, idolatrous and otherwise, adhering to the old ceremonies of birth, marriage, death, wholly ignoring Sunday, etc. Christians in nothing but name."[117]

With some small effort of the imagination, that description could easily be applied to a Protestant parish in England: alcohol-soaked, snobbish to an idolatrous degree, and nominally Christian by almost any standard. The Episcopal churches of the British Isles have a well-known record of attempting to drive away the poor, working people and other unfashionable groups with snobbery, pew-rents, and elitism. On the other hand, Episcopalian parishioners in Britain and Ireland, like the Delhi Chamar Christians, doggedly made use of parochial services, including both the rites of passage popular with working people and the public worship patronized by the more prosperous. The Anglican laity had for centuries struggled to build up elaborate systems of defense against the authoritarian tendencies of their own clergymen. Clergymen had in turn developed as a matter of necessity a kind of ironic tolerance for nominal Christianity. In the Indian imperial setting, the tolerance evaporated.

Lefroy regarded himself as free to define who was and who was not a Christian, and expel from the community those who failed his own tests. As the betrothal incident illustrates, Lefroy's control over Chamar Christians was strictly limited. Discipline would be easier to impose, however, if Christians were turned into tenants of the mission. The mission bought eight houses in Daryaganj, creating a Christian *basti* ("neighborhood") and giving Lefroy control over religious and social practices as the price for admission to this housing. Consequently Lefroy was able to set the standards defining a Christian Chamar, which were: (1) observe Sunday as a day of rest; (2) use exclusively Christian rites for birth, marriage, and death; and (3) abstain from intoxicating drugs (cannabis).[118]

As was so often the case with missionary discipline in India, some Christians refused to be disciplined. Dissension broke out among Chamar Christians, some of whom proposed setting up a test to sort out the truly devout from the purely nominal. A showdown over communal definition occurred at an overnight meeting of the several hundred male representatives of the three main Chamar divisions (Bawanis) centered in Daryaganj (constituting, according to Lefroy, ten thousand to twelve thousand men). Many of the Christian Chamars were bitterly opposed to any division of the community along religious lines, but others at this meeting announced that in the future they would have nothing to do with the Chamar brotherhood as such.

This provocative behavior of the more severe Christians elicited a response from other Chamar leaders who, after an hour or so of discussion, finally announced that there would be a sifting of Christians with a pot of Ganges water. Those who refused to raise it to their heads in an act of veneration would be cut off from communal ties. They began calling a list of names, summoning alleged Christians to raise the water or refuse. By 7:30 A.M. the process was complete, and only eight families of Christians remained to repair to the chapel for worship.

Initially pleased with this small number, Lefroy later discovered that nominal Christianity survived outside the confines of the Christian basti, "a dead weight around our necks,"[119] and grumbled that "even in the case of those who definitely broke the bond, it turns out far more difficult than we had previously expected to say what they have given up and how they now stand."[120] In 1887 another movement to purge the community was initiated, after which (by Lefroy's reckoning) only fifty to sixty Christian Chamars remained. "With a great sweep of the work of years," he wrote, "we start again anew with this remnant."[121]

The dead weight of Chamar Christianity survived Lefroy's on-slaughts, since many Chamars were determined to define themselves as Christians on their own terms. Delhi missionaries (Baptist as well as Anglican) frequently claimed to have "lost" all their Christians, only to find them again later. In 1897, for instance, a Faqir sponsored by the resurgent Hindu cow protection movement reclaimed for Hinduism a group of Baptist Chamars in Daryaganj that were unknown to the Baptist mission until they became objects of contention in a struggle for communal self-definition.[122] But mission strategy made a difference, as prospects for the further spread of Christianity in Delhi were effectively thwarted, at least for the time being. By reducing the Anglican Chamar community to a small group of families dependent on the mission, Lefroy had ensured the irrelevance of this particular mission to the broader Chamar community, by far the largest untouchable community in Delhi. In the entire Delhi district they constituted the second largest of the census caste groupings, with 10 percent of the total population, exceeded in numbers only by the Jats.[123] Their status undoubtedly made them receptive to movements of religious reform, whether that took the form of allegiance to the Chamar Hindu saint Ravidas, or to the Kabir-Panth, or (in the twentieth century) to the leadership of Dr. Ambedkar and the influence of neo-Buddhism.[124] In rural Uttar Pradesh there were mass conversions to Methodist and other forms of Christianity after 1900.[125] But in urban Delhi, thanks to the Cambridge Mission to Delhi, religious reform was not to be Christian.

The CMD was not the only mission with an openly antagonistic relationship with Indian Christians. Antagonism was not a missiological "mistake," but a difference of opinion rooted in nineteenth-century assumptions about the centrality of Christian institutions for the nurturing of genuine Christian faith. In an imperial context power relationships were unequal, but Chamar Christians as we have seen had considerable bargaining power as long as they insisted on calling themselves Christians. Other missions did not share the CMD's heavy emphasis upon institutional conformity. In the very late nineteenth century two missions in Punjab, the (largely British) Salvation Army and the (entirely American) Methodist Episcopal Mission welcomed both Chamar and Chuhra conversions. By that time two other missions had already faced crises in the matter of Chuhra conversions: the (American) United Presbyterian Mission and the Anglican Evangelical Church Missionary Society. In this matter (as in so many others), the clearest fault lines could be seen in the CMS.

COMPROMISE

In the early 1880s rural villagers began to request baptism of Anglican evangelical CMS missionaries near Narowal, a town adjacent to the UP mission territory. Responding to Chuhra initiatives, evangelical Anglicans found themselves trapped between the imperatives of Christian universalism and Christian institutionalism. Narowal was the base of the Rev. Rowland Bateman, who had focused on the conversion of a few high-caste boys who proudly retained their identity as "Bateman's converts" (although Bateman himself hated the phrase, preferring to give the glory to the Holy Spirit). In the 1870s Bateman built a church at Narowal, one of the earliest attempts at the neosaracenic style. In 1878 the beautiful "Cathedral of Narowal" served thirty-six Indian Christian parishioners.[126]

Invalided to England in 1881, Bateman returned in late 1884 to find that the UP mission had spread a network of missions all around Narowal, baptizing hundreds of village untouchable converts.[127] Although willing to baptize Chuhras, Bateman objected bitterly as American marauders baptized thousands in his territory, and objected even more bitterly when UP missionaries (especially the Rev. Samuel Martin) claimed God's guidance in the matter. In the end the UP mission was coerced by their foreign mission board to hand over "their" converts to Bateman.[128]

Faced with fifteen hundred new Christians, Bateman took them in hand, firing schoolmasters and catechists who could not repeat the Apostles' Creed, excommunicating and expelling ordinary believers who could not repeat the Lord's Prayer. But he also began to scramble for new resources, requesting the CMS to redirect funds from their elite institutions to training schools for village catechists and primary schools for village Christian children.[129]

CMS remained divided both in its allocation of resources and its attitude toward untouchable converts. With its evidence of rapid Christian growth, the 1891 census caught the attention of journalists in Britain and proved irresistible as a rhetorical tool to some CMS missionaries who otherwise had no interest in low-caste conversions. Unwilling to praise their own success at gaining converts and then disparage the character of those converts, they attributed to Punjabi Chuhras extraordinary virtues (which had been visible to no missionary before 1870). The Rev. H. E. Clark in 1913 described them as "an exceptionally fine race of men who are rapidly moving towards Christianity. The Chuhras or the village menial type has neither in physical or mental development any trace of deterioration such as is associated with similar occupations in other parts of India."[130]

Just as they were unable to make up their minds about the allocation of resources, missionaries were of two minds about the character of village Christians. For every positive account from a CMS missionary it is possible to find a negative one. In 1892 T. J. L. Mayer described the CMS village settlements at Clarkabad as a failure because "they are Mehtars or descended from Mehtars and therefore know nothing of agriculture; none of them can read or write; very few have any wish to work for their living. Take a man from the London sewerage company and make a farmer of him. That is what you are doing."[131]

Similar ambivalence characterized the Church of Scotland Mission, whose seven thousand Punjabi church members in 1906 came overwhelmingly from Chuhra communities. Pioneer missionary John Youngson worked for years building Christian institutions in and around Sialkot before being caught up in the large-scale conversions of the 1880s.[132] A special report from the Punjab Mission in 1926 identified the biggest problem for the mission as "the low standard of some of our workers and converts," a result of the lack of pastoral care from properly trained missionaries who cannot "be spared from the work in schools, colleges, and hospitals."[133]

Both the CMS and CS admitted their failure to provide pastoral care for Chuhra converts. In the 1930s the thirteen thousand Christians in 250 villages in the Pasrur area were served by sixteen pastors with twelve villages each. A minority of villages had regular Sunday services; some received pastoral visits only two or three times a year.[134] These Christians were not entirely out of touch with institutional Christianity, but the relationship was sporadic. Punjabi Christians were free to develop their own forms of spirituality, piety, and worship with only intermittent clerical interference, and that is what they did.

PIETY AND SONG IN PUNJABI CHRISTIANITY

There are several traditions of judgment on Punjabi village Christianity, all dismissive. Government administrators were entirely indifferent. Caste Hindu, Muslim, and Sikh landowners, and many missionaries, dismissed conversion as nothing more than a change of label in search of higher social status. In his famous novel *Train to Pakistan* (1956), Khushwant Sing described the village setting this way: "There are a few families of sweepers whose religion is uncertain. The Muslims claim them as their own, yet when American missionaries visit

Mano Majra the sweepers wear khaki solar topees and join their women folk in singing hymns to the accompaniment of a harmonium. Sometimes they visit the Sikh temple, too. But there is one object that all Mano Majrans . . . venerate. This is a three-foot slab of sandstone that stands upright under a keekar tree beside the pond. It is the local deity, the *deo* to which all the villagers—Hindu, Sikh, Muslim or pseudo-Christian—repair secretly whenever they are in need of a special blessing."[135] In the eyes of the villagers of Mano Majra, seen through the eyes of Khushwant Sing, sweeper Christians are a small, marginal, faintly ridiculous community, pseudo-Christians not allowed to define their own religion.

Even those missionaries strongly committed to village work often complained that village Christianity was superficial, a judgment repeated by some scholars who rank as "more religious" a religion that is intellectually rationalized and visibly institutionalized. Mark Juergensmeyer, for instance, includes in his chapter "Christianity: The Sweepers Revolt" an account of his early 1970s visit to a village in Gurdaspur near the Pakistani border where one-quarter of the population was Christian. He identifies healthy faith with institutional allegiance and theological knowledge, noting that the villagers did not attend church and that "church officials" nearby seemed unaware of their existence. Village Christians were unable "to identify any of the tenets of Christianity; the only aspect of Christianity they knew was 'Lord Jesu Masih,' Jesus Christ, who sometimes replaces the local gods as the subject of the folk tunes they sing at night."[136]

Juergensmeyer is generally respectful of Punjabi rural Christians, and his book is one of the few to take them seriously and place their conversions in a broader political context. But his assumption that theological knowledge strengthens simple faith, and that church attendance is more desirable than singing Christian hymns, reflects the kinds of dismissive institutional assumptions that produce unfair judgments on Chuhra Christianity. That these villagers remained Christian at all through the tumultuous events of midcentury Punjab is itself remarkable; in many parts of India, especially in Uttar Pradesh, Chamar converts abandoned their Christian allegiance.[137] Even from an institutionalist point of view, the ignorance of church officials would seem to reflect more discredit on the officials themselves than the people of this village. The syncretism that is sometimes cited as evidence of the superficiality of faith could equally be cited as evidence of its strength.

Juergensmeyer's dismissal of Christian "folk tunes" misses the significance of popular hymnody, which was and is at the heart of rural Punjabi piety in India and, especially, in Pakistan. It is in Punjabi hymnody, rather than in the bureaucratic creations of the missions, that one finds the fullest expression of indigenous Punjabi Christianity. In the accounts of both Kushwant Sing and Juergensmeyer, song was associated with women. Mission reports are full of accounts of popular enthusiasm for Christian song, a Church of Scotland report on village Christians observing that "[t]he church, in the past, was gathered in largely by singing and the converts from among the poor can usually sing."[138] The Christians of the Pasrur area may not have been able to conduct their own worship services, but they gathered to sing when it was convenient. Itinerating in the new canal colony area of Jhang Bar in 1911, a CMS missionary reported finding only five Christian households in one Chak (division), but observed that a number of Muslims, male and female, attended Christian prayers and teachings where women and girls from Christian families would sing Christian hymns. He also noted that the "women and girls of the Christians could sing Christian hymns," evidence that instruction was reaching women.[139] When asked to define the importance of Christianity among new converts, a village Salvation Army officer identified cleanliness and song with Christian women: "The women?" "They sing praises to Jesus, they pray with their families morning and evening, they are anxious to keep themselves, their homes, and their families clean."[140]

Women missionaries noted the same phenomenon among Chamar Christian women in and near Delhi, although the male leaders of the SPG mission never took any notice. Miss Fiennes reported from a village near Rohtak a visit to a woman "with I think a vague religious instinct and feelings of her need, seemed greatly taken with a Bhajan I sang and took the utmost pains to learn it by heart, following me from house to house and making me sing it again and again. The words were to this effect: 'without Thee I am helpless / sinners are lost in the deep waters; the righteous have reached the other shore; the sinner too beseeches Thee to take him across.' Yet I could not get that girl to take the slightest interest in what I told her of the Saviour. . . . [Of] the books we sell the most popular are the bhajans."[141] In the 1930s itinerating Baptist women missionaries found scattered Chamar Christians with no formal leader in sixty-three villages around Palwal/Baraut. Miss Thorn reported that in Baraut a Christian village women said, "No one has visited us women for eleven years, but the bari Miss Sahiba taught us 'God so loved the world . . . ,' and 'The wages of sin is death, but the gift of God is Eternal Life' and the Lord's Prayer, and I say these every day before I go to work."[142]

In this matter, as in many others, the United Presbyterians appeared to have the right touch. It was an accident of Scottish and American ecclesiastical history that led to the great popularity of the Punjabi Psalms (Zabur) among rural and urban Christians. This development was rooted, not in the influence of Islam (although the Psalms are canonical for Muslims) but in denominational divisions in the American Midwest, demonstrating once again that Punjabi Christianity cannot be encompassed by labels such as indigenous, foreign, or hybrid. It was a unique social formation, a thing in itself. Unlike the mainstream Presbyterian Church in the U.S.A., the United Presbyterian Church of North America prohibited the singing of hymns in church, allowing the Psalms as the only musical form authorized by Scripture. The 1884 annual report of their Sialkot Mission listed among the Indian ruling elders, catechists, and other "helpers" not only the famous evangelist Ditt but also the equally important "Poet and Catechist" Imad-ud-din Shahbaz.[143] An early UP ordinand, the Rev. I. D. Shahbaz, agreed in the 1880s to translate the Psalms into metric Urdu and set them to Western tunes used in the United Presbyterian Church. The Urdu Psalms were not a hit with rural Punjabi United Presbyterians, but Shahbaz also translated a few of the Psalms into metric Punjabi. When set to indigenous tunes, they became instantly popular.

Realizing the incompetence of missionaries to handle this task, in the mid-1890s the Sialkot Mission had set up a special committee to create a metric Punjabi Psalter with indigenous tunes.[144] Missionaries worked with catechists to transcribe tunes heard in marketplaces, and Imad-ud-din Shahbaz provided a complete Punjabi version of the Zaburs.[145] In 1904 the committee, "at last," reported that it had transcribed tunes for all the Punjabi Zaburs after a final ten-day session with "native singers," and requested Rs 75 to print three hundred copies. By 1905 the 103d Psalm was introduced into a "tentative course for inquirers" along with Urdu passages from the Shorter Catechism, the Lord's Prayer, the Apostles' Creed, and passages in Punjabi from John, Chapter 4. In 1906 the Punjabi Zaburs were printed in Urdu script, with full attribution to the Rev. I. D. Shahbaz.[146]

It is impossible to overestimate the importance of the UP's transcription, translation, and publication projects in shaping the character of Punjabi Christianity. Although they were drawing on indigenous developments that were beyond their control, they recognized what was happening and publicized it. The singing of metrical Zaburs spread across class and denominational boundaries, and was introduced to middle-class urban congregations through hymn and tune books.[147] The annual Sialkot Conventions, modeled on the evangelical and perfectionist Keswick Conventions in England, attracted evangelicals from every denomination who sang from hymnbooks that featured Zaburs prominently. The Anglican *Masihi Git ki Kitab* (Christian Song Book) contained no Zaburs in its 1916 edition, although it did include among its fifty-three ghazals one authored by Dr. Shahbaz. The American Presbyterian hymnal was revised in 1923 as *Zabur aur Git* (Psalms and Songs).[148] Eventually every general hymnbook published for north Indian Christians, even those for congregations entirely beyond the range of Punjabi, and even the dignified *Masihi Git ki Kitab*, would have a section dedicated to Punjabi Zaburs, and in some cases another one dedicated to Punjabi bhajans. The Christian Council of the United Provinces' *Zabur aur Git ki Kitab* (Psalm and Song Book) of 1932 was characteristic in its arrangement: hymns, then ghazals, then bhajans, then Punjabi Zabur.

The metric Psalms were not the whole story of Punjabi hymnody; the Midwestern revivalism of Moody and Sankey played a role as well. The editors of the 1916 *Masihi Git ki Kitab* were perhaps less staid than uninformed in excluding Zaburs, for they were making a good faith effort to make their hymnal useful for rural itineration by including, along with sixty-four tunes from *Hymns Ancient and Modern*, twenty-nine tunes from Ira B. Sankey's *Sacred Songs and Solos*. They included also the British and American Sunday School favorite "Jesus Loves Me" (complaining about the high fee required to reprint it), but it was printed in a flat-footed, literal Hindustani translation, which probably explains why it never became popular in Punjab. Other denominations stepped in to promote the popular hymnody of Anglo-American revivalism, which spread in Punjab along with Dr. Shahbaz's Zabur. *Sacred Songs and Solos* provided the basis for many of the most popular Salvation Army hymns, and the Methodist Episcopal Church (North) provided another conduit for Sankey's hymns as well as their own, many of them by Charles Wesley, in their 1911 *Hindustani Git ki Kitab*.[149] These hymns were taught antiphonally during itineration, with missionary or catechist or Bible Woman singing one line, and the assembled Christians repeating.

With the metric Psalms and *Sacred Songs and Solos* came the harmonium, added to the tabla to produce a Punjabi popular hymnody that makes nonsense of the categories East and West as well as almost every other imaginable binary opposition. It is here, rather than in Native Church Councils or theological training schools or diocesan synods, that one can find the synthesis of East and West to which the Cambridge Mission to Delhi aspired, and the indigenous Indian church longed for by Henry Venn and the CMS. Village Christians could not of course afford a harmonium, which was brought in with itinerant missionaries or catechists, but the ability to play it soon became a mark of honor, one of the visible signs of dignity that marked the links between village Christianity and the universal Christianity propagated by missionaries and Indian Christian catechists and Bible Women.

Missionaries never developed the right touch with Punjabi hymnody, and they recognized their own shortcomings. J. C. Heinrich reported in 1938: "One of our men has put the Synod Bible course into Basic Punjabi Verse with popular Punjabi tunes and these Bible stories that we missionaries have been accustomed to pump into the Punjabis in our dry western way are getting themselves sung into the consciousness of the village church through these Martinpur village traveling bands."[150] The intermittent character of contact between missionary or catechist and village Christian resulted in a pattern of religious observance very different from the weekly church attendance considered the norm in the West. Missionaries of all denominations reported being overwhelmed with converts, leaving them unable to simultaneously provide pastoral care and promote further growth.[151] In the Tarn Taran Mission report for 1907 we discover that seventy inquirers were kept back for years "because there was no one to shepherd them" despite the very heavily staffed institutional presence there.[152]

The shortage of shepherds became even more acute with the migration of village Christians to the new Chenab canal colonies. The opening of new areas of settlement had contradictory effects on the missionary enterprise. The further dispersal of Christians meant that they were even further beyond the reach of missionary discipline, and free to develop their own forms of piety and worship. Dispersal created opportunities for recruitment, and new pressure on mission resources as missionaries tried simultaneously to "find" Christians and enroll them in Christian institutions, and to recruit new Christians. The major missions, along with new competitors from the Roman Catholic Church, attempted to discipline Christians in the canal colonies by enrolling them in their own Christian colonies, where they would be subject to the authority of the mission (see Chapter 9 on Christian canal colonies).

The mildly defamatory treatment that (what is now called) Dalit Christianity has often received from missionaries, novelists, imperialists, and scholars has obscured the emergence of a unique and genuine piety in the convert communities. Everyone involved in religious acts and religious institutions does so with mixed motives, and the motives of Chuhra converts were no more mixed than those of anyone else. Because of the imperial setting, "secular" motives were more transparent, Chuhra concern for education, dignity, and patronage being obvious to everyone. But there was a theological dimension to each concern. The UP missionaries, in particular, never dismissed the desire for dignity as a "secular" concern, and the missionaries' own passion for education, which often appears to be "secular" from a distance, was driven by theological aspirations.

A pattern of religious piety based on formal and informal gatherings for the singing of hymns and Psalms, memorization of Scripture verses, festival visits by dignitaries foreign and Indian, and Christmas observance did not conform to the pattern anticipated by Western missionaries, who envisioned stable parishes and congregations gathering weekly under regular pastoral care. But those missionaries most closely involved with village Christians all admitted that Chuhra Christianity, however defective from their point of view, had taken on a life of its own. Here again we encounter E. P. Thompson's "vast undiscriminating categories" that "obliterate the complexities of the past."[153] If Punjabi Christianity was a "translation" into an "indigenous" Christianity, or an exercise in "transculturation," it was one that embraced large elements of Western Christianity in a community that was envisaged as multinational and multiracial. Far from being merely an exercise in collaboration with imperialism, Punjabi Christianity was a collaborative enterprise created by people who had very good reasons to make their choices, and who produced a religion that bore little resemblance to anything envisaged in any imperial project. From their point of view, rural Christians were not becoming Western, but becoming Christian. Shaped by powerful historical forces, and sprawling across imperial fault lines, Punjabi Christianity assumed a unique character that resists definitive categorization.

6

Gender, Medicine, and the Rhetoric
of Professional Expertise

Missionary narratives of male clerical heroism, which provide the foundation narratives for all subsequent histories of mission work, obscure the cooperative nature of an enterprise that involved extensive collaboration between men and women at all levels from the very first days in Punjab. I have found that a simple assertion that two-thirds of British missionaries worldwide were women by 1900 continues to be greeted with surprise. By 1931, when the practice of counting married women as full missionaries had at last become entirely routine, 70 percent of the 622 Protestant foreign missionaries in northwest India were women (see Table 9). Even before the large influx of unmarried women missionaries in the 1880s and 1890s, mission institutions were heavily dependent on European and Indian female staff in addition to missionary wives.[1]

The nature of male/female collaboration changed in the late nineteenth century, however, and along with the change came a new narrative of heroism: the single woman missionary, acting in India (as at home) as a moral vanguard with a special bond of sisterhood with Indian women.[2] Religion along with education and the family were regarded in the nineteenth century as arenas where women had special qualifications, and in some religious literature the devout English woman pursuing philanthropic or educational work was treated as the highest exemplar of Christianity. In late-nineteenth-century missionary circles, two arguments were added. Women teachers and women doctors used the allegedly unique circumstances of Indian women—locked in the Zenana, unable to attend school, unwilling to see male doctors—as a justification for (1) an extension of women's religious work overseas, which was in turn (2) a field where professional qualifications were essential. New narratives of professional female heroism slighted the work of missionary wives and the extensive work of the amateur women missionaries of all races who preceded the white professional women of the late nineteenth century.[3] In presentations to a

TABLE 9

Foreign Agency in Punjab by Sex and Marital Status, 1931

	Men	Married women	Unmarried women	Total foreign
Punjab	143	110	219	472
NWFP	11	10	21	42
Delhi	21	10	40	71
JAM/KASH	13	11	13	37
TOTAL	188	141	293	622

SOURCE: *Directory of Christian Missions in India, Burma and Ceylon, 1932–1933* (Madras: Christian Literature Society, 1932), 175ff.

NOTE: By 1931 Delhi and the Northwest Frontier Provinces (NWFP) were separate administrative units. The Jammu and Kashmir (JAM/KASH) missions had always been treated as extensions of the respective Punjab missions.

home audience in particular, the rhetoric of women's missions utilized the image of the helpless and dependent victim projected onto all Indian women, in ways very similar to the arguments that Antoinette Burton has documented in her work on British feminists.[4]

The advent of relatively large numbers of unmarried women missionaries coincided with a large expansion of mission institutions in the 1880s and 1890s. Although missions everywhere became increasingly institution-bound, the Punjab had an even larger concentration of medical institutions for women than other mission fields in India and around the world. Just as elite educational institutions were created in response to the high level of non-Christian civilization in Punjab, so were women's medical institutions created in response to the alleged seclusion of Punjabi women in the Zenana.[5] Heavily gendered and multiracial, these institutions and the women who created them deserve separate attention. Just as male missionaries in the mid–nineteenth century found that the defamation of Indian character was a rhetorical technique of limited utility, professional women missionaries in the late nineteenth century found that the trope of a helpless, dependent Indian woman was of little use in situations where they required extensive assistance from and cooperation with Indian women.

The argument for a special mission for women would have met with little success if it had not been rooted in the practical realities of mission work. Some kinds of work could be done only by women. In 1894 Dr. J. O. Summerhayes, unable to marry according to CMS until he passed his second language exam, wrote from Dera Ghazi Khan requesting a waiver of the rule. He not only "finds work in the mountains very lonely," but cannot visit in homes unless accompanied by a wife.[6] Pleas for more women were a staple of nineteenth-century mission correspondence. During its first fifty years the American Presbyterian mission sent seventy women and forty-five men to Punjab, maintaining a rough gender balance at any given time largely because of greater turnover among women.[7] Although they died at roughly the same rate as men, women withdrew from the mission at a greater rate. As early as 1877 the annual meeting of the mission unanimously adopted a report recommending a separate mission conference for unmarried ladies, but in the laconic words of an early official historian, "its recommendations seem to have been overlooked."[8]

GENDERED BUREAUCRACIES

The Protestant missions developed diverse bureaucratic structures to deal with issues of gender and marital status, and the resulting struggles over the allocation of authority and resources to men and women respectively became both chronic and tedious, except on those occasions when they illuminate broader issues of gender and empire. Like the American Presbyterians, the United Presbyterian, Church of Scotland, and American Methodist missions placed unmarried women under the (often nominal) control of the male head of mission with varying degrees of representation. The first single women to join the United Presbyterian Mission officially, Misses Calhoun and Welsh, arrived in 1870. Married women were first listed as missionaries in 1885; by 1904 unmarried (or widowed) women missionaries, and unordained men, had full votes in the mission.[9] In 1906, the UP mission was 70 percent female, with twenty-six men (one M.D.), twenty-three married women, and thirty-eight unmarried women (two M.D.). It was only in 1936 that married women were given voting rights in the mission, although they rarely appeared on mission committees.[10]

Others created separate mission structures for women (Baptist Zenana Mission Society, Church of England Zenana Mission Society, the independent nondenominational Zenana Bible and Medical Mission). High Church Anglicans established religious orders for women, the largest being St. Stephen's in Delhi in the 1880s and St. Hilda's in Lahore in the 1890s. Of the 312 women who worked in Delhi and Lahore in connection with the SPG after 1860, 260 were recruited after 1880 and roughly 200 in the first half of the twentieth century, the heyday of British missionary work in India. In contrast, the Cambridge Mission to Delhi recruited fewer than 50 male missionaries for the entire period 1878–1947. In any given year between 1910 and 1930, roughly 60 European women in connection with the SPG were at work in Delhi and Lahore. The characteristic SPG missionary was an unmarried career woman, from London or a small city in the south of England, who arrived in India during her late twenties and either returned quickly, within a year or two, or served a lengthy term, the mean being twelve years. Those who did not die in India (at least twenty-four did), or marry while in service (at least twenty-three), or move on to missionary service elsewhere (at least fifteen), resigned to return to England.[11]

Even after the missions began to count married women as missionaries, formal classification fails to convey the fluidity of gender boundaries, the chaotic lines of bureaucratic control, and the multiracial and multigenerational character of mission institutions. Just as missionary wives played major roles in institutional management, unmarried women were sometimes commandeered for child care. Missionary children moved seamlessly into the work of some of the missions, appearing occasionally on lists of "Misses." Officially, 20 of 115 AP missionaries in Punjab between 1834 and 1884 were children of missionaries.[12] But in the 1890s Robert Clark's daughter came to Amritsar to "keep house" for her aging father. It is highly unlikely that she refrained from missionary work and equally unlikely that she appeared in the missionary statistics.

OUR INDIAN SISTERS

Women's mission work was never all white. In 1857 two Calcutta societies devoted to the education of Indian women amalgamated as "Indian Female Normal School and Instruction Society," and decided to expand their work beyond Calcutta by sending Miss Jerrom and Miss Branch to Amritsar.[13] At their second station, Jullundur, the first missionary appointed (in 1869) was not a foreigner but an Indian, Miss Golak Nath, the daughter of an Indian Christian Presbyterian clergyman (although as a Bengali, Miss Golak Nath would have been very foreign to the Punjabis of Jullundur). Of forty-three women who worked in some capacity in the Delhi SPG mission before 1880, and who can be identified, at least six (and probably more) were from Eurasian or Indian Christian families; some listed as "country born" may well have been European women permanently domiciled in India.[14] When a new Anglican sisterhood, St. Stephen's Community, was formed in 1886, one of the first sisters recruited was Mary Tara Chand, the daughter of an Indian clergymen ordained before the arrival of the Cambridge Brothers.[15]

An Indian surgeon, Martha Francis, was one of the first head doctors at St. Stephen's Hospital for Women.

Although the progression from "women's work" to "women's professional work" appears in hindsight to be seamless and in some way natural, it is important to keep in mind that women missionaries were fighting on several rhetorical fronts. They were required to defend not only education for women but also education for Indian women, which mixed together gender and imperial/racial anxieties about the transgression of recognized boundaries. A sample of what they were up against came from the English Sanskrit scholar Monier Monier-Williams, who in the missionary journal *The Indian Female Evangelist* sternly warned missionary women that their brains were on the average four ounces smaller than those of men, and that in India we do not "want our educational operations to result in the production of unnatural specimens of womanish men and mannish women."[16]

Although the superiority of the west was taken for granted by almost everyone in nineteenth-century Britain, the view that western men and women had the right to convert or proselytize or even educate people in other cultures was never a hegemonic view in the west, and always subject to widespread suspicion and severe criticism at home. Women missionaries appeared to interfere with established Indian social customs to a greater degree than men, and encountered criticism not merely from critics of the entire missionary enterprise but also from social conservatives within mission institutions. While holding Indian religions to be inferior, the bishop of Lahore, T. V. French, found the social conservatism of Indian society not only compatible with Christianity but even in some respects admirable. French defended polygamy in the church, and the Rev. T. P. Hughes of Peshawar objected to any attempt to interfere with Purdah, which he regarded as a commendable mechanism to protect the purity of women. His magnificent church in Peshawar included an aisle reserved for women in Purdah, secluded from the rest of the congregation with elaborate carved wooden screens. Missionary women found themselves allied with (supposedly helpless and dependent) Indian women in arguments about the role of mission institutions, which Indian Christian women in particular regarded as avenues of social and professional advancement.[17]

Missionary defenders of Purdah, or the Zenana, or seclusion in any form for married women, infuriated missionaries such as Sarah Hewlett of Amritsar, who singled out Purdah as emblematic of Indian treatment of women generally. Her critique of Purdah jumbled to-

gether religious and utilitarian elements. Rooted in the dominant Indian religions, it denied Indian women the opportunity to develop their
personalities through education, leaving them ignorant, indolent, and
unhappy.[18] In these arguments about Purdah, predictable images of separate spheres break down entirely, and the helpless and dependent Indian woman of mission rhetoric becomes instead a strong, intelligent
woman with great potential for advancement. If Indian women were
powerless victims, then what was the point of Zenana visitation, the
characteristic activity of women in the early missionary movement?
"It is supposed," Hewlett argued, that "because the woman of India is
often secluded and kept in a state of ignorance and darkness, that,
therefore, she has no power or influence. The very opposite is the fact.
The women have really great power in their families. . . . [H]usbands
rarely do anything contrary to the known wishes of their wives, especially of wives who are mothers of children. . . . It is sometimes supposed that the women of the Zenanas are wanting in mental power and
intellect; this again is a mistake. . . . Those who really understand
these interesting women, and can converse freely with them in their
own language, generally find them anything but stupid or wanting in
intelligence, and reckon the time spent with them most pleasantly and
happily employed."[19]

Miss E. Bauman reported in *The Indian Female Evangelist:* "It has
been my privilege to do Zenana work in six different Indian cities. . . .
The women in Lahore, at least those whom I have had the pleasure to
teach, are more advanced than the generality of those in the North
West. . . . It is rare to find women here, except in the lowest ranks, who
cannot read either Urdu, Hindi, Gurmukhi or Bengali, whilst some of
our advanced pupils know two or three of those languages, and are
studying English besides. . . . [It] is delightful to find one's pupils, with
very rare exceptions, really keen about study. . . . [E]ducation is much
prized now even among the poorer classes in this city."[20] Many of her
pupils, she claimed, were members of the Brahmo Samaj or Dev
Dharm Samaj, both organizations competing with Christian Zenana
Missions.

Although accounts of Zenana visits are interesting for their contradictions, they do not reflect the great variety of relationships between
European missionaries and Indian women. One would assume from
her rhetoric that Sarah Hewlett spent most of her time battling Purdah, but she saw Indian women mainly in other contexts. In the early
1880s she began a class for one hundred untouchable women in Amritsar. In 1880 she founded St. Catherine's Hospital for women in Amrit-

sar, and in 1884 she began systematic training of Indian midwives. By 1897 she was supervising eleven fellow-workers, sixteen Bible Women, and "several Christian converts in training."[21] Her sympathy with and fondness for her students, employees, and coworkers comes through even in her rhetoric directed to a home audience. As women's institutions grew, the rationale for the attack on the Zenana changed. Instead of the site of indolence and immorality, it became a barrier to the efficient recruitment of employees: "Even women, not Christians, are entering the medical profession. . . . It is clearly out of the question to be at once in a learned profession and a prisoner of the Zenana!"[22]

Despite the diversity of real encounters between European and Indian women, until the early twentieth century much of the discussion of the relationship is set in the scene of a zenana visit. The gap between rhetoric for home consumption and the practical realities of mission work appears throughout these accounts, which are often highly ambivalent. The entry of a missionary to a zenana involved negotiations, often elaborate, between missionary, husband, and wife, with a great deal of speculation about respective motives. On the one hand there is the essentializing theme of the mistreatment of women by their husbands, of Indian women as victims and missionary women as possessors of a special bond of sympathy with them. An SPG missionary working at Hissar reported: "I can only teach work, as her husband, an educated man and accountant in the canal office, attributes his first wife's death to her learning to read."[23] This argument could not be taken too far, however, since the husband was by definition relatively progressive if he allowed zenana visitation. Emily Pilkington spent two years in Delhi in the early 1890s, and reported on her zenana visit in this way: "One woman I [was] teaching Bible verses; her husband became angry and sat in on lessons, contradicting what I said. When he saw that I would not become angry he forbade me to do more than come talk to her of general things, which I do so as not to lose touch. She is 28 with no children, and presented me with a little fan."[24]

Women missionary accounts of zenana visitation show a sense of mutual awkwardness as the missionaries brought in western styles of needlework and the material culture of Victorian Protestantism in the form of Bible verses and illuminated texts. Women missionaries often came from a socially conservative ecclesiastical world. Recruited into mission work through churches and schools, many of them were daughters, nieces, or sisters of clergymen, others from families with a tradition of missionary service. In India they moved into missionary institutions which, if not entirely isolated from those of other Europeans, certainly constituted a separate world. Their relationships with Indians can be classified according to degrees of dependency. In their encounters with orphans, students, and untouchable converts, missionary women were basically in the position of either supervisors or teachers. A zenana visit, on the other hand, was more like a social call or parochial visitation, but the imperial context made it a particularly awkward one with a self-conscious mutual awareness of the incongruity of the situation: "I don't know what they think most peculiar in me," Emily Pilkington asked, "myself, my clothes, or my manners."[25]

Zenana missionaries were distinct in one important respect from the western women travelers and social reformers who swept through India and then wrote books on the condition of Indian women.[26] Zenana visitors often spent years in India. They could converse with Indian women in elementary or even advanced Hindi or Urdu, and upon occasion developed long-term relationship with both Christian and non-Christian Indian women. In 1885 SPG zenana visitors in Delhi included Miss Boyd, who had worked with Hindi-speaking women for fifteen years, and Miss Teasdale, who had five years of experience and was training two newcomers. Miss Henderson gave Christian lessons in Urdu to Muslims, and Miss Henkeley in both Hindi and Urdu. Some Zenana visitors were Indians. Mrs. Ram Chander, a Christian widow, visited Bengali-speaking ladies in Delhi.[27]

Some Indian women who received Zenana visits evidently found the missionaries fascinating and asked questions that the visitor was ill prepared to answer. A zenana teacher provided the opportunity to satisfy curiosity about things English. In Lahore Miss Baumann reported that "Miss Aitken was speaking to one woman when another touched my arm and asked whether that lady and I were M.A. or B.A.!"[28] Other Indian women invited Zenana visitors to educate young girls in the household.

Some Hindu women went to considerable lengths to reassure their missionary visitors that they were Christians at heart in some obscure sense, although whether this was merely a desire to be courteous or a genuine conviction that one religion was as good as another (or both) is unclear. A Baptist in Delhi reported that Hindu women reassure her that "'Yes, there is but one God; you call Him God or Christ, and *we* call Him, Bhagwan, but it is all the same.' It is an opinion with which one can hardly agree, as is the one to which Mohammedans, if in a benevolent mood, will sometimes treat us. 'Hindus,' they say, 'are very different; they, of course, are idolaters, but our religion and yours are the same; we worship the same God as you do, and we consider Jesus Christ a Prophet, only Mohammed was a Prophet also and since he has come since Christ, he has superseded him.' Rather a large and important *only*."[29]

Other women challenged Christian exclusivism, one asking: "Why did not God make us all Christians, and why does not God use His power and convert the whole world at once, so that there need be no leaving of one's loved ones to confess Him?"[30] Miss Hooper reported a list of objections to conversion she had encountered: "Besides the persecution they would suffer . . . [o]ne is the conviction they have that it is wrong to change one's religion, whatever it be, and that if God caused them to be born Hindus, He meant them to remain Hindus. Another obstacle I have to get over in every new house is their idea that our religions and theirs are really the same, only we call God by a different name."[31]

Peering across an imperial and cultural divide, missionary women declared their affection for Indian women in ways that undercut the rhetorical depiction of Indian women as helpless victims. "Those who have never seen India," Miss Hewlett suggested, "would be extremely surprised if they could be introduced into a Zenana. . . . [T]hey would be astonished to find among women who have never been out (and who therefore can know nothing of the ways of the world) refinement, gentle manners, and politeness; and they would also be unprepared to find *themselves* feeling awkward and embarrassed, and continually in danger of making some serious mistake in etiquette."[32]

Once the images of helplessness and dependency that dominate rhetoric for home consumption are put in context, women's accounts of their work with women are suffused with considerable sympathy and, given the popular image of missionary work, a surprising lack of condescension. The phrase "our Indian sisters" appears regularly in missionary literature; the phrase "our Indian brothers" hardly ever. Unlike their clerical male counterparts, women missionaries were exempt from the obligations of direct ecclesiastical discipline, leaving them freer to respond and interact without censorious anxieties about impious motives and spiritual impurity and piety, and allowing SPG missionary Frances May to openly declare that she has developed a "passion for one's own sex out here."[33]

In light of the ultimate missionary goal of creating a multiracial community of faith, however, zenana visitation led nowhere. Furthermore, despite all attempts to be subtle and diplomatic and to avoid direct proselytization, zenana work brought sharp opposition from Muslim and Arya Samaj groups claiming that foreign women were challenging the sanctity of marriage and secretly entering homes. The attacks of opponents illuminated the intrusive, imperial features of zenana work. A "Mohammedan Manifesto" circulated in Lahore in 1888 declared that Zenana visitors were spies and beguilers who come into the house under the guise of providing worldly instruction, and that a non-Muslim woman is the religious equivalent of a man for purposes of Purdah. The circular rebutted the misapprehension that zenana visitors were appointed by the government, and therefore have a legal right of entry. On the contrary: no one is required to admit them, and the government interferes with no one's faith. The manifesto was particularly irate at the practice of teaching non-Christian girls to go about singing Christian hymns.[34]

In Lahore the liberal Hindu Dev Dharm Samaj formed their own zenana mission to counter missionary teaching, demonstrating the worrying effect of even a small number of zenana visitors. A Christian Zenana missionary "attended a women's meeting held in one of her Zenanas, and conducted by a female missionary. We could not but admire the earnest eloquence of the poor woman. . . . They have borrowed their phraseology from Christianity, and a good deal of their teaching is an imitation of the same, but it is all lifeless and unreal, for Christ, who is our Life, is unknown to and unheeded by them."[35] In the view of the Dev Dharma Samaj, zenana work was a good thing—good enough to be carried out by Indians only.

Zenana work stirred up opposition while reaching very few Indian women. A government report of 1873 identified fewer than 2,000 zenana pupils in all of India.[36] At the peak of their zenana work in 1885, the SPG mission in Delhi enrolled 2 Christians, 54 Bengalis, 69 Muslims, and 217 Hindus, for a total of 342.[37] Zenana work subsequently waned, and after 1910 was hardly ever mentioned in mission reports as missionary women became more interested in expanding their influence through schools and hospitals. Women's medical and educational work expanded, not from zenana work, but from early work with dependent women—destitute widows, orphans, lepers, and the blind—who were brought under the care of the missions and cared for by women. These dependent women were at the opposite end of a spectrum of dependency, which ranged from a zenana pupil who could ask a visitor to leave at any time to a destitute famine orphan sent to a mission by the government. Zenana visitation involved a certain degree of cultural deference (B.A. or M.A.?), but a destitute orphan was almost entirely without discretion. In an imperial context, the care of orphans was characterized by a notable moral blindness, which grew in proportion to the degree of subordination of the recipients.

MORAL BLINDNESS: THE CARE OF ORPHANS

American Presbyterians in India attributed their investment in orphanages to the initiative of magistrates who realized that taking orphans was an "act of charity demanded of us as followers of Christ."[38] As early as 1871 the forty girls at the Ludhiana orphanage were receiving the attention of five different missionary wives. I have not been able to estimate the number of orphans brought into the orbit of the Punjab missions, in part because orphanages were often merged into other institutions, or disguised as part of a diffuse parochial structure, or transformed into "industrial training schools" and such like. Mission orphanages were more important in other parts of India, such as the United Provinces, which contained sixteen Christian orphanages in 1938, whereas Punjab and Delhi together had only three.[39]

In the matter of orphans, the corruptions of imperial power appear on a broad screen and in Technicolor. The care of widows and orphans had been an historic obligation of the Christian churches, and the nineteenth century a period of massive expansion of Protestant philanthropy. But in India the hand of the government was everywhere, especially during famine. During the grueling famine of 1900, for instance, the United Presbyterian mission accepted a group of "famine boys" from the United Provinces. Miss Emma Dean Anderson took them to Gujranwala, where the government gave land tax free for an industrial school. This later became, not an orphanage, but an industrial training school for Punjabi Christians, teaching weaving, tailoring, and shoemaking.[40] The fact that government and mission were cooperating to put Hindu or Muslim children into Christian missions was not lost on Indian public opinion. I have found no evidence that a single missionary comprehended the moral implications of using famine as an opportunity for making Christians. Even a liberal missionary such as Isabel Angus, a Baptist in Bhiwani, spoke of what amounted to religious child stealing as a desirable act: "Competition is very keen nowadays. Hindus and Muslims have awoke to the danger of letting Christians slip in to claim the children. . . . Principle forbade our buying children, though some parents wished to sell; but others were less scrupulous, and it

was said that Mohammedans everywhere had been beforehand in securing the *girls*, by what means and to what end one does not like to
contemplate."[41]

The moral dilemmas involved were thoroughly obscured by the des-
perate need of the orphans, and the anxious attempts of a distracted
government concerned with public order. In addition to the general
Christian obligation to care for the needy, the care of women and girls
had been a prominent rhetorical justification for women's mission
work. The care of defenseless or abandoned widows and orphans was
part and parcel of the parochial work expected of women missionaries.
Orphans were often left by persons unknown in the care of the Ludhiana
Mission Hospital, where they first lived in the compound and were later
sent to Christian families or put in the care of missionary schools.[42] At
St. Catherine's Hospital in Amritsar, Miss Hewlett claimed that mission workers "heard the voice of God, saying, 'Take these children and
nurse them for me,' and are now reaping great joy in the happy and
promising lives of these little ones."[43]

The Baptist Zenana Missionary Society claimed that its settlement
at Palwal "deals with the flotsam and jetsam, the backwash of poor Indian 'womanity,' and the doors are always open for the woman who
wants a home."[44] But during famine, self-proclaimed widows found
themselves subject to the cold hand of charity as the mission demanded some confirmation of their status as widows: "[We] have had
some stormy scenes and shall doubtless have more."[45] Orphans were of
course exempt from this moral scrutiny.

The moral legitimacy of care for widows and orphans lay not only in
the long Christian history of charity but also in the interest of the Indian Christian community in sustaining their status. The descendants
of widows and orphans quickly became respected and even distinguished members of the Christian community. Despite the stormy
scenes at the Baptist mission near Delhi, seven of the women taken in
were baptized, and four of those married Indian Christians.[46] As early
as 1884, the American Presbyterian mission counted among the former orphans in the Indian Christian community six ordained ministers, and "a dozen or more" employed as catechists or teachers. Orphan girls included the wife of a licentiate preacher and ten wives of
ordained native ministers, as well as "about as many more" wives of
catechists or employed as teachers or Bible Women. Among the sons
of ten ministers whose wives came from the orphanage were the head
master of Mission High School; another who had just finished his edu-

cation for the bar after graduating with honor at an English university;
one theology student; and one ordained missionary. The daughters of
these ten ministers include three ministers' wives, one superintendent
of Mission Bazaar Schools; one teacher in Girls Boarding School; one
medical student; and one wife of an ordained missionary. One of the
third generation was "recognized as a Native Lady Missionary."[47]

The presence of orphans and their offspring was diluted as the Indian Christian community became larger, the sources of conversion
more diverse, and Christian institutions more complex. But early converts were often prestigious converts. Work with orphans created one
of many imperial fault lines. It was impossible to unmask the imperial
associations of Christian orphanages without impugning the respectability of Indian Christians and the legitimacy of Indian Christianity.
But missionaries could hardly complain if some Indians noticed the
convergence of interests of mission and government, then confused
the missions with the government. The missions appeared to be using
their position in India to transgress the boundaries of religious competition established by the colonial state itself. The actions of the missions during the famines, especially the turn-of-the-century famine,
provided another powerful incentive for indigenous rivals to the missions to act, not merely in the provisions of orphanages but also in the
provision of other institutions for women. In Bhiwani, where "competition was very keen" for orphans in 1901, Miss Isabel Angus welcomed in 1903 the opening of the first Hindu schools for girls, an "honorable rival" to the Baptists in what she apparently regarded as a common task of educating Indian women.[48]

Care for the helpless and dependent extended to the blind and to
lepers. As Zenana work was de-emphasized, work with the helpless
was increasingly professionalized along with other forms of women's
work and mission work in general. The first specialized school for the
blind in India was founded in Amritsar in 1887 by Annie Sharp after
she came from England to visit her sister Frances, a missionary doctor
at St. Catherine's Hospital, and was "brought . . . from a life of self-
centred ease to a dedication as real as that of her sister." After a period
in England for training in Braille and specialized education of the blind,
she returned to Amritsar to establish an "industrial school" for the
blind associated with St. Catherine's. The Sharp sisters, along with another sister, Emily, moved the school as a private undertaking to Raj-
pur (near Mussoorie) in 1903, and it was eventually taken over by the
ZBMM in 1932.[49]

ITINERATION AS ENTERTAINMENT

The history of women's missions from the 1880s is largely the history of growing institutions and higher professional standards. In the management of institutions, single women without family responsibilities could devote themselves single-mindedly in a way that married missionaries could not. With institutions came independence and autonomy from male clerical control. But before looking at that story, it is important not to forget another aspect of post-Zenana women's work: itineration. Married missionaries often accompanied men on village tours, holding women's meetings and singing hymns while a separate men's meeting was going on. Freedom from childcare meant that unmarried missionaries itinerated more often, and often with other women. Some missionary women, such as Miss Clay of the CEZMS, moved out into a village in order to have a convenient base for itineration. Miss Clay is treated in mission literature as the characteristic pioneer, one of a group of English ladies who "went forth alone, trusting in God, to build their houses in the villages, away from all European support."[50] But Miss Clay could have done no itineration without ample support from Indians in a multiracial enterprise. By 1880 she had been joined in her pioneering work at Jandiala by "a native Christian lady, Miss Ellen Lakshmi Goreh"; by 1881 she supervised more than seven centers worked by a staff of fifty "missionaries, assistants and native Bible women."[51] In 1894 Miss Clay wrote home that "Miss Singh, Miss Toussaint and I have paid 706 visits in the 106 villages in the Khutrain and Thoba part of the district during the course of the year. . . . During the mela there was no need for us to go to it, as the women came to us."[52]

Itineration accounts stress repeatedly the hospitality offered in village after village. They demonstrate inadvertently that itinerating women missionaries had considerable entertainment value in the varied religious landscape of the countryside. Miss Jansen arrived at a village at sunset: "As we drive slowly . . . we are followed by crowds of children and barking dogs, while the men, sitting in groups round their huqqas, turn to look at us with various remarks. . . . Our arrival is a great excitement to the children, who peep in; and when we look at them, scamper away, screaming, only to return, however in greater numbers! It will be difficult to sleep to-night."[53] After a morning visiting in the village and an afternoon dispensing medicines from the tent, she prepared one of the endless reports for the home audience: "As I write a crowd of faces presses against the tent door. These are some of the remarks that are being made: 'Look well and long! They are the big unmarried girls!' 'One has a big face, one has a little face.' 'I suppose they read all night.'" A Sadhu showed up and pitched his tent close to them, and "lay stretched out on a bed, with a grand umbrella over him, to receive his worshipers, and their offerings. This evening his puja has been going on, the women bringing him their choicest foods, whilst a most horrible noise of drums and cymbals and monotonous singing is kept up unceasingly."[54]

Some missionary women obviously enjoyed itineration enormously, complete with the spectacle they created, and despite the hardships and the difficulty of measuring their effectiveness. Isabel Angus of the Baptist Mission at Bhiwani (where she was for a time the only European resident) itinerated regularly, and was often gratified to discover years later upon returning to a scene of her labors that some women could sing Hindi hymns for her.[55] She not only enjoyed her work but also enjoyed itinerating on her own. Other women missionaries simply could not take the very real hardships of living in India, and returned home after a probationary period. Miss Muriel Saunders, a probationer of the CMS, "seems to find a difficulty in appreciating Indians, because she is too English."[56] Other than ethnocentrism, reasons for dismissal from SPG work in India included "broke down," "unfit for work in India," or "too old to learn the language."[57] Others embraced work in India with an enthusiasm that seemed to vary with the degree of independence from clerical control, or the degree of independent authority over institutions.

INDEPENDENT FOREIGN WOMEN

The figure of the missionary hero provided an opportunity for the transgression of the limits of separate spheres. Unmarried missionaries moved into mission work from a world of very gradually expanding opportunities for women in Britain and the United States to pursue careers with some degree of financial independence. Presbyterian and Anglican missionaries in particular were highly educated by the standards of the day. Of the 312 women who worked in Delhi and Lahore in connection with the SPG after 1860, forty claimed a B.A. or M.B. (a medical) degree or its equivalent. As many as 113 mentioned some kind of secondary education, usually a girls' high school (at least five attended Cheltenham Ladies College, and four each Bedford High School and the Godolphin School).[58] At least 81 had some instruction at one of the Church of England deaconess training institutions.[59]

A United Presbyterian missionary from Iowa, Kate Hill, began nearly a half-century of service in Punjab in 1896 at the age of twenty-three. A graduate of Newton High School, she had received teacher training at Amity College in College Springs, Iowa. During her early days of itineration, her letters to her mother and sister play on the theme of missionary heroism in the face of hardships including the heat, dirty cooks, the necessity of cutting off her bangs, the ordeal of reading *Pilgrim's Progress* in Urdu, and the snobbery of the English: an English doctor, after refusing to shake hands with her because he thought she was a Eurasian nurse, asked her if there were any "natives" in America.[60]

In this Scotch-Irish United Presbyterian family, the unmarried daughters taught first at local common school, and hoped to move up either to High School teaching or church work of some kind, the most glamorous being a missionary. "I guess each one of us had to teach a school at the corners of Jasper County to see how well we turned out," Kate wrote to her sister Bessie, and she chided her sister Susie for setting her sights too low by attending the State Normal School at Cedar Falls instead of a private college where she could receive an education suitable for a high school teacher.[61]

Hill did not escape hierarchies of status upon becoming a UP missionary. When stationed in settled missionary centers, Hill found herself looked down upon by women medical doctors, and pressed into child care when married missionaries with small children fell ill. It is little wonder that, in spite of great discomfort and periodic depression, she preferred to be out in the villages itinerating with other young unmarried women, and writing tales of her exploits to her schoolteacher aunts and sisters in Iowa. Although itineration provided autonomy and independence for women, it did not provide status. Like zenana work, it was thought to be suitable for any educated person with some language skills. Kate Hill intended to move from itineration to a secure position in the mission educational bureaucracy. The growth of mission educational and medical institutions provided autonomy and independence for women as a class within the mission, but also led to the introduction of levels of hierarchy and status among missionary women and their Indian coworkers, students, and patients, Christian and non-Christian. As mission institutions became more complex, the abject dependency of the destitute orphan was replaced by a spectrum of relationships between women missionaries and a diverse array of Indians recruited into or attracted to mission institutions, as students, teachers, patients, nurses, doctors, and missionaries.

The missions opened schools for girls whenever they could. In the early eighties the Anglo-Indian novelist and teacher Florie Annie Steel surveyed girls education for the government of Punjab. She discovered fifty-eight municipal girls schools in Ludhiana, Lahore, Amritsar, and Gujranwala, with 1,647 on the rolls, 1,133 of them in Amritsar. The missions sponsored fifty-five schools with 1,344 on the rolls, half of them in Lahore under the IFNS and American Presbyterian missions.[62] The Baptists, she noted in passing, had a "non-aided low caste school" in Delhi with fifty-six pupils, and almost all of the missions were engaged in girls' education that was too informal to merit government inspection. Steele had a low opinion of Indians generally, but for what it is worth she argued that mission schools were superior to government schools in both "thoroughness of teaching" and "intelligent supervision."[63]

Opinions on the relative efficiency of mission and government education varied, but school inspectors and women teachers were of one opinion on the importance of professionalization. The informal gathering of women and girls for instruction never ceased within the mission, but the importance of formal classroom instruction with properly trained instructors, both foreign and Indian, grew steadily in importance and became a measure of the success or failure of a mission. Competition among the missions reinforced the commitment to high professional standards. As early as 1872 Indian Female Normal School missionaries were sent to Punjab to supplement the "labors of the wives of our missionaries of the CMS" and establish a teacher training college in order to head off potential competition from the Anglo-Catholic sisterhoods inside the Church of England, who were alleged to spread "perverted and unscriptural Catholic teaching on the proper role of women."[64] Despite his evangelical background, Bishop French's fear of Roman Catholic competition, in the form of convent schools and orphanages, led him to approve in 1882 the establishment of a High Church Anglican sisterhood in Murree where three Sisters of St. Denys were put in charge of a school. They immediately caused controversy, and reinforced the worst fears of CMS evangelicals, by requesting that the (CMS) bishop hear their confessions.[65]

Upon arriving in Delhi in the 1880s the Cambridge Brothers reorganized the already extensive SPG women's work around an Anglican sisterhood, the Community of St. Stephen, and attempted to recruit ordained deaconesses with professional training as teachers. St. Stephen's Community in the 1890s was centered in a five-acre compound outside the old city walls in the civil lines, with a home for missionaries, boarding school for Christian girls, St. Mary's Refuge for women, and four closed carriages for transporting women in Purdah. In the cold weather the daily routine began at six with *chota haziri*, an early small breakfast, followed by service at seven in the mission church, St. Stephen's in Old Delhi. After returning to the compound, the women would have prayers with the servants, then their own service in the chapel, then breakfast. The school and zenana workers would depart for five hours of teaching; those learning Urdu would join their munshis. The work day ended with midafternoon prayers, then a walk or a drive before dinner at seven. After spending an hour with each other in the drawing room, the women would observe compline and retire or, during the hot weather, go "up to the roof to study and stars and hope for some slight breeze."[66]

In 1899 an English deaconess, Katherine Beynon, created yet another Anglican women's community, St. Hilda's in Lahore. Beynon used her personal wealth to subsidize the construction of a large new deaconess house on the cathedral grounds (each room named for a single virtue, such as Honesty, Truth, and Courage), and the SPG supplied qualified teachers for the new cathedral school system that was attracting non-Christian students. According to Beynon, St. Hilda's deaconesses "[w]ere to be, not free lances, but trained and disciplined women working with the Bishop's license under the direction of the Chaplains. Marriage at a very early age is not the only thing to which a girl looks forward after leaving school, as it used to be."[67]

Even as they were established, St. Stephen's and St. Hilda's communities found themselves threatened with fragmentation from the increasing institutional specialization of women's educational and medical missionary work. Delhi and Punjab were the sites of pioneering medical work by women, a geographical concentration that one study attributes to the "larger proportion of Purdah women" in north India.[68] Medical missions were thought of as a method of entry into the relatively closed worlds of Muslims and caste Hindus. There is a strong contrast between the heavy emphasis placed upon the image of the zenana in mission rhetoric and the practical realities of women's missionary work in India. In medical care as in education, the overwhelming majority of Indian women served by mission institutions did not live in seclusion. The image of the zenana, however, served as a powerful recruiting tool and accounts (along with the accidents of missionary entrepreneurship) for the distinctive concentration of women medical missionaries in India in comparison to other mission fields, and in northwest India in contrast to the rest of India.[69]

RELIGION AND HEALING

Medical work itself was rarely controversial within the missionary movement, despite its lack of any obvious connection to conversion. Jesus healed people; he neglected to set up schools and colleges. The benefits of medical care were clear and unchallengeable to almost everyone in the west, convinced as they were of superiority of western science and technology. A convergence of interests emerged between medicine and religion in the missionary movement, standing in sharp contrast to the battle fought between doctors and clergymen over their relative moral authority in Great Britain and the United States.[70] Furthermore, unlike educational results, medical results could be quantified and tabulated in a satisfying form: number of babies delivered, number of women admitted to hospital, etc. By the end of the century, with the advent of anesthesia and antiseptic surgery, missionaries, patients, and donors at home could feel a common sense of satisfaction at the results of medical mission work. The fact that Jesus' medical methods were not based on the germ theory of disease was conveniently overlooked.

Early missionaries, male and female, conducted a good deal of highly informal medical care along with their other activities, following the advice of Rowland Bateman: "Become a quack specialist. I asked a medical friend to put me up to the diagnosis of the commonest eye troubles of these villagers, and their remedies in the early stages, and the result is that I have obtained quite a reputation for the number of people whose sight I have saved."[71] The Church of Scotland Foreign Mission Committee placed an order in 1886 for sulfate of magnesia, precipitated sulfur, sulfate of quinine, castor oil, gutta percha (for teeth), wafer papers (for nauseous medicines), and enema apparatus, evidence that missionaries proclaimed the Word along with a good deal of purging, patching, and dosing with quinine.[72]

At the Punjab Mission Conference of 1864, Robert Clark advocated the formation of a Punjab Medical Mission Association to cooperate with the Edinburgh Medical Missionary Society to provide trained doctors as missionaries. There is every reason to believe that the missions would have appointed trained women with medical degrees if they had been available. From Britain, only men were available until the late nineteenth century, and the CMS appointed William J. Elmslie, a Presbyterian of Aberdeen, to the Kashmir Medical Mission in 1864. When Elmslie approached the London Zenana Committee in 1871 to ask for female medical missionaries, Elizabeth Garret Anderson had been licensed only six years before. Elmslie argued of medical missions: "Were there no other reason . . . than that of the humane endeavour to lessen human pain and save human life, that ought to speak loudly and persuasively to every pitiful and compassionate heart. . . . The death rate amongst Indian women and children is enormous and quite out of proportion." Furthermore, the sheer presence of women missionaries is "*a key which may be said to fit every lock.* She would find an entrance where the educational missionary would find it closed. She would soften bigotry, remove prejudice, dispel ignorance, drive away gloom, and unobtrusively but effectually deposit the all-pervading leaven of the Gospel in numberless hearts and homes."[73]

The barriers posed to women doctors in Great Britain and the United States by the metaphors of separate spheres simply vanished in India. Although there were endless debates in mission circles about the level of qualifications proper or necessary for a female medical missionary, and extended debate over who should or should not have authority over women medical missionaries in India, I have never encountered in mission circles a principled missionary objection to the presence of women medical missionaries in India. The practical difficulties remained formidable, but women confronted them under the cover of the rhetoric of missionary heroism. The IFNS responded to the appeal for medical missionaries by sending in 1873 an English nursing sister, Lucy Leighton, and a Scots widow, Mrs. Crawford, neither qualified as a doctor. Lucy Leighton was ill when she left, and the ship "pitched so badly in the Bay of Biscay that she was dead before Gibraltar."[74] Mrs. Crawford dropped dead after three months in Bombay despite the protections afforded by the topi, spine-pad, and woolen cholera belt. The IFNS persevered, placing Elizabeth Beilby in Lucknow in 1875, although she returned home in 1876 "a physical wreck." She was back in Lucknow in 1878 with her sister Alice, who died within a month. Beilby succeeded in training Sarah Hewlett, the society's next medical missionary, who in 1880 founded a hospital (later known as St. Catherine's) in Amritsar.

In 1884 at least twelve women missionaries were listed as primarily medical missionaries, with or without qualifications, compared to only eight men (five British, three American).[75] Dr. Maria White, a qualified American physician sponsored by the Methodist Episcopal Church (North), began medical work at a hospital in Sialkot in 1875.[76] A daughter of Punjab missionaries, Dr. Jessie Carleton of the American Presbyterian (AP) mission returned to the bungalow in Ambala where she had been born and opened her practice in 1887.[77] The medical missionary enterprise was multiracial from the first, although Indians in subordinate positions are often left unnamed in mission records. Miss Bose of Tarn Taran made it onto the official CMS mission list as a medical missionary, and the AP mission dispensary in Lahore was under the supervision Dr. Esa Das, who "bears a high Christian character, and is an elder of the church." Other AP Indian Christian clergy practiced irregularly, including "[t]he Rev. Ahmed Shah, having some knowledge of the old Grecian system of medicine."[78] When opening medical institutions, the missions made use of Indian men and women with medical qualifications. The first head surgeon at St. Stephen's Hospital for Women in Delhi was Martha Francis, a surgeon whose formal qualifications were listed only as "Indian doctor" but who served until 1932 as a surgeon at Delhi or Riwari.

In its rush to recruit Indian clergy, the CMS ordained not only educated Indians but at least one Indian medical practitioner. A second-generation Christian, John Williams was serving in the government medical service on the frontier when he was, according to CMS history, "found" by T. V. French conducting prayer-meetings for English soldiers quartered in "a desolate little fort built out in the howling waste."[79] Williams was recruited from government service into the CMS as a medical missionary at Tank, where he conducted a medical mission and supervised a hospital for over twenty-five years. Ordained deacon in 1872 and priest in 1893, Williams did no evangelism but was featured regularly in CMS literature as an exemplar of the bricks and mortar strategy of Christian witness.[80] In CMS racial taxonomy, Williams was listed under "native clergy." Another Indian doctor, Henry Martyn Clark, was described in the CMS register as "An Afghan of Peshawar" but was nonetheless included in the list of "foreign missionaries" serving in India, presumably on the basis either of his medical degree from the University of Edinburgh or his status as the adopted son of CMS missionaries Robert and Elizabeth Clark.[81] Accepted as a missionary by the CMS in 1881 to begin a medical mission in Amritsar, Clark was soon presiding over an empire of medical networks in and around Amritsar with duties that included (at least nominally) the supervision of trained English women medical missionaries.

As professional qualifications grew in importance and medical institutions became more complex, racial stratification became more prominent. Opened in 1880 with six beds, St. Catherine's Hospital for women in Amritsar served forty-two in-patients in 1887 with more than one hundred people living on the premises and a staff of eleven fellow-workers, sixteen Bible Women, and "several Christian converts in training." By 1896 the hospital reported 200 in-patients, 38,000 out-patients, and 2,000 home visits.[82] By that time the CEZMS and ZBMM between them sponsored a broad network of Indian and foreign women's medical personnel throughout Punjab (staff with formal qualifications are *italicized*).[83] Miss Kheroth Bose ran a dispensary in Baharwal Atari with 153 in-patients and 13,000 outpatients; the Star Dispensary and Hospital in Batala had been founded by and operated by Miss Dixie until her marriage in 1897, when she was succeeded by *Dr. Maria Sharp (hon.; MD Brux., LSA)*. At Jandiala a tiny dispensary founded by Mrs. Parthinkar was transferred to Miss Lacey, an assistant surgeon trained at Madras (it is not clear if she was country-born European, Eurasian, or Indian Christian). The Misses Catchpool and Reuther in Narowal supervised a dispensary with "fully trained nurse and dispensary" (in 1900 Miss Ruth Verana and Miss Annie Sher Singh, Indian Christians trained at Ludhiana). The Tarn Taran dispensary and hospital (with *Miss Vines, LRCP*) was an extension of the Amritsar mission with a "Leper Village, Sunday Schools for Christian, Muhammadan, and Hindu children, a School for Blind Women, Bible readings for English people from the station, a Converts' School, a Creche, and regular Servants' Bible Readings."[84]

In the dreaded outpost of Dera Ismael Khan ("Dreary Dismal Khan") a trained nurse, Miss Rose Johnson, "held the Medical Mission fort alone for ten years" until replaced in 1896 by *Miss Adams, LSA*. In Peshawar the Duchess of Connaught Hospital (CMS) was opened in 1884 and rebuilt after 1891. *Miss Mitcheson (LRCP)* began medical work there, then left for England for further training. In 1898 she was joined by *Miss Holst MD Brux, LSA*. In Quetta *Dr. Charlotte Wheeler (MD)* had opened a "pleasant little hospital." In Kashmir CMS work was funded by the famous traveler Isabella Bird, who built a hospital there in memory of her husband. *Dr. Fanny Butler (LSMW, MD)*, who became the first fully trained medical doctor from Britain to practice in India, in 1880, was transferred to Kashmir in 1887.[85] Under Anglican evangelical auspices alone, six fully qualified foreign doctors had worked in Punjab by the turn of the century.

In Delhi the "medical zenana work" of Miss Engellman had evolved into a specialization in midwifery. At the time of the arrival of the Cambridge Brothers in 1880, she was delivering hundreds of babies a year. With a passion for Christianity embodied in institutions, Miss Engellman and the Cambridge Brothers established St. Stephen's Hospital for Women. By 1888 she and her Anglo-Indian assistant, Alice King, lived in a new thirty-bed hospital overlooking the Queen's Gardens in Delhi, and a branch hospital had been established in Karnal. In 1888 the aggregate number of patients seen at Delhi and Karnal (including out-patients) was reported as 19,790.[86] St. Stephen's Hospital became the heart of the women's missionary effort in Delhi in the 1890s. With the new hospital came a new emphasis on professionalism, and a renewed emphasis on the missionary value of the sheer presence of Christian institutions in India. Another medical zenana worker, Jenny Muller, went for training to Calcutta Medical College in 1888, and returned in 1891 to serve as the hospital's first qualified doctor. Probably born in India, she had been educated at the Lawrence Military School at Sanawar Asylum. The progression in mission institutions from unqualified country-born missionary to qualified English missionary is neatly demonstrated by the arrival from England in 1893 of St. Stephen's second qualified doctor, Mildred Staley, M.B. London, a bishop's daughter who "gave up a lucrative practice for Christ's sake, at first in order to fill the need in Karnal."[87]

PROFESSIONAL WOMEN

In 1896 she was joined by Charlotte Hull (M.B., B.Sc. London), who returned to London in 1901 to deliver a speech to women in medical training—an appeal to join her in mission work in Delhi. Forget about the old and already outdated image of the missionary, she argued, the "unconscious survival of our childish picture of the pith hat and the big Bible under the palm tree." At a time when the number of unmarried women physicians, surgeons, and general practitioners in England and Wales amounted to only 167, she argued that India offered an opportunity to exercise the highest level of medical skill.[88] "There are few places where such a variety of practice, and especially surgical practice, can be obtained by a medical woman as in our Delhi Hospital." Furthermore, do not worry about being forced to proselytize. "Is not the spirit and aim with which the work is done more than the actual work itself, more at any rate than the actual preaching, which constitutes its missionary aspect?"[89]

In 1906 the foundation stone was laid for a new hospital in the civil lines north of Old Delhi, paid for in part by the sale of the old buildings. By 1916 St. Stephen's Hospital had a European staff of five doctors, two evangelists, two housekeepers, five nursing sisters, and an Indian staff of twenty-seven. By one estimate there were only 60 unmarried career women doctors practicing in England in 1911.[90] Of the 312 female foreign missionaries affiliated with the SPG in Delhi or Lahore after 1860, 24 claimed the title of doctor.[91] At one time just after World War I there were nine women doctors affiliated with the Delhi Mission alone, although not all were in residence in India at once.

Given their strong commitment to professionalization, it is perhaps not surprising that women missionaries showed little curiosity about, sympathy for, or willingness to draw on Indian medical practices. Indian medical knowledge was portrayed as a static traditional monolith, rooted in superstition and in practice either quaint or lethal. At the Baptist Zenana Mission Annual Breakfast in 1897, Dr. Ellen Farrer praised Indian civilization as "very different from our western one, but in many respects not unworthy of the name." But medical practice was not an aspect of Indian civilization to be admired. "Some of their Hakims possess a system of medicine too, professing to be Greek in origin, but reminding one of the accounts one reads of the state of medical science in our own land in centuries now happily long past. Bleeding, cupping, leeching, burning with red hot irons, potions and plasters containing such ingredients as stags horns, lamp-black, red-earth, and various conglomerations of vegetable origin, seem to figure largely in the treatment prescribed by these gentlemen. . . . Such surgery as there is in the hands of barbers, as it used to be long ago in England."[92]

Especially in respect to obstetrics and the care of children, Indian medical practice was regarded as positively menacing. "This is the place to see miserable babies," Jenny Muller wrote of St. Stephen's dispensary, while lamenting the small number she saw that day because of an eclipse of the sun and fear of new plague regulations.[93] The doctors' and nurses' abilities to effect visible good for Indians very quickly gave them an impregnable sense of the superiority of their own approach in contrast to that of their indigenous enemies: "[T]he fearsome old mother-in-law, the filthy old family mid-wife, and the foolish old family medicine men."[94] In 1894 the Civil Surgeon at Karnal assembled the local Dais, Indian midwives, for a lecture from Miss Muller on hygiene. "Anything more gruesome and horrible for a person trained in antiseptic principles to behold than that crowd of dirty women can hardly be conceived," she wrote.[95]

Early surgical reports from St. Stephen's and St. Elizabeth's Hospital in Karnal report, along with the usual bones set, abscesses drained, and cataracts removed, an emphasis on gynecological and obstetric operations, including the disheartening late-term "reduction of the fetus" that was so often judged necessary to save the life of the mother.[96] Medical practice was unspecialized, with a heavy emphasis on antiseptic surgery with chloroform, and with doctors at the beck and call of patients during emergencies.[97] At the Baptist hospital in Bhiwani, a small institution compared to St. Stephen's in Delhi or St. Catherine's in Amritsar, Dr. Ellen Farrer arrived from England in 1891 to face her first emergency operation on a boy of ten, done in an open courtyard and successful despite "an inopportune dust-storm which rendered aseptic precautions useless."[98]

In more than forty years of practice in Bhiwani, Ellen Farrer treated tetanus, burns, hernias, perforations, tonsillitis, cataracts, tumors, abscesses, ovarian cysts, and uterine polyps; performed Caesarean sections and blood transfusions; prescribed medicines and regimens of treatment for the plague, malaria, pneumonia, whooping cough, syphilis, and flatulence. On January 5, 1902, she was called away from the Sunday morning sermon by her Indian Baptist pastor to treat an infant of three days near death, a "feeble little specimen of humanity in a poor Chamar house."[99] A few days later she was called out at 2:30 A.M. for a confinement case, "a transverse presentation and we were in time to save (humanly speaking) both lives."[100] Remaining each year through the hot weather, reserving her holidays for the fall, she conducted in July of 1904 an operation for sinus and glands in the neck, a "long and gory business."[101] Later that month she reported that, during a Sunday afternoon congregational meeting, a "mother took my (five year old) tetanus patient away, to my great disappointment and grief."[102]

Ellen Farrer kept extensive diaries and maintained a huge correspondence (in 1904 alone she wrote 527 letters and 113 postcards), which documents her pleasure in the practice of medicine and concern for the well-being of her patients. In a practice punctuated with the melancholy refrain "arrived too late," she never lost her self-mocking sense of incongruity, her compassion for her patients, or her astonishment at the unpredictable demands on her skills. Shortly after Christmas in 1901, at his request, she "gave Khalib chloroform and circumcised him."[103] In 1919 she "went to the dispensary and had a lively time with two small operations as a new nurse misunderstood an order and cut off a 'supernumary digit' instead of the beads on a baby . . . and I had to make the best of the business!"[104]

Although often accused of proselytization, Christian medical practitioners did very little to press Christian views on patients. By utilitarian standards, Ellen Farrer was simply a doctor who found in Bhiwani a good place to practice medicine. From a missionary point of view, however, the building of medical institutions represented the most admirable of the third and most important forms of missionary witness: (1) preaching the word, (2) publishing the word, (3) making the word visible in Christian institutions. Anticipating objections, Ellen Farrer addressed the Baptist Union on women's medical practice shortly before her departure for India in 1891. "If to some the practical element seems to be too prominent in what I have to say, I can only beg them to remember that *the subject is essentially practical in its nature*, and that a medical woman can hardly be expected to regard it from any other than a practical and matter of fact point of view."[105] Given her own experience, professionalism and religious commitment fit seamlessly: "We have a duty to our Master to give Him workers as fully trained and as well equipped as possible."[106]

Raised in a prosperous and cultured Nonconformist family, members of Heath Street Baptist Church in Hampstead, Farrer explained that "the call to be a missionary grew up in me from childhood and through girlhood. But it was to my mother that I owed my decision to train as a doctor and to go as a medical missionary. I had won prizes and scholarships at school and at college, and she suggested that God had not given me the ability to do this without meaning me to do something with it."[107] After Bedford College, she received her MBBS from the London School of Medicine for Women and the Royal Free Hospital. "As nine of us had graduated M.B. London in the Autumn of 1890, we did a canvas of the Royal Free Hospital Staff with the object of getting posts as House Surgeons and Physicians opened to us there in our own hospital, but in vain!"[108]

Farrer worked in various hospital and free clinics, including the Medical Mission at Kentish Town, and served four months as Resident Medical Officer at the New Hospital for women on Euston Road. She always insisted that, despite obstacles, there were opportunities for women medical practitioners at home. Her decision to become a missionary (where she would be in complete charge of a hospital) was not from her point of view primarily a question of careerism, but of spiritual discernment in the face of a divine call. A frequent diary entry was "I dare not choose my lot/I would not if I might/Choose Thou for me my God/So shall I walk aright."

If the personal and spiritual choices required painful acts of discernment, the imperial contradictions of the missionary movement rarely surfaced in Ellen Farrer's public rhetoric or private diaries. But those contradictions were evident to others, including students at the London School of Medicine for Women and the organizers of the Countess of Dufferin's Fund to provide medical care for the women of

India. Although founded by pioneers in the opening up of medical practice for women, including Dr. Sophia Jex-Blake and Dr. Elizabeth
Blackwell, the London School of Medicine for Women was initially associated with the missionary movement. The first two women to begin studies at the LSMW in 1874 were in training to be missionaries,
and the school continued to train missionary women in search of
medical qualifications. In 1875 Dr. Elizabeth Garrett Anderson accepted a lectureship, and for twenty years after 1883 served as dean.
Under her leadership, the LSMW exhibited a relentless professionalism, which involved distancing the institution from the missionary
enterprise. As the only recognized medical school for women, the
LSMW had obvious reasons for stressing professionalism rather than
religion. From 1895 to January of 1897, eight of twenty-one appointments listed for graduates were for mission work, but from 1897 to
1900 the numbers fell noticeably.[109] The opening of the Edinburgh
School of Medicine for Women in 1886 provided another British opportunity for regular professional training, but women who aspired to be
medical missionaries continued to train in a variety of other venues,
some of them subprofessional, including Dr. Griffith's Training School
and Hospital for Female Missionaries, later renamed (1887) the Zenana
Medical College, where students could receive a diploma in midwifery.
This institution was a particular object of Dr. Garrett Anderson's ire.[110]

SECULAR IMPERIALIST MEDICINE

If some women regarded women's medical missions as a threat to
hard-won professional legitimacy of women doctors, others (including
Queen Victoria) regarded medical missions as a threat to the legitimacy of British imperial rule in India. In the 1880s the imperial tensions within the women's medical enterprise broke into the open with
the formation of the Countess of Dufferin's Fund, which provided a
clear, secular imperialist alternative to the missionary movement in
Punjab.[111] In 1881 medical missionary Elizabeth Beilby returned to
London to receive formal medical training, and secured an interview
with Queen Victoria, who received from her a large silver locket containing a petition from the Maharani of Punna pleading with her to
send female doctors to India. The Queen, having "expressed my deep
interest and hope that something might be done in the matter," sub-
contracted her concern to the Countess of Dufferin, who in 1883
toured India to organize official support, especially from the wives of
the lieutenant-governors, for a charity to provide western education to

the women of India. In 1885 the National Association for Supplying Female Medical Aid to the Women of India was organized with the queen as patron, the viceroy as patron in India, the viceroy's wife as president, and the governors and lieutenant-governors of the provinces as vice-president.[112] At a meeting at the Mansion House in support of the Countess of Dufferin's Fund, Lord Hobhouse dismissed the work of the missionaries as "some ladies sent out by the zealous missionary bodies in England and America who have practised medicine with a considerable amount of skill, though far from professing a full professional equipment."[113]

The association claimed to receive no direct aid from the government, although the medical officers of the government were authorized to supervise the work of the association's employees. Among the first objects of its charity was Miss Beilby, who after obtaining a medical degree in 1885 jumped ship from the missionary movement and became the director of the Lady Aitchison Hospital for Women in Lahore, opened by the Countess of Dufferin in 1888. In 1893 the fund claimed sixty-five hospitals and dispensaries in India "in connection" with the association and a staff of thirteen lady doctors (European), forty-two female assistant surgeons, and forty-five female hospital assistants.[114] Despite the centrality of antimissionary sentiment in this enterprise, Lady Dufferin complained that "there is something very uncharitable in the way some few persist in talking and writing of my fund as if it was an anti-missionary and anti-Christian institution."[115]

The intervention of the Countess of Dufferin's Fund reflected understandable confusion about the motives and purposes of missionary medicine. The *Times* argued: "In an indirect way, the same good that is aimed at by medical missionaries, will be attained by the Lady Doctor pure and simple."[116] Missionaries could never accept the *Times*'s argument that a medical doctor "pure and simple" could achieve the same goals as a missionary doctor. On his departure for Kashmir, Dr. Ernest Neve received a letter reassuring him that the CMS parent committee "are sure that you are going with the purpose of being a medical *missionary* and not merely a medical *man*."[117] This was the heart of the matter. A medical missionary was intrinsically a missionary, but only if his or her motives sprang from love of God and love of the people of India. This conviction allowed missionaries to steer a course between supporters at home, who often demanded evidence of direct proselytization in medical work, and imperialist and Indian critics, who accused them of using medical work as a cover for proselytization.

From the points of view of mission and imperial administrators, the Lady Aitchison Hospital in Lahore was run on one set of principles and the Baptist Hospital at Bhiwani on another, despite the fact that the medical care provided was identical. The Christian ethos of the hospital was assumed to "rub off" even on non-Christian staff. The doctors at the Baptist hospital in Bhiwani were recruited by local officials to conduct classes for dais (midwives) "on modern lines" at the City Municipal Office. Officials paid the dais two annas (a day's wage) per attendance plus Rs 1–5 for calling a doctor to a difficult case. As a result mission doctors and midwives became great friends. "We were in their homes for many hours," and "countless opportunities for Christian talk and advice were presented." The missionary in charge of the Baptist hospital at Bhiwani believed that one of the most popular midwives "was at heart a sincere believer in Christ although she did not openly confess him."[118]

Ellen Farrer's career as a dedicated doctor in Bhiwani showed little evidence of a desire for self-aggrandizement or a passion for influence and honor that infected many missionaries. But the outward conformity in professional standards made the Bhiwani hospital little different (except in scale) from the Lady Aitchison Hospital in the practical business of running a hospital. Ellen Farrer was a doctor who enjoyed practicing medicine, and had the additional satisfaction of divine sanction for her calling. But she was, in her everyday activities, a medical doctor, which meant in this context a hospital administrator, which meant that she was, in her relationship to Indians, an employer. It was there that missionaries and Indian Christians encountered the unyielding imperial fault line running through the missionary movement, the imperialism of greater resources and superior professional qualifications.

PROFESSIONALISM AND RACIAL STRATIFICATION

European women were freed from the blight of clerical professionalism, which forced male clergy into the role of ecclesiastical disciplinarians. Women did not have to manipulate, mold, evict, and excommunicate Indian Christians. But as the scale of mission institutions grew, women missionaries were less likely to encounter Indians as colleagues in mission or church work, or as social equals in zenana work, and were more likely to encounter them as patients, students, or employees. In India, as in Great Britain and the United States, patients, students, and employees were people to be managed, disciplined, or discharged. A patient in the Bhiwani Baptist Hospital whose pain was relieved, or whose baby was saved from death or disfigurement, would no doubt have found it very bewildering to be told that, beneath the surface of compassion and commitment, Ellen Farrer was contributing to a complex discourse of subordination whose ultimate purpose was the maintenance of western superiority. But there were aspects of the missionary commitment to professionalism that led in that direction.

The trajectory of professionalism is clearer in the career of Dr. Edith Brown, another Baptist doctor who sailed to India with Ellen Farrer in 1891. In 1887 the Baptist journal *Our Indian Sisters* issued an appeal for funds for the medical training of Edith Brown, who stood second in all England at her final High School Examination, passed with distinction a three-year course at Girton College, and was at that time a teacher of science in the Girls High School in Exeter.[119] The appeal must have been successful, for by the time of her departure for India in 1891 Edith Brown had secured a medical diploma from Scotland and an M.D. from Brussels.[120] Assigned first to the Charlotte Hospital (AP/FES) in Ludhiana, she reported "happy early days ... because of a daily walk with Miss Pogson who was helping her to learn Urdu and the history of Ludhiana."[121] She was then ordered to begin practice in the city of Palwal, where her happiness evaporated.

Edith Brown had never heard of Palwal, and the remoteness of it horrified her. After a twenty-six-mile ride first in a tum-tum, and then in a springless ekka, she found awaiting her a cold, largely windowless house in a town where (she confided in her diary) there were no European residents outside the mission compound, the roads were narrow and filthy, the houses dilapidated, and the vernacular Hindi unintelligible to her despite her study of Urdu.[122] There was no operating room, and the primary medical practice was handing out quinine. This was clearly unsuitable for a Girton graduate with a medical degree. It had already occurred to her in Ludhiana, by analogy with the ecclesiastical principle of a "native church for the natives of India," that Indian patients could best be reached by Indian doctors and nurses. In Palwal she soon came to a conclusion: "Why should we not have a Christian Medical School attached to one of the Mission Hospitals and ourselves train suitable Indian girls?"[123]

For Edith Brown, founding a Christian medical school for Indian women became the quickest way out of Palwal. In 1893 she organized a Conference of Women Medical Missionaries in Ludhiana, attended by fourteen women (eight with M.D. or MBBS) representing the principal mission societies in Punjab and Delhi.[124] The women circulated a prospectus among the missionary societies appealing for financial support for interdenominational medical school to train female native assistants for female medical mission work: "We wish friends clearly to understand that however humbly the School may begin its work, a full curriculum of five years and a Government Diploma such as is open to men are steadily contemplated."[125]

With £50 in hand, and the promise of £50 a year for the next three years (note how small sums of western currency could go a long way), Brown opened a medical college for women in Ludhiana in January of 1894 with four Christian medical students, two dispenser students, five nursing students, and four midwifery students. Staff in addition to Miss Brown, the principal, included Miss Balfour (FES), M.D., L.R.C.P.S., lecturer (who remained in charge of the Charlotte Hospital) and two women from the American Presbyterian mission, both with M.D. degrees, Miss Allen and Miss Caldwell, who taught chemistry, osteology, and materia medica. Teaching was in English except in the midwifery course, which was in Urdu.[126]

Brown began a long career as fundraiser and medical administrator, bombarding her home committee, the government, and private donors with requests for everything from a cow to a new hospital, all in the name of increased efficiency. In 1898 the first wards of the E. A. Greenfield Memorial Hospital were opened by the lieutenant governor of Punjab, Sir Mackworth Young, and Lady Young. This expansion was financed by the provision of private rooms for wealthy patients, who were transported to the hospital in secluded dhoolies and housed in a wing where husbands and female relatives could enter without seeing other relatives. In 1904 the government of Punjab offered a regular yearly grant for the work, and in 1915 women medical students were transferred from Government College, Lahore, to Ludhiana, which was then recognized as the Women's Christian Medical College, with which was incorporated the Punjab Medical School for Women.[127] By 1931 the College had awarded 210 medical diplomas (licentiates of the State Medical Faculty of the Punjab) and trained 122 compounders, 158 nurses, and 329 nurse dais.[128]

While Ellen Farrer was laboring in relative obscurity at her small hospital in Bhiwani, Edith Brown had created a medical training empire in Ludhiana that made her well known in the community and in mission circles. When returning to Ludhiana from the Edinburgh Missionary Conference in 1910, she was met at the station at midnight by the entire staff of the college, placed on a crimson-draped elephant, and marched through town in procession to her rooms.[129] As her fame

spread, she was awarded the Silver Kaiser-i-Hind Medal, the government of India's civilian honor, in 1911, and the Gold Kaiser-i-Hind
Medal in 1922. In 1931 she was created Dame Commander of the British Empire. By 1942, when she stepped down (unwillingly) at the age of
seventy-seven, the Christian Medical College for Women had become
one of the best known educational institutions in colonial India.

By 1931 there were twenty-nine mission hospitals in the Province of
Punjab, more than any other Indian state or province except Madras.
Of those, women missionaries staffed sixteen. In the broader area
served by the Punjab missions, including Punjab, Delhi, the North
West Frontier Province, and Kashmir, there were thirty-eight mission
hospitals, twenty-one staffed by women. The Countess of Dufferin's
Fund provided staff for only five women's hospitals in the same area.[130]
Of roughly 622 foreign mission agents in northwest India in 1931, 43
were qualified female doctors and 11 qualified male doctors.[131] But
these foreign practitioners were almost matched in number by Indian
doctors, male and female, who numbered 59 by 1935, and by the nearly
400 nurses who staffed Christian medical institutions.[132] Beyond the
nurses were incalculable numbers of hospital and dispensary staff,
some Christian and some not, including Bible Women, compounders
and dressers, cooks and laundresses, cleaners and sweepers.

An Indian woman who came into the orbit of the missionary
movement by 1930 would encounter, not a foreign agent, but a mission institution staffed by Indians. At the Bhiwani Hospital, "[t]he
work has tended to center more and more on the hospital—the chief
reason for this being lack of staff to cope with increased work. Very re-
gretfully both the city dispensary and the one at Hansi have had to be
closed for this reason. Now all out-patients are seen at the hospital. . . .
It is regretted that time cannot be found to visit villages. . . . [We] have
tried to send a staff nurse regularly to a village three miles away, but it
has not always been possible for her to go."[133] Evangelism was the responsibility of a succession of blind Indian hospital evangelists who
also performed massage, and were charged with the task of having
quiet talks with patients on Christian themes. The work of the missionaries, insofar as it did not involve surgery, came to involve more
and more the training and supervision of staff. Instead of an Indian
church for the people of India, the missionary goal became the creation
of a corps of efficient and high-minded Indian nurses for the people of
India.

In the early days of mission work the relationship of missionary to

staff was informal, resembling in some respects the relationship between a missionary and a Bible Woman during cold weather itineration. In the early days of the Ludhiana Medical College, "[t]he life
which Principal and students lived . . . was simple and intimate. It was
Dr. Brown who gave the call which fetched them from their beds in the
early morning, and who cared for every detail of their well-being. Their
health was one of her main considerations, and she was not only their
lecturer, but made herself responsible for Bible teaching and so arranged their time-tables that each one's quiet time for prayer was safe-
guarded."[134] Such informal relationships with staff became impossible
as the scale of medical work grew. By 1900 the CMS Medical Sub-
Conference was outlining an elaborate bureaucratic scale of pay and
duties for Indian medical personnel.[135] From the point of view of an Indian Christian woman, the mission became an educational and professional bureaucracy, with all the hazards and opportunities of any such
bureaucracy including upward mobility and the satisfaction of a profession worth doing.[136] By the eve of World War II, mission hospitals
provided the bulk of training for nurses throughout all India, and the
small Christian community supplied the overwhelming majority (by
one estimate, 90 percent) of all trained nurses.[137]

The relationship was inevitably one of subordination. Missionaries
regarded their charges as raw material to be shaped into professional
and moral efficiency. Retiring after thirty-three years as a doctor at St.
Stephen's Hospital in Delhi, Dr. Minna Bazley wrote to the Baptist
Zenana Missionary Society offering her services as a supply physician
at Palwal. She pointed out that she was not only proficient in the Delhi
dialects of Hindi, but highly skilled at the training of nurses: "I . . .
have a very thorough knowledge of . . . the amount of energy needed to
get knowledge into the average nurse's mind. I don't mean to disparage
the Indian girls, but in our Mission hospitals we aim at helping many
girls who start life handicapped and need special teaching and coach-
ing."[138] The handicaps might include widowhood or untouchability, for
the missions recruited nurses from both Chamar and Chuhra communities. In 1928 when the government launched a scheme for village
dispensaries with a subassistant surgeon and midwife nurse, most of
the nurses hired were poor Christian widows of outcaste origins. In-
sulted because of their caste and subject to attempts at conversion or
reconversion from Arya Samaj missionaries, they nonetheless had
marketable skills from their mission training.[139]

INDEPENDENT INDIAN WOMEN

Just as western women missionaries were in principle subordinate to men but in practice often independent, Indian staff soon developed skills and assumed institutional responsibility that put them beyond the practical control of western women missionaries. In the 1920s Dr. Brown would tour India "inspecting" the work of her former students. What comes through in her accounts, despite her maternalist tone and characteristic use of first name only, is the practical autonomy and high morale of her former students. Tara, for instance, originally an orphan girl, worked alone in a village where "Women, rich and poor, for miles around were coming to her dispensary, a converted garage, partitioned to provide consulting room and a waiting room, while outside stood her steriliser—two kerosene-oil tins full of boiling water."[140] Premi, a child of Christian parents, served initially as assistant to a male missionary doctor who then was transferred, leaving her in full charge of a thirty-bed hospital. "Single-handed she performed operations having no assistant but Indian nurses, whom she was training herself. Attached to her hospital was a large out-patients department needing her supervision, and just beyond the Hospital compound in the High Schools were found a hundred boys and two hundred girls receiving medical oversight from her. In the city itself three Health Centres had been established by her, while the fees she had earned that year in response to private calls amounted to more than half the required income and every rupee was paid in by her for that purpose."[141]

Rebecca graduated from a mission school and married a catechist with whom she bore four children. But in order to meet the medical needs of their villages, "by mutual consent she placed the children in a Mission School, bade farewell to her husband for two years and went to Ludhiana to take the dispenser's course, combined with midwifery. . . . With what joy Rebecca greeted her Principal, and with what pride she showed us her little dispensary—a low mud-floor room, scrupulously clean." She also managed a school. "Girls must be taught," Rebecca explained, "so my eldest daughter gathers the girls together in our home."[142]

Edith Brown hoped to sustain the special bond of sympathy, the passion for "our Indian sisters" that inspired the early unmarried women missionaries. Some of that survived the growth of institutions, as missionaries remained important and sometimes loved figures in the Indian Christian community. But it is likely that Indian women caught up in mission institutions, whether Christian or non-Christian, encountered missionaries at a distance, not as metaphorical sisters but as teachers or doctors with superior western training and qualification. "The English people I knew as a child," wrote Anita Desai, "were the teachers in my school, Queen Mary's, in Old Delhi. They were the Grey Sisters (in grey cotton dresses with white collars and buttons, unmarried and austere) of the Cambridge Mission that had founded the school, as well as St. Stephen's Hospital over the wall. These teachers and doctors lived busy lives inside the grey walls of their institutions, and did not go much beyond their compound except to service at St. James's Church in Kashmere Gate."[143]

Professionalism and racial difference were mutually reinforcing. Medical work for women at Bhiwani was initiated by an Indian. Miss Angus and Miss Theobald began zenana work in the 1880s, and included in their rounds weekly visits to the Municipal Hospital where the absence of women led them to appeal for medical workers. The first, in 1890, was Maryam, "an old Delhi school girl who had been trained in the medical school at Agra." She opened and managed a dispensary for fourteen months before leaving to marry Lal Muhammed.[144] In 1891 Ellen Farrer arrived, with degrees from Bedford College and the London School of Medicine for Women. Five years after her arrival she sent "our first Indian girl for medical training to Ludhiana after I had coached her in arithmetic and Urdu for a preliminary exam." In 1908 separate living quarters were constructed for Miss Josephine Jacob, an Indian assistant doctor trained at the Ludhiana Medical College.[145]

Whether Miss Jacob preferred to live in racially segregated quarters is unclear, although in larger institutions there is no reason to believe that Indian staff would prefer to live with Europeans who were in effect either employers or supervisors. But in 1933 Dr. Farrer's successor wrote that the "Indian Christian assistant doctor has given us a pleasant surprise by asking to live with us and share our meals. We thought that she was far too conservative to have done such a thing. It seems that these better class Indian girls are happier living with us than living alone in special quarters of their own. I think that on the whole it is good for us to get to know the Indians better by living in closer contact. Years ago I should not have agreed to this, but after years of experience out here I think we have not yet got into close enough contact with some Indians."[146]

Close contact with Indians was one of the rationales for the missionary movement. What sustained the medical work in Bhiwani instead was the sense of professional achievement by both Europeans and Indians, backed with the further sanction of religious faith. Beyond that, defining the specifically Christian character of their work led into frustrating contradictions. Edith Brown's attempt to impose an evangelical confession of faith on all Christian students and staff at Ludhiana failed ultimately because of the combined opposition of the government and the missionary societies.[147] In 1940 the Bhiwani Hospital, in urgent need of a temporary physician, offered the post to a Sikh and a Czech Jewish refugee, but drew the line at a Roman Catholic on the grounds that it would make things difficult for the local church.[148]

Missionaries sincerely believed that they had provided a model of public-spirited behavior for the entire community. New nonmission hospitals were built in Bhiwani in 1929 and 1933, funded by Chhaju Ram (who had also donated to the mission hospital) and Rai Sahib Kishan Lal Jalan. According to the Baptist Missionary Society, "The generous work of these two gentlemen may be rightly accredited to Dr. Farrer and Dr. Bissett who imbued into them the spirit of public service."[149] But this assertion was difficult to justify and easy to rebut. When peering beyond the daily evidence of good works in the practice of medicine, and the genuine satisfaction found in training competent nurses and doctors, thoughtful missionaries upon occasion found it difficult to identify precisely the Christian character of their work, which lay ultimately beyond the utilitarian calculations of cost and benefit. Perhaps it is musing of that sort that lies behind the confession found in the Bhiwani Hospitals circular letter for 1942: "Work has been going on steadily in Bhiwani for over 50 years now, and there is so little to show for so much labor. I have been reminded of the hymn which says 'But the slow watches of the night not less to Him belong.' Perhaps the long watch is near an end and the dawn about to break."[150]

7

The Many Faces of Christian Education

Missionary strategy in Punjab was rooted in the culture of the nineteenth-century European and American churches. Faced with the prospect of a loss of influence in the face of competition from other institutions, the churches could no longer ignore popular indifference to their claims. Challenged ideologically by positivism and secularism,[1] and confronted with the task of expansion in non-Christian lands, the men and women of the churches adopted a variety of strategies. Some withdrew inward and held fast to the truth; others engaged in aggressive membership recruitment; almost all of the churches built institutions, especially schools, in hopes of maintaining and extending religion's hold on society. Missionary strategy included preaching the word, publishing the word, and setting forth the word through the construction of Christian institutions. As the bishop of Lahore argued: "It was the formation of character which they wanted to get at. If St. Paul had the command of missionary agencies he would have set up schools in Corinth and Ephesus."[2]

In an imperial setting, the building of schools was pursued with dogged intensity even while generating bitter controversy. Criticism of medical missions, and especially of medical missions by women, came mainly from outside the missionary movement; criticism of educational policy came as often from the inside. Some evangelicals wished to concentrate purely on proclamation through word and scripture (although they ended up building institutions, too). Others found no biblical mandate for schools. Missionaries themselves, frustrated with bureaucratic routine, often took out their frustration on the most visible institutional embodiment of routine, the schools. Home supporters of missions wondered, not unreasonably, why the missions were educating large numbers of non-Christian students. Despite the tensions and outright contradictions, the Punjab missions (and missions throughout India) remained deeply committed to Christian education throughout the colonial period and beyond.[3]

Educational work expanded with the growth of the missions, facilitated by the educational policies of successive provincial governments of Punjab. In educational as in medical policy, government and the missions had different goals and aspirations, but in matters of education there was a notable convergence of interests. Even as Sir Charles Wood's educational dispatch of 1854 banned Bibles from government schools, setting off a bitter response in mission circles, the imperial government authorized a grant-in-aid approach that allowed mission schools access to government funding. The provincial government of Punjab had wide latitude in setting educational policy, and its theoretical and practical concerns varied according to personnel. With their characteristic faith that the appearance of an improvement in the condition of the people justified imperial rule, Punjab School administrators of the first provincial government in 1849 set as their goal the provision of an elementary school in every village. By 1854 government high schools existed in the cities of Amritsar, Rawalpindi, and Gujrat, but the CMS and AP missions were in the field earlier than the government at the secondary levels with schools in Amritsar, Kangra, Kotgarh, Ferozpur, Ludhiana, and Ambala.[4]

A complete change of policy was effected in 1856 by the first director of public instruction (DPI), W. D. Arnold, the brother of Matthew Arnold. Arnold was an orientalist fantasizer who wanted to scrap the entire system of popular education and replace it with a new system of general education based, not on English, but on elite languages, Persian and Urdu.[5] His views, which confused unpopularity with success, were offensive to the public and ignored by his successors, who were happy enough to have teaching in Hindi or Urdu, depending on circumstances, or even upon occasion in Punjabi (which contradicted official policy). Punjab educational administrators were united, however, in their suspicion of any existing school taught in a mosque or other building of a religious character, and attempted to create government-run scales with teachers paid on a regular salary scale. By 1871 the Punjab government was teaching in its own schools roughly 3.5 percent of the school-going cohort.[6]

NON-CHRISTIAN DEMAND FOR MISSION EDUCATION

The government supplied funds to religious schools only if they met (or attempted to meet) government standards of professional competence. For several decades, this policy favored the missionaries, who were also committed to western standards of professional competence, and who soon discovered that Christian education was often (although not always) acceptable to non-Christian families. Vernacularists in principle, mission educators became Anglicizers in practice largely in response to student demand for English education. Government critics of missions took heart when many scholars at the Sialkot government school refused, upon its closure, to transfer to the Church of Scotland School, but even in the Muslim stronghold of Peshawar, where the government school also closed, the new CMS high school "numbered among its scholars the sons of mullahs and men of good family."[7] The sequence of events reported by Theodore Pennell (CMS) in Quetta is a familiar one:

> "Any parent sending his son to the mission school will be excommunicated" was the *fatwa* of the Mullahs at Bannu when the mission school was inaugurated. The delinquent would be unable to get priestly assistance for marriages, for burial, or for the other rites so essential to a Muhammadan's religious safety. But parents and boys alike were desirous of availing themselves of the advantages of the school, so the Mullahs relented, and said, "Let the boys go to school, but beware lest they learn English, for English is the language of infidelity, and will certainly destroy their souls." But without English all the best government appointments were unattainable, and their boys would have to be content with inferior posts and inferior pay; so pressure was again brought to bear on the Mullahs, and the fiat went forth: "Let the boys read English, so long as they do not read the Christian Scriptures, for the Christians have tampered with those books, and it is no longer lawful for true Muhammadans to read them."
>
> Again a little patience and a little gaining of confidence, and the Mullahs tacitly retracted this restriction too, and now many of the most prominent Mullahs themselves send their sons to the mission school. The Muhammadan lads compete zealously with the others for the Scripture prizes, and in 1907 two Muhammadan officials gave prizes to be awarded to the boys who were most proficient in Scripture in the matriculation class.[8]

Although the mission schools were teaching a small percentage of the number of students taught in government schools (about 10 percent in 1871; see Table 10), the Punjab government conceded the higher quality of mission secondary schools, noting in particular that the AP school in Lahore "is considered the best in the Panjab Province."[9] The pattern of mission domination of secondary (and later higher) education lasted for several decades. In 1871 the government high schools in Lahore, Amritsar Delhi, and Hoshiarpur were outnumbered by mission high schools in Lahore, Delhi, Amritsar, Peshawar, Rawalpindi, Sialkot, Ambala, and Ludhiana.[10] The Punjab DPI at this

TABLE 10

Educational Statistics, Punjab, 1871

	Pupils (schools)		
	Male Anglo-vernacular	Male vernacular	Female not including zenanas
AP	3,487	412	162
BMS	100	234	
CMS	2,163	159	547
CS	535	197	49
OTHER		140	40
SPG	424		174
UP	705	80	376
ZBMM			202
TOTAL	7,414 (69)	1,222 (42)	1,550 (42)
1861	2,174	1,121	282
1850	178	488	35

SOURCE: Calcutta Missionary Conference, *Statistical Tables of Protestant Missions in India, Ceylon, and Burma for 1871* (Calcutta: Baptist Mission Press, 1873), reworked from tables.

time, Captain W. R. M. Holroyd, took a dim imperialist view of mission education based on government grants, and regarded government policy as "a wide departure from English principles, and from religious neutrality, when the entire education of large cities was handed over to religious societies with the power of making religious instruction compulsory."[11] By 1881 Holroyd had succeeded in nearly matching the missions by expanding the number of government English-language high schools to ten.[12] He cut back on girls' education in order to shift resources into teacher training programs, inadvertently opening the door for an expansion of mission schools for girls.[13] Although committed from the first to education for women, the pioneer male missionaries concentrated first on schools for boys largely because they were convinced that girls were inaccessible and had no idea how to attract them to schools. The women of almost every mission station, however, attempted some type of education for girls, even if the number was small, the methods informal, and the statistics unreported. As the missions became more heavily female, women's education became more prominent.

Holroyd was trapped by the grant-in-aid system he so disliked, which allowed the missions to replicate their early advantage in secondary education at the collegiate level. The Punjab government founded colleges in Lahore and Delhi in 1864. Government College in

Lahore flourished, despite the competition from Punjab's first mission college (later Forman Christian College), but the Delhi college languished and was closed in 1877, leaving an opening for the Cambridge Mission to Delhi to open St. Stephen's College.[14]

The missions' high level of bureaucratic organization, combined with the considerable demand from non-Christians for mission schools, allowed them to take advantage of grants-in-aid, combine them with student fees and local contributions, and call on the mission funds only for the salaries of missionary teachers. Mission supporters in the Punjab government like William Mackworth Young and Charles Aitchison were usually strict voluntarists in matters of religion, just as strict as the secularist Holroyd in their own view, but they saw nothing wrong with encouraging the missions to initiate or expand mission work as long as grants were available on a "blind to religion" basis to all faiths, and to none. The Church of Scotland's College in Sialkot first opened in 1889 at the request of "one of the European government officials"—that is, Sir Charles Aitchison.[15] For eighteen years the Sialkot college languished as a "second grade" institution with no government grant, but in 1906 the government dangled before the Scottish Mission the prospect of affiliation with Punjab University if they would only remedy major defects in the College within the next two years. The Church of Scotland foreign mission committee redirected to the college a bequest of £2,000 left in 1883 by Miss Agnes Murray for the purpose of evangelizing India.[16] The renamed Murray College at once received RS11,000 from the government for a new building.[17] By 1918 62 percent of Murray College's budget came from student fees, and 34 percent from government grants-in-aid.[18]

A similar pattern emerged in the founding of the two most prestigious of the mission colleges, St. Stephen's in Delhi and Forman Christian College in Lahore. The Cambridge Brothers arrived in the 1880s committed to building a "new Alexandria" on the banks of the Jumna, but soon after their arrival they were deep into plans for a Christian college for non-Christian students. A plan to build up a Christian community in Delhi became instead a plan to promote Christian influence among the non-Christian elite by creating Christian institutions to serve them. The Church of England served elites at home without inquiring too closely into their piety, and building important institutions to serve the non-Christian elites of Delhi seemed natural and normal.

St. Stephen's College was founded in 1882, the same year as Punjab University (India's fourth), and the college was brought into the same relationship with the university as Government College, Lahore. By 1885 the province was providing 80 percent of St. Stephen's College budget, and the Delhi municipal government another 10 percent; the students included 48 Hindus, 4 Muslims, 3 Christians, and 1 Parsi.[19] As the number of students grew (221 by 1914), and a new campus opened on government-donated land near Kashmiri Gate, the college remained largely Hindu with small Muslim and Christian minorities.[20]

The Cambridge Brothers' initial profession of reluctance to countenance government grants followed by wholehearted acceptance of them was characteristic of all the missions, reflecting their ambivalence about the relationship between mission and government.[21] American Presbyterians in Lahore at first expressed reservations about government grants and competed vigorously with government schools, even to the point of trying to drive them out of business, but they later adopted a cooperative relationship.[22] The Presbyterian Forman Christian College in Lahore competed for prestige with the Government College at Lahore and achieved a level of prestige among mission colleges second only to St. Stephen's. By 1931 the missions had founded six colleges in Punjab, Delhi, and the Northwest Frontier: St. Stephen's, Delhi (SPG); Forman Christian College, Lahore (AP); Murray College, Sialkot (CS); Edwardes College, Peshawar (CMS); Gordon College, Rawalpindi (UP); and Kinnaird College for Women, Lahore (AP and others). Although the overwhelming majority of mission college students were non-Christians, these institutions were strongly supported by the Indian Christian community, who not only took pride in them but also sent their children to them when possible. In 1935, 10 of 183 students at Edwardes College, Peshawar, were Christians, 50 of 1,075 at Forman College, Lahore, and 64 of 508 in Murray College in Sialkot.[23]

CHRISTIAN EDUCATION FOR NON-CHRISTIANS

Mission supporters in Britain and the United States often found these statistics perplexing and troubling. If the purpose of the missionary enterprise is the evangelization of India, why were mission resources being used to found institutions for non-Christians? Twenty-first-century scholars confront the same question, and often resolve the dilemma by implying that missionaries abandoned their commitment to conversion in order to build schools, as if they did not know what they were doing. From the point of view of missionary educators in India, however, there was no conflict to resolve. The methods of evangelization included preaching the word, publishing the word, and demonstrating the reality of the word through the building of Christian institutions. Responding to a query from the home board in 1918 about the low number of Christian students, the Church of Scotland mission wrote: "If Non-Christians were the only responsibility of our Punjab Mission our conscience would be at peace with our present policy of higher education."[24]

Even while taking government grants, missionaries repeatedly contrasted their schools favorably with secular government schools, which many missionaries regarded as a greater threat to India's future than Hinduism or Islam. The key issue, as the bishop of Lahore argued, was the formation of character, and religion was essential to that task. Theodore Pennel justified the teaching of Hindus and Muslims with no direct proselytization on the grounds that "[it] is a terrible thing to take away a boy's faith, even though it be a faith in a mistaken creed, and I think the man who has argued or bantered a young fellow out of his faith without bringing him to a higher faith has incurred a grave responsibility. The real enemy of the Christian faith is not so much Islam or Hinduism, but infidelity and a gross materialism. When I first went to India I had a prejudice against mission schools, and protested against a medical missionary having to superintend one; but I have become convinced that the hope of India is in her mission colleges and schools, for it is in their *alumni* that we find young men who have been able to acquire western knowledge without losing the religious spirit, learning without moral atrophy, mental nobility without a conceited mien and disrespect for their parents, and breadth of view without disloyalty and sedition."[25] Pennell was neither a theological liberal nor a religious relativist. Committed to the Christianization of India, he took a characteristically long view in which the institutional expansion of Christianity was a step in the moral progress of the nation. Christianity would be an eventual and inevitable stage in that progress.

Government support came with a cost. Missionary administrators spent many tedious hours mediating between officials of the Department of Public Instruction, who insisted upon accountability for its grants and efficiency in school administration, and the home mission boards who insisted on accountability in spiritual as well as financial matters. Missionaries were prepared in good conscience, and even with enthusiasm, to teach non-Christian students in order to extend the Empire of Christ; government officials were prepared to extend mission teaching among non-Christian students in order to strengthen the

Empire of Britain. But a convergence of interest reflected no identity of interests. Conflicts between government and mission, and between the contradictory goals of the missions, set off periodic crises of accountability revolving around imperial and spiritual issues.

Evangelical CMS administrators in London grasped the problem early but were never able to resolve it. CMS directives to their India missions alternately authorized a capitulation to the enticements of government grants and plaintively warned their agents of the dangers of excessive entanglement of mission and government. As early as 1855 the CMS, under the guidance of Henry Venn, recognized the imperial trap into which they were falling, and their Committee of Correspondence explained:

> They are anxious, as a general principle, to point out that their educational work is still *Missionary*. The Society are willing to accept the aid of Government, so far as they will give it. But they consider themselves as doing their own work, and not as standing in the position of Schoolmasters to the Government; and in reference to the fear expressed as to the secularizing tendency of the system, they feel every confidence that their Missionaries will be alive to the paramount importance of maintaining the Missionary principle intact, and that they will watch unto prayer, lest any injurious influence, arising from the encouragement given to the secular branch of their teaching, obtain any advantage over them. The Committee are alive to the difficulty, but cannot abandon the line of operation opening before them without a trial. It is one which admits of no remedy but that which is derived from on high; and they are unwilling to believe that it will be withheld.[26]

NON-CHRISTIANS AS MISSION AGENTS

Unable to discern the precise details of the workings of God's Providence in these matters, the CMS remained sufficiently convinced of its presence to regard government grants as providential openings: the Punjab government continued to award them, and mission schools grew rapidly after 1870. In order to accommodate the doubling of the number of students by 1890, mission schools resorted to the hiring of non-Christian teachers to teach more than 20,000 mostly non-Christian students. Seventy percent of the roughly 750 mission schoolteachers were non-Christian, the most unfavorable ratio in all of India.[27] Missions schools were not only multiracial but also multireligious.

Under those circumstances, some critics found it difficult for the missions to sustain the claim, however firmly asserted, that India would be gradually Christianized as non-Christian students were brought under the sway of teachers with a Christian ethos. One consequence was the creation of a very favorable labor market for trained Indian Christian teachers, male and female. Another was the attempt to make sure that children were taught Christian Scripture even in schools with non-Christian staff, although sheer pressure of resources (as well as parental opposition) made this impossible in some cases. In 1890 the bishop of Lahore asked the Rev. T. R. Wade to conduct an examination of the religious teaching in Anglican mission schools in the diocese. In a flagship school at Peshawar, Edwardes High School, Wade found that in the lower classes and branch schools Scripture was not taught at all because no Christian masters were available. "The students examined appeared to be generally ignorant of scripture history," Wade observed, and in one class "not one could tell where Jesus was born, nor how he died." He goes on to note, however, that "[t]his school has had great influence and done much good. Old pupils are now occupying high positions of trust and responsibility under the British government."[28]

Wade noted with some alarm cases where non-Christian teachers appeared to be doing a better job at Scripture teaching than Christians. Christian teachers provided Scripture instruction at the Simla CMS Boys School (Upper Primary), where "no boys in the class could tell me where Christ was born, the name of his mother, or how he died." At the Batala City Mission School, however, where the boys performed well on the Scripture exam, the headmaster was the only Christian and shared Scripture teaching with a Muslim. Some non-Christian staff were hopefully identified as either "secret Christians" or earnest seekers after the truth. At Bhawalpur CMS Middle School, the headmaster, L. Remal Das, a Hindu graduate of the school, was identified as one of the secret Christian fellow travelers that missionaries discerned in mission institutions. "He appears to be using his influence and energy for the good of the school. I have had a long private talk with him, and he has promised to pray to God for help and to think about becoming a Christian."[29]

At a minimum, mission school teaching of non-Christians must have spread some knowledge of some characteristics of Christianity among the literate sectors of the population. At Dharmsala CMS Upper Primary School, most of the boys could recite the Lord's Prayer and the Ten Commandments. The thirty-nine girls at Kangra Girls' School all knew the Ten Commandments and Lord's Prayer and could repeat at least one text. But missionaries, with their emphasis on character, hoped for more than mere knowledge. Many of them believed that the sheer atmosphere of Christian schools could have an almost involuntary effect on everyone in the room. Addressing readers of *The Indian Female Evangelist*, Miss Wauton described Rahnat Bibi, a Muslim teacher in Amritsar, as "a strict Mussulmani, and had it not been for her singularly open honest face, which seemed a sure index of a candid, straightforward mind, I should have feared her influence counteracting the effect of Christian teaching. . . . The other day she asked for a book to write hymns in, one of her favourites being some verses sung to a very sweet plaintive native air, describing in detail our Lord's sufferings on the Cross; a part of the Gospel which is entirely at variance with the teaching of the Koran. In these matters Rahnat Bibi's pupils have influenced her far more than she has influenced them. . . . Gospel truth is like light reflected and refracted by the objects with which it comes in contact, shedding its beams far and wide, carried from pupil to teacher, from teacher to pupil, from the child-scholar into the home; its sunny rays shine on and on, and we know not into how many hearts they are bringing warmth and comfort."[30]

The situation was far more complex than readers of *The Indian Female Evangelist* might suppose. The need to hire Muslim teachers for Christian girls' schools in Lahore and Amritsar produced awkward negotiations. Miss M'Phun reported from Lahore: "There is no difficulty in getting Mohammedan women to volunteer to become teachers. Of late several have asked me to begin schools in their houses."[31] There is no reason to believe that Muslim and Hindu teachers were acting in bad faith by attempting to secure employment in mission schools, and missionaries had a variety of rationalizations for the practice, ranging from sheer necessity to the "secret Christian" label. But the situation was so fraught with imperial contradictions that accusations of deception or betrayal were inevitable. Miss M'Phun went to one school and found only three students, and the teacher "with tears in her eyes, informed me that she could not keep the school any longer, as their religious teachers objected to her having anything to do with Christians. . . . A short time before, I had nailed up Scripture texts and pictures upon the walls of the room in which the children were taught, to make it look more cheerful. I noticed the texts had been taken down—only the pictures remained: they had been afraid to leave the texts."[32]

A letter circulated among Muslims in Punjab objecting to schools for Muslim girls: "Mohammedan teachers in these schools, who are only nominal Mohammedans, by pretending to teach the Quran, draw our daughters into their schools, and then teach them the gospel and hymns. For a little while they may teach the Quran; but when the missionary lady comes in, they hide it under a mat, or throw it into some unclean place, into which, if a man had thrown it, he might have been sent to prison. And as long as the lady is present they teach Christianity and expose Mohammedanism."[33] While some Muslims accused non-Christian teachers in mission schools of fraudulently teaching what they do not believe, missionaries attributed to them secret Christian beliefs. Miss Wadsworth justified the opening of a school in Multan with reference to a potential teacher who, "besides being intelligent, is inclined to Christianity, if, indeed, she is not a secret believer; so that whatever was taught the children from the Gospels, she would be a help in encouraging them to remember."[34]

The need for trained teachers led into another set of contradictions. As part of its program to create a unified educational system in Punjab, the government created normal schools for teacher training, initially at Delhi, Lahore, and Rawalpindi.[35] Although the Christian Vernacular Education Society sponsored a Normal School, the missions found themselves increasingly dependent on the government normal schools in order to provide the trained teachers required for the retention of government grants. If non-Christian teachers had not been trained in a Christian atmosphere, how could they impart a Christian atmosphere in the classroom?

This particular fault line over pedagogical ethos led to a remarkably bitter fight in 1886 between two entrenched and immovable branches of the mission bureaucracy, the CMS Punjab Mission and the CMS Parent Committee in London. The Punjab missions in general had a large degree of autonomy, rooted in part in their independent fundraising capacities. When the Christian Vernacular Education Society announced plans to close its Normal School in 1886, Robert Clark moved quickly to secure funds from a private patron in the Indian Civil Service in order to reopen the school as a CMS Christian Normal School in Amritsar that would train Christian and non-Christian teachers in a Christian atmosphere. But the CMS Parent Committee in London, upset with the growing prevalence of non-Christians in mission schools, vetoed Clark's initiative.

This decision led to an outpouring of protest from missionaries and supporters of missions in Punjab. Sir Charles Aitchison, a member of the viceroy's council who would later be lieutenant governor of Punjab, declared to Clark that he was "ready on my return to England to go to Salisbury Square [CMS headquarters] and plead with your committee on my knees" to avoid so great a calamity.[36] The sheer centrality of mission schools in the mission enterprise was the heart of their argument. One missionary wrote the Parent Committee that it is better to "send forth teachers who shall have received a fair knowledge of Christianity even if they have not been led to accept the Gospel in its fulness. Even if they never become Christians in name, it will be impossible for them to obliterate from their consciences all remembrances of the words of Christ."[37]

The secretary of the Parent Committee, who had been led to believe that non-Christian teachers were a temporary expedient, met these objections with a certain degree of incomprehension. Pointing out that the Normal School, although Christian, enrolled thirty non-Christians and three Christians, the CMS secretary asked: "Is such a moral atmosphere good for the three? When, after all, these non-Christian students have been for years getting non-Christian teaching and remain non-Christians still, is it likely that the moral tone of their teaching afterwards can be much relied upon?"[38]

For the Parent Committee, the creation of an indigenous Indian church was more important than maintaining mission schools for non-Christians. For many Punjab missionaries, and some Punjab imperial administrators, the building of a network of Christian institutions was at the heart, not only of missionary movement but also of Christian strategy in the modern world. Robert Clark responded to the Parent Committee's decision to uphold their veto with a bitter anonymous pamphlet, "The Downfall of Christianity in Punjab," authored by a twentieth-century historian a century after the momentous decision to allow the normal school to close. After that decision, teacher training fell into the hands of secularists, infecting young Indians with the ideas of John Stuart Mill. As a result of imperial intervention in India, and the failure of the missions to respond wisely, the nation was lost to Christianity forever.[39]

The Parent Committee won this skirmish, but it had little effect on the inexorable growth of Christian institutions requiring staff who required training. By the late 1920s the Punjab missions sponsored only two fully accredited normal schools: Kinnaird College Teachers Training Class at Lahore and an American Presbyterian Training School for teachers at Moga. But each of the missions improvised, either by training their own teachers below the government standard in special training classes or summer schools, or by organizing middle schools for women that served as feeder schools for the government normal colleges.[40] Parent Committee critics of mission educational policy were misrepresenting the situation when they complained about the focus on non-Christians at the expense of Indian Christians, for Indian Christians as well as foreign missionaries were deeply involved in mission educational institutions.

INDIAN CHRISTIANS AND THE DILEMMAS
OF SOCIAL CLASS

The policy of institutional expansion created a demand for the labor of Indian Christians as teachers, nurses, and doctors. Indian Christian employees complained with justice about their dependence on foreign missionaries, but it was offset by their leverage in the labor market. The headmaster of Baring Christian High School in Batala complained in 1888 that the demand for Christian masters was so great that they coiuld get double the salary of non-Christians. Mission educational strategy produced a considerable over-representation of Christians in colleges that were among the best secondary and collegiate institutions in the province. The over-representation was particularly striking since Christian students were for the most part drawn from the small urban middle-class minority among the Christian minority. Christian college students, if they could afford it, lived in Christian hostels, and the missions opened boarding schools at the secondary level for boys and, especially, for girls. Although some of them were short-lived, at one time or another girls' boarding schools for Indian Christians were established by nearly every Punjab mission.[41]

When creating boarding schools, all of the missions ran squarely into the contradictions of social class. Outside the Salvation Army, mission educational policy was unashamedly elitist. The American Presbyterians hoped to create a Princeton in the Punjab, and the dependence of the Cambridge Brothers on the Cambridge model is evident today in the layout of the high table at St. Stephen's College. Baring High School (CMS) in Batala published a prospectus explaining that the school "was founded and is maintained at considerable expense with a view to giving a sound religious training and first class secular education to the sons of Christians of the upper classes of North India. The advantages of the public school system have been proved in England, and those to be derived from it are even more conspicuous in a country where contact with non-Christian boys in Day Schools frequently has an injurious effect on Christian boys."[42] The prospectus touted the building, "formerly the palace of Maharaja Sher Singh," and the opportunity for students to attend as "parlour boarders" who took

meals with the matron, unlike those who could pay only the ordinary
Rs 5 per month.

A similar concern with class distinctions characterized the CMS
Alexandra School for Girls in Amritsar. Both the Baring High School
for Boys and the Alexandra School for Girls were meant by the CMS to
serve as the educational counterparts of the ecclesiastical arm of the
Punjabi church, the Punjab Native Church Council. Distinguished lay
Indian Christians would control an evangelical Episcopal church
through the church council, educate their children at Baring and Alexandra, and constitute a Christian church equal in social dignity to
Hinduism, Islam, and Sikhism. "The time has arrived when communities are forming themselves among us," Robert Clark wrote in 1891.
"Our Christians . . . are becoming little bands all over the country. . . .
The Church of Christ in India must be formed in India of Indian people. We cannot always hope that the streams of Christian liberality
will go on flowing from England. It may at any time diminish, or even
cease. We want to leave behind us native workers, able and willing to
take our place, and to carry on our work. We look to *our institutions* to
form them."[43]

As educational theory, Clark's social elitism mirrored his ecclesiastical commitment to early ordination. His snobbery was linked to his
antiracism. If English Christians had elite schools, then Indian Christians should have them too, and as early as possible. The enormous
Alexandra School building was built outside the Ram Bagh gate in Amritsar, which led from the old city to the new civil lines, as an architectural challenge to the physical presence of other religions. From the
time of its foundation, critics of the Alexandra School charged that it
was overly ambitious for the infant Indian church and, even worse,
educated girls above their station in life. That was precisely Clark's intention. He argued that "the time is coming when Christians will be of
high estate and dignity, schools worthy of their daughters will be
needed, and when their young men want wives, they will look for dignified, refined ladies, and for them I found this school. Boys and girls
bred in large surroundings are large-hearted; those brought up in a narrow way are apt to be poor-spirited."[44] Clark hoped to see a complex of
Christian institutions in Amritsar that would be comparable to the
new Aligarh Muslim University founded by Sir Syed Ahmed Khan,
who exchanged compliments with Clark on the respective flourishing
of their institutions.[45]

The Alexandra School never worked as Clark intended, despite his
repeated assertions to the contrary. Instead of the daughters of wealthy

and influential Christian laity (who hardly existed in Punjab), Alexandra students were the daughters of Christian pastors and headmasters. The scattering of students from the homes of pleaders and government doctors was overwhelmed by the daughters of mission employees—pastors and catechists, headmasters and doctors, even a Christian fakir "of no fixed abode."[46] For the most part these families could not afford the Alexandra School's fees, and applied for reduced rates. While agonizing over which Indian Christian families deserved assistance in paying fees, CMS leaders found to their dismay that the very small group of families for whom they had created the school found it socially below them. The Alexandra headmistress listed those Christian families who have "not yet thought our school good enough": Kanwar Haman Singh, brother of the Rajah of Kapuithalla; Mr. Abdullah Athim; Mr. George Lewis, EACA; Mr. Mya Das; Mr. Chandra Lal, whose son is M.A. "The highest class children," she complained, "are now either educated at home or else are sent to the English Girls School in Simla or other hill stations, where they pay 30 or more Rupees per month and return to their homes neither native nor Europeans."[47]

In creating the Alexandra School, the CMS was caught in the contradiction between its desire to serve the Indian Christian community and its anxieties about unseemly upward mobility and dependency, twin phobias of the Victorian upper middle classes that were especially strong among the clergy.[48] The result was the founding of what appeared to be a very good school for girls that was the target of periodic outbursts of criticism from its founders, supporters, and staff, who feared that it was educating girls above their station and, in an imperial context, denationalizing them.[49]

CMS attempts to confine upward mobility among Christian girls led to the creation of a social hierarchy of schools, and confused attempts to negotiate the fault lines of social class by allocating girls to the correct school. They created a new "lower middle class school" for girls who "from the social standing of their parents, ought not to be in the Alexandra School," but even below that was the girls boarding school at Clarkabad, the Christian agricultural settlement near Lahore.[50] Usually styled an "orphanage," this school had become a combination of orphanage and boarding school for rural Christians of untouchable background. Committed in principle to education for girls regardless of race, class, gender, or caste, the CMS found itself unable to settle on a suitable pedagogy for untouchable village Christian girls for fear of "educating them above their station." Even though serving an entirely different set of girls, the school faced the same accusations from social conservatives as the Alexandra School. The Rev. H. E. Perkins described the Clarkabad school as a "permanent menace to the prosperity of the indigenous church. . . . Naturally, every sweeper who found his daughter educated beyond her sphere, and made a lady, who was not asked to do manual labor, was taught a fine language, and dressed in fine clothes at merely nominal cost, was only too thankful to have her there. . . . The puzzle as you well know is that the smallest education lifts a pauper out of the social scale she has been in, and though it is necessary to run the risk of this, up to the point of teaching her to read her Bible, and write a simple letter, anything more than this is an evil."[51]

CMS reactionaries were forced to recognize that even the daughters of sweepers had bargaining power in the Punjabi church. The headmistresses of the Clarkabad School in the 1890s attempted to crack down on the girls by forcing them to do field work, wash their own clothes, clean the wheat, make butter, pick and spin cotton, beat out the Indian corn, and beat the rice husks too heavy for young children. The result was a series of student rebellions, including one in 1895 when the girls all claimed to be sick, and refused to wash their own clothes, do field work, carry wood, or tidy up. Others threatened to run away, and in the end the school admitted defeat because the fall in enrollment made it difficult to keep the building clean.[52]

Indian Christian families and students regarded mission attempts to restrict upward mobility in the girls' schools as a nuisance, and they found allies among middle-class Indian Christian women and some foreign missionaries who regarded upward mobility as a good thing, even evidence of the success of their work. After graduating from the Alexandra School, medical training at St. Catherine's Hospital, Amritsar, and a two-year medical course in London, Miss Kheroth Bose was put in full charge of the CEZMS medical mission station at Bahrwal and later became a mission publicist.[53] Despite concerns about her questionable social origins, Alexandra graduate Miss R. M. Phailbus trained in medicine for five years at St. Catherine's, Amritsar, then began medical work in Bengal, and by 1900 was placed in full and independent charge of a mission station.[54]

It is more difficult to trace the fate of the girls at the Clarkabad School. Despite the determination of certain missionaries to turn them into wives of village ploughmen, other missionaries took a proprietary interest in the well-being of their students. As early as 1891, Miss G. L. West, the matron of the Clarkabad orphanage, defended herself against charges of educating girls above the level of potential husbands: "If the young men who have been brought up in the orphanage since childhood can neither read nor write . . . why then, as I told Mr. Holden, I should not feel inclined to throw my girls away on them."[55] In the twentieth century, education for village Christian girls flourished at Clarkabad under the direction of Miss Minnie Warner, whose middle school enrolled 60 boarders and 130 day-girls who could take advantage of a junior Vernacular Teachers' Training Class.[56]

If educational elitism was thwarted in some respects by Indian Christians and their missionary allies in the CMS, the hierarchies of class and caste triumphed in other ways in the SPG mission in Delhi. The Victoria School for Girls served as a boarding school for the daughters of Indian Christian catechists and clergy, and St. Elizabeth's School enrolled the daughters of Chamar Christians. Some SPG women missionaries, like their counterparts from the CMS at Clarkabad, dedicated their lives to the education of girls from stigmatized backgrounds, and they were deeply proud of their work. Miss Payne looked back on thirty years of work on the occasion of St. Elizabeth's "Old Girls Day" in 1934: "All these people are from outcaste families . . . broadly speaking, women who, left without Christianity, would be living in great poverty if not degradation . . . but of this material has grown a capacity for disinterested love and loyalty—pride and enthusiasm and unity. And this is what we are striving to foster . . . devotion to the Church and Christian brotherhood and above all to Him by whose grace and spirit it exists at all."[57] This spiritual egalitarianism created even deeper contradictions in the SPG than in the CMS, for the Delhi Mission was the most elitist in principle of all the missions in northwest India. In the early twentieth century the mission's educational strategy for girls was refocused on Queen Mary's School, opened in 1912 under the direction of Helen Jerwood, a clergyman's daughter and graduate of Cheltenham Ladies College, who donated £1,000 toward the cost of a new building.[58] The school's purpose was to give "an education which will fit the girls to be companions of 'English educated' men."[59] It was so thoroughly under the direction of women that "Miss Jerwood's School" allowed no men on the premises at all except on one occasion, an official visit by the viceroy.

The Alexandra School had been opened in the 1880s in the hope of serving an Indian Christian elite that would rival the elites of other communities. Recognizing that the Christian elite could not stand on the same footing as non-Christian elites, Miss Jerwood limited access to Indian Christian girls in order to maintain the social standing of her school. She explained that the school was for the "daughters of Indian gentlemen who are able and ready to pay fees toward the cost of their children's education. Great care is taken in the selection of girls per-mitted to attend the school."[60] By Indian gentleman she was not refer-ring to Indian Christians, even if they were able to pay. "We have to re-fuse Christians fairly frequently on account of class. Christian parents value education . . . so they are willing to make great sacrifices to send their children here. We don't intend to ever have more than 25% Christians here, in fact probably in the future we shall have only 20%."[61] Queen Mary's enthusiastically accepted the new conscience clause instituted by the imperial government in 1918, which required mission schools to exempt non-Christians from religious training, as another mechanism to make the school more acceptable to non-Christian elites.

It is important to understand that religion as well as class remained central to the mission of Queen Mary's. Queen Mary's was competing with the new Roman Catholic convent schools opening in Delhi (as well as Lahore and Sialkot).[62] Both denominations had discovered the appeal of a "convent educated" girl, an appeal that rested on morality as well as simple class snobbery. The Christian mission of Queen Mary's was to be found in the ethos of its teachers. Miss Jerwood claimed that all of the teachers were Christians, and that those Chris-tian students admitted to the school were of good family, including the daughter of a professor at St. Stephen's College and the niece of the first Indian Archdeacon. She stressed the importance of Christian teachers on the non-Christian girls at Queen Mary's, who studied Urdu, Hindi, English, Persian, math, geography, history, domestic economy (including sick nursing and care of infants), needlework, drawing, and physical exercises.[63] The focus on the languages, math, history, geography, and, for women, domestic arts was characteristic of secondary and higher education in most mission schools regardless of denomination.

SCIENCE AND RELIGION

The absence of the physical and natural sciences reflected no princi-pled missionary objection to the teaching of science, even in "convent schools." In principle, missionaries regarded the teaching of western science as an ally in the struggle to spread true religion. The difficul-ties were practical ones. Until well into the twentieth century, the missions were unable to recruit missionary teachers trained in sci-ence.[64] Although physical and natural science were not mandatory subjects of the degree examinations, the Punjab government often threatened to make science teaching a condition for receiving grants. There was the additional problem of laboratories, notoriously expensive to build and maintain. When new university chemical laboratories were constructed in Lahore in 1922–23, Forman College was forced to propose a new B.Sc. pass degree for work at their inferior labs, but this arrangement proved unsatisfactory and instruction had to be arranged with staff at the university laboratories.[65] The CMS's Edwardes College in Peshawar began offering B.A. classes in 1910, with teaching in mathematics, history, Arabic, and Sanskrit, but in 1928 there was still no science department. The Education Department of the Northwest Frontier Provinces Government offered to pay the full cost of science instruction if the mission would provide a "science missionary," but the home committee saw "no hope" unless the government met the full cost of the stipend.[66]

Government policy was confused by a lengthy internal debate over how to teach science in India. Educational orientalism continued to flourish in the Punjab because of the influence of G. W. Leitner. In 1864 he became principal of Government College, Lahore, and in 1870 head of the Oriental School (later the Oriental Institute) in Lahore, where he remained through the century a vigorous advocate of the rejuvenation of Indian culture through the study of Arabic, Sanskrit, and Persian. Untrained in the teaching of science even in English texts, missionaries were wholly unprepared to teach science in the Urdu translations, sponsored by Leitner, of Huxley's *Physiology*, Fowler's *Logic*, Roscoe's *Chemistry*, Todhunter's *Statics*, and a Gurmukhi (Punjabi) treatise on psychology.[67] Most missionaries came from a background in the humanities or at best mathematics, and they naturally taught what they knew best. When Thomas Valpy French opened St. John's College, Agra, in 1853, with classes in mathematics and English, the curriculum included Thierry's *Norman Conquest*, Sir James Macintosh's *History of England*, Guizot's *Life of Charles I*, Herodotus in translation, Malkin's *History of Greece*, and readings in Milton and Cowper.[68] Missionaries in the Punjab colleges followed in his footsteps, teaching mainly history and literature.

The smaller mission colleges—Edwardes, Murray, and Gordon—never achieved the pre-eminence of Forman and St. Stephen's, and often ran into financial difficulties that threatened them with closure or amalgamation.[69] But the tenacity with which both missionaries and Indian Christians struggled to keep them open illustrates their importance both as sources of status for the Christian community and as

central institutions in the mission strategy of extending Christian influence. In response to a threat by the Church of Scotland's Foreign
Mission Committee to close Murray College and redeploy missionaries in village evangelism, missionary William Scott laid out the theory
of diffusion and influence clearly in 1918. His arguments, when juxta-
posed with the Sermon on the Mount, illustrate clearly the fault lines
of mission educational policy:

> One's position in the college gives a standing in the city, affords one
> access to the best families, and enables one to exert a personal influ-
> ence upon officials and men in position in the district. This is un-
> doubtedly denied to the ordinary missionary or even to the ordinary
> school manager. One's students secure responsible positions in various
> departments and grades of service and in many cases the influence of
> the college continues. As a rule they consider that the Mission College
> Code of Honour has to be maintained. In other words the mission that
> lacks a college in this country cannot exercise an all round influence
> upon the community and therefore cannot do the best work. But this
> needs no arguing.[70]

This unsavory combination of a passion for influence with snobbery
is perhaps a not entirely unexpected response from a class of professional educators, hired as professional educators, who were threatened
by remote bureaucrats taking a high moral line and proposing to redeploy them at tasks for which they were in fact unfit. In their support
for maintaining Christian education, they had behind them the solid
backing of the Indian Christian community, united at all levels in a
desire for more and better schools although bitterly divided from missionaries over how educational funds should be allocated and controlled. Behind their common tenacity was also the unique theory of
Christian education in which ethos and morality were indissolubly
linked, and could only be linked in a Christian context.

NON-CHRISTIAN COMPETITION

By the early twentieth century, Christian schools, and even colleges,
were competing not only with government schools but also with Arya
Samaj, Anjuman (Muslim), Khalsa (Sikh), and privately financed non-
Arya Samaj Hindu schools both at the secondary and collegiate level,
especially in Lahore. In 1877 the Arya Samaj began its Anglo-Vedic
High School and College in Lahore; in 1890 the most influential Muslim educational society, the Anjuman-i-Himayat-i-Islam, founded the
Islamia College for men; the Sikh Khalsa College was founded in Amritsar in 1892; another Hindu College in Lahore, the Sanatan Dharma

College, opened in 1916.[71] Gail Minault has noted that missionary competition was the incentive for the Muslim middle classes of Lahore to open girls' primary schools in the late nineteenth century: "Thanks to the Anjuman-i-Himayat-i-Islam and the competitive intellectual and religious atmosphere of Lahore in the 1880s and 1890s, Muslim girls' education was more advanced in the Punjab capital than in Delhi or Aligarh at that time."[72]

In the early twentieth century, European churches began to struggle with the high costs of maintaining institutions developed for nineteenth-century purposes in the face of competition from government, secular, or other religious alternatives. In Punjab, mission schools continued to benefit disproportionately from the grant-in-aid policy, but their competitive advantage diminished in the face of competition. In 1910 the principal recipients of government building grants were the Kinnaird Girls School, Lahore; the T'alim-ul Islam High School, Qadian; the American Presbyterian Mission Girls School, Ambala; the Scotch Mission High School, Gujrat; the Dayanand Anglo-Vedic High School (Arya Samaj), Rawalpindi; and the Loreto Convent School, Simla.[73] The government observed that the Arya Samaj and Sikhs were now the most active in founding schools while "the muslim Anjumans and Christian missions have been less prominent."[74] By 1922 there were Sikh Khalsa high schools for boys in Tarn Taran, Baba Bakala, Sarhali Karan, and Moga; a Dev Samaj High School in Lahore; an Anglo-Sanskrit high school in Ambala and privately funded Hindu schools in Sonepat, Moga, Ferozepore, and Dharmkot; and new girls' high schools in Amritsar (Hindu) and Ferozepore (Sikh).[75] Government education expanded rapidly in Punjab in the 1920s; between 1917 and 1922 the overall numbers of students in Punjab Province grew from 149,952 to 626,690.[76] In some regions even Christians began to make use of government rather than Christian schools as the Christian share of Punjab's educational enterprise began to shrink.[77]

MANLY IMPERIALIST CHRISTIAN EDUCATION

The proliferation of competition did nothing to shake the faith of missionary and Indian Christian educators in the unique virtues of Christian education. They dug in their heels, insisting on the unique Christian ethos of their particular school and citing as evidence activities as varied as Bible teaching, the study of literature, and even, in the case of the CMS High School in Srinigar, Kashmir, athletics. With the arrival of C. E. Tyndale-Biscoe in 1891, the school became an extreme example of sheer imperialist indoctrination through the mechanisms of organized games and "social service" schemes. With such methods the Kashmiri Pandits (Brahmins) who attended the school were to be turned into "good citizens, imbued with the spirit of serving the Universal Father by following the example of Christ in serving their fellows."[78]

Tyndale-Biscoe declared that "the school is not intended to westernise the boys," but he obviously failed to recognize late Victorian obsessions with cleanliness and manliness as "western." T. V. French attempted to force his students in Lahore to abandon western clothing for "native dress"; Tyndale-Biscoe embarked on a campaign to rid the Pandit students of their Kashmiri clothing on the grounds that it was both unhygienic and unmanly: "[It] has been asked: 'What can you expect of a people whose national costume is a night-gown?'"[79] His method was compulsory games. The Kashmiri long robe was unsuitable for the horizontal bar, and so replaced by trousers. The nose ring succumbed to boxing, and earrings fell victim to a game called H. cockaloram, jig jig jig, which required boys to ride on the shoulders of others and hold on with the knees. Clogs proved to be unsuitable for football.

Although it had powerful supporters, this school proved upon more than one occasion to be an embarrassment to the CMS. After being briefed with a map of the life of Christ in which every good deed was marked with an X, students were enrolled in compulsory "social service" projects such as fighting fires, visiting food shops to ferret out false weights, and ministering to cholera victims.[80] Some tasks were chosen because they included contact with blood or feces and were regarded as polluting by Brahmins. When Annie Besant heard of Tyndale-Biscoe's "sanitation corps," she set up a rival theosophical high school across the street that emptied the school of all but six students in 1901.[81] It is not clear why parents allowed their children to be subjected to such harassment in school in the first place, and it is not surprising that the CMS received a letter of complaint requesting them to transfer Mr. Biscoe, "for he is an exceedingly bad man, illiterate, deceitful, ill-mannered, uncultured, cunning, and a man too much fond of cricket."[82] Biscoe, however, thought that parents would do almost anything to gain for their children a knowledge of English with its prospects for government employment. Sometimes ignorant, usually fanatical, but never lazy, Biscoe went to work to rebuild the school, and enrollment rebounded. Perhaps the Pandits, who obviously regarded the education he provided as worth the trouble of dealing with him, got the best of Biscoe after all.

LIBERAL FEMINIST CHRISTIAN EDUCATION

Although sports and physical education were important in many mission schools, Biscoe's combination of anti-intellectualism and overt propaganda on behalf of imperial manliness was uncharacteristic of mission schools, many of which were run by Americans and women. Kinnaird Christian College provided another model of ethos in Christian education, that of female professionalism and public service. Originally an interdenominational high school for Christian girls founded in Lahore in 1864, it survived under various names with the support of the Zenana Bible and Medical Mission. In 1913 the Kinnaird High School for Women began offering college classes as an interdenominational Christian college with support at various times from AP, CMS, UP, and ZBMM funds. The only college for women in Punjab, Kinnaird grew steadily, affiliating with the University of Punjab in 1917 and celebrating its first two graduates in 1919.[83]

Michelle Maskiell's thorough study of the changes in the student body at Kinnaird in the twentieth century stresses the leadership of Miss I. T. McNair, the daughter of a Scottish Congregationalist minister who received her M.A. in Germanics from Glasgow University and served as Kinnaird's principal from 1929 to 1950.[84] McNair supervised Kinnaird's transition from a college primarily for Christian students to one serving the western-oriented Hindu middle class of Lahore.[85] The result was a college that, in Maskiell's words, "became integrated into the social training patterns of the Punjabi Hindu professional class," and whose degrees were "weighed in the exacting scales of Punjabi marriage markets."[86]

Maskiell also stresses, as did McNair, the Kinnaird staff's sense of its own unique ethos, which was rooted in the values of early-twentieth-century liberal Protestantism. Competing with the four government colleges for women founded between 1919 and 1943, Kinnaird teachers both Indian and foreign stressed the value of communal harmony based on a commitment to the value of female participation in public life.[87] Kinnaird's Christian teachers taught, as did their counterparts in Britain and the United States, that women could be citizens as well as wives, and that everyone who acted as a good citizen was acting in ways that reflected Christian ethics.

Before concluding that Christianity had been secularized as a form of good citizenship, and Kinnaird merely captured by the progressive Hindu or Arya Samajist middle class, it is important to recognize that for many Anglo-American liberal Protestants good citizenship had a strong theological foundation. Religion should, in the first instance, be defined by those engaging in religious activity. Social ethics lay at the heart of liberal Protestantism, more important as an index of Christian commitment than propositional assent or private devotion or sacramental piety. From their own point of view, the Kinnaird staff were not de-Christianizing Kinnaird, but spreading the influence of Christianity. With their slogan of "a liberal education for all," Kinnaird continued another missionary conviction, the belief that a liberal education had strong moral consequences, and in and of itself made students more likely to perceive Christian truths.[88]

ROMANTIC LITERATURE AND RELIGIOUS ETHOS

Although the ultraimperialist Rev. C. E. Tyndale-Biscoe and the feminist liberal Miss I. T. McNair appear to have little in common, they shared a belief that ethos set Christian education apart from other kinds of education, government, Hindu, Arya Samaj, Muslim, or theosophist. They assumed that a full liberal education was only possible under Christian auspices, and shared with the missionary innovator Alexander Duff of Calcutta the belief that the government attempt to promote morality through secular education was fundamentally flawed.[89] Gauri Viswanathan attributes to Duff a "staggering" influence on the direction of English education through his advocacy of the moral basis of educational practice.[90] In Punjab, however, educational bureaucrats such as W. D. Arnold, W. R. M. Holroyd, and G. W. Leitner were serenely confident in the moralizing power of secular liberal education, and had no need to be taught the importance of morality by missionaries. Where they differed with missionaries was not so much in curriculum but in their assessment of the efficacy of a Christian ethos in imparting liberal knowledge. They also differed fundamentally about the intention of education, which was in one case civic and therefore imperialist, and in the other religious and from the missionary point of view only incidentally imperialist.

Viswanathan perhaps overstates her case when arguing that "[at] a glance it appears that government and missionary schools adopted two mutually exclusive curricula, one heavily classical and the other predominantly Romantic."[91] But she has succinctly defined an essential feature of the widely shared missionary faith in the power of literature, especially Romantic literature, as a path to Christian truth: "As various missionary publications point out endlessly, the power of the Bible lies in its imagery. If images could be regarded as arguments, reason, and demonstrations that illustrate and reinforce the truth, the best means to conversion was, accordingly, through an appeal to the imagination. . . . The truth of Christianity was presented in vain unless it was *seen*, unless it was *felt*."[92] As bishop of Lahore, T. V. French was asked to help draw up examination papers for the new Lahore University. In 1879 he wrote: "For the last fortnight you would have seen my tables strewn with Hallam, Bacon, Shakespeare, Spenser, Chaucer, Macaulay, and such like books for the purpose of drawing up examination papers for our Lahore University. . . . Hallam and Schlegel were my great holdfasts. I have had to work at Chaucer as I never did before, and I think I see how true a father of English poetry he was. . . . My favourites will always be, I think, Spenser, Tennyson, and Wordsworth, after Shakespeare."[93] French recalled the early days of St. John's College, Agra, where in poetry, "Milton was the great book, and interesting it was to hear some of the students repeat verbatim page after page of *Paradise Lost*. Cowper was read, but it was found much more difficult to the students from its more peculiar English character."[94]

The Cambridge Brothers in Delhi, unlikely to be influenced by Alexander Duff, taught the handful of new B.A. students at St. Stephen's College in 1883 Kingsley's *Hypatia*, Macaulay's *Essays on Chatham and Pitt*, Shakespeare's *Hamlet*, Milton's *L'Allegro* and *Il Penseroso*, and Tennyson's *Passing of Arthur*. G. A. Lefroy attempted to guard against the dangers of westernization by requiring the students to wear what he called "Urdu dress" on St. Stephen's Prize Day.[95] St. Stephen's teachers complained (in comments reminiscent of Dickens on utilitarianism) that the routine grammatical and rote nature of the Indian education system had left Indian students without the speculative faculties necessary to understand Wordsworth. A definition of missionary "success" as the inculcation of an ability to make judgments from a Wordsworthian point of view would have struck most home supporters and contributors to the British missionary movement as peculiar and perhaps even unintelligible. But there is no doubt about the Cambridge Brothers' commitment to that point of view as they shaped the curriculum of St. Stephen's College. The Cambridge Mission's Annual Report for 1887 reported on the success of the mission by quoting from a letter received from a non-Christian graduate, Shiv Narayan, now extra assistant commissioner, the "highest post open to Indians in uncovenanted civil service":

> Often on a cloudy morning when I go for field inspection it is pleasant to see all around a spectacle of verdure and fertility. The rural scenery is sometimes very picturesque, where a man of Wordsworthian mood

would like to be in a state of "wise passiveness" and "silent medita-
tion."

The citation was included to "enable you to judge a little of the extent to which Christian teaching has influenced his character" and
"indicates quite a new departure in its incipient appreciation of scen-
ery to which the Indian student is as a rule quite a stranger."[96]

Viswanathan commented on the difficulty of assessing the long-
term effect of curricular decisions on students or society in general:
"There are no simple lessons to be derived from this history, least of
all the lesson that imperialism can be swiftly undone merely by hurl-
ing away the texts it institutionalized."[97] After attributing a large influence to Alexander Duff on government schools, she puts government educational policy at the center of the stage by invoking the
master narrative of secularization. In that story, government is at the
center of history and religion at the margins, and with religion go missionaries and Indian Christians. But the prominent role of mission institutions in secondary and higher education in Punjab raises questions
about the differential impact of government and mission schools, and
the particular impact of mission schools in Punjab.

Over the last two decades I have asked in an informal way several
dozen educated Indians and Pakistanis, all non-Christian and a majority of them women, this question: "[D]id you attend a high school or
college that was associated, or formerly associated, with a Christian
mission?" The answer is often yes. But to the follow-up question—
"[D]id that religious affiliation make a difference?"—the answer is almost always "no."[98] The assumption is that the missions were simply
providing education, perhaps more prestigious than others, but no different in kind. The Christian ethos so important to mission educators
is either ignored or taken for granted. The Indian *Dictionary of National Biography* entry for the Punjabi nationalist leader Lala Lajpat
Rai mentions that he studied at Mission High Schools at Ludhiana and
Ambala, but takes the lack of influence of Christianity through that
medium for granted.[99] Of the charismatic Gandhian Muslim leader
from the Frontier Province, Abdul Ghaffar Khan, the DNB notes his attendance at the mission high school in Peshawar, where "he was greatly influenced by the missionary spirit of the Principal of his School,
Rev. Wigram, and resolved to serve his community as his Principal had
served his faith in a missionary spirit."[100] This is not exactly the sort of
missionary spirit that mission educators had in mind. But the conventions of Indian historiography, where the missionary presence is either

taken for granted or dismissed as a foreign intrusion, make direct assessments of mission influence in the history of Punjab rare.

Maskiell's detailed work on Kinnaird College alumnae makes it clear that this particular mission college played an important role in middle-class Hindu and Indian Christian social life in Lahore. In addition to the six mission colleges, nine girls' boarding schools, and seven boys' boarding schools, missions in the area of the old Punjab Province in 1931 reported twenty-four day high schools (six for girls and eighteen for boys); another count in 1935 listed six colleges with 2,643 students, and twenty-nine high schools with 8,873 students.[101] By this time the government had assumed fundamental responsibility for education in these provinces, and beginning in 1923 they made special efforts targeted at a population that had been mostly left to the missions and Arya Samaj, depressed class (untouchable) students.[102]

Despite the ascendancy of government numbers, the history, prestige, and social location of the mission high schools and colleges gave them an importance that far outweighed their numbers. The far-flung CMS Anglo-vernacular boys' high schools in Bannu, Multan, Dera Ishmael Khan, Dera Ghazi Khan, and Tank provided educational opportunities identified by Amit Chaudhuri as a characteristic feature of preindependence mission schools: "One of the reasons for the good health of the vernaculars in pre-Independence India had been the spread of good education and, paradoxically, the teaching of good English in even some of the remotest areas. Those dreaded figures, the missionaries were often responsible for this. . . . Thus, Indians from a variety of backgrounds learnt English as a second language and acquired a deep feeling for it; English represented to them social mobility and choice."[103] With Christian or non-Christian students in mission schools, there is little evidence of the crisis of being caught between two cultures that so worried missionaries obsessed with the "denationalization" of their students, and that has been written about from a student point of view so forcefully by Edward Said and others.[104]

The effects of mission education lay in matters more mundane than Milton or Wordsworth: not only in upward mobility in government service or the marriage market but also in the "social service" and extracurricular activities stressed by missionary educators who were "too much fond of cricket." Kinnaird College staff placed a huge emphasis on community service and extracurricular activities, including drama, and Sara Suleri remembers the postindependence years when "theater and Kinnaird sat cheek by jowl in the imagination of

Lahore."[105] The UP Gordon College in Rawalpindi survived the pre–World War I threat of amalgamation with Forman College, and the period of missionary retrenchment in the 1930s, prospering despite falling mission contributions because of increased enrollment. Gordon's 753 students on the eve of World War II (356 Hindu, 202 Muslim, 167 Sikh, and 28 Christian) continued to take Bible classes unless they objected under the conscience clause. Despite a pass rate for Punjab University degrees considerably higher than average, and a library of 13,493 volumes, Gordon's prestige never matched Forman's. However, it sponsored the most important basketball tournament in Punjab, the "Stewart Quadrangular" with Forman, Murray, and Gordon Colleges, and the United Presbyterian Christian Training Institute in Sialkot.[106]

At the beginning of the twenty-first century, *India Today International* listed St. Stephen's College as one of the top ten in India: "[T]his last repository of the Oxbridge culture has slipped this time. But few colleges can still match its fierce work culture."[107] Missionary and Indian Christian educators hoped for more than Oxbridge culture and a work ethic. The ultimate success of educational and extracurricular effort depended on the impact of the Christian ethos on students, Christian and non-Christian. Missionaries hoped that students would recognize the higher purposes of mission education, and would make the connection between the motives of the missionaries and their everyday tasks of institution management. Anita Desai makes precisely that connection in her fictional depiction of the teachers at Queen Mary's, Delhi, in the 1940s:

> Tara could not suppress a baleful look as she observed them bustling about the classrooms, cracking open the registers or working out algebraic problems across the blackboards, blowing whistles and rushing across the netball fields, organising sports days and annual school concerts, leading the girls in singing hymns and, every so often, dropping suddenly to their knees, burying their faces in worn and naked hands, and praying with most distinguished intensity. Tara wondered uneasily if hers were one of the lost souls they prayed for.[108]

The reserved and decidedly nonevangelical Grey Ladies of the SPG would never drop publicly to their knees in prayer, and it is unlikely that they prayed for the salvation of particular lost souls. They would no doubt have been pleased, however, to see any student, even a fictional one, make an association between their mundane teaching duties and their deeply held religious commitments, for that connection was at the heart of mission education strategy. It was also a source of worry and anxiety for missionaries who pondered the results of their life's work. The principal of Gordon College, James Cummings, summed up those worries after a survey of the college's interwar achievements: "Unless we can change things so as to win the genuine loyalty and affection of our students, I should favor closing the college."[109] This was only one of the many and varied forms of missionary discontent, frustration, and occasional outright rebellion in the twentieth century.

PART III

Confronting Imperialism / Decolonizing the Churches, 1900–1940

8

Embracing India

Missionaries and Indian Christians Confront Imperial Fault Lines

The designation of the missionary enterprise as "imperialist" is no anachronism. Indian critics of missions, Indian
Christians, and missionaries alike recognized elements of social, cultural, and political imperialism in the missionary enterprise. As early
as 1879 the Rev. G. A. Lefroy moaned: "I believe that our position as
the ruling power puts a dead weight on the missionary enterprise
which nothing but the direct grace of God can possibly enable us to
lift."[1] The imperial boundary was seen at different times as (1) the cultural gap—racial, religious, political, and academic—between foreigner
and Indian; (2) the association of the mission presence with foreign
rule; (3) the disproportionate material resources and professional status accorded to foreigners in mission institutions. The last was by far
the most alarming to missionaries, for the ultimate purpose of their
presence in India depended upon some degree of sympathy between
foreigners and Indians based on common spiritual commitments. It
was that sympathy that the Rev. Golak Nath declared impossible in
his statement to the Lahore Missionary Conference in 1863: "I have
failed to discover how an European or American missionary *can* secure
the *full* sympathy of Native converts. . . . [T]here can . . . scarcely be
any fellow-feeling between them."[2]

This was an imperial problem, and recognized as an imperial problem by conference participants. If there could be no fellow-feeling between foreign missionaries and Indians, then the missionary movement was foreordained to fail. There was an imperial gulf lying between the aspiration to create a church that would survive the revolutions of empire, and the missionary commitment to building strong,
attractive, durable, decently funded Christian institutions—churches,
schools of every imaginable sort, publishing houses, conference centers, hospitals, clinics, leper asylums, reading rooms. Golak Nath im-

plied that missionaries had not merely fallen into some kind of imperial trap, but were active agents in creating the gulf between Europeans and Indians.

In the late nineteenth century the imperial divide was increasingly likely to crystallize around a rhetoric of race. As Laura Tabili has reminded us, race is a "relationship" rather than a "thing,"[3] and it was in the context of relationships inside institutional settings that racial rhetoric emerged in the mission context. The presence of racial antagonism often has to be deduced from a reading of internal mission debates, since Indian Christians were not only on occasion dependent upon but also possessed of considerable affection for missionaries, who found accusations of racial prejudice extremely painful. Racial rhetoric had little utility for missionaries, who attributed the deficiencies of Indian civilization to its removable cultural and religious defects. Genuinely committed to building up what Jean and John Comaroff refer to as "the multiracial Christian commonwealth of missionary fantasy,"[4] they resisted the hardening of racial rhetoric in the late nineteenth century, although very much aware of it. There is no evidence that their depictions of Indians conform to Patrick Brantlinger's general description of a trend toward portraying natives as "ignoble and bestial in late Victorian thinking."[5]

The imperial divide hardened in some ways, however, as mission institutions grew and professional and clerical stratification fell along racial lines. Furthermore, missionaries often failed to comprehend the Indian Christian perception that a combination of white skin with control over resources was a source of gratification for missionaries, one that provided a sense of superiority in their everyday encounters with nonwhites. Writing with the elitist self-confidence of a fully trained Indian Christian professional woman, and the widow of a European missionary, Alice Pennell wrote to the CMS in 1925 declining to return to the hospital in Bannu because of conflict with the CMS over accommodation for a European doctor: "Your fears for Dr. Martin's status and comfort . . . help me to see that it would be hopeless to try to prove that the CMS does not put race first. . . . Your missionaries will, I feel sure, be happier with their own people as colleagues and with Indians of a lower social status than themselves."[6]

Indian Christians, as we have seen, could no more write off the missionary presence as a hopeless failure than could missionaries. As long as missionaries were present, working together with Indians in Christian institutions, the imperial divide was simply there: a presence that could neither be ignored nor banished. It had to be lived with and talked about and negotiated. The early ordination of Indians had been one approach, but its most notable consequence was to bring the imperial divide out into the open by providing Indian clergy with the right of criticism. Experiments with Indian ecclesiastical self-government represented an ongoing attempt to create circumstances where sympathy was possible, but as we have seen they were for the most part failures that could not be abandoned. Some missionaries and Indian Christians counseled patience, drawing historical analogies from the rhetorical storehouse of ecclesiastical history.

For other missionaries and Indian Christians, the imperial divide was too great an evil to tolerate. The more work they did to build up Christian institutions, it seemed, the greater the divide between foreigner and Indian. "Try as I will I cannot get them to look upon me as other than a Sahib," one missionary complained. "Now that was not for a moment my intention when I left England . . . longing to make myself the friend and brother of my people. But this 'master and servant' relationship that seems expected of me all day long is chilling me. . . . If it were not for my wife and children, I would alter at once my manner of life, and start to live like my people and among my people."[7] A missionary nurse in Delhi, Beatrice Ponzoni, was frustrated with the distance required by professionalism: "I long to know them better and above all to give them the message of Incarnate love. In hospital there has been so little opportunity, the work takes up all one's time and energy. . . . If there had only been any one in hospital ready to accept the love and fellowship I was longing to for . . . but not in the hospital—there the rush of work has gone on unrelieved."[8]

MOVING OUT

In every mission of any size there are cases of missionaries, especially unmarried women, responding to this frustration with the simple step of moving out. Although Miss Tiede had served the American Presbyterian mission in Ludhiana as an indefatigable worker for fifteen years, she had never been to a village. When missionaries "discovered" six native Christians in Waga in 1885, she persuaded male missionaries to allow her to live there. She built "three mud huts such as the natives live in, though somewhat larger," subsisted on dhal, rice, and chappatis, and worked exclusively with the untouchable Christians, who by 1888 numbered forty-seven. When a Christian was killed just outside her door, and she herself was threatened, some missionaries from Lahore went there to bring her back to the city. When the proposal was made to her she did not say a word, but simply raised her eyes to heaven and pointed upward.[9]

Moving out required some means of support. When Miss Bengough moved into her own house in Delhi in 1923, hoping to get in touch with Indians by doing independent work, she was shocked to find herself threatened with termination by the mission.[10] After twenty-four years of Baptist work in Palwal and Delhi, Miriam Young concluded that mission structures had thwarted her aspirations: "However hard we have tried to change the institution into a 'community' . . . the institution has remained."[11] She too moved out of the mission, although her critique of institutionalism was based on liberal rather than evangelical theology. She objected to "mere proselytism," preferring "witness" in the form of doing Christian work in India. "Witness" for her meant carrying on her former work as a Montessori teacher in a nonecclesiastical setting, a school opened by Mr. Raghubin Singh, a Hindu formerly of St. Stephen's College.[12] The distinction between witnessing for Christ by teaching in a Christian school, and doing the same but more effectively by teaching in a Hindu school, eluded other BZMS missionaries, and Young herself admitted that "I was being logically forced into the Quaker position and to that extent . . . I am . . . up against organized Christianity."[13]

IMPERSONATION

One step beyond moving out was impersonation. At the 1863 Punjab Missionary Conference, the Rev. Golak Nath suggested that "[if] the missionary, renouncing his refinement, and coming down from his social position, would adopt the life of a Hindoo fukeer, retire from his family and friends, and live in a dhurmsala with his converts, sympathy could easily be secured."[14] Sympathy was not so easily won. Nineteenth-century missionaries who attempted to follow the Rev. Golak Nath's advice and live as Indians frequently succeeded only in magnifying the imperialist dimensions of missions. CMS literature hails the Rev. George Maxwell Gordon as a "born Fakir" missionary, but his enthusiasm for solo itineration dressed as an Indian was matched by his enthusiasm for British imperial expansion. Attempting to overcome one form of imperialism, he was brought down in the service of another. Volunteering as an acting chaplain in the Afghan Wars of 1878 and 1880, he was "killed in the historic sortie at Candahar, endeavouring under hot fire from both sides, to bring in some wounded men lying some 400 yards from the gate."[15]

Other impersonators lacked Gordon's open enthusiasm for imperial expansion, but the Kim-like romanticism of other missionary "fakirs," notably Rowland Bateman and Theodore Leighton Pennell, gave their outreach efforts a marked imperial stamp.[16] Bateman's attempts to "live like an Indian" in Narowal included not only wearing a turban and riding a camel but also establishing a cricket league. Pennell once bicycled across North India in the garb of a "fakir," living on alms. But he showed no interest in the problems of untouchables, and always hoped that the Christianization of India would begin with the elites and help reconcile India to "the more peaceful aspects of British rule."[17]

The psychosexual gratifications of impersonation and mimicry that characterized the famous imperial impostors of the nineteenth century, Richard Burton and Kimball O'Hara, have drawn the attention of postcolonial scholars and are also evident in Gordon, Pennell, and Bateman to some extent.[18] The gratifications of "going native" were not purely theological. Bateman reported with some glee an occasion when he used his status as a "fakir" to persuade a highway robber to leave him alone. Many influential missionaries recognized the marginality, the unpersuasiveness, and the outright hypocrisy of European Christian "fakirs," arguing instead that missionaries should live honestly as what they were: English clergymen in a foreign land.[19] To Robert Clark of the CMS, "going native" was a form of hypocrisy, and authenticity would bring more respect despite opening the missionary to charges of luxurious living.

There are important differences, however, between Richard Burton's imperial imposture and the missionary's adoption of Indian dress. Burton succeeded when he fooled an Oriental. A missionary succeeded when an Indian recognized him as a foreigner attempting to show his good faith, and gained the sympathy of Indians. Rowland Bateman's posing as a "fakir" strikes us as imperialist role-playing, but it did not prevent him from becoming an important and beloved figure among the Indian Christians or Narowal, and an important mentor in the development of an indigenous Indian Christian clergy. Pennell was genuinely respected for the devotion with which he built up a hospital at Bannu under extremely difficult circumstances, and it was his widow (an Indian medical doctor from the Sorabji family of Poona) who launched a vigorous attack on the CMS for racism.

The path from missionary to fakir was very different from Burton's path from orientalist to oriental. Samuel Stokes arrived in India from Philadelphia in the very early nineteenth century to assist a missionary working in a leper asylum, but he soon became disillusioned with the missionary lifestyle, which prevented him from having any rapport with Indians or any spontaneity in his relationships: "It made me feel as if 'a great gulf were fixed,' and that neither of us could draw near to each other, and I hated my Western customs and longed to cast them aside."[20] He cast aside his western clothing, the most visible sign of his foreignness, moved into a cave, bathed only in cold water, and emerged as a Christian Sadhu "with a beard and a long saffron choga (long loose dress) and polas (hemp slippers) on his feet. He had few worldly possessions—a blanket thrown over his shoulder, a lota for keeping water and a degchi to cook and eat in."[21] Ultimately even this extreme form of identification with India proved unsatisfactory for Stokes, who married an Indian woman and later became a Hindu, going so far as to break off ties with Christian friends in order to maintain caste distinctions.

THE CHRISTIAN FAKIR

If western missionaries remained frustrated in their ability to show sympathy for Indians, perhaps an Indian could transgress the imperial divide by developing and putting on display truly Indian forms of Christian piety. As the hopes faded for an influential Indian clergy, a flourishing self-governing Indian church, and a new Alexandria on the banks of the Yamuna, missionaries continued to look for the satisfactory Indian Christian fakir or Sadhu, a mendicant with special religious charisma living on alms who could communicate Christianity in a special way to Indians while the professional multiracial clergy went about their business of baptizing infants and building schools.[22]

Although thought by missionaries to be a characteristic form of Indian religious expression, the "Christian fakir" proved to be of more interest to missionaries than to the majority of Indian Christians, who for the most part preferred a more conventional "padri." For missionaries, deference to the Christian fakir was a means of showing sympathetic interest in India and things Indian, and allowing Indians to develop indigenous forms of piety. A few Indian Christians agreed. One of the first projects of the CMS Punjab Native Church Council was a donation of land to support Bande Shah, described by the Rev. Mian Sadiq as a "great Christian fakir at Chhelowal." Many travelers, both learned and illiterate, were said to stop to take tobacco or draw water from his well. Sadiq hoped that the Christian fakir would do great things in the future, and help deal with the problems he and other edu-

cated Indian Christian pastors faced in their dealings with poor and illiterate Christian villagers.[23]

For denominations committed to ecclesiastical order and bureaucratic regularity, any claim to autonomous spiritual authority could
spell trouble, and the Christian fakir was no exception. In 1887 the
Rev. Robert Clark relayed hopeful reports of 150 conversions in a village near Clarkabad among followers of a Christian fakir, Chet Ram.
They had built a church for their Sadhu and were pleading for Christian teaching.[24] But the CMS catechist at Clarkabad, Sant Shah, wrote
shortly afterward claiming that these Christians believe in Christ as a
God and Chet Ram as his incarnation.[25] As events in another mission
would demonstrate, the Christian fakir need not fall into outright her-
esy to challenge mission and church discipline.

In the normally placid Baptist mission compound at Bhiwani, five
English Baptist women were in charge of a mission hospital and constituted a significant portion of a small Baptist congregation presided
over by an Indian pastor. Christian fakirs occasionally preached at
Sunday services, and one lived in the neighborhood: Jitu, who had been
baptized in 1904.[26] One of the missionaries, Bertha Scoresby, began in
1915 to exhibit signs of a common missionary longing to strike out
and live directly with the people in order to serve them better. She
opened a school for the Christians in Bhiwani's Chamar neighborhood,
and later moved out of the hospital compound to live among them.
Conducting her own religious services, which attracted all of the "outside Christians" in Bhiwani—that is, those who did not actually live in
the mission compound—she created a schism in the Bhiwani church
by instructing her followers to call themselves "Christian" rather than
"Baptist."[27]

From the other missionaries' point of view, Miss Scoresby's behavior up to this point had been unwise and disturbing but recognizable.
She soon passed the boundaries of respectability, however, by leaving
Bhiwani on January 29 with the intention of marrying Fakir Jitu. The
missionaries rushed to Hissar in order to persuade missionaries and
magistrates there to refuse to conduct a marriage ceremony. The missionaries then resorted to kidnapping and drugging. As Miss Scoresby
and Jitu returned from their attempt to marry at Hissar, according to
Dr. Farrer, Indian Christians (presumably the "inside" Christians)
"abducted Jitu and brought him forcibly to the Babu's house, and he is
now locked up there. But before this was accomplished his boy pupils
went and told Miss Scoresby, and she rushed after and clung to him.
Annie was sent for, and found them locked in each other's arms, while

the Christians were trying to separate them, a terribly unseemly sight. Her hair was down, her topi off, and she looked pale and disheveled, and tried to scratch or bite anyone who tried to get her away. By the time I got there Jitu was locked up, and Miss S. was lying on a charpoi in the yard guarded by the preachers and others, and still resisting everybody. She scratched me when I tried to get her to be reasonable, so I went home and fetched my boy, and administered a strong dose of morphine. Its comparatively slight effect rather confirms the idea that she really is mad now, and looks it too."[28]

These steps persuaded Jitu to leave the locality. Miss Scoresby returned to the Chamar *basti* and reopened her school. Two months later another fakir appeared on the scene, Faqir Mirza Amir Husain, a friend of the well-known Baptist missionary in Delhi, G. A. Smith. Miss Scoresby was by this time reduced to eating plain chappatis with no lentils or vegetables, and Faqir Mirza offered to help get her away from Bhiwani. The next day they eloped, and Ellen Farrer wrote: "We think she must be insane, but it is a peculiar and limited kind of insanity for which it would be even more difficult to get a patient 'certified' out here than at home!"[29]

Miss Scoresby began a life of itinerant evangelism with Faqir Mirza, holding meetings wherever possible, wearing a sari and sandals, eating Indian food, and living on whatever people gave them.[30] Mirza apparently regarded heroic and dangerous preaching as part of the fakir's role, for in September they were being "hounded from place to place by government officials on account of the strong religious feelings he stirs up amongst the Mohammedans. It is very foolish of him to be so controversial in his sermons and addresses, but I gather from what I have heard that he likes to pose as martyr. He is known to have prophesied an attempt on his life."[31] At last report, they had come to the attention of Bishop Azariah of Dornakal, who evidently persuaded them to engage in a civil marriage ceremony. They were reported to be desperately poor, but had either joined or at least been persuaded to join the Salvation Army.[32]

Insanity is a category commonly used to understand or stigmatize religion, and the Salvation Army was often treated by rival denominations as a safe haven for the mentally disturbed. But Scoresby Mirza and Faqir Mirza were acting squarely within Christian traditions well known in Baptist and Methodist circles. The heroic itinerant evangelist with charismatic spiritual authority, persecuted by the authorities and hostile crowds, might have been Wesley or Whitefield. The impulse both to "go native" and "get in touch with the people" was endemic in mission circles. Interracial marriage, although not routine, was far from unknown in mission and Indian Christian circles. Scoresby Mirza and Faqir Mirza took things a few steps too far, but they were not the first or the last to take their interpretation of the principles of evangelical and sectarian Christianity at face value, and act on them. Dr. Farrer could stigmatize them to her heart's content, but she could not prevent the Salvation Army from co-opting them.

Miss Scoresby's belief that embracing true Indian Christianity meant embracing a fakir (evidently any fakir) was emblematic of the continuing hope among missionaries that the emergence of the Christian fakir or Christian sadhu would provide the key to unlock the spiritual world of India. Much more successful at appealing to that missionary hope, especially when compared to the unfortunate Jitu or the persecuted Faqir Mirza, was Sadhu Sundar Singh. From a respectable and prosperous Sikh family of Patiala State, Sundar Singh was converted in a mission school at Rampur through close reading of the Bible under the tutelage of an American Presbyterian missionary.[33] This was the ways things were supposed to happen, but rarely did, in mission schools. Sundar Singh's conversion, in 1904 at age fifteen, was both unusual and full of Christian resonance. A Hindustani-speaking Christ appeared directly to him, asking, "Why do you persecute Me? Remember that I gave My life for you upon the Cross."[34] Persuaded by the scars that the appearance was genuine, and always insisting that it was an "appearance" and not a "vision," Sundar Singh was changed in the same way that St. Paul was changed on the Damascus Road by an earlier appearance. Full of both joy and peace, he began his mission to transmit the good news of the living Christ to others.

Following the usual persecution by family members, he took refuge with Presbyterian missionaries, engaged in desultory theological study, and was eventually baptized into the Anglican Church of India at Simla. Hoping that Sundar Singh would become a truly Indian but nonetheless settled and respectable Anglican cleric, Bishop Lefroy of Lahore gave him a license to preach. But Sundar Singh adopted the role of wandering Indian sadhu, armed with the near-Apostolic authority of direct communion with the living Christ. As a symbol of his mission, he donned a sacred saffron robe.

Sundar Singh posed a potential challenge to ecclesiastical authority in India, but he always regarded himself as an Anglican communicant and never challenged clerical authority directly, merely ignoring it when it suited his purposes. Many missionaries, and western Christians in the missionary movement, regarded him as the fulfillment of their hopes. Here was a figure who combined the indigenous cultural forms of the "other" with charismatic Christian authority, behaving in ways that were simultaneously fully Indian and fully Christian. His admirers could hardly restrain their praise of someone who appeared to be a combination of Guru Nanak with Luther, Paul, or perhaps even Jesus, wandering homeless from village to village, withdrawing periodically for solitary contemplation in the hills.[35]

Sundar Singh was masterful in combining elements of orientalist imagery, charismatic Christian tradition, Victorian geo-religious romanticism, and biblical allusion. His tours included persistent attempts to "penetrate" Tibet, Nepal, Kashmir, or Afghanistan. After months he would return to the Christian lecture circuit with implausible tales of heroic fasting, miraculous conversions, Christian martyrdom, and faith healing.[36]

Tales of the miraculous constituted Sundar Singh's greatest rhetorical risk. Protestants generally took a dim view of latter-day miracles, and liberal Protestants rejected them altogether. A German liberal pastor psychoanalyzed Sundar Singh as a neurotic, with other morbid traits such as sadism, whose obsessive love for Christ was caused by "repressed infantile sex-complexes."[37] Roman Catholics regarded the miracle-worker genre as their own, and were sufficiently alarmed by Sundar Singh's spreading fame to launch an extensive attack on him as an "imposter" and an "oriental deceiver." But for most Protestant missionaries, Sundar Singh was simply too good to be true. To the conservative bishop of Lahore, Sundar Singh appeared to be the fulfillment of the dreams of the Cambridge Mission, an expression of Christianity in indigenous Indian forms, the beginnings of a New Alexandria on the banks of the Jumna. To C. F. Andrews, "The whole future of the Christian faith in India seemed to centre in the ideal he put before us."[38]

Sundar Singh was befriended by Samuel Stokes, who had also had a vision of Jesus Christ "toilworn and travel-stained, trudging on foot along an Indian high road." In 1910 Sundar Singh, Stokes, and F. J. Western of the Cambridge Mission to Delhi formed a new religious community, the Brotherhood of the Imitation of Jesus, committed to service, itineration, and periodic retreat for prayer and contemplation. As Bishop Lefroy laid hands on them in Lahore Cathedral, he "looked upon the founding of the new Order as the greatest event that had happened to the church in the Punjab during his episcopate."[39] Stokes went to work at the leper asylum at Sabathu, Western to live among the poor of Delhi, and Sundar Singh to wander barefoot among the villages of Punjab. To Bishop Lefroy's bitter disappointment, the Brotherhood of the Imitation of Jesus lasted barely two years. On the road to outright conversion to Hinduism, Stokes married an Indian as a "fierce protest" against "ancient racial prejudices" in the church.[40] The celibate Bishop Lefroy, reportedly heartbroken, dissolved the order in 1911 amidst embarrassing acrimony and charges of racism.

Sundar Singh remained celibate and Christian, unscathed by scandal and on friendly terms with Bishop Lefroy. His fame began to grow in 1912 after he was discovered senseless in a wilderness area near Dehra Dun where he had been fasting. He began yearly itinerations in the mountains, interspersed with appearance to groups of Indian Christians including large assemblies among the divided Syrian Christians in Kerala. In 1920 he embarked on his first tour of Europe, addressing large crowds of several denominations—Anglican, Congregationalist, and Baptist—as well as an assembly of seven hundred Anglican clergy including the archbishop of Canterbury. Few speakers would find an equally warm welcome from the Society of Friends, the Anglo-Catholic monks of Cowley, and stern Baptist evangelicals of C. H. Spurgeon's Metropolitan Tabernacle. Similar acclaim greeted him in the United States and Australia. Sundar Singh was a kind of ecclesiastical counterpart to Tagore in the literary world and Gandhi in the political world, a representative Indian, although one whose influence was limited to the world of the Christian churches. Another tour in 1921 took him to Palestine, Egypt, and Switzerland (where he spoke to three thousand people at Tavannes and ten thousand at Neuchâtel), a pilgrimage to Wittenberg, and several days of consultation with Archbishop Söderblom at Uppsala.[41]

Sundar Singh had become an ecumenical celebrity, both in India and in Europe, complete with charges that he had been corrupted by success and detached from his true Indian roots. His rhetorical skills lay in addressing Christians, and the core of his message to Europe was one that had been popular in missionary circles since the time of William Carey: Europe is not truly Christian, any more than India. Attacks on the materialism and superficial Christianity of the west were a staple of mission rhetoric, and they were all the more persuasive coming from an Indian in a saffron robe who bore an uncanny resemblance to the stained glass Jesus of the western Protestant churches. Furthermore, Sundar Singh knew that his rhetoric was linked to his behavior, and after his European tours returned to his Himalayan itinerations. In 1929 he disappeared for good in Tibet.

Sundar Singh's appeal was to those already Christian, and in particular to western Christians, missionaries, and church leaders. There is little evidence that his message had any relevance to the village untouchables who constituted the majority of the church in Punjab, or to the urban, middle-class Christians who led it. Both groups were intimately tied to a missionary presence that was important to their communities, despite the bitter conflicts that broke out periodically between Indian Christians and missionaries. Sundar Singh of course preached against caste, but it was an abstract denunciation that held little practical relevance to the circumstances of labor servitude in Punjabi agriculture. His celebrity served, like mission institutions, to give the urban Indian Christian community some status, particularly as the rise of the national movement in the twentieth century left them more vulnerable to charges that they were "denationalized" by their Christianity.

Despite perennial rumors of his involvement with secret orders of Christian Sannyasis (holy men learned in Sanskrit), Sundar Singh founded no order and left no successor. His prophetic teaching in some ways reinforced the quietist and perfectionist teachings of the evangelical Sialkot Convention (see below). Sundar Singh was one model of how to be an Indian Christian, but it was one of limited practical applicability, and one that left intact the everyday practical fault lines of race, culture, and power that bedeviled the complicated Indian church.

That Sundar Singh was aware of the limits placed on his charisma by his Christian faith is evident in his account of yet another supernatural appearance—from Satan himself. In 1918 Sundar Singh addressed two large assemblies of South Indian Christians, chastising crowds numbering in the tens of thousands for keeping the Gospel of Christ to themselves and forcing God to send in strangers from Europe and America to do the work of evangelism. At the peak of his influence, he withdrew into the jungle to pray, and was approached by a man who addressed him:

> Pardon me for interrupting your solitude and devotions, but it is one's duty to seek the good of others; hence I have come, for your pure and unselfish life has deeply impressed. Many other God-fearing people have been similarly impressed. But though you have consecrated yourself heart and soul to the good of others, you have not yet been sufficiently rewarded. My meaning is this: by becoming a Christian your influence has affected some thousands of Christians, but it is limited to this, and even some of them regard you with distrust. Would it not be better for you as a Hindu or Mussulman to become their leader? They are in search of such a leader. If you consent to my suggestions, you will soon see that millions of Hindus and Moslems in India will become your followers, and will actually worship you.[42]

With his characteristic allusion to a recognizable story, Sundar Singh responded much as Christ did to Satan when offered all the kingdoms of the world: "Get thee hence, Satan!"[43] The lure of fame through politics was one of the greatest temptations of Sundar Singh's life, and his rejection of anti-imperial politics was rewarded by an appearance of Christ as a glorious being clothed in light. For him, the contradictions between Christian faith and the realities of imperial power could be resolved only supernaturally. As a potential leader in an Indian Christian community faced with growing anxieties about their political status, Sundar Singh had little to offer beyond prayer and personal holiness.

GOING NATIVE

It is notable that Sundar Singh, although striving for an Indian expression of Protestantism, did not reject the messengers of God sent from Europe and America. The early twentieth century was the high point of missionary intervention in Delhi and Punjab, with more than six hundred foreign missionaries at work in the late 1920s (see Table 9), and the influx of foreigners heightened the contradiction between a foreign institutional presence staffed by "strangers" and the urgent need to generate an indigenous Indian Christian church. Nineteenth-century attempts to create a regular Indian church with ordained Indian clergy all foundered on the practical realities of funding: the foreign missions controlled the funds that staffed the institutions. Missionaries were not prepared to turn over control of foreign funds to Indians, although they were happy to extend to Indians control over funds raised in India. This irresolvable problem was confronted with characteristic self-confidence by the Salvation Army, which engaged in the broadest of all attempts to break down the barriers of culture by "going native." Like Sundar Singh, Salvation Army officers confronted the temptations of power and fame, although their tempters were imperial officials rather than the nationalist masses.

Throughout the period of Sundar Singh's ascent to prominence, another fakir named Singh was also prominent as a Christian leader in Punjab and throughout India: Commissioner Fakir Singh of the Salvation Army.[44] Fakir Singh was the Indian name adopted by Frederick de Lautour Tucker, an Indian civil servant who had been converted during a revival meeting conducted by the American evangelist Dwight L. Moody. Frustrated at his inability to proselytize while a civil servant, Tucker heard of the new Salvation Army and traveled to London to meet General William Booth, its founder. He was so impressed that, to his wife's horror, he resigned from the civil service to become head of the Salvation Army in India, their first mission field. Booth instructed his disciple (who later changed his name to Booth-Tucker) to "become all things to all men, in order that you may win them to your Master. This must mean, if anything at all, that to the Indians you must be Indian."[45]

The Salvation Army had a special flair for publicity, which was nowhere more in evidence than in Booth-Tucker's arrival in Bombay in 1882. Traveling with four companions who adopted Indian names and wore a kind of half-Indian dress including turbans and long yellow coats, they issued press releases announcing a Salvation Army "invasion" of India. Expecting large numbers of Salvationists to march around Bombay in the manner of the east end of London, local authorities mobilized the police to prevent the Salvationists from stirring up riots. Fakir Singh was allowed to address indoor meetings, but the police began to block public processions and arrest the Salvationists. As Fakir Singh was marching with two associates and a banner through one Bombay street, he encountered a deputy police commissioner and the superintendent of police, who ordered him taken to jail, the first of several incarcerations in Bombay that made his reputation.[46] Public support for his right to march, coming even from protonationalist and Brahmo Samajist journalists who enjoyed seeing imperialists at odds with each other, made him unjailable.

Salvation Army officers had in their own minds a clear sense of the difference between the Empire of Christ and the Empire of Britain. From the first, they met the rhetorical objection that as westerners they had no right to proselytize in India with an argument by counter-assertion: they were not there to promote a western way of life but to put the love of God into action through service. An outward and visible sign of that commitment was an attempt to go native with Indian dress and an Indian style of life. One of Commissioner Fakir Singh's successors as Salvationist commissioner in India, Commissioner Bullard, came to India as an ordinary missionary officer, took the name Jai Singh, wore his version of Indian dress, shaved his head, and went with bare feet. In his first interview after becoming commissioner in 1920, he declared that he had no problems with Indian nationalism, and that everyone must recognize that "[c]olour is only skin deep."[47] The Salvation Army first organized the major cities of India, including Lahore, and used them as bases to extend Salvationist work into the countryside.

Commissioner Fakir Singh found that he was much less welcome among the other Christian churches than Sadhu Sundar Singh. Promiscuous opportunism in matters of recruitment led to bitter conflict with other Christian groups. Converts were sometimes listed in official statistics as "prisoners taken," and growth was achieved in part by the straightforward method of poaching from other Christian churches. A CMS missionary reported from the Punjab canal colonies that "skirmishes from the Salvation Army have also appeared. They absent themselves from worship, and when our bell rings set to work with drums and bhajans, and so attract and intercept ordinary worshipers."[48]

After being released from prison, Commissioner Fakir Singh held public meetings in Amritsar and Lahore, where he established a permanent Salvationist presence in 1882. In the 1890s their "invasion" of Amritsar was condemned by the bishop of Lefroy, and was met with a virulent pamphlet by CMS missionary Henry Martyn Clark, who claimed that all Salvationist converts were from other Christian denominations. Salvationist growth in Punjab in fact combined new converts and poaching.[49] It took little time for them to discover the readiness of Chuhra villagers to embrace Christianity in some parts of Punjab. They worked in districts previously worked over by American Presbyterians (Doda and Ambala) and the Anglican Church Missionary Society (Batala and Gurdaspur), claiming in rebuttal to angry protests that there was plenty of opportunity for work remaining there. The Salvation Army recorded 3,236 Salvation soldiers in Punjab in 1900, 7,345 in 1907, and more than 18,000 in the official census of 1911, 35 percent of the Salvationists in India. They claimed (not unreasonably) that the true number of adherents in Punjab was closer to 25,000.[50] In 1899 Punjab was separated as a territorial command of the army under the direction of Brigadier Catherine Bannister (Yuddha Bai).

Salvation Army work in Punjab was distinguished by its opportunism, by its egalitarianism with respect to gender and race, and by the working-class background of its European missionaries. The Salvation Army's Promoted to Glory (PTG) file lists among the male Salvationists who died in Punjab a baker, cabinetmaker, carpenter, clerk, cook, draper, engineman, farmer, ironmonger, mechanic, plumber, Salvation Army employee, stock-keeper, tailor, and woolspinner, two coal miners, two soldiers, and two shop assistants. At least one cowboy, and one lion tamer, also served. Most women listed "wife" as former occupation, but about one-third of the women (in this case from all of India) listed a distinct occupation, including a cashier, chauffeuse, clerk, dye-worker, factory worker, forewoman, machinist, matron, munitions worker, papercounter, ringspinner, shopkeeper, shorthand writer, teacher, three dressmakers, four typists, five shop assistants, eight domestics, and nine nurses.[51]

It is at least possible that the class composition of the Salvationists provided them with greater flexibility. Punjabi villagers were unable to distinguish working-class from middle-class Britons, or for that matter Britons from Swedes, who constituted a significant minority of Salvationists. But the very fact of their adherence to the Salvation Army was testimony to a Salvationist willingness to avoid the snobbery, professionalism, and bureaucratic clericalism that characterized male Anglican and Presbyterian missionaries. Salvationists had no desire to recruit from the top down, and avoided the tedious anti-Hindu and anti-Muslim polemics of Bishop Lefroy and his predecessors. A typical Salvation Army address was much more direct: "The source of the Ganges is the Himalayas; it is a wonderful river, it fertilizes the country. Jesus is the source of my joy, my life, my all. There are other rivers, but Christ is the mainstream. Get better acquainted with God, get more of his Spirit, God bless the Salvation Army."[52]

If class composition gave them more flexibility, so did their attitude to gender. The Salvation Army was not democratic, but it was egalitarian, and women were given leadership roles from the very first. A majority of women Salvationist missionaries were married, but the Salvation Army ethos discouraged women from using family responsibilities as an excuse for neglecting responsibilities to Indians. In other societies missionary mothers were primarily mothers when their many children were young, and their missionary roles were diminished in the twentieth century by the influx of unmarried women. An obituary for a Salvationist missionary, Mrs. Pinchbeck, noted that she raised four children but "never allowed those responsibilities of home and work to lessen her contact with the women around her for whom she had a sincere affection."[53]

The Salvation Army made efficient use not only of European women workers but of Indian men and women workers as well. From the very first the Salvation Army was officially antiracist (as all the missionary societies were), but more antiracist in practice than other missionary societies, recruiting Indian men and women into positions as officers. From one point of view, all Europeans, and all European missionaries, were racist, unable to escape the broad structures of racism that governed the imperial enterprise. It would no doubt be possible to document a considerable record of hypocrisy in the Salvationist approach to race. A ringing declaration in 1901 that "No distinction or difference is to be recognized between European and Indian staff officers on account of nationality" was followed with a qualifier: "except as regards financial requirements."[54] But from the Salvation Army's own point of view, some Europeans were more racist than others, and they could point to a documented record of success at promoting Indian participation. Of the eighty top officers in India in 1893, ten years after their "invasion" of Bombay, fifty-three were European and twenty-seven Indian, a record of recruiting Indians into the higher clergy (Salvation Army style) far surpassing that of any other western missionary society.[55] (The first non-European Protestant Bishop of Lahore was consecrated in 1968.) Racial intermarriage among officers, although not common, was no bar to becoming an officer, and it is not entirely surprising that Miss Scoresby and Faqir Mirza eventually took refuge in the Salvation Army after being driven away from the Baptist Mission at Bhiwani. There was even a black Salvation Army missionary in Punjab, an American named Zulu John. A lion tamer by profession, Zulu John was converted by the Salvation Army in the east end of London, enrolled as a missionary, sent out to India, given an Indian name and a turban, and sent out barefooted into the villages for evangelistic work.[56]

A combination of egalitarianism, opportunism, and an authoritarian command structure gave the Salvation Army a competitive edge in denominational competition in rural Punjab. Their particular form of "going native," dressing as Indians and living simply, was simultaneously a moral statement, a response to the imperial fault line dividing Europeans from Indians, and an element of the Salvationists' well-known commitment to showmanship. Coal miners from the West Midlands and clerk-typists from suburban London attracted considerable attention in Punjabi villages as they marched barefoot and dressed in turbans and saris. One Salvationist reminisced about the early days in this way:

> In those days, we wore no shoes and no topi. Our allowance was Rs 2 a month for incidental expenses, and we begged our food from the village people. Those were hard days. . . . Once I remember that were 3 days with nothing to take but a little buttermilk. . . . The first time I went out collecting, I went with bare feet and no topi, but of course, taking with me an umbrella. I remember that I stayed with a mission lady at Ajmir, and she happened to have a gathering of missionaries at her house just at that time; the house was full of ladies and gentlemen, and there I was in my bare feet, and in my sari. In another place a lady said to me, "I will give you Rs 5 for the army work, and Rs 5 for you to buy

another pair of shoes for yourself, if you will put them on. I told her I could not accept this. She gave me that Rs 10, which I put into the fund. In those days, although we were so poor, we were very happy. When Miss Lucy (Commissioner Ruhani) came, she arranged that we should have a little more comfort, and gradually things became a little easier for non-Indian officers working in India.[57]

Showmanship was combined with skill at providing Indian Christian converts a sense of dignity and self-esteem, and Salvationists paid special attention to women. Indian Salvationist women wore the same red coats as men and held posts as village officers. Like men, they were put to work in accordance with the Salvationist maxim: "Never allow a single emotion to evaporate without extracting from it some practical service."[58] Salvationists created a "band of widows" sent from Pandita Ramabai's home near Poona to remarry Punjabi Christian men and work together as specialists in village women's meetings.[59] The sheer aggressiveness of the Salvation Army provided a sense of protection for village untouchables, who felt in some places that they could call on Salvationist officers for assistance in dealing with threats of violence or extortion by the police. One observer claimed that as early as 1905, in some parts of Gurdaspur, "Walking on any of the roads, one is almost bound to meet a red-coated Salvationist, either soldier, cadet, or officer."[60] At the yearly Christian mela in Batala, village Christians would gather in red coats with musical instruments for singing, wrestling, and tract distribution. New Year's Eve festivities at Dehra Baba Nanak village consisted first of a drama of the prodigal son produced and acted by Salvation Army officers, then singing of Punjabi Psalms, then a march through the villages to shouts of "Victory to the Name of Jesus and Hallelujah."[61]

Salvationists used fireworks on their village tours, and were among the first to use cinema in rural Punjab, with showings of the life of Christ, the coronation of George V, and Salvation Army drill. On an even grander scale, the Punjab Annual Easter Congress in Lahore in 1913 featured 850 officers all dressed in bright uniforms for a wedding that was combined with a mass dedication of infants, sermons, singers from Lahore Girls School, and an "Open Air Bombardment," that is, tract distribution in nearby villages. In the 1920s they distributed posters of General Booth for veneration as the "Christian Mahatma."[62]

Older officers of the Salvationist community in Pakistan today remember with great fondness the openness of public debate and peaceful religious competition in the 1920s and 1930s—days when, as one retired brigadier put it, "we had great speakers who could best our opponents, the Akalis and Arya Samaj."[63] The contradictory nature of the missionary movement is on clear display in the Salvationist story. To interpret the interaction of European and Indian in the 1920s and 1930s as sheer imperialist intrusion makes no sense from the point of view of village Salvationists. Nor does it make sense to portray a huge gap between west and nonwest (as the Comaroffs do in their treatment of African Christianity) in which the nonwest encounters western religion and makes it over into something wholly new.[64] European Salvationists were important to the Salvationist communities, just as European missionaries were important to almost all Indian Christian communities.

The Salvation Army's Christian message and aggressive methods spoke to the condition of some sections of Punjab's Chuhra community, but village work was not the sum of Salvation Army work in Punjab. In India as in Great Britain, the Salvation Army portrayed itself as an agent of social transformation for society's outcasts. For all of their genuine enthusiasm for embracing India, and their willingness to challenge government power when it interfered with their public spectacles, Salvationists had a blind spot when dealing with other issues of government power. The very enthusiasm of their attempt to storm the boundaries of race and culture set them up for a highly visible and in some ways disastrous entanglement with the principalities and powers of imperial rule.

SOCIAL SALVATION AND IMPERIAL POWER

In 1890 Frederick Booth-Tucker published *Darkest India. A Supplement to General Booth's "In Darkest England and the Way Out,"* in which he claimed that "the gospel of social salvation, which has so electrified all classes in England, can be adopted on this country almost as it stands."[65] Applying his antiracist environmentalism to what he thought were Indian conditions, Booth-Tucker suggested numerous schemes for the reorganization of labor, including a beggar's brigade, a prison gate brigade, a drunkard's brigade, a rescue home for the fallen, an industrial village, a suburban farm, a dairy colony to supply a major city, and a country colony for the "congested mass of low caste laborers in need of organization."[66] In order to combat the plague in the 1890s, Booth-Tucker sent to India an entire shipload of cats. During the famine of 1908 he promoted tapioca, shipping it in and trying to persuade merchants to stock it. The Salvation Army also manufactured and distributed its own new model "swadeshi" automatic looms for sale cheaply in "factory," "village," and "popular" models.[67]

In theory the Salvation Army made a clear distinction between the Empire of Christ and the Empire of Britain. In his first direct encounter with authority during a street procession following his arrival in Bombay, Booth Tucker encountered a deputy police commissioner who called out: "In the name of Her Majesty, Queen of England and Empress of India, I order you to disperse." He replied: "In the name of His Majesty, King of kings and Lord of lords, I command you to stand aside."[68] But it was one thing for temptation to appear to Sadhu Sundar Singh in the form of Satan offering political fame and influence. It was another thing for temptation to appear to the Salvation Army in the form of Sir Louis Dane, the lieutenant governor of Punjab, offering government aid.

The Salvationist flair for publicity in a search for "what works" paid off in the form of an extended and fruitful cooperative relationship with the government of Punjab. In 1908 Dane placed a large abandoned fortress in Ludhiana at the Salvation Army's disposal.[69] *The Indian War Cry* reported a "government grant for a Weaving School and Industrial Home to instruct and employ a certain fraternity over whom the government likes to keep a fatherly eye, as owing to kleptomania and other propensities they are requested to call at the Government Offices to register their latest address in case they are 'wanted' at any time. . . . [T]hese people will now have a chance of learning and trade and becoming industrious members of the community."[70] Punjabi prisoners were assigned by the courts to the fort and paid wages for their weaving. The Salvation Army kept the profits they earned as prison subcontractors for the government of Punjab. By 1911, with six hundred looms, the Sir Louis Dane Weaving School was the largest hand-loom weaving school in India.

Salvationists assumed responsibility not only for the compulsory vocational re-education of criminals but also the supervision of entire villages designed by the government as "Criminal Tribes." Under the Criminal Tribes Acts of 1871 and 1911, local governments were empowered to declare a "tribe, gang, or class of persons" a criminal tribe, and request the governor general in council to restrict their movements to a specified area. In 1910 the Salvation Army opened the Ummedpur Criminal Settlement for ninety persons of the Sansia caste, whose women had been described in the 1881 census as "especially depraved."[71] The women were set to work weaving while the men constructed military letter boxes to fill a government contract. That same year an entire village of one thousand persons was designated the Karampur Criminal Tribes Settlement and put under the charge of three Salvation Army officers.[72]

Interested in securing canal colonies in western Punjab where their landless village converts might secure some independence from land-owners, the Salvation Army found themselves encouraged by the provincial government to develop even more criminal colonies, or even horse and mule breeding farms for the military.[73] In 1911 the lieutenant governor of Punjab, while praising the Salvation Army for their work, pressed them to investigate the possibility of a criminal settlement near "Changa Manga Forest, west of Lahore, where the Forest Department was finding great difficulty in raising the necessary labor to carry out fellings."[74] The Salvation Army of course responded to this reasonable request to help provide a cheap and efficient labor supply for a repressive colonial government, and opened in 1912 a criminal settlement at Changa Manga with thirty houses for Sansias who engaged in tree felling from October to March, and silk growing the rest of the year.[75]

Bringing the fruits of workers in their eight industrial establishments to the heart of empire, the Salvation Army put on an exhibit in Simla in July to enable those attending the yearly holiness meetings to inspect a wide range of products including oranges, apples, pears, jams, pickles, honey, marmalade, eggs, maize, beans, trees and timbers, milk, poultry, wheat, barley, fodder, raw silk, shirts, sheets, mercerized table cloths, serviettes, silk Turkish towels, bath and face towels, aprons, uniforms, coats, drawn thread, and needlework.[76] In 1917 Booth-Tucker lectured on "criminocurology" at Forman Christian College in Lahore to an audience that included the lieutenant governor, Sir Michael O'Dwyer, who responded by unveiling plans for more cooperative work and appealed to other missionary societies to follow the example of the Salvation Army.[77] By that time the man who had been arrested by imperial authorities in 1882 for challenging them as a representative of the Empire of Christ had been invested with the gold Kaiser-i-Hind medal of the Empire of Britain.

The Salvation Army eventually paid a price for this praise from the heights of power and influence. Their work with criminal tribes in particular drove a wedge into the heart of Salvationist work in India, affecting the morale of ordinary Salvationist missionaries. In 1920 the *Indian War Cry* reported that "we hear occasionally comrades deploring the fact that while they came to be 'missionaries' they find themselves engaged in work which hardly comes up to their ideals in this respect."[78] Perhaps the writer was referring to Reuben Moss, a coal miner who arrived in India to find himself in charge of criminals at the Ludhiana weaving shed; or Albert Walker, a cabinet maker put in charge of a criminal tribe in Punjab in 1914, only to return to work in Scotland in 1919; or Albert Britton Mabe, a carpenter in charge of the new Chawa Criminal Settlement in 1910; or Adam J. Pettiford, a soldier drafted into the Salvation Army in order to be a prison guard at the Danepur Dairy.[79]

Salvation Army officials responded to this disquiet with rhetoric familiar in missionary circles, drawing clear distinctions between government policy and Salvation Army policy, pointing out the distinctive motives, purposes, and goals of their cooperative work. But once their criminal tribes policy had to be openly defended in a new political climate of the 1920s, it became indefensible theologically and politically. In 1928 the Weaving School at the Ludhiana fort was closed without comment.[80] In 1935 the Punjab government restored persons in the criminal tribes to full citizenship. With no further legal responsibility for their charges, the Salvation Army announced plans to set up regular corps at Kot Adhian and Kassowal to carry on purely spiritual work.

The title of the standard celebratory history of the Salvation Army in India is *By Love Compelled*.[81] Bearing in mind the prevalence of mixed motives, I have no doubt that the author's description of the dominant motive of most Salvationist missionaries is precisely accurate. But in working through the story of the Salvation Army in Punjab, watching coal miners being turned into prison guards, the most obvious lesson to be learned is how easily well-intentioned men and women can be seduced by the lure of imperial power in its bluntest form. The Salvationist leaders appeared to be particularly blind to the dangers of zealous cooperation with the state, and acted as if the decades of thought on this subject, especially in the CMS, had never occurred.[82] But in the 1920s Salvationists in the Punjab found themselves condemned by their own standards, based on their own point of view, as they quietly wound up their criminal tribes work and re-emphasized their work with villagers who chose the Salvationist path freely and with enthusiasm.

ANOTHER GOSPEL

Having dealt with the more visible and colorful attempts to transgress the imperial fault line, it is important to keep in mind that other missionaries and Indian Christians worked quietly and privately to deal with imperial boundaries, often taking refuge from the frustrations and corruptions of routine institution-management in purely individual quests for spiritual purity and closeness to God. Evangelical moralists frequently warned of the dangers of identifying God's work with the work of institution-building, and this spiritual impulse found its own institutional setting in the annual Sialkot Conventions, which eventually drew up to twenty-five hundred Indian and European attenders each year to a week of attention to a deeper spiritual life, and joyous singing of both Ira B. Sankey's hymns and the Punjabi Psalms of Dr. I. B. Shahbaz. The Sialkot Convention had been founded in 1904 by John Hyde ("Praying Hyde") of the American Presbyterians, R. McCheyne Paterson of the Church of Scotland, and George Turner of the YMCA.[83] Although resembling the Anglican-dominated Keswick Convention of England, and sharing with it a holiness/neoperfectionist theology, the Sialkot convention was heavily influenced by the Chicago institutional milieu of Dwight L. Moody. Evangelical missionaries and Indian Christians alike wrote repeatedly of what they described as a time of "spiritual refreshment" in Sialkot.

Liberal Protestants like Miriam Young, equally frustrated by an inability to turn institutions into communities, found no comparable institutional refuge. Leaving mission institutions to embrace the world on religious grounds, they found themselves isolated and confused. After leaving the mission to teach in the Montessori School in Delhi, Young set up household with Miss Budden, and they adopted two Indian children. She continued to send defensive reports to Baptist Missionary Society officials in London, claiming: "Though there is nominally nothing Christian or religious about the school, I feel that the ideals it embodies are emphatically and pre-eminently Christian and that anyone helping in the school is doing a real piece of work for the Kingdom of Christ." Furthermore, "One of the chief attractions of this post is that in it I should be working with Indians to further, not my schemes but *theirs* and that where we do not work as equals it is *I* who should occupy the subordinate place."[84] A year later she complained that her teaching duties were so onerous that "I hardly ever have opportunities of presenting Christ to people," but she laid out a scheme of intensive prayer for Indians.[85] Although she found it satisfying to have relationships to Indians that being a missionary would make impossible, she lamented the lack of definite Christian work and the absence of the fellowship provided by a missionary society.[86] In 1931 she returned to London so that Miss Budden could take a course in the LSE, and she could lay plans for a scheme of child guidance work in

North India. By 1937, however, at the age of sixty, she wrote a letter of apology to the BMS, confessing to fifteen years of guilt over her resignation: "[T]he mistake was sheer sin and disobedience."[87]

Liberals who remained with mission institutions attempted to reinterpret their institutional work in the light of the social gospel.[88] Liberals and evangelicals continued to work side by side building Christian institutions. For liberals, the old methods were given a new significance. The building of Christian institutions ceased to be one of the methods that would lead to the Christianization of India, and became instead a substitute for proselytization. The good done through Christian institutions became the end rather than the means of God's work in India. Despite liberal objections to proselytizing, liberal Protestant mission theory remained strongly rooted in the assumptions of nineteenth-century evangelical institution-building, the gospel of bricks and mortar. Traditional mission activities were seen in a new light.

One example of this was the American Presbyterian literacy campaign carried out from their school at Moga, which received good-faith support from missionaries and Indian Christians of widely varying theological opinions. Another was the attempt of liberal United Presbyterian missionary J. C. Heinrich to transform the UP settlement at Martinpur into a "rural village uplift center." In 1934 he wrote to the UP Foreign Mission Board proposing a rural uplift scheme in accord with the liberal theology of missions as a partnership in helping the foreign church instead of converting foreign heathens. Although suspicious of liberal theology, the mission board was also suspicious of missionary paternalism and respected Heinrich because of his outspoken advocacy of greater autonomy for the Indian church.

The division between evangelicals and liberals looms large in the history of twentieth-century Protestantism, and it was important in the Punjab mission. But the primacy of bricks and mortar over theology was evident in the United Presbyterian response to Heinrich's plans for village uplift at Martinpur. W. B. Anderson explained to Heinrich that in his opinion modernists in the missionary movement represent "another gospel," but that there is no time to quarrel with them.[89] Heinrich's social gospel included familiar community-building activities: new wells, the promotion of latrines, a competition for success in removing manure piles from the streets, a village wrestling tournament, the "Heinrich Challenge Cup" for the cleanest village, and a Boy Scout religious education class. To make these activities sound modern and scientific, Heinrich promoted his methods in the light of Adlerian social psychology, an alternative to conversion as a means of promoting "self-esteem" among village untouchables. He detected abnormal behavior among village Chuhras, including the "sheer joy of minimizing and undervaluing others," which resulted in an unwillingness to pay decent salaries to Indian Christian pastors. This "hysterical indirect reaction," based on "repressed rage and anger" shaped between the age of two and six, required scientific treatment and a change in mission policy.[90] Heinrich summarized his insights about untouchability and development as follows: the "abnormal love of authority and power manifest in depressed class groups particularly in the older leaders of the village is a large factor in restraining the initiative of younger and progressive groups."[91]

Here we have the authoritarian and manipulative rhetoric of objective social science used to justify the work of an authoritarian and manipulative American missionary, creating an impenetrable orientalist stew of defamatory half-truths about untouchable "character" all designed to justify Heinrich's utterly conventional scheme of settlement management. The goal of offering hope to people was of course unexceptional and worthwhile; there is no reason to believe that untouchable Christian boys received anything but good from winning the 1933 Punjab Scout jamboree boxing trophy. It might even have produced, as Heinrich hoped, a "more hopeful outlook on life."[92] But the stigmatization of an entire class as wounded, deficient, abnormal, and neurotic provides a clear picture of manipulative "love of power and authority" clothed in the language of scientific objectivity.

Liberals like Heinrich, Miriam Young, and C. F. Andrews shared an anxiety about the marginal status of the missionary movement and a desire to embrace India by bringing Christianity into the "mainstream" of Indian life.[93] Unable to take advantage of the consolations of the Sialkot Convention, Heinrich sought instead the prestige of academic affiliation, and petitioned Forman Christian College to request permission for him to be named to the Forman College staff as "an honorary member for development of extension work" with special expertise on hybrid varieties of wheat seed.[94] After returning from a 1936 tour of America delivering lectures on "Social Engineering in Indian Villages,"[95] Heinrich launched an even more ambitious scheme in cooperation with the government and with Sikh landowners near Martinpur, opening a grandiosely titled Center for Rural Reconstruction to promote what he called "The Gospel of Good Seed."[96] With the assistance of a bagpipe band, "The Pride of Martinpur," he persuaded enough Christian cultivators to adopt his rust-resistant wheat seed to add, he claimed, Rs 500,000 to the value of the 1939 wheat crop in

Christian villages. Pointing out that the amount was one and a half times the total field budget of the United Presbyterian mission boards in Punjab, he proclaimed his seed project an evangelistic success: "The amount of gospel preaching that would come out of this as a by-product would I am sure be more than we are getting done now."[97]

This was the social gospel at work in Punjab. Heinrich attempted to embrace India and was full of praise for Gandhi, but his desire for mainstream status had driven him directly into the arms of the colonial government. He found the mainstream in rural development work, and became an interpreter of the untouchable mind to the general public in India and the United States. In the summer of 1934 he delivered lectures in Simla on the "Psychology of Untouchability" to missionaries, government officials, and American Christians. His pamphlet on the depressed classes was reprinted by the government of Punjab and circulated in the departments of education, health, cooperative societies, police, irrigation, and rural reconstruction.[98]

Other liberals succeeded in gaining the academic affiliation that Heinrich craved, and gradually transformed the old anti-Muslim apologetics into the study of comparative religions. BMS missionary Lewis Bevan Jones, known as expert on Islam, arrived in Lahore in 1930 as head of the new Henry Martyn School of Islamics, a scheme promoted by William Paton of the National Christian Council of India. Indian Christians showed little enthusiasm for this new academic innovation. Every single Indian member of the CMS Church and Mission Central Council resigned in protest when the CMS offered one of the bungalows at St. John's College to the staff of the Henry Martyn School. The mission prevailed, however, and Jones wrote several books in the 1930s in which he extended to Islam the fulfillment theology approach that had been popularized by J. N. Farquhar's book on Hinduism.[99] In 1940 Jones was joined in Lahore by a Canadian Islamic scholar, Wilfred Cantwell Smith, who had already written a monograph on Islam in India that had been rejected as a thesis at Cambridge because of "its sharp Marxist critique of the British Indian imperium."[100]

CHRIST IN THE INDIAN NATIONAL CONGRESS

The best known liberal Christian to emerge from a Punjab mission was the Rev. C. F. Andrews, whose praise for Gandhi and desire to see Christianity in the mainstream led him on a unique spiritual and political journey. Andrews joined the Cambridge Mission to Delhi in

1904. The Westcottian ideal of a synthesis of East and West had never been entirely lost among the Cambridge Brothers, but the ideal had been deferred if not entirely submerged in the practical business of building mission institutions in Delhi. The Cambridge Brothers naturally adopted the role of the higher Anglican clergy at home, chaplains to wealthy and influential people. That the wealthy and influential people in Delhi were not Christians did not, in some respects, matter, and especially through St. Stephen's College the Cambridge Mission acted as chaplains to and teachers of the children of influential Indians.

Initially the most enthusiastic of all the missions about Indian participation, the Cambridge Mission had by 1900 become the most reluctant to extend positions of leadership to Indian Christians. The Indian Christian church was from their point of view a marginal institution in India, and the Cambridge Brothers had a passion for influence at the centers of power. The best way to exert Christian influence was to exert it among the elites, and since Indian Christians were not among the elite, the Indian church was duly neglected or ignored (and their daughters later excluded from Queen Mary's School). Andrews reacted sharply against this practical conservatism and became close friends with S. K. Rudra, whose appointment as head of St. Stephen's College was opposed by influential members of the mission.

Andrews shared with his conservative colleagues, however, a sense of Christian expansion as geo-religious triumphalism. God was at work throughout Asia, they believed, and God worked through important people at the center, not in remote villages where despised untouchables huddled together for Christian worship in mud huts, or outdoors. The Cambridge Brothers were always on the lookout for the "signs of the times," evidence that God was at work in the politics and diplomacy of Asia. Shortly after arriving in India, Andrews was involved in a controversy with Henry Whitehead, bishop of Madras, who advocated reorienting the church's work away from education and toward the untouchables. While welcoming untouchables, Andrews claimed that far more important was "the welcome given by the Mikado and the great statesmen of Japan to the Christian delegates at the Tokio Conference" which has "had a great effect upon the educated classes, and taught them that Christianity may become a national religion in the East as well as in the West."[101]

It was less the Mikado than the Indian national movement that drew Andrews's theological attention, and after attending the 1908 Indian national congress meeting he began to discern in the national movement the work of God, the "seed of Christian ideas beginning to spring forth from the soil." "It is easy," he argued, "to take a superficial view and call the whole movement secular. Yet I cannot see how this can be maintained by anyone who holds intelligently the faith of the Incarnation, and who believes that Jesus is the Son of Man. If the Christian nations are faithful to high principles, and the Christian messengers make clear their message, then it may come to pass that, amid the shaking of the nations of the East, we shall see the Son of Man coming in His glory, and, before this generation pass away shall welcome 'one of the days of the Son of Man.' "[102]

The decision to build a new capital in Delhi caused Andrews great excitement, and he began to spin out grandiose schemes for an aggressive Christian architectural presence at the center of imperial power.[103] Yet the more Andrews became involved in the national movement, and in particular after the failure of his brotherhood experiment with Samuel Stokes and Sundar Singh, the more frustrated he became with a missionary movement that appeared to be left behind by history. Discerning the signs of the times, he concluded that they pointed away from the Cambridge Mission to Delhi. The educated classes were only now abandoning Hinduism and Islam for science and nationalism, he argued, but Christianity had yet to be presented to them in a truly national guise. By early 1914 he wrote to Tagore: "I know and recognize now how insolent and vain I was when I first came to India ten years ago, coming to teach instead of to learn and writing and speaking at first in the evil patronizing way."[104] Early that same year he traveled to South Africa to participate in Gandhi's campaign of civil disobedience among the Indians of Natal, where he discovered in Gandhi the fullest expression of the Christian ideal for India.

Andrews preached a farewell sermon to a crowded congregation of Anglican friends in Lahore Cathedral in early May 1914, giving an account of his reasons for leaving the Cambridge Mission to enter Tagore's retreat at Santineketan:

> In South Africa I found Christ's presence more wonderfully near to me in all its beauty (moving me to adoring worship) among the patient, gentle Hindu ladies, just released from prison, speaking kindly to their gaolers, than in the churches of the wealthy in that land where doors were practically closed to coloured people. . . . And the question came upon me with a sad, a terrible insistence, as I travelled across many seas, past many shores, whether the modern, aggressive wealthy nations of the world, armed to the teeth against each other, trafficking in the souls of men for gain, can be for long the dwelling place of the meek and lowly Christ, whether the hour may not be near, when he will say unto them, as he said unto Bethsaida and Chorazin of old,

"Woe unto you," and will turn instead to the poor and downtrodden people of the earth, and say unto them, "Come Unto Me." For in his Kingdom there are many that are last that shall be first and first that shall be last.[105]

In his subsequent life in India, as publicist for both Tagore and Gandhi, Andrews never abandoned his own sense of vocation as a missionary, as someone doing Christ's work in India. Like Miriam Young, he never found an institutional context for that work, other than the national movement itself. In the late 1920s he wrote that the missionary movement "appeared to me to be out of keeping with the character of Christ Himself and be unworthy of His name."[106] But in the 1930s his disagreements with Gandhi over conversion provided an opportunity to outline an explicit vision of a legitimate missionary role in India, one that was entirely consistent with his pre-1914 arguments.[107] Andrews drew a sharp line between bearing public witness to one's faith on the one hand and direct persuasion, or proselytism, on the other. He believed that Christians should bear witness to their faith through service to others, and look for opportunities to explain the Christian motivation for that service while engaging in respectful dialogue with men and women of other faiths. Like Stokes and Sundar Singh, he had a vision of Christ, but discerned the presence of Christ already in India: "There is an experience which has happened to me so frequently in India that I have no longer come to look upon it as strange or unusual. It is this. Continually, when I come into new surroundings and meet new faces, the consciousness of the presence of Christ among those I meet is borne in upon me. If one may dare to express what happens in words, it is as if I saw Christ in their faces and knew that He was present. They reveal Christ to me. This is, I am aware, mystical language, but I can express the reality in no other adequate manner."[108] In his own distinctive way, Andrews believed that in embracing India he was embracing Christ.

9

Christianity and the National Movement

In the 1920s and early 1930s the missionary movement reached the peak of its influence in Northwest India. In 1871 there had been roughly eighty foreign agents in Punjab and Kashmir; in 1931 there were well over six hundred in Delhi, Punjab, the Northwest Frontier Provinces, and Kashmir (see Tables 2 and 9). In cooperation with large numbers of Indians, not all of them Christian, they presided over six colleges, at least twenty-two high schools, twenty-eight hospitals, and Indian churches with more than 300,000 members or affiliates.[1] A count of Indian agents associated with the missions in 1935 found 2,565 people, including 278 ordained clergymen, 59 doctors, and 396 nurses (see Table 11).

In some ways the influence of the missions was waning. They no longer dominated higher education to the extent that they had in the 1870s, and had long ago ceded to the government responsibility for the general education of the region. Furthermore, they faced vigorous competition almost everywhere from Arya Samaj, Khalsa, and Islamia schools. The influential Anjuman-i-Himayat-i-Islam of Lahore expanded into girls' secondary education in 1925, and opened the Islamia College for Women in Lahore in 1939.[2] Competition was in some respects a measure of missionary influence if not of their success. The missions had succeeded in establishing an important educational role at both the top and the bottom of the established social hierarchy. St. Stephen's College and Forman College were rivaled in prestige only by the Government College in Lahore; Kinnaird College for Women was the pioneer college for women in the province; the medical college for women in Ludhiana was a pioneer in training women for medical careers.

The missions also played a central role in the education of Punjab's untouchable children. The Punjab government claimed a larger enrollment than the missions of students of untouchable background, who had been the target of recruitment campaigns by government schools beginning in 1923, but their own statistics for the 1930s show

TABLE 11
Indian Agency, Punjab and All India, 1935

	Punjab & Delhi	Northwest Frontier Provinces	Kashmir	Total	All India
Ordained men	266	7	5	278	2,403
Unordained men	281	3	14	298	9,784
Women (church)	309	1	5	315	5,030
Male teachers	1,204	84	21	1,309	21,992
Women teachers	349	13	3	365	7,454
TOTAL	2,409	108	48	2,565	46,663
Doctors	49	4	6	59	310
Nurses	350	29	17	396	2,997

SOURCE: *Directory of Christian Missions and Churches in India, Burma and Ceylon* (Nagpur: National Christian Council, 1938), 22–25.

rapidly falling enrollments in government schools.[3] While the growth of Christian membership perhaps falls short of J. S. Grewal's "spectacular success,"[4] since Christians never constituted more than 2 percent of the total population of Punjab, the community had grown from roughly 4,000 in 1881 to more than 300,000 in 1921. Conversions continued in the 1920s, with 22 percent growth in the Protestant community in Punjab.[5] However the numbers are arranged, by the 1920s the Christian community in northwest India, despite their small numbers, had important and influential social locations in higher education and medicine, and were playing an important role in the redefinition of untouchability.

The early 1930s represented the high point of both institutional advancement and membership growth. The British missions began facing retrenchment in the post–World War I economic slump,[6] and in the longer term from the institutional and membership declines of the British Protestant churches, which could no longer raise the money to sustain their early-twentieth-century missionary effort.[7] After 1929 financial support for the American missions declined because of the Great Depression, which caused further waves of retrenchment in the British missions as well.[8] For the first time in the 1930s, the number of foreign missionaries began to fall (by nearly 15 percent, from 622 in 1931 to 523 in 1938), despite the "reinforcements" received from Australian and Canadian Anglicans, New Zealand Presbyterians, the American Associate Reformed Synod, the Danish Pathan Mission, and the Seventh Day Adventists. Membership growth leveled off as well, as the "mass movements" of the 1920s proved to be the last large-scale infusion of membership into the churches of Punjab. The Christian percentage of the population remained more or less stable for the rest of the twentieth century.[9]

In some ways this is a success story. The missionaries did what they intended to do—that is, build institutions that would serve the Indian Christian church and provide a broader Christian influence in Indian society. The number of converts remained relatively small, but missionaries and the urban Christian middle class were unable to provide adequate parochial care even for the numbers on hand, and they had no way of knowing in the early 1930s that there would be little further membership growth. In two important ways, however, the missionary enterprise had been a failure by its own standards. The first was the failure of its elite institutions, however prestigious, to shape the course of Indian history in a Christian direction. The second was the obvious lack of progress in the 1930s toward the missionary ideal of a self-governing, self-supporting, and self-extending Indian church.

The pioneer missionaries had intended to align Christianity with the mainstream of Indian history. Elitists from established or dominant denominations, they saw their role as directing the entire Indian nation in a Christian direction. Especially after the waves of nationalist agitation in 1905–7 and 1919–21, missionaries and Indian Christians attempted to come to terms with a national movement that regarded Christianity as irrelevant at best and an offensive imperial intrusion at worst. Nationalist tensions were particularly demoralizing to the Cambridge Brothers in Delhi, whose commitment to an elitist strategy of Christianizing educated Indians was undercut by the attractions of nationalism, brought home to them by nationalist agitation among students in Christian colleges. In a 1909 sermon the Rev. C. F. Andrews lamented the rejection of Christianity by the educated:

> We see that in India today a strange and terrible thing has happened, a change has taken place. Christ the great giver of emancipation, Christ, who has revealed the light of progress to India, is being rejected by educated Indians today in this the hour of their awakening. Instead of India becoming the brightest jewel in the Crown of Christ, India, in her educated classes, is standing gloomily aloof, resisting His appeal. Educated India, which in Keshub's times was hovering on the brink of Christian decision, almost ready to acknowledge the new light which had come to her through Christ, has now shrunk back from Him. He is more and more regarded by them as a foreigner, as One alien to their nation, as One who will ruin her country's ideals, as One who comes not to fulfil but to destroy, as One who comes not to give life but to bring death.[10]

In despair over the missionary movement, Andrews eventually embraced the national movement as the work of Christ. Even his colleagues who remained behind in the Cambridge Mission to Delhi became demoralized, however; in 1931 the Rev. Hugh King wrote privately: "The Brotherhood . . . has served its purpose and can sing its *Nunc Dimittis.*"[11]

Rank and file missionary and Indian Christian attitudes toward the national movement (which have been examined by scholars in detail) can be placed on a spectrum ranging from outright support through suspicious anxiety to reactionary opposition.[12] Any investigation of whether the missionary movement contributed to or resisted the national movement, with its implied binary moral judgment of "nationalism for or against," misses an essential point: the major goal of missionaries was to maintain their institutional position in India through whatever political upheavals and revolutions of empire might come their way. Missionaries who took a definite political position one way or another might find themselves isolated. The Reverend H. J. Hoare was eased out of the CMS in 1914, after serving for nearly a quarter of a century, in part because his antinationalist attitude made him too conservative for the "spirit of the age." His reactionary political attitudes were linked to his opposition to the promotion of Indian Christians to positions of authority.[13]

WAR AND ITS AFTERMATH

The jingoist wing of the CMS got its revenge in 1919 with the dismissal of the Rev. A. D. Dixey, whose employment file was filled with complaints from other missionaries and government officials. He objected to singing "God Save the King" in Church during the war, and claimed that the English were no better than the Germans. Furthermore, his "Christian socialist views encourage a challenge to authority," and his pronationalist views led a local government official to claim that "his influence with Indians is purely mischievous."[14] As in the case of Hoare, Dixey's general political views were tied up with attitudes toward Indian Christians. The Rev. Ihsan Ullah wrote that "Indian Christians love him and he loves them. . . . [He] is one of the very best missionaries," and Dixey himself claimed that "my only conflict is with older colleagues who do not want to see Indians take their rightful place."[15]

In the Punjab political disturbances after 1907, and the political violence of 1919 in Amritsar, Indian Christians were not targeted as they had been in 1857. The Indian Christian community had developed sufficient public identity to allow them to be distinguished in some respects from missionaries. Mission institutions, however, were attacked in Amritsar, and it is reasonable to assume that an unusual concentration of prowar activity by CMS missionaries in Amritsar contributed to the identification of mission institutions as foreign institutions.

CMS missionaries were not alone in being caught up in a war frenzy. Several hundred thousand Indians (including the eighty-five thousand dead commemorated by New Delhi's India Gate) fought in a war whose goals included the redrawing once again of the boundaries of Alsace-Lorraine, the plundering of the Turkish Empire by the British Empire, and the suppression of "disturbances" in the North West Frontier Province. The surge of ultrapatriotic sentiment in the CMS during the war put on display the blindness of a particular group of missionaries to their own political vulnerability in India. CMS institutions in Amritsar became targets of violence after the unusually brutal Jallianwallah Bagh massacre of 1919, in part because CMS missionaries had during the war abandoned any attempt to distinguish mission and government, and embraced the wartime effort with characteristic Anglican vigor. The secretary of the Punjab Mission, C. M. Gough, essentially offered the services of the mission as military recruiters.[16] In 1916 the CMS Parent Committee refused to allow missionaries to act as military recruiters, but by 1918 the CMS Punjab mission had virtually made themselves into a recruiting arm of the military.[17] Dr. A. Neve went off with a specially recruited Punjabi Christian Regiment to fight in Mesopotamia along with the other missionary doctor in Srinigar, Dr. James Freer Richardson.[18]

No doubt the abandonment of any sense of vigilance about the distinction between government and mission was justified by reference to the magic word "war," which sanctions all sorts of behavior that would otherwise be regarded as criminal or depraved as well as merely unwise. Gough failed to make any connections between his wartime behavior and postwar politics as he reported to the CMS in 1919, in the wake of the rioting associated with the General Dyer's Jallianwallah Bagh massacre; "The CMS church in Amritsar is only bare walls. Everything inside is destroyed including the register from the beginning of the mission. Also destroyed apparently, or at least damaged, were the boys high school and the girls middle schools."[19] Missionaries were all safe, he reported, "except Miss Sherwood of CEZMS, badly attacked on bicycle and injured, rescued by some leading Hindus. Miss Cresswell was fetched from Tarn Taran in a motor car dispatched by District Commissioner of Amritsar. I (Gough) went to fetch ladies at Asrapur and Clarkabad in an armored car with machine guns."[20]

It was the attack on Miss Sherwood that led to the notorious punishment of alleged perpetrators, who were forced to lick blood on the site (the good efforts of "leading Hindus" doing little to assuage the British military's thirst for sadistic revenge).[21] It was obvious to missionaries that political agitation was reaching into parts of Punjab that had been largely untouched, at least from their point of view. In the Sikh stronghold of Tarn Taran near Amritsar, the CMS missionary claimed that only town people are hostile, while the "outlook in the villages is most promising, and people are as friendly as ever," but the CMS Tarn Taran mission report for 1921 noted that agitation among the Sikhs was "most painful."[22]

From the relatively remote Baptist mission in Bhiwani, Dr. Ellen Farrer commented on the wave of political agitation of 1919–22 as if it were some mysterious change in the weather. In early January of 1919 she reported new village baptisms regularly, but after rioting began around Punjab in April they ended. The next spring there was a strike in Bhiwani over peace terms for Turkey, and their dispensary in Hansi was vandalized. In October 1920 there was a huge Congress Mela in Bhiwani with the Ali brothers and Gandhi: "Such crowds we had never seen in Bhiwani before . . . but nothing worse happened to us than that some of the crowd seemed more disposed to stare at us than salaam us. Probably some of the village folk had hardly ever seen an English woman before."[23] In February of 1921 she reported a strike over the Duke of Connaught's visit to Delhi, and in 1922 "Misses Slater and Theobold with the 2 evangelists were mobbed in the city when looking at a house in which to open a chamar school. Had to give up the idea for the present. Political feelings are strong."[24]

That was her last reference to political interference with her mission work, which then proceeded in Bhiwani as if nothing had happened. Church of Scotland missionaries reported that by 1923 political hostility had receded.[25] In contrast to 1857, no missionaries had been killed and there were no attacks on Indian Christians. The hard hit CMS discussed closing its Amritsar girls' school and concentrating on friendlier small towns, but decided to rebuild everything, conceding only the wisdom of putting the new girls' middle schools in a "less public position."[26] Missionary political analysis of the situation remained naive or ambivalent; a CMS report on the 1919 riots characteristically declared the emergency powers under the Rowlatt "justified but misunderstood" and nationalist agitation "well meaning but misguided."[27]

Some missionaries responded to the imperial fault line by taking refuge in prayer. Miss Helen Maud Scott served the Christian Girls Boarding Schools at Amritsar. "Her own contribution was not so much in the classroom as in the individual mothering of the girls. It was the firm belief of those who passed with her through the terrible experience of April 1919, when only a frail wooden door hid her and them from a maddened mob, that they owed their rescue entirely to her prayer; and that incident was never forgotten, so that servants, children and staff turned to her as one whose prayers would certainly be heard." After the amalgamation of the two schools, she took charge of the McKenzie hostel "and there exercised a deep and pervasive influence, the secret of which was her own childlike spirit . . . and her own constant living in the nearness of God's presence."[28]

Prayer and nurturing are not often seen as a response to politics, but they belong among the array of responses by Europeans in Amritsar alongside the soldiers forcing Indians to lick blood off the street, and the Rev. C. M. Gough rescuing the ladies of Clarkabad and Asrapur in an armored car. Furthermore, many missionaries recognized the need to do more than take refuge in prayer, or simply redouble their efforts to extend the Gospel with bricks, mortar, and medical clinics. In Tarn Taran, forty to fifty Indian Christian men gathered after Sunday service to decide what response should be made to the Sikh political agitation. The mission reported: "We are still trying to organize the work in this district on proper and permanent lines, and as far as possible we strive to eschew all western ideas."[29] The efforts to elude the imperial trap by establishing a self-governing Indian church had failed, but the effort to create an indigenous Indian Christianity could never be abandoned, and required new ideas and new initiatives in the twentieth century.

Like missionaries, Indian Christians were forced to come to terms with resurgent nationalism; like missionaries, their main concern was in defining their own community and its institutions in relationship to the dominant culture. Discussion of their relationship to British and Indian culture had been going on for decades among Indian Christians, leaving them with a sense of vulnerability and marginality that was reinforced by their preference for western dress and in some cases western names. "Who of us," asked Mr. Chandu Lal at an early meeting of the CMS Native Church Council, "has not many a time heard ignorant and semi-civilized friends taunt us often respecting our baptism;

and ask us what promotion of rank and pay we have received by adopting the religion of the *sahib log*?"[30] A quarter of a century later a Christian student at St. Stephen's College, Satish C. Chatterji, was asking similar questions, lamenting the denationalization of Indian Christians caused by their own preference for western hymn tunes and western methods of administration. Strong family ties within a socially heterogeneous community, he argued, meant that Christians often had difficulty socializing with other Christians. Social relations with missionaries had always been awkward, and there was a "practical absence of all social relations between Indian Christians and non-Christians."[31] Nationalism merely added a new and urgent dimension to the problem, for Indian Christians were now separated from the national movement.

These problems afflicted urban middle-class Christians, whose problems were very remote from the majority of Punjabi Christians in the villages. The outward and visible signs of this imperial identity problem would become much less important later in the twentieth century, as the Hindu and Muslim urban middle classes adopted western ways with little anxiety about losing their Indian identity. In some ways Congress Party nationalist politicians were as "denationalized" as urban middle-class Christians. The heart of the matter, though, was religion. How does one define a Christian in India? This problem centered on the emergence of an indigenous, self-governing Indian church. Just as racial language appeared in debates about the relationship between missionaries and Indian Christians in the 1880s and 1890s, so did the language of Indian nationalism appear after the turn of the century. In the ongoing struggle over resources and control in mission institutions, Indian Christians conducted their own internal nationalist struggle with the sanction of the principles of Henry Venn.[32]

Both sides in this struggle faced insoluble problems. Missionaries committed to an indigenous church and to the building of religious institutions found the two incompatible. Indian Christians lobbied for increased spending on the Indian Christian community and found themselves saddled with institutions that they could not sustain. When the Church of Scotland Foreign Mission Committee complained about the scale of the plans for new building in Daska put forward by the Rev. A. Nicholson, he responded by arguing that the mission, even in a time of general retrenchment, can no longer neglect the housing needs of mission employees when constructing new buildings: "Nowadays Indians notice these things and point at the Mission House and then at the Servants Houses; I do not mean to suggest any blame; it is just that times are changed." Also at issue was expenditure for a motor godown, additional kitchen, and verandah. The need to maintain a fleet of automobiles added considerably to the cost of the mission, improving their ability to move around from one institutional compound to another. The enormous Daska compound, completed in 1931, included the solid physical presence of a divinity school, a school, a mission house, a ladies' house, a servants' house, a main boarding house, a Christian hostel, a pastor's house, a headmaster's house, a kitchen, a Hindu kitchen, and a church, all built around fields, and all eventually bequeathed complete with maintenance costs to the poverty-stricken independent church in Pakistan.[33]

The Scottish mission was responding to comments such as those of S. C. Lall of the CMS: "We never read in the scripture that the Disciples of Christ lived in a big bungalow as bara sahibs and were waited on by servants."[34] The glacial pace of Indianization, and the heated rhetoric that surrounds the struggle of Indian Christians to battle their way into middle management, obscure the fact that mission institutions were gradually being turned over to Indians out of both political and economic necessity. UP missionary J. G. Campbell commented in 1943: "Ours is a very conservative group when it comes to transferring responsibility to Indians ... the Scotch having Indian missionaries who sit in mission meetings and live in mission bungalows." He conceded the inevitability of Indian control, for "with nationalism coming on ... with us it looks like a foreign show."[35] When the United Presbyterians finally granted the status of "district missionary" to an Indian—that is, assigned Indian pastors the supervisory functions of foreign missionaries—they were the last of the Punjab missions to take that step.[36]

The shape of an Indian church for the people of India was becoming clear in these negotiations. The urban Christian middle class would have extensive institutional responsibility for managing former mission institutions and the top levels of the church; the base of the church would consist of village Christians recruited from stigmatized communities. There was inevitably a large gulf between the two. Middle-class Christians occasionally "discovered" the true nature of the church, to their dismay, and like their missionary predecessors mulled over schemes to raise the social status of rural Christians. After a meeting of the Punjab Christian Council in 1938 devoted to the condition of village Christians, B. L. Rallia Ram, secretary of the Lahore YMCA, commented: "This fact has come home with a tremendous force. Twenty years ago if there had been the same realization as we have today many of us would have preferred to devote our lives to the work in the villages."[37]

CANAL COLONIES

Rural Christians were also affected by politics, but not in a straight-forward or predictable way. By the mid-1930s, the waves of untouch-able conversion to Christianity had come to an end in Punjab, and the reasons for that end have remained something of a puzzle in mission literature. One reason appears to be the heavy pastoral emphasis of the missions and Indian Christian clergy in the 1920s and 1930s, as they faced even further dispersal of an already scattered rural Christian community. Disruption was exacerbated by the opening of new canal settlements in western Punjab, and by intensified denominational competition, especially from the Salvation Army and the Roman Catholic Church.

Treated by imperial apologists as a triumph of colonial economic development, the canal enterprise was extraordinarily conservative both socially and politically.[38] The government was determined to rep-licate the existing rural social structure in the new colonies, and fur-ther the interests of the (mainly Jat, in their view) landowners in their battle against the alleged evils of "Hindu moneylenders." By the Land Alienation of 1901, the government of Punjab limited land ownership to fourteen tribes or castes. Designed to prevent the transfer of land to Hindu moneylenders, it had the effect of excluding Chuhras and most Christians from land ownership (although some became tenants of Jat landholders).[39] Chuhra, Christian, and Musali "village menials" being essential to the agricultural enterprise, they naturally migrated with the landholders. In the areas where almost all Chuhras had become Christians, there was a large-scale exodus of Christians to the west. In the 1931 census the number of Christians in Montgomery district was twice as large as the number of "Hindu Chuhras," and more than three times as large in Lyallpur District (see Table 7). In sections of the new canal colonies, "village menial" meant "Christian."

The CMS and UP struggled to divide up the new settlements, but faced competition everywhere from the Salvation Army. In 1900 the CMS was responsible for the ecclesiastical supervision of more than 750 villages in a fifteen-hundred-square-mile tract in the Jhang Bar where nearly half of the Christians they had "found" were from the neighborhood of Narowal. At least one hundred villages had Christians with no minister to marry them, and no place of Christian assembly except the open air.[40] Emigration continued throughout the early twentieth century as Christians spilled over into the "frontier" areas worked with such intensity and such failure by the CMS in the mid-nineteenth century. A CMS missionary in 1925 reported two thousand Christians in the Multan Bar, mostly illiterate, with "Rev. Buta Singh doing what he can with three workers." Mrs. Elwin "found a good number of Christians" working for the municipality in Dehra Ishmael Khan and "is looking after them," and forty "Punjabi village types" in Peshawar looking for work were baptized.[41] In 1929 the CMS requested an assistant bishop for the mass movement areas with episcopal oversight of 880 Christian congregations, and a year later complained that since 1918 the CMS had sent no one for village evangelism.[42]

Committed to parochial care, they neglected recruitment. As the overall Christian percentage of the population leveled off, denominational competition intensified among those already Christian. Many Punjabi Christians had a weak sense of denominational loyalty. One new denomination, the Associate Reformed Synod from the American South, worked closely with the United Presbyterians to divide up the new mission fields, but both Roman Catholics and the Salvation Army ignored the comity agreements and recruited Christians from other denominations. Roman Catholics were the institution-builders par excellence of the mission field, making even the Protestant commitment to bricks and mortar pale by comparison. After the creation of a new diocese of Rawalpindi in 1887, they opened convent schools and, in 1898, bought land in the new canal colony for a Christian agricultural settlement.[43]

The Protestant missions were furious at the Catholic intrusion, and regarded their Flemish-speaking missionaries, not as allies but as competitors in the same category as the Hindu Arya Samaj. The Roman Catholic church at this time did not regard Protestants as Christians, giving them a license not only to convert Protestants but also to annul Protestant marriages. In 1900 the United Presbyterians objected to any further government grants of land to the Roman Catholics on the grounds that they use the land to proselytize Protestant converts.[44] They were correct, but all of the missions were in a bidding war to maintain their position in the Christian community. The overwhelmingly foreign nature of the Roman Catholic presence (the first indigenous priest was ordained in 1945) demonstrates the irrelevance of most Protestant attempts at "indigenization." Village Christians of Punjab had no objections whatsoever to making use of institutions run by foreigners if it suited their purposes, and had little interest (at least initially) in the incompatible denominational claims on the label "Christian."

One element in the bidding war was the purchase by the missions of canal colonies to settle Christian cultivators. Although very few Christian settlers actually lived in the colonies (a few thousand at any one time), they are important for two reasons. Small in numbers, the Christian colonists were large in symbolism, for they provided visible evidence that the missions could act on behalf of their despised and dispossessed adherents. At the same time, they demonstrated the limits placed on the missions' ability to expand by their commitment to institution building. The first missions' attempts to settle Christians on land were the CMS Clarkabad settlement, and the Church of Scotland's Hunterpore (or Hunterpur) settlement at Sialkot. Robert Clark hoped that Clarkabad, founded in 1875, would be owned by Christian investors who would act as both patrons and landlords for Christian cultivators. Both settlements ran into serious difficulties because of a lack of Christian cultivators. At Hunterpur the first settlers were non-Christian Meghs. Clarkabad also granted land to non-Christians, who farmed around Christian institutions, in a characteristic attempt to bring non-Christians into a Christian sphere of influence. By 1887 the cultivators were two-thirds non-Christian, and Clarkabad provided insoluble administrative headaches for the CMS for decades.[45]

In the 1890s the missions began negotiating with the government to secure tracts of land for Christian settlers in the new canal districts of western Punjab. Although Christians were moving to these districts to work for migrating landowners, the government had no interest at all in providing land for Christians, and the Christian settlements had to be negotiated on an ad hoc basis between individual missions and government officials.[46] There was consequently a large amount of confusion over the terms of tenancy. Were the landholders to become tenants of the government, or landowners in their own right, or tenants of the mission? What was clear was the authority of the missions to choose the cultivators, which meant that the only way a village menial could become a landholder in the new canal regions was to become a Christian. The missions of course attempted to reward long-standing Christian families in the older mission areas,[47] but once Christians arrived in the canal colonies they encountered opportunities to play one mission off against another. In 1901 a CMS official complained that CMS tenants at Montgomerywala, faced with insecurity over their status, were "dallying with the Roman Catholics for money. We cannot use threat of eviction to keep them. Bateman is mourning over their ingratitude and covetousness."[48]

To be fair, the CMS wished their own tenants to become hereditary landholders while the government in this case wished to vest ownership in the CMS, but it is characteristic of the missions to put themselves in the position of landlord, then complain of ingratitude from their tenants, who were simply looking after their interests as tenants. The missions sponsored at least a dozen agricultural settlements (not counting those used for incarcerating "criminal tribes") with three kinds of land tenure: (1) land held by the cultivators in one form or another with the missions given various rights of representation, including in some instances "Lambardari" rights, which included the right to build a church, control the village square, and represent the village with the government; (2) land granted to the mission to act as landlords; and (3) land owned originally by the mission and used for the settlement of Christian cultivators.[49] Land conflict was most severe at the second type. There were rent strikes at Santokh Majra (AP) in 1903, and a lengthy rent strike at Clarkabad from 1904 to 1906 that led to four hundred defections to Islam followed by evictions.

The missions hoped that "the mere possession of land by Christians would work wonders in the character and result in wonderful advance,"[50] but the settlements were an enormous drain on resources, time, and energy. Even the highly efficient United Presbyterians found that their Martinpur settlement was described in 1934 as "the despair of the mission."[51] With title vested in cultivators rather than the mission, the local church suffered chronic internal conflict leading to a breakdown of the church session after the Indian pastors and headmaster had been forced out. If the missions had so little control over their settlements, they had even less over the dispersed groups of Christians in both old and new areas of Christian conversion and settlement. With missionaries concentrated in urban and centralized institutions, the missions redoubled their effort to supply Indian catechists and Bible Women for village Christians. As usual, the United Presbyterians were better prepared to train and supply catechists than the other denominations. Their Christian Training Institute at Sialkot was already in place with thirty-eight students in 1882, recruited from Chuhra converts and trained along with twenty-two wives and daughters who would serve as Bible Women.[52] The UP also saw the most success at insisting on "self-support" for their catechists and village pastors in the 1920s and 1930s. Partly out of sheer stubbornness, UP missionaries forced catechists and village pastors to make village Christians pay.

The provision of catechists and Bible Women raised all the old issues of dependency, missionary control, and self-support, for there can be little doubt that missionaries were formally in charge. At every level, however, there were negotiations based on levels of mutual respect and the vagaries of the labor market. Missionaries were just as dependent on catechists as catechists were dependent on missionaries. That the United Presbyterians persuaded impoverished village Christians to pay anything at all to support their catechists demonstrates the importance of these catechists to rural Christians. In the 1930s a UP village pastor near Pasrur summarized the complex negotiations that surrounded his attempt to raise his own salary:

Some Christians see that Roman Catholics do not pay any contribution and the marriage fee is also less, then they turn to Catholicism. . . . Some Christians marry their children at an early age and compel the pastor to marry them. If the pastor does a thing like that then he makes himself liable to criminal proceedings; if he does not hold the marriage ceremony then the congregation gets angry and he gets nothing as a contribution.

Some Christians keeping two wives do not want to be excommunicated. If the pastor takes action against them, then they make a group whose business becomes not to pay anything to the Church.

When some Christians are prosecuted for stealing or other crimes and are punished by Government, and if the pastor with all his efforts fails to save them, the whole burden falls on him and the contribution is stopped.

If the daughter or daughter-in-law of a Christian runs away and the pastor is unsuccessful in getting her back, then too the contribution is stopped.

Thus a hundred and one matters creep in which form the basis for not paying anything. As for instance, in Badumali there was a Christian servant of a zamindar. One day the marriage party of the daughter of the zamindar came to the B. Railway Station. The zamindar told his Christian servant it would be very nice if you get the Sahib's (missionary) motor lorry to convey the party to the house. The Christian went to Mr. Clements and asked for the conveyance. Mr. Clements in reply said that my lorry is not for hire nor am I servant to any zamindar and that he should arrange for the lorry elsewhere. The Christian of course could not do anything more but stopped his contribution to the pastor for three years. On enquiry by the pastor the reply was that you Sahib had not helped me so why should I pay anything.[53]

CELEBRITIES

Catechists, missionaries, even bishops were important to the rural Christian community. Missionaries wanted to be disciplinarians; they became instead celebrities. In communities of CMS and SPG Christians, elaborate ceremonies revolved around the very occasional episcopal visitations. When Henry Matthew, second bishop of Lahore, first visited Narowal, he was met at the River Ravi by a triumphal procession of Indian Christians with a beautifully worked banner bearing the Urdu text, "Neither as being lords over God's heritage but being ensamples to the flock," an inscription that Bateman had inscribed over the door in the vestry in the Narowal Church as an exhortation to clerical humility.[54] The heavy mission-studies emphasis on the emergence of indigenous Christianity throughout the world has obscured the extent to which missionaries were important in communities of converts, even if not important in precisely the way that missionaries preferred. Visits became festivals for village Christians, occasions (like Christmas) for a show of the visible signs of dignity that came with conversion. These festivals sprawled across the normally impermeable boundaries created by Orientalism and imperialism, and even across the boundaries of caste, class, and nationality within Punjabi Christianity.

At Asrapur the CMS sponsored a multireligious but Christian-sponsored community celebration, the Prem Sangat Mela, which began according to the bishop of Lahore as a result of "educated Indian Christian initiative." The bishop went on to warn that "I am conscious of the possible dangers of such gatherings as conceivably tending to give the idea that all faiths are equally true."[55] But with characteristic Anglican elitism he justified it to himself as something beyond "peasant ignorance." Clearly the middle-class Indian Christian was interested in portraying the Christian community as one on equal standing with other faiths. A CMS missionary looked on in envy at the 1913 mela as a catechist and his son began the festival at noon with an antiphonal sermon, answering each other in alternative verses, which "made me wish that I could preach in a way so obviously acceptable to the audience." At two o'clock it was announced that anyone might have twenty minutes to praise or sing his own faith, but must not speak against the faith of others. A Sikh spoke first, then the secretary of the Amritsar Temperance Association.[56] The presiding dignitary was often a Sikh, although in 1913 the president was a missionary, Mr.

Guilford, and people of all religions "welcomed a topi-wala who could speak to them in Punjabi."[57]

The roughly one thousand Christians in and around Asrapur, although unusually laden with Christian institutions, were not educated or middle class. The majority were Chuhra or Mazhabi Sikh converts. In the surrounding villages, Christian panchayats had been established, and each member given a silver medallion with the name of the village stamped on it. On the first Sunday of each month, all preachers, panchayat members, and as many men as could come, except for those baptized by the Methodists, gathered for Bible instruction.[58] Women participated freely with men. Miss K. M. Bose reported that "a Hindu woman sitting by me saw a low caste Christian girl and asked her to sit elsewhere. My answer: 'My dear friend she is one of the Prem Sangat; if you are not you had better get up and sit elsewhere yourself.' There was a laugh from the neighbors, and the Punjabi woman . . . joined in the laugh, and sat contentedly ever after." Husbands would never allow such mixing by women, she observed, "if it were not a religious assembly."[59]

There are multiple levels of complexity in this encounter, which includes a good example of the rhetoric of missionary egalitarianism. Miss Bose was an Indian, but as a Bengali working in Punjab, she was as much of a foreign missionary in her neighborhood as the Punjabi-speaking topi-wallah from England. The adoption of Christianity did little to erase caste divisions. The stigma of untouchability remained in the eyes of the majority of rural Punjabis, along with dependent labor relations. The Prem Sangat Mela did not even abolish the class divide between urban Christians and untouchable converts. But it does illustrate some of the ways in which mission staff, European and Indian, male and female, were important in rural Christian life, and contributed to the good name of the community.

Even in Asrapur, an area heavily worked by missionaries, Indian Christian clergy grumbled that the rigidity of ecclesiastical and clerical institutionalism was a barrier to expansion. The Rev. Wadhawa Mall of Asrapur complained that the CMS Pastorate Committee rules "bind us as with ropes. Non-Christian villagers have a Mullah or Granthi. If only we could appoint a help to give teaching in spare time, a Lambardar of the village or member of the Panchayat, or some other true and faith Christian who would be content with rs 2–5 a month, some less." The Asrapur Church built by Mr. Perkins, he added, can only hold 130 on the floor.[60]

In the new canal colonies, institutional connections were even more intermittent. In their search for dispersed Christians in the Jhang Bar canal area, the Rev. Ihsan Ullah and the Rev. Warris-ud-din used large-scale assemblies with antiphonal singing of hymns, sometimes gathering thousands of Christians and almost everywhere finding a few hundred. Bishop Lefroy toured the area in 1905 with a new traveling set of communion vessels, administering Holy Communion at one assembly where seventeen hundred gathered. Those honored as communicants had been carefully prepared by the clergy to kneel upright when receiving the elements rather than bowing to authority. The usually censorious Lefroy, concerned with order above all else, wrote in the mission record book that "the demeanor and answers of the people showed that solid work had been done in bringing this scattered multitude of mainly illiterate Christians into something like an organized condition."[61]

COMMUNAL ELECTORATES AND
CHRISTIAN IDENTITY

Bishop Lefroy would have been the last person to consult for accurate information on the state of organization of the Punjabi church; it would be more accurate to say that rural Christians were organizing themselves, making use of catechists, missionaries, and bishops to order their community. Like missionaries confronting the Amritsar crisis, and urban Indian Christians mulling over their relationship with the national movement, village Christians were affected by politics. Unlike urban Christians, village Christians were not in fear of being singled out and left behind by nationalists because of their alleged denationalization. New to the politics of village Punjab after the passage of the Government of India Act in 1919 was the competition for untouchables who were wanted to swell the numbers in various sections of the communalized electorate, in which Sikhs, Hindus, and Muslims were given separate representation. This was a very complex system imposed upon an even more complex system of communal self-identification that was only vaguely represented by the census. After the fading away of the noncooperation movement, politics in Punjab began to take a communal turn with the elections to the provincial Legislative Assembly in 1921. Having been defined by the imperial government as communal, Indians began to act politically in a communal way. Violent competition for control of Sikh shrines that accompanied the rise of the Akali Dal movement led to the Sikh Gurd-

waras Act of 1925.[62] The Hindu "Shuddhi" movement, which attempted to re-enroll untouchables as Hindus, ran into violent opposition from Muslims who objected to Hindu attention to Musalis. The
1931 census, responsible for classifying everyone by community, was
heavily politicized, all the more so for occurring during a revival of
Congress Party's appeal.[63]

What the census documents are the new political constraints on the
ability of Christianity to expand in the Punjabi countryside. While missionaries concentrated on maintaining elite institutions, and finding
and providing pastoral care for rural Christians, Hindus and Sikhs alike
were hunting for formerly despised untouchables to enroll in their respective political communities. The abandonment of Kebir Panth,
Balmiki, and Lal Begi self-ascription continued rapidly in the 1920s (see
Table 12), but Christians had more competitors for the allegiance of
former untouchables, competitors driven by politics. In Sialkot and
Gujranwala nearly all Hindu Chuhras became Christians between 1880
and 1910. In 1921 there remained in other parts of Punjab nearly 700,000
"Hindu Chuhras," a number that declined dramatically in the 1920s. If
they had become Christians, rather than something else, Christianity
would have grown at an unprecedented rate. Instead, as the very inexact
Table 13 shows, although Christianity was growing, the largest rates of
growth came in the categories of "Sikh Chuhra" and Ad-Dharm, both
Chamar and Chuhra. "Sikh Chuhra" represented a straightforward Sikh
political embrace of Chuhras in Sikh-dominated areas. The Ad-Dharm
was a new player, an attempt to set up a separate electorate for Hindu
Chuhras with the new respect of having their own communal form of
identification in the Ad-Dharm Mandal.[64] The Ad-Dharm naturally
made little progress in the Christian heartland of central Punjab where
Christianity was strongest (see Table 7).

TABLE 12

The Decline of "Saint Worshippers and Sects
of Low Castes," 1921–31

	1921	1931	Percent loss	Net loss
Kebir Panth	37,111	12,780	65.6	24,331
Balmiki	221,027	155,738	29.5	65,289
Lal Begi	437,295	58,897	86.5	378,398
Ram Dasia	239,869	84,092	64.9	155,777
Bala Shahi	3,330	1,227	63.2	2,103
TOTAL NET LOSS				625,898

SOURCE: Census of India 1931, *Punjab Part I, vol. 17*, Khan Ahmad Hasan Khan
(Lahore: Punjab Government, 1933), 301.

TABLE 13

Changes in Communal Self-Ascription in Punjab, 1881–1931

	1881	1891	1901	1911	1921	1931
Hindu Chuhra	613,434	859,571	934,553	777,821	693,393	368,224
Sikh Chuhra	40,501	90,321	21,673	49,937	40,345	157,341
Ad-Dharmi Chuhra						86,548
Hindu Chamar	931,915	1,029,335	1,089,003	909,499	968,298	684,963
Sikh Chamar	100,014	106,328	75,753	164,110	161,862	155,717
Ad-Dharmi Chamar						256,349
Indian Christian	3,351	18,626	36,856	158,383	306,498	395,629

SOURCE: Census of India 1931, *Punjab Part I, vol. 17*, Khan Ahmad Hasan Khan (Lahore: Punjab Government, 1933), 308, 311, 321.

The extent to which categories of religion were being imposed upon a population in ways that were baffling and in many cases tyrannical is obvious from the census reports, where the mocking and humorous tone adopted by census officials about public confusion over religious categories implies that it is all the fault of the enumerated rather than the enumerators. In many localities self-ascription was a matter of political and economic pressure. The census enumerator noted that "the menial classes, mainly Chamars and Chuhras in the central Punjab, in order to consolidate their position wanted to return their religion as 'Ad-Dharmi.' A tug-of-war started in some districts, and Ad-Dharmis were required by Sikhs and Hindus not to return themselves as Ad-Dharmis. Particularly in Ambala, Ludhiana, Ferozepore, and Lyallpur the Sikh landowners employed all sorts of measures, in some cases bordering on terrorism."[65]

The problem for Sikh landowners, according to the census officials, was the desire of "menials" to return Ad-Dharm, demonstrating among other things a considerable degree of political awareness. Missionaries echoed this change in politics. "There is a new feature this time which was not present in the old Chuhra mass movement effort," noted J. G. Campbell. "It is the nationalist attitude of the reform sects of both Hindus and Mohammedans which leads them to follow our every move and try to checkmate it as they wish these people to swell their proportionate representation in the assemblies."[66] Christianity became an even riskier option politically when the mainstream political leaders began taking up the cause of untouchability. By the mid-1930s Dr. Ambedkar was recommending that untouchables in Punjab become Sikhs,[67] and Gandhi, who had begun to address the issue by protesting the exclusion of untouchables from temples in Travancore, was targeting "Harijans" as a special responsibility of the Indian national movement. As one missionary put it: "In proportion as the National Party succeed in championing the untouchables, will our influence decrease, for that party considers it one of its tasks to counteract, where it can, the work of organized Christianity."[68]

If Christianity reached a high-water mark in the 1930s, it also reached a level of stability that sustained it through the political crises and mass slaughter of the 1930s and 1940s. The majority of Christians in Indian and Pakistani Punjab remained poverty-stricken, illiterate, and powerless, but they also remained Christian. Their piety was unsatisfactory to almost everyone else, from missionaries to middle-class Christians. Instead of regular Sunday worship there were intermittent and impromptu gatherings for song. Instead of a deep prayer life there was the most common topic of religious conversation, the family genealogies of Christians that defied denominational boundaries.[69] A steady stream of rural Christians had found their way into the medical professions, and into leadership positions in the church. The legacy of the missions to the church leaders of independent Pakistan and India was heavily institutional and elitist. It was several decades after independence that the churches of South Asia would make a sustained attempt to come to terms with their history as "Dalit Christians."[70]

Although missionaries and Indian Christians had succeeded in making some progress toward the multiracial commonwealth of missionary fantasy, there remained a sense of something important missing: "the affectionate freedom, the warm, confiding, brotherly feeling, and the intimate and sweet communion, which should be found among brethren in Christ," that an American Presbyterian missionary had defined as their goal in 1863.[71] Despite the many friendships forged across racial boundaries, missionaries and Indian Christians remained divided by permanent disputes over control of the mission institutions they had built together. "Why can't we be friends now?" was the plaintive question asked by one of E. M. Forster's characters at the end of *A Passage to India.* "It's what I want. It's what you want."[72] To paraphrase Forster's own answer, it was the schools and colleges and clinics and hospices and hospitals that "said in their hundred voices, 'No, not yet.'"

Notes

CHAPTER I

1. Although there were no critical, scholarly, published histories of the domestic missionary movement available in the 1980s, pioneering work on missionary recruitment and training had appeared in three dissertations of the 1970s: Frederic Stuart Piggin, "The Social Background, Motivation, and Training of British Protestant Missionaries to India, 1789–1858," Ph.D. dissertation, London (King's) (1974); Sarah Caroline Potter, "The Social Organization and Recruitment of English Protestant Missionaries in the Nineteenth Century," Ph.D. dissertation, London (econ.), 1975; Cecil Peter Williams, "The Recruitment and Training of Overseas Missionaries in England between 1850 and 1900," M. Litt. thesis, Bristol (1976). Since then more scholarly work has been done on the social history of domestic missionary movement. See especially F. Stuart Piggin, *Making Evangelical Missionaries, 1789–1858: The Social Background, Motives and Training of British Protestant Missionaries to India.* Evangelicals & Society from 1750, 2 (Abingdon, Oxfordshire: Sutton Courtney Press, 1984); Brian Stanley, *The Bible and the Flag: Protestant Missions and British Imperialism in the Nineteenth and Twentieth Centuries* (Leicester, Eng.: Apollos, 1990); Brian Stanley, *The History of the Baptist Missionary Society, 1792–1992* (Edinburgh: T. &T. Clark, 1992); Steven S. Maughan, *Regions beyond and the National Church: Domestic Support for the Foreign Missions of the Church of England in the High Imperial Age, 1870–1914,* Ph.D. dissertation, Harvard University (1995); Susan Thorne, *Congregational Missions and the Making of an Imperial Culture in Nineteenth-Century England* (Stanford, Calif.: Stanford University Press, 1999).

2. Sir Lewis Namier, *The Structure of Politics at the Accession of George III,* 2d ed., reprint, 1929 (London: Macmillan, 1952), x.

3. The United Presbyterian Church of North America merged with its old rival, the Presbyterian Church in the U.S.A., in 1958. The merged body adopted the name United Presbyterian Church in the U.S.A., creating havoc with library catalogs.

4. Antonio Monserrate, *The Commentary of Father Monserrate, S.J., on His Journey to the Court of Akbar: Translated from the Original Latin by J. S. Hoyland, and Annotated by S.N. Banerjee* (London and Bombay: Oxford University Press, 1922).

5. For a celebratory account see Frederick and Margaret Stock, *People*

Movements in the Punjab, with Special Reference to the United Presby-terian Church (South Pasadena, Calif.: William Carey Library, 1975), chs. 6–8.

6. R. Maconachie (late I.C.S.), *Rowland Bateman: Nineteenth Century Apostle* (London: CMS, 1917).

7. A partial account is in CMS G2/I4/O3/188/1889: "Resolution in Re-gard to Giving up to the CMS Certain Territory in Riah Tahsil. Adopted by the Sialkot Mission of the United Presbyterian Church of North Amer-ica," 27 Mar. 1889, Sialkot.

8. Ibid., marginal note.

9. Stock, *People Movements*, 64–67.

10. Antoinette M. Burton, *Burdens of History: British Feminists, In-dian Women, and Imperial Culture, 1865–1915* (Chapel Hill: University of North Carolina, 1994); Mrinalini Sinha, *Colonial Masculinity: The 'Manly Englishman' and the 'Effeminate Bengali' in the Late Nineteenth Century.* Studies in Imperialism (Manchester, Eng.) (Manchester; New York: Manchester University Press; New York: St. Martin's Press, 1995); Jane Hunter, *The Gospel of Gentility: American Women Missionaries in Turn-of-the-Century China* (New Haven: Yale University Press, 1984); Ruth Compton Brouwer, *New Women for God: Canadian Presbyterian Women and India Missions, 1876–1914.* Social History of Canada, 44 (Toronto; Buffalo: University of Toronto Press, 1990); Modupe Labode, "From Heathen Kraal to Christian Home: Anglican Mission Education and African Christian Girls, 1850–1900," in *Women and Missions: Past and Present: Anthropological and Historical Perceptions*, edited by Fiona Bowie, Deborah Kirkwood, and Shirley Ardener (Providence and Oxford: Berg, 1993), 126–44; Leslie Flemming, "New Models, New Roles: U.S. Presbyterian Women Missionaries and Social Change in North India, 1870–1910," in *Women's Work for Women: Missionaries and Social Change in Asia*, edited by Leslie Flemming (Boulder, Colo.: Westview Press, 1989), 35–57; Gauri Viswanathan, *Outside the Fold: Conversion, Modernity, and Belief* (Princeton: Princeton University Press, 1998); Jane Haggis, "'A Heart that Has Felt the Love of God and Longs for Others to Know It': Conventions of Gender, Tensions of Self and Constructions of Difference in Offering to Be a Lady Missionary," *Women's History Review* 7, no. 2 (1998): 171–92.

11. Dana Lee Robert, *American Women in Mission: A Social History of Their Thought and Practice. The Modern Mission Era, 1792–1992* (Ma-con, Ga.: Mercer University Press, 1996).

12. The microfilm records of the Society for the Propagation of the Gospel, marketed as the complete records, fail to include the records of the SPG's Committee on Women's Work. See SPG E Series, Annual Re-ports 1856–1900, India.

13. It helps when the hymns have been translated into Hindi from the original Moody and Sankey, and the Psalms appear in the missionary's fa-vorite Urdu script—that is, Latin!

14. Avril A. Powell, *Muslims and Missionaries in Pre-Mutiny India*. London Studies on South Asia No. 7 (Richmond, UK: Curzon Press, 1993); Gail Minault, *Secluded Scholars: Women's Education and Muslim Social Reform in Colonial India* (New Delhi: Oxford University Press, 1998); J. S. Grewal, *The Sikhs of the Punjab*, rev. ed., *The New Cambridge History of India*, II.3 (Cambridge: Cambridge University Press, 1999); Kenneth W. Jones, *Arya Dharm: Hindu Consciousness in 19th-Century Punjab* (Berkeley: University of California Press, 1976).

15. Viswanathan, *Outside the Fold: Conversion, Modernity, and Belief*; Saurabh Dube, *Untouchable Pasts: Religion, Identity, and Power among a Central Indian Community, 1780–1950*. SUNY Series in Hindu Studies (Albany: State University of New York Press, 1998); Susan Billington Harper, *In the Shadow of the Mahatma: Bishop V. S. Azariah and the Travails of Christianity in British India* (Grand Rapids, Mich.: Eerdmans, 2000).

16. Antony Copley, *Religions in Conflict: Ideology, Cultural Contact and Conversion in Late Colonial India* (New Delhi: Oxford, 1997); Gerald Studdert-Kennedy, *British Christians, Indian Nationalists and the Raj* (Delhi: Oxford University Press, 1991); Gerald Studdert-Kennedy, *Providence and the Raj: Imperial Mission and Missionary Imperialism* (New Delhi: Sage Publications, 1998).

17. Lamin O. Sanneh, *Encountering the West: Christianity and the Global Cultural Process: The African Dimension*. World Christian Theology Series (Maryknoll, N.Y.: Orbis Books, 1993), ch. 1; Harper, *In the Shadow of the Mahatma: Bishop V. S. Azariah and the Travails of Christianity in British India*, preface.

18. Sydney Smith, "Indian Missions," *Edinburgh Review*, Apr. 1808.

19. Bernard Porter, *The Lion's Share: A Short History of British Imperialism, 1850–1995*, 3d ed. (New York: Longman, 1996); Denis Judd, *Empire: The British Imperial Experience from 1765 to the Present* (London: HarperCollins, 1996); William Roger Louis, gen. ed., *The Oxford History of the British Empire*, vols. I–V (Oxford: Oxford University Press, 1998–99).

20. Andrew Porter, ed., *Atlas of British Overseas Expansion* (London: Routledge, 1991); Andrew Porter, "Cambridge, Keswick, and Late Nineteenth-Century Attitudes to Africa," *Journal of Imperial and Commonwealth History* 5, no. 1 (1976): 5–34; Andrew Porter, "Evangelical Enthusiasm, Missionary Motivation and West Africa in the Late Nineteenth Century: The Career of G. W. Brooke," *Journal of Imperial and Commonwealth History* 6 (1977): 23–46; Andrew Porter, "The Hausa Association: Sir George Goldie, the Bishop of Dover and the Niger in the 1890s," *Journal of Imperial and Commonwealth History* 7 (1979): 149–79; Andrew Porter, "Religion and Empire: British Expansion in the Long Nineteenth Century, 1780–1914," *Journal of Imperial and Commonwealth History* 20, no. 3 (1992): 370–90; Andrew Porter, "'Commerce and Christianity': The Rise and Fall of a Nineteenth-Century Missionary Slogan,"

Historical Journal 28 (1985): 597–621; Andrew Porter, "Religion, Missionary Enthusiasm, and Empire," in *The Nineteenth Century*, vol. 3 of *The Oxford History of the British Empire*, edited by Andrew Porter, Wm. Roger Louis, gen. ed. (Oxford: Oxford University Press, 1999), 222–46.

21. Jane Hunter, *The Gospel of Gentility: American Women Missionaries in Turn-of-the-Century China* (New Haven: Yale University Press, 1984); Patricia Grimshaw, *Paths of Duty: American Missionary Wives in Nineteenth-Century Hawaii* (Honolulu: University of Hawaii Press, 1989); Leslie Flemming, "New Models, New Roles: U.S. Presbyterian Women Missionaries and Social Change in North India, 1870–1910," in *Women's Work for Women: Missionaries and Social Change in Asia*, edited by Leslie Flemming (Boulder, Colo.: Westview Press, 1989), 35–57; Ruth Compton Brouwer, *New Women for God: Canadian Presbyterian Women and India Missions, 1876–1914*. Social History of Canada, 44 (Toronto; Buffalo: University of Toronto Press, 1990); Rosemary R. Gagan, *A Sensitive Independence: Canadian Methodist Women Missionaries in Canada and the Orient, 1881–1925* (Montreal: McGill-Queens University Press, 1992); on Anglican High Church women in Africa and India, see Modupe Labode, "From Heathen Kraal to Christian Home: Anglican Mission Education and African Christian Girls, 1850–1900," in *Women and Missions: Past and Present: Anthropological and Historical Perceptions*, edited by Fiona Bowie, Deborah Kirkwood and Shirley Ardener (Providence and Oxford: Berg, 1993), 126–44; and Jeffrey Cox, "Independent English Women in Delhi and Lahore," in *Religion and Irreligion in Victorian Society: Essays in Honor of R. K. Webb*, edited by R. W. Davis and R. J. Helmstadter (London: Routledge, 1992); on British evangelical women in the Middle East, see Billie Melman, *Women's Orients: English Women and the Middle East, 1718–1918: Sexuality, Religion and Work*, 2d ed. (Basingstoke: Macmillan, 1995).

22. Mark Harrison, *Public Health in British India: Anglo-Indian Preventive Medicine 1859–1914*. Cambridge History of Medicine (Cambridge: Cambridge University Press, 1994); David Arnold, *Colonizing the Body: State Medicine and Epidemic Disease in Nineteenth-Century India* (Berkeley: University of California, 1993).

23. See B. D. Basu, *Rise of the Christian Power in India* (Calcutta: Brahmo Press, 1923) for antimissionary nationalist history, an argument continued recently in Arun Shourie, *Missionaries in India: Continuities, Changes, Dilemmas* (New Delhi: ASA Publications, 1994). For Gandhi's characteristically complex attitude to missionaries, see M. K. Kuriakose, ed., *History of Christianity in India: Source Materials* (Madras: Christian Literature Society, 1982), 362–63; and Charles Freer Andrews, *The Testimony of C. F. Andrews*, edited by Daniel O'Connor (Madras: Christian Literature Society, 1974), 118–22.

24. Partha Chatterjee, *Nationalist Thought and the Colonial World: A Derivative Discourse* (London: Zed Books, 1986).

25. *Subaltern Studies* (Delhi; New York: Oxford University Press, 1982); Sumit Sarkar, *Modern India 1885–1947* (Delhi: Macmillan India, 1983).

26. Mary Louise Pratt, *Imperial Eyes: Travel Writing and Transculturation* (London; New York: Routledge, 1992); Gauri Viswanathan, *Masks of Conquest: Literary Study and British Rule in India.* The Social Foundations of Aesthetic Forms Series (New York: Columbia University Press, 1989); Burton, *Burdens of History*; Sinha, *Colonial Masculinity.* Viswanathan acknowledges the influence of Alexander Duff on colonial educational policy, but his presence in Calcutta is taken for granted.

27. Imran Ali, *The Punjab under Imperialism, 1885–1947* (Princeton: Princeton University Press, 1988).

28. Edward W. Said, *Orientalism*, 1st ed. (New York: Pantheon Books, 1978); Edward Said, *Culture and Imperialism* (New York: Vintage Books, 1993).

29. John M. MacKenzie, *Orientalism: History, Theory, and the Arts* (Manchester; New York: Manchester University Press; New York: St. Martin's Press, 1995); Aijaz Ahmad, *In Theory: Classes, Nations, Literatures* (London: Verso, 1992).

30. Joseph Esherick, *The Origins of the Boxer Uprising* (Berkeley: University of California Press, 1987), 91.

31. *Subaltern Studies* (Delhi; New York: Oxford University Press, 1982), 8.

32. T. O. (Thomas O.) Beidelman, *Colonial Evangelism: A Socio-Historical Study of an East African Mission at the Grassroots* (Bloomington: Indiana University Press, 1982); Jean and John Comaroff, *Of Revelation and Revolution: Christianity, Colonialism, and Consciousness in South Africa* (Chicago: University of Chicago Press, 1991).

33. Beidelman, *Colonial Evangelism*, 5–6. Reviewers have commented on the tendency of Beidelman and the Comaroffs to marginalize or functionalize the religious point of view of Africans. R. Gray, "An Anthropologist on the Christian Kaguru," *Journal of African History* 24, no. 3 (1983): 406: "[Beidelman] seems quite unaware of the ability of the Kaguru, and other Africans, to distinguish between Christianity and the missionaries"; J. Peel, "The Colonization of Consciousness," *Journal of African History* 33, no. 2 (1992): 328, notes the Comaroffs' "strangely wilful indifference to the subject of religion."

34. Comaroff, *Of Revelation and Revolution*, xiv.

35. E. Said, letter, *Times Literary Supplement*, Mar. 19, 1993, 15. Said identifies Thomas Hodgkin as the "author" of that view.

36. Comaroff, *Of Revelation and Revolution*, 15.

37. Between 1945 and 1981 doctoral students in North America completed 943 dissertations on missionary work. See E. T. Bachman, "North American Doctoral Dissertations on Mission, 1945–1981," *International Bulletin of Missionary Research* 7, no. 3 (1983): 98. The field has grown

rapidly since. The Currents in World Christianity project has done much to promote mission studies research and make it accessible. See http://www.divinity.cam.ac.uk/carts/cwc/.

38. David Barrett, ed., *World Christian Encyclopedia: A Comparative Survey of Churches and Religions in the Modern World, A.D. 1900–2000* (Nairobi; New York: Oxford University Press, 1982); *International Bulletin of Missionary Research* (Ventnor, N.J.: Overseas Ministries Study Center, 1981–).

39. Kenneth Scott Latourette, *A History of the Expansion of Christianity* (New York: Harper, 1937–45); Kenneth Scott Latourette, *Christianity in a Revolutionary Age* (New York: Harper, 1957–61).

40. Andrew F. Walls, *The Missionary Movement in Christian History: Studies in the Transmission of Faith* (Edinburgh: T. & T. Clark, 1996).

41. For an example that deals with Punjab, see John C. B. Webster, *The Christian Community and Change in Nineteenth Century North India* (Delhi: Macmillan of India, 1976).

42. Stanley, *Bible and the Flag*; Sanneh, *Encountering the West.*

43. R. E. Frykenberg, "India," in *A World History of Christianity*, edited by Adrian Hastings (Grand Rapids, Mich.: Eerdmans, 1999), 183.

44. Andrew Porter, "Religion and Empire," 382.

45. Norman Etherington, "Missionaries and the Intellectual History of Africa: A Historical Survey," *Itinerario* 7 (1983): 116–43.

46. For a recent example, see James T. Campbell, *Songs of Zion: The African Methodist Episcopal Church in the United States and South Africa* (New York: Oxford University Press, 1995). The sheer complexity of the missionary story is made clear in his account of African-American missionaries to South Africa. British missionaries, however, are treated largely as imperialist obstacles to the building of an authentic African church, despite the fact that most Africans in this period remained in mission churches.

47. Comaroff, *Of Revelation and Revolution*, 32.

48. Edward Said, *Culture and Imperialism*, 39–40.

49. Ibid., 40, emphasis mine.

50. Ibid., 41.

51. Edward W. Said, *Orientalism*, 204.

52. Homi K. Bhabha, "Signs Taken for Wonders: Questions of Ambivalence and Authority under a Tree Outside Delhi, May 1817," *Critical Inquiry* 12 (autumn 1985): 144–65; a different use of the term "hybridity" may be found in Sara Suleri, *The Rhetoric of English India* (Chicago: University of Chicago Press, 1992); Anne McClintock attempts to transgress imperial boundaries through psychoanalytic categories in *Imperial Leather: Race, Gender, and Sexuality in the Colonial Conquest* (New York: Routledge, 1995); Laura Ann Stoler uses Foucauldian categories in *Race and the Education of Desire: Foucault's History of Sexuality and the Colonial Order of Things* (Durham, NC: Duke University Press, 1995).

53. Pratt, *Imperial Eyes.*

54. Ibid., 4.

55. Ibid., 6.

56. Ibid., 100, quoting Peter Hulme. Although Pratt's interest in this topic was whetted by stories of David Livingstone that she encountered in her Canadian childhood, she has no interest in missionaries.

57. Thomas Babington Macaulay, *Macaulay: Poetry and Prose*, compiled by G. M. Young (Cambridge, Mass.: Harvard University Press, 1967), 729.

58. E. M. Forster, *A Passage to India*, reprint, 1924 (Harmondsworth: Penguin, 1974), 317.

59. Billie Melman, in *Women's Orients: English Women and the Middle East, 1718–1918: Sexuality, Religion and Work*, ultimately concludes that women travelers in the Middle East could escape the confines of Orientalism, but missionary women could not. Kumari Jayawardena's *The White Woman's Other Burden: Western Women and South Asia during British Rule* (New York: Routledge, 1995) judges missionary women in South Asia by the feminist content of their work (see p. 10).

60. *Report of the 21st Annual Meeting of the Punjab CMS District Native Church Council, Amritsar, Apr. 11–13 1898* (Lahore? 1898), n.p.

61. Solveig Smith, *By Love Compelled: The Salvation Army's One Hundred Years in India and Adjacent Lands* (London: Salvation Army, 1981).

62. Cited in C. Peter Williams, "British Religion and the Wider World: Mission and Empire, 1800–1940," in *A History of Religion in Britain: Practice and Belief from Pre-Roman Times to the Present*, edited by Sheridan and W. J. Sheils Gilley (Oxford: Blackwell, 1994), 400.

63. Bernard S. Cohn, *Colonialism and Its Forms of Knowledge: The British in India*. Princeton Studies in Culture/Power/History (Princeton: Princeton University Press, 1996).

64. Julian Pettifer and Richard Bradley, *Missionaries* (London: BBC Books, 1990), 7.

65. Gyan Prakash, "After Colonialism," in *After Colonialism: Imperial Histories and Postcolonial Displacements*, edited by Gyan Prakash. Princeton Studies in Culture/Power/History (Princeton: Princeton University Press, 1995), 6.

66. Cited in Wallace Earle Stegner, *Angle of Repose*, reprint, 1971 (Penguin, 1992), 475.

CHAPTER 2

1. Eugene Stock, *The History of the Church Missionary Society: Its Environment, Its Men and Its Work* (London: Church Missionary Society, 1899), vol. 2, 195.

2. The Rev. Herbert Alfred Birks, M.A., *The Life and Correspondence of Thomas Valpy French, First Bishop of Lahore*. 2 vols. (London: John Murray, 1895); Robert Clark, *The Missions of the Church Missionary Society and the Church of England Zenana Missionary Society in the Pun-*

jab and Sindh, edited by Robert Maconachie (London: Church Missionary Society, 1904 ed.); Henry Martyn Clark, *Robert Clark of the Punjab: Pioneer and Missionary Statesman* (London: Andrew Melrose, 1907); Andrew Gordon, *Our India Mission: A Thirty Years History of the India Mission of the United Presbyterian Church of North America, Together with Personal Reminiscences* (Philadelphia: Andrew Gordon, 1886); Arthur Lewis, *George Maxwell Gordon M.A., F.R.G.S., the Pilgrim Missionary of the Punjab: A History of His Life and Work 1839–1880* (London: Seeley & Co., 1889); *Historical Sketches of the India Missions of the Presbyterian Church in the United States of America, Known as the Ludiana, the Farrukhabad, and the Kolhapur Missions: From the Beginning of the Work, in 1834, to the Time of Its Fiftieth Anniversary, in 1884* (Allahabad: Allahabad Mission Press, 1886); John C. Lowrie, *Travels in North India: Containing Notices of the Hindus; Journals of a Voyage on the Ganges and a Tour to Lahore; Notes on the Himalaya Mountains and the Hill Tribes: Including a Sketch of Missionary Undertakings* (Philadelphia: Presbyterian Board of Publications, 1842); Cecil H. Martin, *Allnutt of Delhi: A Memoir* (London: Society for Promoting Christian Knowledge, 1922); Alice M. Pennell, *Pennell of the Afghan Frontier: The Life of Theodore Pennell, M.D., B.Sc., F.R.C.S.* (London: Seeley, Service & Co., 1914); H. F. Lechmere Taylor, *In the Land of the Five Rivers: A Sketch of the Work of the Church of Scotland in Panjab* (Edinburgh: R. & R. Clark, 1906); John F. W. Youngson, *Forty Years of the Panjab Mission of the Church of Scotland, 1855–1895* (Edinburgh: R. & R. Clark, Ltd., 1896); R. Maconachie (late I.C.S.), *Rowland Bateman: Nineteenth Century Apostle* (London: CMS, 1917); H. H. Montgomery, *The Life and Letters of George Alfred Lefroy D.D., Bishop of Calcutta and Metropolitan* (London: Longmans, Green & Co., 1920); for comments on some of the pioneer missionaries in Punjab and their initial reactions to other religions, see Antony Copley, *Religions in Conflict: Ideology, Cultural Contact and Conversion in Late Colonial India* (Delhi: Oxford University Press, 1997), 125–39.

3. Stock, *History of CMS*, vol. 2, 195.

4. D. A. Washbrook, "India, 1818–1860: The Two Faces of Colonialism," in *The Nineteenth Century*, in *The Oxford History of the British Empire*, edited by Andrew Porter, Roger Louis, gen. ed. (New York: Oxford University Press, 1999), 419; Imran Ali, *The Punjab under Imperialism, 1885–1947* (Princeton: Princeton University Press, 1988).

5. Montgomery, *Life and Letters of Lefroy*, 14.

6. Henry Martyn Clark, *Robert Clark*, 50, 61.

7. Daud Ali, "Recognizing Europe in India: Colonial Master Narratives and the Writing of Indian History," in *Contesting the Master Narrative: Essays in Social History*, edited by Jeffrey Cox and Shelton Stromquist (Iowa City: University of Iowa, 1998), 95–130.

8. Sita Ram Goel, *History of Hindu-Christian Encounters* (New Delhi: Voice of India, 1989).

9. Edward W. Said, *Orientalism*, 1st ed. (New York: Pantheon Books, 1978), 204.

10. Birks, *Life and Correspondence of French*, vol. 1, 160–61.

11. Arun Shourie, *Missionaries in India: Continuities, Changes, Dilemmas* (New Delhi: ASA Publications, 1994), cited on p. 61.

12. John C. B. Webster, *The Christian Community and Change in Nineteenth Century North India* (Delhi: Macmillan of India, 1976); Gerald Studdert-Kennedy, *Providence and the Raj: Imperial Mission and Missionary Imperialism* (New Delhi: Sage Publications, 1998).

13. CMS G2/I4/02/295/1886. R. Clark, Report on a visit to Kotgarh, 17–21 Sept. 1886.

14. William Carey, *An Enquiry into the Obligations of Christians, to Use Means for the Conversion of the Heathens in Which the Religious State of the Different Nations of the World, the Success of Former Undertakings, and the Practicability of Further Undertakings, Are Considered* (Leicester, 1792), 79; I discuss Carey further in Jeffrey Cox, "The Nineteenth Century Missionary Movement," in *Nineteenth Century English Religious Traditions*, edited by Dennis Paz (Greenwood Press, 1995), and "Religion and Imperial Power in Nineteenth Century Britain," in *Freedom and Religion in the Nineteenth Century*, edited by R. W. Davis and R. J. Helmstadter (Palo Alto: Stanford University Press, 1997).

15. CMS G2/I4/07/127/1891. R. Clark, Feb. 25, 1891, Dera Ishmael Khan.

16. Francis G. Hutchins, *The Illusion of Permanence: British Imperialism in India* (Princeton: Princeton University Press, 1967).

17. E. S. Wenger, *Missionary Biographies in Four Volumes*, unpublished manuscript (Serampore: Carey Library, 1936), IV, 224 ff.

18. Baptist Missionary Society, *Annual Reports*, being a continuation of the Periodical Accounts relative to the Society (London, 1809–98), 1839, 20.

19. Stock, *History of CMS*, vol. 1, 199.

20. Homi K. Bhabha, "Signs Taken for Wonders: Questions of Ambivalence and Authority under a Tree Outside Delhi, May 1817," *Critical Inquiry* 12 (autumn 1985): 144–65.

21. For a clear and useful summary of the denominational and social background of AP missionaries, see John C. B. Webster, *The Christian Community and Change in Nineteenth Century North India* (Delhi: Macmillan of India, 1976), ch. 2.

22. Ibid., 13.

23. Ibid., 46.

24. The Associate Presbyterian Church of North America merged in 1858 with the Associate Reformed Presbyterian Church to form the United Presbyterian Church of North America.

25. Henry Paget Thompson, *Into All Lands: The History of the Society for the Propagation of the Gospel in Foreign Parts 1701–1850* (London:

SPCK, 1951), 153; Brian Stanley, *The History of the Baptist Missionary Society, 1792–1992* (Edinburgh: T. & T. Clark, 1992), 145. The best known Christian convert in Delhi, Professor Ram Chandra of the Hindu College, narrowly escaped death; see Avril A. Powell, "Processes of Conversion to Christianity in Nineteenth Century North-Western India," in *Religious Conversion Movements in South Asia: Continuities and Change, 1800–1900,* edited by Geoffrey A. Oddie (Richmond, UK: Curzon, 1997), 24–31.

26. Youngson, *Forty Years,* 75.

27. Webster, *Christian Community,* 52,192–93.

28. For a recent addition to the mutiny literature, see Andrew Ward, *Our Bones Are Scattered: The Cawnpore Massacres and the Indian Mutiny of 1857* (New York: Henry Holt and Co., 1996).

29. Kenneth E. Hendrickson, *Making Saints: Religion and the Public Image of the British Army, 1809–1885* (Madison, N.J.: Bucknell University Press, 1998).

30. For a recent celebratory treatment of missions and the mutiny, see Stephen Neill, *A History of Christianity in India, 1707–1858* (Cambridge: Cambridge University Press, 1985), 431.

31. Jeffrey Cox, *The English Churches in a Secular Society: Lambeth 1870–1930* (Oxford University Press, 1982); Mark (Mark A.) Smith, *Religion in Industrial Society: Oldham and Saddleworth, 1740–1865.* Oxford Historical Monographs (Oxford: Clarendon Press; New York: Oxford University Press, 1994); S. J. D. Green, *Religion in the Age of Decline: Organisation and Experience in Industrial Yorkshire, 1870–1920* (Cambridge: Cambridge University Press, 1996); Arthur Burns, *The Diocesan Revival in the Church of England c. 1800–1870.* Oxford Historical Monographs (Oxford: Clarendon Press, 1999).

32. Stock, *History of CMS,* vol. 2, 208.

33. There is a large literature on the Punjab School. For recent studies from different points of view, see Peter Penner, *Robert Needham Cust, 1821–1909: A Personal Biography.* Studies in British History, vol. 5 (Lewiston, N.Y.: Edward Mellen Press, 1987); Lewis D. Wurgaft, *The Imperial Imagination: Magic and Myth in Kipling's India* (Middletown, Conn.: Wesleyan University Press, 1983); on the twentieth century, see Clive Dewey, *Anglo-Indian Attitudes: The Mind of the Indian Civil Service* (London and Rio Grande: Hambledon Press, 1993).

34. See, for example, Stock, *History of CMS,* vol. 2, 201.

35. Stanley Elwood Brush, "Protestants in Conflict: Policy and Early Practice in the British Punjab," *Al-Mushir* 17, no. 4–6 (June 1975): 91.

36. Henry Martyn Clark, *Robert Clark,* 147.

37. Ainslee T. Embree, "Christianity and the State in Victorian India: Confrontation and Collaboration," in *Religion and Irreligion in Victorian Society: Essays in Honor of R. K. Webb,* edited by R. W. and R. J. Helmstadter Davis (London: Routledge, 1992), 151.

38. Robert Frykenberg, "The Construction of Hinduism at the Nexus of History and Religion," *Journal of Interdisciplinary History* 23, no. 3

(1993): 523–50; Arjun Appadurai, *Worship and Conflict under Colonial Rule: A South Indian Case.* Cambridge South Asian Studies. 27 (Cambridge, Eng.; New York: Cambridge University Press, 1981); Kenneth W. Jones, *Socio-Religious Reform Movements in British India: The New Cambridge History of India* III, 1 (Cambridge, Eng.; New York: Cambridge University Press, 1989).

39. Gauri Viswanathan, "Coping with (Civil) Death: The Christian Convert's Rights of Passage in Colonial India," in *After Colonialism: Imperial Histories and Postcolonial Displacements*, edited by Gyan Prakash. Princeton Studies in Culture/Power/History (Princeton: Princeton University Press, 1995), 183–210; Gauri Viswanathan, *Outside the Fold: Conversion, Modernity, and Belief* (Princeton: Princeton University Press, 1998).

40. Stock, *History of CMS*, vol. 2, 214–16; Stanley Elwood Brush, "Protestants in the Punjab: Religion and Social Change in an Indian Province in the Nineteenth Century," Ph.D. diss., University of California at Berkeley, 1964, passim.

41. Private support by officials for the American Presbyterians is documented in Webster, *Christian Community*, Table 1, 14; for the CMS in Stock, *History of the CMS*, chs. XLIV–XLVII.

42. Lahore Missionary Conference, *Report of the Punjab Missionary Conference Held at Lahore in Dec. and Jan., 1862–63* (Ludhiana: American Presbyterian Mission Press, 1863).

43. Kenneth W. Jones, *Arya Dharm: Hindu Consciousness in 19th-Century Punjab* (Berkeley: University of California Press, 1976); J. S. Grewal, *The Sikhs of the Punjab*, rev. ed., *The New Cambridge History of India*, II.3 (Cambridge: Cambridge University Press, 1999); Gail Minault, *Secluded Scholars: Women's Education and Muslim Social Reform in Colonial India* (New Delhi: Oxford University Press, 1998).

44. *Talks on India: An Outline of Six Missionary Instructions with Illustrations and Recitations for Young People* (London: Church Missionary Society, 1908), 5.

45. B. D. Basu, *Rise of the Christian Power in India* (Calcutta: Brahmo Press, 1923), vol. I, xli–xliv.

46. Arun Shourie, *Missionaries in India: Continuities, Changes, Dilemmas* (New Delhi: ASA Publications, 1994), 80; cf. Gauri Viswanathan, *Masks of Conquest: Literary Study and British Rule in India.* The Social Foundations of Aesthetic Forms Series (New York: Columbia University Press, 1989) on the convergence of interests of government and missionary educational policy; for an Indian Christian response to Shourie, see Vishal Mangalwadi, *Missionary Conspiracy: Letters to a Postmodern Hindu*, 2d ed. (Mussoorie, India: Nivedit Good Books Distributors, 1996).

47. Shourie, *Missionaries in India: Continuities, Changes, Dilemmas*, 58.

48. Gyan Prakash, "After Colonialism," in *After Colonialism: Imperial Histories and Postcolonial Displacements*, edited by Gyan Prakash.

Princeton Studies in Culture/Power/History (Princeton: Princeton University Press, 1995), 6.

49. Sydney Smith, "Indian Missions," *Edinburgh Review*, Apr. 1808.

50. Viswanathan, "Coping with (Civil) Death," 186.

51. Shourie, *Missionaries in India: Continuities, Changes, Dilemmas*, 109; Stock, *History of CMS*, vol. 2, 259.

52. Zenana Bible and Medical Mission, *The Indian Female Evangelist*, vol. 13, no. 86, Apr. 1893 (London: Indian Female Normal School and Instruction Society), 50.

53. Dev Samaj, *European Sympathy with the Deva Dharma Mission* (Lahore: New Lyall Press, 1892); Dev Samaj, *General Information Regarding the Dev Samaj* (Lahore: Dev Samaj Head Office, 1915).

54. *Talks on India.*

55. Hans Cnattingius, *Bishops and Societies: A Study of Anglican Colonial and Missionary Expansion 1698–1850*. Published for the Church Historical Society (London: SPCK, 1952), 52.

56. Robert Stewart, *Life and Work in India: An Account of the Conditions, Methods, Difficulties, Results, Future Prospects and Reflex Influence of Missionary Labor in India, Especially in the Punjab Mission of the United Presbyterian Church of North America* (Philadelphia: Pearl Publishing, 1899), 27.

57. Henry Martyn Clark, *Robert Clark*, 101.

58. Birks, *Life and Correspondence of French*, vol. 1, 250.

59. Ibid., vol. 1, 66.

60. Wenger, *Missionary Biographies*, 224.

61. Webster, *Christian Community*, 209–14.

62. Henry Martyn Clark, *Robert Clark*, 100.

63. Ibid., 101.

64. Thompson, *Into All Lands*, 355, 611.

65. Youngson, *Forty Years*, 168–69; Gordon, *Our India Mission*, 207.

66. Macaulay, *Prose and Poetry, Selected by G. M. Young* (Cambridge: Harvard University Press, 1967), 729; how this aspiration was worked out in practice is documented in Gauri Viswanathan, *Masks of Conquest: Literary Study and British Rule in India*. The Social Foundations of Aesthetic Forms Series (New York: Columbia University Press, 1989).

67. *Report of the Third Meeting of the Punjab C.M.S. Native Church Council Held at Umritsur from the 27th to the 30th of December 1878* (London, 1879), 5.

68. Birks, *Life and Correspondence of French*, vol. 1, 43.

69. Ibid., vol. 1, 250–51.

70. Ibid., vol. 1, 219.

71. Ibid., vol. 1, 236.

72. Ibid., vol. 1, 301.

73. C. Peter Williams, *The Ideal of the Self-Governing Church: A Study in Victorian Missionary Strategy*. Studies in Christian Mission, vol. 1 (Leiden; New York: E. J. Brill, 1990); Wilbert R. Shenk, *Henry Venn, Mis-*

sionary Statesman. American Society of Missiology Series, no. 6 (Maryknoll, N.Y.: Orbis Books, 1983), foreword.

74. On the American Congregationalists Rufus Anderson, see Wilbert R. Shenk, "Rufus Anderson and Henry Venn: A Special Relationship," *International Bulletin of Missionary Research* (Oct. 1981): 168–72; on the English Baptist E. B. Underhill, see Brian Stanley, *The History of the Baptist Missionary Society, 1792–1992* (Edinburgh: T. & T. Clark, 1992), 149–56.

75. Henry Venn, *The Missionary Life and Labours of Francis Xavier, Taken from His Own Correspondence: With a Sketch of the General Results of Roman Catholic Missions among the Heathen* (London: Longman, Green, Longman, Roberts, & Green, 1862); Cox, "Religion and Imperial Power."

76. Henry Venn, *To Apply the Gospel: Selections from the Writing of Henry Venn*, ed., Max Warren (Grand Rapids, Mich.: William B. Eerdmans, 1971), 63, extract from a letter to a missionary in North India, the Rev. R. M. Lamb.

77. Church Missionary Society, *Laws and Regulations of the CMS: Part IV: Organization of Native Churches* (London: CMS, 1883); Shenk, "Rufus Anderson," 171.

78. Venn, *To Apply the Gospel*, 28, 63.

79. Mary Louise Pratt, *Imperial Eyes: Travel Writing and Transculturation* (London; New York: Routledge, 1992), 7.

80. T. B. Macaulay, *The History of England from the Accession of James II*, vol. 2 (Chicago: Belford, Clarke & Co., 1889).

81. Birks, *Life and Correspondence of French*, vol. I, 327 ff.

82. Ibid., vol. 1, 329.

83. *The Indian Church Directory for the Province of India and Ceylon* (Calcutta, 1890), 220.

84. Birks, *Life and Correspondence of French*, vol. 1, 347, 353.

85. Punjab Mission News, Jan. 15, 1888, quoted in Birks, *Life and Correspondence of French*, vol. 1, 360.

86. Ibid., vol. 2, 333.

87. Ibid.

88. Ibid.

89. T. E. Yates, *Venn and Victorian Bishops Abroad: The Missionary Policies of Henry Venn and Their Repercussions upon the Anglican Episcopate of the Colonial Period, 1841–1872* (Uppsala, 1978).

90. *A Native Church for the Natives of India, Giving an Account of the Second Meeting of the Punjab CMS Native Church Council Held at Umritsar, 24–27 December 1877* (Lahore, 1878), 8.

91. *A Native Church for the Natives of India, Giving an Account of the Formation of a Native Church Council for the Punjab Mission of the Church Missionary Society, and of the Proceedings of Their First Meeting at Umritsar, 31 Mar.–2 Apr. 1877* (Lahore, 1877); *A Native Church for the Natives of India, Giving an Account of the Second Meeting of the Punjab*

CMS Native Church Council Held at Umritsar, 24–27 Dec. 1877 (Lahore, 1878); *Report of the Third Meeting of the Punjab C.M.S. Native Church Council Held at Umritsur from the 27th to the 30th of Dec. 1878* (London, 1879); Jeffrey Cox, "On Redefining 'Crisis': The Victorian Crisis of Faith in the Punjab, 1880–1930," in *Victorian Faith in Crisis: Essays on Continuity and Change in Nineteenth-Century Religious Belief,* edited by Richard J. Helmstadter and Bernard Lightman (London: Macmillan, 1990), 315–41.

92. Cnattingius, *Bishops and Societies,* 201.

93. Ibid., 75.

94. Montgomery, *Life and Letters of Lefroy,* 10.

95. B. F. Westcott, *On Some Points in the Religious Office of the Universities* (London: Macmillan, 1873), 41.

96. CMS G2/I4/PI/166/1882. Bishop French's letter to the editor, clipped from unidentified publication.

97. *The Story of the Delhi Mission* (London: Society for the Propagation of the Gospel, 1908); F. J. Western, *The Early History of the Cambridge Mission to Delhi,* typescript (1950); *One Hundred Years in Delhi* (Delhi: The Brotherhood of the Ascended Christ, 1977); C. M. Millington, *"Whether We Be Many or Few": A History of the Cambridge/Delhi Brotherhood* (Bangalore: Asian Trading Corporation, 1999).

98. Robert Clark, *Missions of the CMS,* 53 ff.

99. Zenana Bible and Medical Mission, *The Indian Female Evangelist* (London: Indian Female Normal School and Instruction Society), Jan. 1873; Mar. 1901. Miss Fuller was assigned to Lahore in 1867; Miss Archer to Jullunder in 1869, where the work was being carried on by Miss Golak Nath in 1873. Miss Henderson and Miss Urquart were sent to Lahore to establish a Normal School in 1873, Miss Swainson to Lahore for unspecified work, and Miss Wauton and Miss Hasell assigned to the Lady Henry Lawrence School in Lahore.

100. For instance, in the 1860s and 1870s an SPG missionary couple, Richard and Priscilla Winter, administered a mission with a substantial female presence in Delhi, bringing in Eurasian and "country born" staff and Anglo-Indian (that is, European civilian) volunteers to do Zenana visitation and teach schools for Indian and Eurasian women. See Jeffrey Cox, "Independent English Women in Delhi and Lahore," in *Religion and Irreligion in Victorian Society: Essays in Honor of R. K. Webb,* edited by R. W. Davis and R. J. Helmstadter (London: Routledge, 1992), 166–68.

101. Jane Haggis, "'A Heart That Has Felt the Love of God and Longs for Others to Know It': Conventions of Gender, Tensions of Self and Constructions of Difference in Offering to Be a Lady Missionary," *Women's History Review* 7, no. 2 (1998): 171–92; Modupe Labode, "From Heathen Kraal to Christian Home: Anglican Mission Education and African Christian Girls, 1850–1900," in *Women and Missions: Past and Present: Anthropological and Historical Perceptions,* edited by Fiona Bowie, Deborah Kirkwood, and Shirley Ardener (Providence and Oxford: Berg, 1993), 126–

44; Rosemary Fitzgerald, "'Rescue and Redemption'—the Rise of Female Medical Missions in Colonial India during the Late Nineteenth and Early Twentieth Centuries," in *Nursing History and the Politics of Welfare*, edited by A. M. Rafferty, J. Robinson, and R. Elkan (London: Routledge, 1996), 64–79.

102. Youngson, *Forty Years*, 92.

103. English Report, 1880.

104. Maconachie (late I.C.S.), *Rowland Bateman*, 43.

105. Report of the Seventh Meeting, 1883.

106. Birks, *Life and Correspondence of French*, 143, speech to the Reading Church Congress, 1883.

CHAPTER 3

1. E. S. Wenger, *Missionary Biographies in Four Volumes*, unpublished manuscript (Serampore: Carey Library, 1936), 224. Thompson used only initials in his publications; he is identified as Joseph T. Thompson in the British Library catalog, and as John Thomas Thompson in some mission records.

2. Henry Martyn Clark, *Robert Clark of the Punjab: Pioneer and Missionary Statesman* (London: Andrew Melrose, 1907), 62–63.

3. John F. W. Youngson, *Forty Years of the Panjab Mission of the Church of Scotland, 1855–1895* (Edinburgh: R. & R. Clark, Ltd., 1896), 120, 137.

4. SPG, Mission Reports, 3 Winter to Tucker, 17 Feb. 1885.

5. R. S. McGregor, *Outline of Hindi Grammar*, 2d ed., reprint, 1972 (Oxford: Clarendon Press, 1986), xi–xii.

6. *Report of the Sixth Meeting of the Punjab CMS Native Church Council Held at Umritsar, 25–27 Dec. 1881* (Amritsar? 1882), 49.

7. Sialkot Mission Annual Report, 1884, 7–8.

8. CMS G2/I4/0/312/1890; *Historical Sketches of the India Missions of the Presbyterian Church in the United States of America, Known as the Ludiana, the Farrukhabad, and the Kolhapur Missions: From the Beginning of the Work, in 1834, to the Time of Its Fiftieth Anniversary, in 1884* (Allahabad: Allahabad Mission Press, 1886), 47.

9. The Rev. Herbert Alfred Birks, M.A., *The Life and Correspondence of Thomas Valpy French, First Bishop of Lahore.* 2 vols. (London: John Murray, 1895), vol. 1, 141.

10. Ibid., vol. 2, 135.

11. R. Maconachie (late I.C.S.), *Rowland Bateman: Nineteenth Century Apostle* (London: CMS, 1917), 30–31.

12. Birks, *The Life and Correspondence of Thomas Valpy French, First Bishop of Lahore*, vol. 1, 189.

13. Sialkot Mission, Minutes, 1897, n.p.

14. S. S. Hewlett, *Daughters of the King* (London: James Nisbet and Co., 1886).

15. SPG, "Roll of Women Missionaries"; see Jeffrey Cox, "Independent

English Women in Delhi and Lahore," in *Religion and Irreligion in Victorian Society: Essays in Honor of R. K. Webb*, edited by R. W. Davis and R. J. Helmstadter (London: Routledge, 1992), note 1.

16. CMS G2/I4/P3/46/1900. Minutes of Medical Sub-Conference, CMS, 6–7 Nov. 1899.

17. M. E. Gibbs, *The Anglican Church in India 1600–1970* (Delhi: Indian Society for the Promotion of Christian Knowledge, 1972), 245.

18. Clark, *Robert Clark*, 108.

19. Wenger, *Missionary Biographies*, IV, 224.

20. Church Missionary Society, *Register of Missionaries (Clerical, Lay, & Female) and Native Clergy from 1804 to 1904* (London: Printed for Private Circulation, 1905), 492.

21. J. T. Thompson, *A Dictionary in Hindi and English*, reprint, 1846 (Calcutta: Sangbada Jnanaratnakara Press, 1870), v–vi.

22. See J. D. Bate, *A Dictionary of the Hindee Language* (Benares: Medical Hall Press, 1875), preface.

23. *Report of the General Missionary Conference Held at Allahabad, 1872–73, with a Missionary Map of India* (Madras: Seeley, Jackson, and Halliday, London, 1873), 525.

24. *Historical Sketches of the India Missions of the Presbyterian Church in the United States of America*, 46–48. In 1883, forty-three thousand books and tracts were issued; after that year the Presbyterian depository was merged with the Punjab Bible and Religious Book Society in Lahore, an outpost of the British and Foreign Bible Society.

25. Bate, *A Dictionary of the Hindee Language*.

26. John C. B. Webster, *The Christian Community and Change in Nineteenth Century North India* (Delhi: Macmillan of India, 1976), 41.

27. *Imperial gazetteer of India, Punjab*, reprint, 1908. Provincial Series (New Delhi: Usha publications, 1984), vol. 1, 150.

28. L. Janvier, *Dictionary of the Punjabi Language* (Ludhiana: For the Ludhiana Mission, 1854); James Croil, *The Noble Army of Martyrs and Roll of Protestant Missionary Martyrs from A.D. 1661 to 1891* (Philadelphia: Presbyterian Board of Publication, 1894), 109.

29. David Kopf, *British Orientalism and the Bengal Renaissance: The Dynamics of Indian Modernization, 1773–1835* (Berkeley: University of California Press, 1969); V. Ravindiran, "Reverend Robert Caldwell (1814–1891): The Bard of the Dravidians," unpublished paper, Dept. of History, University of Toronto (1997); V. Ravindiran, "Discourses of Empowerment: Missionary Orientalism in the Development of Dravidian Nationalism," in *Nation Work: Asian Elites and National Identities*, edited by Timothy Brook and Andre Schmid (Ann Arbor: University of Michigan, 1999).

30. Amrit Rai, *A House Divided: The Origin and Development of Hindi* (Delhi; New York: Oxford University Press, 1984).

31. Avril A. Powell, *Muslims and Missionaries in Pre-Mutiny India*. London Studies on South Asia no. 7 (Richmond, UK: Curzon Press, 1993).

32. J. T. Thompson, *The Psalms of David, Translated into the Hindee Language by J. T. Thompson* (Serampore, 1836); J. T. Thompson, *A Commentary on the Gospel of Matthew in Oordoo* (Calcutta: Baptist Mission Press, 1850).

33. Church Missionary Society, *Register of Missionaries (Clerical, Lay, & Female) and Native Clergy from 1804 to 1904*, respective entries.

34. *Dictionary of National Biography*, vol. 57, 280. The British Library catalogue has 142 separate entries of books published by A.L.O.E. (A Lady of England) between 1854 and 1893.

35. Sialkot Mission, Annual Reports of the United Presbyterian Mission in India, Sialkot, 1882, 18; Webster, *Christian Community*, 33.

36. H. U. Weitbrecht, *The Urdu New Testament*. Bible House Papers, no. 3, ATLA monograph preservation program and ATLA fiche 1987–2938. (London: British and Foreign Bible Society, 1900).

37. Worthington Jukes, *Reminiscences of Missionary Work in Amritsar 1872–1873 and on the Afghan Frontier in Peshawar 1873–1890*, typescript (Peshawar: Edwards High School, 1925), 64–65.

38. *Delhi Mission News* (Delhi: Cambridge Mission to Delhi, 1895–1931), July 1895.

39. Birks, *The Life and Correspondence of Thomas Valpy French, First Bishop of Lahore*, vol. 2, 135.

40. *Delhi Mission News*, July 1895.

41. Powell, *Muslims and Missionaries*.

42. Church Missionary Society, *Register of Missionaries (Clerical, Lay, & Female) and Native Clergy from 1804 to 1904*, 52–53.

43. Birks, *The Life and Correspondence of Thomas Valpy French, First Bishop of Lahore*, vol. 1, 72.

44. Conversion with Martin Reixinger of the London School of Economics, who is doing work on Sana Ullah Amritsari.

45. Tribune, 12 Aug. 1894; CMS G2/I4/P3/404/1894.

46. H. H. Montgomery, *The Life and Letters of George Alfred Lefroy D.D., Bishop of Calcutta and Metropolitan* (London: Longmans, Green & Co., 1920), 80, 93–95.

47. SPG, Report of T. Williams, Riwari, Oct.–Dec. 1889.

48. Kenneth W. Jones, *Arya Dharm: Hindu Consciousness in 19th-Century Punjab* (Berkeley: University of California Press, 1976).

49. Sita Ram Goel, *History of Hindu-Christian Encounters* (New Delhi: Voice of India, 1989).

50. Sialkot Mission, Annual Reports of the United Presbyterian Mission in India, Sialkot, 1882, 18 ff.

51. Andrew Porter, "Late Nineteenth Century Anglican Missionary Expansion: A Consideration of Some Non-Anglican Sources," in *Studies in Church History*, edited by Keith Baker (Oxford: Blackwell, 1978).

52. C. Peter Williams, *The Ideal of the Self-Governing Church: A Study in Victorian Missionary Strategy*. Studies in Christian Mission, vol. 1 (Leiden; New York: E. J. Brill, 1990).

53. Montgomery, *The Life and Letters of George Alfred Lefroy D.D., Bishop of Calcutta and Metropolitan*, 92.

54. Youngson, *Forty Years of the Panjab Mission*, 19, 31.

55. G. A. Lefroy, "The Moral Tone of India," *East and West: A Quarterly Review for the Study of Missions* 1 (1903), 123.

56. Charles Freer Andrews, *North India*. Handbooks of English Church Expansion (Oxford: Mowbray, 1908), 78–79.

57. Hewlett, *Daughters of the King*, 101.

58. Montgomery, *The Life and Letters of George Alfred Lefroy D.D., Bishop of Calcutta and Metropolitan*, 47.

59. Rudyard Kipling, *Kim*, reprint, 1901 (New York: Dell, 1959), 139.

60. Antoinette M. Burton, *Burdens of History: British Feminists, Indian Women, and Imperial Culture, 1865–1915* (Chapel Hill: University of North Carolina, 1994); Barbara Ramusack, "Cultural Missionaries, Maternal Imperialists, Feminist Allies: British Women Activists in India, 1865–1945," *Women's Studies International Forum* 13, no. 4 (1990): 309–21; Janaki Nair, "Uncovering the Zenana: Visions of Indian Womanhood in Englishwomen's Writings, 1813–1940," *Journal of Women's History* 2, no. 1 (spring 1990): 8–34.

61. Charles Freer Andrews, *The Testimony of C. F. Andrews*, edited by Daniel O'Connor (Madras: Christian Literature Society, 1974), 13.

62. Robert Needham Cust, *Essay on the Prevailing Methods of the Evangelization of the Non-Christian World* (London: Luzac and Co., publishers to the India Office, 1894), 40.

63. Daniel O'Connor, *Gospel, Raj and Swaraj: The Missionary Years of C. F. Andrews 1904–14*. Studies in the Intercultural History of Christianity, vol. 62 (Frankfurt/M., Bern, New York, Paris: Peter Lang, 1990), 78–79; Jeffrey Cox, "George Alfred Lefroy: Anglicans, Untouchables, and Imperial Institutions," in *After the Victorians: Essays in Honor of John Clive*, edited by Susan Pedersen and Peter Mandler (London: Routledge, 1994), 55.

64. Martin Maw, *Visions of India: Fulfillment Theology, the Aryan Race Theory, and the Work of British Protestant Missionaries in Victorian India*. Studies in the Intercultural History of Christianity (Frankfurt am Main: Peter Lang, 1990).

65. Birks, *The Life and Correspondence of Thomas Valpy French, First Bishop of Lahore*, vol. 1, 281.

66. Jukes, *Reminiscences*, 22–23.

67. Ibid., 24, 35.

68. *Church Missionary Intelligencer* (London: Church Missionary Society, 1851), vol. 2, no. 2, 30.

69. "Trumpp, Ernst," in *Allgemeine Deutsche Biographie*, vol. 38 (Leipzig, 1894), 687–89.

70. Ernest Trumpp, trans. and ed., *The Adi Granth, or Holy Scriptures of the Sikhs* (London: W. H. Allen, 1877), vii.

71. *Church Missionary Intelligencer*, vol. 2, no. 7, 148.

72. Youngson, *Forty Years of the Panjab Mission*, 50.

73. C. H. Loehlin, *The Sikhs and Their Scriptures* (Lucknow: Lucknow Publishing House, 1958); J. S. Grewal, *Contesting Interpretations of the Sikh Tradition* (New Delhi: Manohar, 1998).

74. Kabir, *The Bijak of Kabir*, translated and edited by Linda Hess and Shukdev Singh, reprint, 1983 (Delhi: Motilal Banarsidass, 1986).

75. Birks, *The Life and Correspondence of Thomas Valpy French, First Bishop of Lahore*, vol. 1, 295.

76. SPG Series E, Report of Yaqub M. Singh, 30 Sept. 1883; Report of T. Williams, 30 Sept. 1888.

77. *A Brief Life-Sketch of Shri Dev Guru Bhagwan (from His Birth to His Taking up the Great Mission of His Life* (Lahore: Jiwan Press, 1913), 8–13.

78. Jones, *Arya Dharm*; Kenneth W. Jones, *Socio-Religious Reform Movements in British India. The New Cambridge History of India*, 1 III (Cambridge, Eng.; New York: Cambridge University Press, 1989).

79. Youngson, *Forty Years of the Panjab Mission*, 26.

80. *Lahore Civil and Military Gazette*, 26 Aug. 1890.

81. Cox, "Independent English Women in Delhi and Lahore."

82. Report of the SPG and Cambridge Mission to Delhi, 1903, 47.

83. Ibid.

84. Rosemary Fitzgerald, "'Rescue and Redemption'—the Rise of Female Medical Missions in Colonial India during the Late Nineteenth and Early Twentieth Centuries," in *Nursing History and the Politics of Welfare*, edited by A. M. Rafferty, J. Robinson, and R. Elkan (London: Routledge, 1996), 64–79; Rosemary Fitzgerald, "A 'Peculiar and Exceptional Measure': The Call for Women Medical Missionaries for India in the Later Nineteenth Century," in *Missionary Encounters: Sources and Issues*, edited by Robert A. Bickers and Rosemary Seton (Richmond, UK: Curzon Press, 1996), 174–96.

85. CMS G2/I4/o/415/1890. A. Neve to Baring Gould, Kashmir, 17 Sept. 1890.

86. Maconachie (late I.C.S.), *Rowland Bateman*, 87.

87. Henry Whitehead, "The Progress of Christianity in India and Mission Strategy," *East and West* 5 (Jan. 1907): 26.

88. Youngson, *Forty Years of the Panjab Mission*, 92.

89. Ibid., 78.

90. Ibid., 85.

91. Ibid., 94, emphasis mine.

92. Clark, *Robert Clark*, 119.

93. Youngson, *Forty Years of the Panjab Mission*, 126, 137.

94. Brooke Deedes, *An Account of the Visit of the Lord Bishop of Calcutta to the Peshawar Mission, Contributed by His Chaplain the Rev. Brooke Deedes, M.A.*, printed for private circulation (CMS G1/I4/PI/371882, 1881).

95. Ibid.

96. Church Missionary Society, *Register of Missionaries (Clerical, Lay, & Female) and Native Clergy from 1804 to 1904*, 136.

97. SPG, Mission Reports, 3, A. Haig report, Karnal, Michaelmas 1891.

98. Cambridge Mission to Delhi, *Annual Report* (Delhi, 1878–1904), 1888, 6.

99. Montgomery, *The Life and Letters of George Alfred Lefroy D.D., Bishop of Calcutta and Metropolitan*, 111.

100. CMS G2/I4/PI/117/1882. T. P. Hughes to Parent Committee, n.d.

101. *Lahore Civil and Military Gazette*, church supplement, 5 Jan. 1884.

102. SPG, Mission Reports, Series E, R. R. Winter to W. H. Bray, Delhi, 24 Nov. 1875.

103. SPG, Mission Reports, Series E, Winter to Tucker, 24 Feb. 1885.

104. *The Indian Church Directory for the Province of India and Ceylon* (Calcutta, 1890).

105. SPG, Committee on Women's Work, Annual Reports, Lahore, 1908.

106. CMS G2/I4/02/223/1883.

107. CMS G2/I4/02/215/1885. T. Bomford to Gray, Multan, 4 Sept. 1885.

108. CMS G2/I4/0/81/1890. Examination of Mission Schools in the Diocese of Lahore by the Rev. T. R. Wade (ms.).

109. Clark, *Robert Clark*, 121.

110. CMS G2/I4/O2/25/1883.

111. CMS G2/I4/02/180/1887.

112. J. S. Grewal, *The City of the Golden Temple*, 2d ed. (Amritsar: Guru Nanak Dev University, 1996), 24–25.

113. J. S. Grewal, *The Sikhs of the Punjab*, rev. ed., *The New Cambridge History of India*, II.3 (Cambridge: Cambridge University Press, 1999), 148–49.

114. Church Missionary Society, *Register of Missionaries (Clerical, Lay, & Female) and Native Clergy from 1804 to 1904*, 159; Clark, *Robert Clark*, 134, 314.

115. National Library of Scotland, Church of Scotland. Letter Book of the Secretary of the Foreign Missions Committee, John T. Maclagan, manuscript no. 7545, 1881–90, letter from William Harper, Sialkot, 5 July 1883; National Library of Scotland, Punjab and Murray College papers, plans, etc., acc 7548 D–17, 1917–28. Correspondence concerning Dr. John Hutchinson of Chamba.

116. SPG, Mission Reports, Series E, Katherine Beynon, Lahore; SPG, Committee on Women's Work, Letters Received, India, CWW 146, obituary of Deaconess Katherine Beynon, 1924.

117. BMS, IN/54, F. W. Hale, clipping, "Our Institutional Work: A Plea for a Forward Policy," paper read to Triennial Conference of Indian Missionaries, Feb. 7–15, 1896.

118. Maconachie (late I.C.S.), *Rowland Bateman*, 131.

119. Ibid., 107.

120. Ibid., 114, 118,123.

121. The Rev. Herbert Alfred Birks, M.A., *The Life and Correspondence of Thomas Valpy French, First Bishop of Lahore*. 2 vols. (London: John Murray, 1895), vol. 1, 133.

122. Clark, *Robert Clark*, 320.

123. Cecil H. Martin, *Allnutt of Delhi: A Memoir* (London: Society for Promoting Christian Knowledge, 1922), iii.

124. United Presbyterian Church of North America, Sialkot Mission, *Minutes*, 1905, 38.

125. Cust, *Essay on Prevailing Methods*, 213; Peter Penner, *Robert Needham Cust, 1821–1909: A Personal Biography*. Studies in British History, v. 5 (Lewiston, N.Y.: Edward Mellen Press, 1987).

126. CMS G2/I4/PI/1866, Dr. A. Jukes, Dera Ghazi Khan, 18 Apr. 1892.

127. Dana Lee Robert, *American Women in Mission: A Social History of Their Thought and Practice. The Modern Mission Era, 1792–1992* (Macon, Ga.: Mercer University Press, 1996).

128. United Presbyterian Church of North America, Records of the Board of Foreign Missions 1833–1966, Presbyterian Historical Society, Record Group 209, Series I, Box 7, Missionary and General Correspondence, India, Folder 32, Dorothy Cumming, Rawalpindi, 28 Mar. 1943.

129. *The Scotsman*, 23 Aug. 1906.

130. See *The Missionary Controversy: Discussion, Evidence and Report* (London: Wesleyan Methodist Book Room, 1890), which contains a summary of evidence on the missionary standard of living in India.

131. National Library of Scotland, Church of Scotland. Letter Book of the Secretary of the Foreign Missions Committee, John T. Maclagan, manuscript no. 7545, 1881–90. Letter to William Harper, Sialkot, 2 Apr. 1883; letter to John Youngson, 22 Oct. 1885; Minutes of the Church of Scotland Foreign Missions Committee, 298/10, 1887, 8; 298/10, 6 Mar. 1888, 17, 298/11, 5 July 1892. Salaries for Africa ranged from £225 to a maximum of £350. Conversion into rupees at 13.73/£ in the 1880s.

132. CMS G2/I4/02/250/1883. Rules Respecting Allowances to CMS missionaries in Punjab and Sindh Mission (printed).

133. Clark, *Robert Clark*, 341.

134. Maconachie (late I.C.S.), *Rowland Bateman*, 35.

135. CMS, Incoming Letters, G2/I4/O/1889, T. Bomford to R. Clark, Multan, 24 & 30 Nov. 1889.

136. Youngson, *Forty Years of the Panjab Mission*, 139.

137. Society for Promoting Female Education in the East, *Female Missionary Intelligencer*, vol. 16, Apr. 1896, new series (London, 1881–99), 56.

138. UP, Records of the Board of Foreign Missions (RG 209, Series I), Box 7, Missionary and General Correspondence, D. Emmet Alter to "Raymond," 28 Mar. 1935, Berkeley, California.

139. UP, Records of the Board of Foreign Missions (RG 209, Series I), Box 7, Missionary and General Correspondence, Emma Dean Anderson to W. B., Chakwal, 23 Oct. 1936.

140. Clark, *Robert Clark*, 168.

141. Maconachie (late I.C.S.), *Rowland Bateman*, 76.

142. *Historical Sketches*, 92.

143. Ibid., 93.

144. Lahore Civil and Military Gazette, "The Mission College, Lahore," 14 Dec. 1891.

145. Anita Desai, *Clear Light of Day* (New York, 1980), 124–25.

CHAPTER 4

1. H. H. Montgomery, *The Life and Letters of George Alfred Lefroy D.D., Bishop of Calcutta and Metropolitan* (London: Longmans, Green & Co., 1920), 20.

2. J. S. Grewal, *The Sikhs of the Punjab*, rev. ed., *The New Cambridge History of India*, II.3 (Cambridge: Cambridge University Press, 1999), 130.

3. John C. B. Webster, *The Christian Community and Change in Nineteenth Century North India* (Delhi: Macmillan of India, 1976); T. O. (Thomas O.) Beidelman, *Colonial Evangelism: A Socio-Historical Study of an East African Mission at the Grassroots* (Bloomington: Indiana University Press, 1982); Lamin O. Sanneh, *Encountering the West: Christianity and the Global Cultural Process: The African Dimension*. World Christian Theology Series (Maryknoll, N.Y.: Orbis Books, 1993).

4. Eugene Stock, *The History of the Church Missionary Society: Its Environment, Its Men and Its Work* (London: Church Missionary Society, 1899), vol. 2, 488.

5. Antoinette M. Burton, *Burdens of History: British Feminists, Indian Women, and Imperial Culture, 1865–1915* (Chapel Hill: University of North Carolina, 1994).

6. Edward Said, *Culture and Imperialism* (New York: Vintage Books, 1993), 40.

7. Lahore Missionary Conference, *Report of the Punjab Missionary Conference Held at Lahore in Dec. and Jan., 1862–63* (Ludhiana: American Presbyterian Mission Press, 1863), 159–88.

8. Ibid., 159, 162–63.

9. Ibid., 166–67.

10. Edward W. Said, *Orientalism* (New York: Pantheon Books, 1978), 204.

11. Missionary Conference, *Report*, 167.

12. See, for example, G2/I4/02/127/1888. Notes of (Native) Church Council Session, 27 Feb. 1888.

13. Henry Venn, *To Apply the Gospel: Selections from the Writing of Henry Venn*, Max Warren (Grand Rapids, Mich.: William B. Eerdmans, 1971), 63.

14. Missionary Conference, *Report*, 180.

15. Ibid., 172, 166–67.

16. *Account of a Society for Mission to Africa and the East Instituted by Members of the Established Church* (London, 1799), 8.

17. C. P. Williams, "'Not Quite Gentlemen': An Examination of 'Middling Class' Protestant Missionaries from Britain, 1850–1900," *Journal of Ecclesiastical History* 31, no. 3 (July 1980).

18. Missionary Conference, *Report*, 181–82.

19. Ibid., 168.

20. SPG Series E, Missionary Reports, Delhi, "Three Months in the SPG Mission, Delhi" (manuscript), the Rev. T. W. H. Hunter, assistant secretary.

21. Ruth Compton Brouwer, *New Women for God: Canadian Presbyterian Women and India Missions, 1876–1914*. Social History of Canada, 44 (Toronto; Buffalo: University of Toronto Press, 1990).

22. Zenana Bible and Medical Mission, *The Indian Female Evangelist*, vol. 5, no. 31, Apr. 1880 (London: Indian Female Normal School and Instruction Society, 1872–1901).

23. Gail Minault, *Secluded Scholars: Women's Education and Muslim Social Reform in Colonial India* (New Delhi: Oxford University Press, 1998), 303.

24. Gauri Viswanathan, "Coping with (Civil) Death: The Christian Convert's Rights of Passage in Colonial India," in *After Colonialism: Imperial Histories and Postcolonial Displacements*, edited by Gyan Prakash. Princeton Studies in Culture/Power/History (Princeton: Princeton University Press, 1995), 183–210; Gauri Viswanathan, *Outside the Fold: Conversion, Modernity, and Belief* (Princeton: Princeton University Press, 1998).

25. Irene H. Barnes, *Between Life and Death: The Story of C.E.Z.M.S. Medical Missions in India, China, and Ceylon* (London: Marshall Brothers, 1901), 181.

26. CMS G2/I4/o/383/1899. Autobiography of Munshi Qutb-ud-Din, candidate for ordination. Translation of Statement to A. H. Storrs, CMS, Tarn Taran; CMS G2/I4/o/193/1901, Autobiography of Mr. Paras Nath; CMS G2/I4/o/110/1903. Biography of Munshi Fazlud Din, head catechist, Amritsar; CMS G2/I4/o/210/1903. Biography of Theodore C. Haube; CMS G2/I4/o/113/1913. "An Account of My Life." Buta Singh Peter.

27. Imad-ud-din, *A Mohammedan Brought to Christ: Being The Autobiography of a Native Clergyman in India: To Which Is Added His Treatise on Justification by Faith in Christ*, from the Hindustanee (London: Church Missionary Society, 1869); Imad-ud-din, *A Mohammedan Brought to Christ: Being the Autobiography of the Rev. Imad-Ud-In, D.D.*, new ed., tr. Robert Clark (London: Church Missionary Society, 1884); see Avril A. Powell, "Processes of Conversion to Christianity in Nineteenth Century North-Western India," in *Religious Conversion Movements in South Asia: Continuities and Change, 1800–1900*, edited by Geoffrey A. Oddie (Richmond, UK: Curzon, 1997), 36–42.

28. Imad-ud-din, *A Mohammedan Brought to Christ: Being the Auto-biography of the Rev. Imad-Ud-Din, D.D.*, 3.

29. CMS G2/I4/P3/261/1896. Ihsan Ullah, Narowal, 18 Apr. to PC.

30. Denzil Ibbetson, *Panjab Castes*, Chapters from the Census Report of 1881 on "The Races, Castes, and Tribes of the Panjab," reprint, 1916 (Delhi: Meeraj, 1984); Thomas R. Trautmann, *Aryans and British India* (Berkeley: University of California Press, 1997).

31. Patrick Brantlinger, *Rule of Darkness: British Literature and Imperialism, 1830–1914* (Ithaca: Cornell University Press, 1988), 39.

32. For one group of American Presbyterians, see Webster, *Christian Community*, 83 ff.

33. The Rev. Herbert Alfred Birks, M.A., *The Life and Correspondence of Thomas Valpy French, First Bishop of Lahore*. 2 vols. (London: John Murray, 1895), vol. 1, 365.

34. *A Native Church for the Natives of India, Giving an Account of the Formation of a Native Church Council for the Punjab Mission of the Church Missionary Society, and of the Proceedings of Their First Meeting at Umritsar, 31 Mar–2 Apr. 1877* (Lahore, 1877), 31.

35. Edward Said, *Culture and Imperialism*, 40.

36. *A Native Church for the Natives of India, Giving an Account of the Second Meeting of the Punjab CMS Native Church Council Held at Umritsar, 24–27 Dec. 1877* (Lahore, 1878), preface.

37. *Report of the Sixth Meeting of the Punjab CMS Native Church Council Held at Umritsar, 25–27 Dec. 1881* (Amritsar? 1882), 71.

38. For a list of occupations of a similar American Presbyterian elite see *Historical Sketches of the India Missions of the Presbyterian Church in the United States of America, Known as the Ludiana, the Farrukhabad, and the Kolhapur Missions: From the Beginning of the Work, in 1834, to the Time of Its Fiftieth Anniversary, in 1884* (Allahabad: Allahabad Mission Press, 1886), 59.

39. Robert Clark, *The Missions of the Church Missionary Society and the Church of England Zenana Missionary Society in the Punjab and Sindh*, ed. Robert Maconachie (London: Church Missionary Society, 1904 ed.), 44–45.

40. CMS Incoming Letters I4/O/348, T. R. Wade, Abbotabad, 3 Oct. 1892.

41. *Report of the 21st Annual Meeting of the Punjab CMS District Native Church Council, Amritsar, Apr. 11–13 1898* (Lahore? 1898), 30.

42. Sanneh, *Encountering the West*; Mary Louise Pratt, *Imperial Eyes: Travel Writing and Transculturation* (London; New York: Routledge, 1992).

43. E. P. (Edward Palmer) Thompson, *"Alien Homage": Edward Thompson and Rabindranath Tagore* (Delhi; New York: Oxford University Press, 1993), 69.

44. Edward Said, *Orientalism*, 204.

45. CMS G2/I4/02/213/1886. Memo from J. D. Tremlett, Member of

the Corresponding Committee, on Rules governing Punjab Native Church Council.

46. Jeffrey Cox, "On Redefining 'Crisis': The Victorian Crisis of Faith in the Punjab, 1880–1930," in *Victorian Faith in Crisis: Essays on Continuity and Change in Nineteenth-Century Religious Belief,* edited by Richard J. Helmstadter and Bernard Lightman (London: Macmillan, 1990), 315–41.

47. *Report of the Eighteenth Meeting of the Punjab CMS District Native Church Council Held at Amritsar, 27–29 Mar. 1895* (Lahore, 1895), 127.

48. CMS G2/I4/02/227/1888. Letter by the chairman to members of the Punjab and Sindh Native Church Council.

49. CMS G2/I4/02/146/1888. Dina Nath's letter of resignation from CMS, to Weitbrecht, Ajnala, 3 Mar. 1888.

50. T. E. Coverdale to Clark, Lahore, 29 Feb. 1888.

51. CMS G2/I4/02/151/1884. Miss Bose to Miss Wauton, Dehra Doon, 9 May 1884.

52. CMS G2/I4/02/150. Clark to Gray, Dalhousie, 17 May 1884.

53. CMS G2/I4/02/209. Miss C. V. Bose, M.A. to Miss Wauton, Calcutta, 30 July 1884.

54. G2/I4/0/170–172/1892, G2/I4/0/215/1892. Proceedings of Corresponding Committee, 26 Mar., and Minutes of Punjab District Church Council, 11–12 Mar.

55. *A Native Church for the Natives of India, Giving an Account of the Second Meeting of the Punjab CMS Native Church Council Held at Umritsar, 24–27 December 1877,* 72.

56. Stock, *The History of the Church Missionary Society: Its Environment, Its Men and Its Work,* vol. 3, 148; see Cox, "On Redefining 'Crisis': The Victorian Crisis of Faith in the Punjab, 1880–1930," for more details.

57. Henry Martyn Clark, *Robert Clark of the Punjab: Pioneer and Missionary Statesman* (London: Andrew Melrose, 1907), 306–7.

58. C. Peter Williams, *The Ideal of the Self-Governing Church: A Study in Victorian Missionary Strategy.* Studies in Christian Mission, vol. 1 (Leiden; New York: E. J. Brill, 1990).

59. Emmanuel Ayankanmi Ayandele, *The Missionary Impact on Modern Nigeria, 1842–1914: A Political and Social Analysis* (London: Longmans, 1966).

60. Andrew Porter, "Cambridge, Keswick, and Late Nineteenth-Century Attitudes to Africa," *Journal of Imperial and Commonwealth History* 5, no. 1 (1976): 5–34.

61. Church Missionary Society, *Abstract of Replies to the Circular Letter of the Conference Secretaries* (London: CMS, n.d., c. 1900), passim.

62. R. Maconachie (late I.C.S.), *Rowland Bateman: Nineteenth Century Apostle* (London: CMS, 1917), 80–82.

63. CMS G2/I4/02/240/1885. Bateman to Wigram, Narowal, 7 Sept. 1885.

64. CMS G2/I4/04. Dr. Datta to Bateman, Karnal, 15 Dec. 1886.

65. Lahore Civil and Military Gazette, supplement, 14 Nov. 1892.

66. CMS G2/I4/P3/152/1903. Minutes of Joint Committee of Conference and Native Church Council.

67. CMS Precis Book, G2/I4/P6/89 1910–19 Dr. N. P. Datta, Gurgaon, 21 May 1916.

68. CMS G2/I4/P7/26/1919. C. M. Gough, Lahore, 21 Jan. 1919 to PC.

69. CMS G2/I4/P7/69/1920. W. P. Hares to PC, Gojra, 13 May; "H and FC" resolution 13 July 1920.

70. Zenana Bible and Medical Mission, *The Indian Female Evangelist*, Annual Returns for 1891.

71. J. K. H. Denny, *Toward the Sunrising: A History of Work for the Women of India Done by Women from England, 1852–1901* (London: Marshall Brothers, 1901), 240–41.

72. Society for Promoting Female Education in the East, *Female Missionary Intelligencer*. New Series (London, 1881–99), Dec. 1881, 98–99.

73. Zenana Bible and Medical Mission, *The Indian Female Evangelist*, Apr. 1889, 89.

74. Society for Promoting Female Education in the East, *Female Missionary Intelligencer*, June 1893, 85.

75. Maconachie (late I.C.S.), *Rowland Bateman: Nineteenth Century Apostle*, 47.

76. Birks, *The Life and Correspondence of Thomas Valpy French, First Bishop of Lahore*, vol. 1, 247.

77. CMS G2/I4/0/148/1892. St. John's Divinity School and Hostel, Lahore. Annual Letter, 1891.

78. *Directory of Christian Missions and Churches in India, Burma and Ceylon* (Nagpur: National Christian Council, 1938), 399, 402.

79. Zenana Bible and Medical Mission, *The Indian Female Evangelist*, July 1880, 161–62.

80. Zenana Bible and Medical Mission, *The Indian Female Evangelist*, Jan. 1876, 20.

81. *Our Indian Sisters: A Quarterly Magazine of the Ladies Zenana Mission in Connection with the Baptist Missionary Society* (London: Baptist Zenana Mission, 1886–89), Jan.–Apr. 1886, 51, 99.

82. Ibid., Jan. 1887, 7.

83. *A Native Church for the Natives of India, Giving an Account of the Second Meeting of the Punjab CMS Native Church Council Held at Umritsar, 24–27 Dec. 1877.*

84. *After One Hundred Years: North India Mission, 1836–1936* (Bangalore: Scripture Literature Press, 1936), 87.

85. *Nai Masihi Git Ki Kitab*, 7th ed., hymnal (Hindi) (Delhi: Indian Society for the Promotion of Christian Knowledge, 1987), 4.

86. *After One Hundred Years: North India Mission, 1836–1936*, 128.

87. Zenana Bible and Medical Mission, *The Indian Female Evangelist*, July 1875, 357–58.

88. Hymns from *Sacred Songs and Solos* in the Karachi Masihi Convention, *Git Ki Kitab,* 3d ed., hymnal (Roman Urdu) (Karachi: Joint Christian Convention Committee, 1959) include "Almost Persuaded," "Pass Me Not," "Only Trust Him," "Near the Cross," "When the Roll Is Called up Yonder," "Precious Blood," and "O Happy Day."

89. Baptist Zenana Mission, *Jubilee 1867–1917: Fifty Years' Work among Women in the Far East* (London: Carey Press, 1917), 48.

90. *Our Indian Sisters: A Quarterly Magazine of the Ladies Zenana Mission in Connection with the Baptist Missionary Society,* 70.

91. Zenana Bible and Medical Mission, *The Indian Female Evangelist,* vol. 2, no. 15, July 1875, 313.

92. Cambridge Mission to Delhi, *Annual Report* (Delhi, 1878–1904), 1880, 10.

93. *A Native Church for the Natives of India, Giving an Account of the Second Meeting of the Punjab CMS Native Church Council Held at Umritsar, 24–27 Dec. 1877,* 55.

94. Mrs. J. D. Bate, Allahabad, comp., *The North India Tune-Book, Containing Bhajans and Ghazals with Native Tunes, as Usually Sung,* hymnal (Roman Urdu) (Allahabad: North India Tract and Book Society Depot, 1886), iii.

95. Ibid., iv.

96. Ibid., v–vii, ix.

97. *After One Hundred Years: North India Mission, 1836–1936,* 131.

98. Ibid.

99. CMS G2/I4/02/127/1888. Notes of Church Council Session, 27 Feb. 1888.

CHAPTER 5

1. Andrew Gordon, *Our India Mission: A Thirty Years History of the India Mission of the United Presbyterian Church of North America, Together with Personal Reminiscences* (Philadelphia: Andrew Gordon, 1886), 450.

2. *The Nineteenth Annual Report of the Board of Foreign Missions of the United Presbyterian Church of North America,* presented to the General Assembly in May 1878, 53.

3. J. S. Grewal, *The Sikhs of the Punjab,* rev. ed., *The New Cambridge History of India,* II.3 (Cambridge: Cambridge University Press, 1999), 130.

4. Census of India 1931, *Punjab Part I,* vol. 17, Khan Ahmad Hasan Khan, ed. (Lahore: Punjab Government, 1933), 317.

5. Christianity accounted for 1.36 percent of the total population of Pakistan in 1951, and roughly 2 percent of the population of Punjab Province.

6. J. Waskom Pickett, *Christian Mass Movements in India: A Study with Recommendations* (New York: Abingdon Press, 1933); J. C. Heinrich, *The Psychology of a Suppressed People* (London: George Allen and Unwin, 1937); Frederick and Margaret Stock, *People Movements in the*

Punjab, with Special Reference to the United Presbyterian Church (South Pasadena, Calif.: William Carey Library, 1975); John C. B. Webster, *The Dalit Christians: A History* (Delhi: Indian Society for Promoting Christian Knowledge, 1992).

7. Gordon, *Our India Mission*, 422.

8. Ibid.

9. *The 55th Annual Report of the American United Presbyterian Mission in India for the Year 1910*, Mysore: Wesleyan Mission Press, 1911, 14. Obituary of the Rev. Samuel Martin, D.D., 1836–1910.

10. Gordon, *Our India Mission*, 422.

11. Ibid., 423.

12. Ibid.

13. I am indebted to Mary Beth Dewey of Iowa City, and other informants from United Presbyterian homes, for enlightening me about this denomination.

14. R. Maconachie (late I.C.S.), *Rowland Bateman: Nineteenth Century Apostle* (London: CMS, 1917), 52; *Report on Public Instruction in the Punjab and Its Dependencies for the Year 1890–1891*, compiled by J. Sime, DPI (Lahore, 1891), lvii.

15. Robert Stewart, *Life and Work in India: An Account of the Conditions, Methods, Difficulties, Results, Future Prospects and Reflex Influence of Missionary Labor in India, Especially in the Punjab Mission of the United Presbyterian Church of North America* (Philadelphia: Pearl Publishing, 1899), 57.

16. Gordon, *Our India Mission*, 427.

17. Webster, *The Dalit Christians: A History*, 75.

18. See United Presbyterian India Mission, *Annual Report*, 1910, 16.

19. John C. B. Webster, *The Christian Community and Change in Nineteenth Century North India* (Delhi: Macmillan of India, 1976), cited on p. 60.

20. Denzil Ibbetson, *Panjab Castes*, Chapters from the Census Report of 1881 on "The Races, Castes, and Tribes of the Panjab," reprint, 1916 (Delhi: Meeraj, 1984), 293.

21. Ibid., preface.

22. H. A. (Horace Arthur) Rose, *A Glossary of the Tribes and Castes of the Punjab and North-West Frontier Province: Based on the Census Report for the Punjab, 1883, by the Late Sir Denzil Ibbetson and the Census Report for the Punjab, 1892, by Sir Edward Maclagan* ([Patiala]: Languages Dept., Punjab, 1970); Kenneth W. Jones, "Religious Identity and the Indian Census," in *The Census in British India: New Perspectives*, edited by Gerald N. Barrier (New Delhi: Manohar, 1981), 73–101; on this topic, see Bernard Cohn, *An Anthropologist among the Historians and Other Essays* (Delhi: Oxford University Press, 1987); Bernard S. Cohn, *Colonialism and Its Forms of Knowledge: The British in India*. Princeton Studies in Culture/Power/History (Princeton: Princeton University Press, 1996).

23. On the "invention of caste" more generally, see Nicholas B. Dirks,

The Hollow Crown: Ethnohistory of an Indian Kingdom (Cambridge, UK: Cambridge University Press, 1987); Nicholas B. Dirks, "The Invention of Caste: Civil Society in Colonial India," *Social Analysis* 25 (1989): 42–52.

24. Mark Juergensmeyer, *Religion as Social Vision: The Movement against Untouchability in 20th-Century Punjab* (Berkeley: University of California Press, 1982), intro., part 1; Eleanor Zelliot, *From Untouchable to Dalit: Essays on the Ambedkar Movement* (New Delhi: Manohar Publications, 1992); James Massey, *Dalits in India: Religion as a Source of Bondage or Liberation with Special Reference to Christians* (New Delhi: Manohar Publishers & Distributors and ISPCK, 1995), part I.

25. Ibbetson, *Panjab Castes*, 290.

26. Census of India 1931, *Punjab Part II*, vol. 17, Khan Ahmad Hasan Khan (Lahore: Punjab Government, 1933), 278–79, 281, 287, 289.

27. On the United Provinces, see Charlotte Melina (Viall) Wiser, *Behind Mud Walls, by Charlotte Viall Wiser and William H. Wiser* (New York: Smith, 1930); Charlotte Melina (Viall) Wiser, *Behind Mud Walls, 1930–1960, by William H. Wiser and Charlotte Viall Wiser*, with a foreword by David G. Mandelbaum (Berkeley: University of California Press, 1971).

28. E. D. and F. Thakur Das Lucas, *The Rural Church in the Punjab: A Study of Social, Economic, Educational and Religious Conditions Prevailing amongst Certain Village Christian Communities in the Sialkot District*. Research Studies in the Economic and Social Environment of the Indian Church (Lahore, 1938), 15–17.

29. Census of India 1931, *Punjab Part II*, vol. 17, 278–79, 281, 287, 289.

30. Ibid., *Part I*, vol. 17, Khan Ahmad Hasan Khan (Lahore: Punjab Government, 1933); *Delhi*, vol. 16, Khan Ahmad Hasan (Lahore: Government of India, 1933); Census of India 1931, *North West Frontier Province*, vol. 15, G. L. and A. D. F. Dundas Mallam (Peshawar: Government of India, 1933); Stock, *People Movements*, figure 15, 114. The Census of India 1931 enumerates 391,270 Indian Christians in Punjab, 11,673 in Delhi, and 4,601 in the Northwest Frontier Province for a total of 407,544. Stock lists 462,681 "Chuhra" Christians in Punjab in 1931, citing "census reports for the whole Punjab." Census enumerators were, with good reason, confused about changes in religious self-ascription in 1931, and their tables are often inconsistent.

31. Census of India 1911, *Punjab*, vol. 14, *Part I: Report*, Pandit Harikishan Kaul (Lahore: Civil and Military Gazette, 1912), 131–33; Census of India 1921, *Punjab and Delhi, Part I: Report*, L. Middleton, and S. M. Jacob (Lahore: Civil and Military Gazette, 1923), 176.

32. Census of India 1921, *North-West Frontier Province*, R. B. Bhai Lehna Singh (Peshawar: Government Press, 1922), 102.

33. Ibid.

34. Ibbetson, *Panjab Castes*, 294.

35. Ibid., 269.

36. Ibid., 295.

37. Sialkot Mission, Annual Reports of the United Presbyterian Mission in India, Sialkot, 1884, 21.

38. Stock, *People Movements*, ch. 2.

39. John F. W. Youngson, *Forty Years of the Panjab Mission of the Church of Scotland, 1855–1895* (Edinburgh: R. & R. Clark, 1896), 168.

40. *Report of the SPG and Cambridge Mission in Delhi and the South Punjab*, title varies (1882–1931), 1904, 85, 1905, 62.

41. Pieter Streefland, *The Sweepers of Slaughterhouse: Conflict and Survival in a Karachi Neighbourhood* (Assen: Van Gorcum, 1979).

42. S. S. Hewlett, *Daughters of the King* (London: James Nisbet and Co., 1886).

43. Lucas, *Rural Church in the Punjab*, 10.

44. Sialkot Mission, Annual Reports of the United Presbyterian Mission in India, Sialkot, 1884, 42.

45. CMS G2/I4/o/117/1892. Report of the Bahrwal Mission, by H. E. Perkins.

46. CMS G2/I4/o/53. Tarn Taran Report for 1925.

47. Ibid.

48. CMS G2/I4/o/1925. Jhang Bar Report, 1925.

49. Sialkot Mission, Annual Reports of the United Presbyterian Mission in India, Sialkot, 1884, 34. The Rev. A. B. Caldwell; CMS G2/I4/o/17/1892. Report of the Bahrwal Mission, by H. E. Perkins.

50. CMS G2/I4/o2/110/1888. Rules of Central Punjab Village Mission Board (proceedings).

51. CMS G2/I4/o/53/1926. Tarn Taran Report, 1925. See also United Presbyterian Church of North America, Records of the Board of Foreign Missions (RG 209, Series I), Box 7, Missionary and General Correspondence, E. V. Clements to Dr. White, Badomali, 27 July 1933.

52. *Indian War Cry*, Apr. 1939.

53. Sialkot Mission, *Annual Reports of the United Presbyterian Mission in India* (Sialkot, 1882–84), 1884, 17, 21.

54. CMS G2/I4/P7/113/1921. C. M. Gough to PC, 9 June 1921.

55. E. S. Wenger, *Missionary Biographies in Four Volumes*, unpublished manuscript (Serampore: Carey Library, 1936), vol. 3, 51.

56. Maconachie (late I.C.S.), *Rowland Bateman*, 101.

57. *Report of the Eighteenth Meeting of the Punjab CMS District Native Church Council Held at Amritsar, 27–29 Mar. 1895* (Lahore, 1895).

58. UP, Records of the Board of Foreign Missions (RG 209, Series I), Box 7, Missionary and General Correspondence, J. G. Campbell to Dr. Dodds, 18 May 1993, Pasrur.

59. CMS G2/I4/o/117/1892.

60. Ibbetson, *Panjab Castes*, 295.

61. Bapsi Sidhwa, *Ice-Candy Man*, reprint, 1988 (London: Penguin, 1989), 181.

62. Lucas, *Rural Church in the Punjab*, iii.

63. Punjab Mission Council. A reply to the committee question regard-

ing the future of the Murray College, c. 1918. National Library of Scotland, Punjab and Murray College papers, plans, etc., acc 7548 D-17, 1917–28.

64. CMS G2/I4/o/56/1913. Report of the CMS Mission, Toba Tek Singh, Jhang Bar, District Lyallpur, Punjab, 1912.

65. Census of India 1911, *Punjab*, vol. 14, *Part I: Report*, 181–82.

66. Webster, *The Dalit Christians: A History*, 75.

67. Maconachie (late I.C.S.), *Rowland Bateman*, 101–2.

68. CMS G2/I4/o2/110/1888. Rules of Central Punjab Village Mission Board (proceedings).

69. BMS IN/42. Copy of a letter for the Southport Sunday School, 21 Nov. 1880; IN/54, Frederick William Hale, "Great Days at Delhi. A Record of Revival," clipping from Mar. 1918 *Missionary Herald*.

70. CMS G2/I4/o/144/1889.

71. Ibbetson, *Panjab Castes*, 294–95.

72. Streefland, *The Sweepers of Slaughterhouse: Conflict and Survival in a Karachi Neighbourhood*, passim.

73. *Indian War Cry*, Mar. 1939.

74. CMS G2/I4/o/127/1912. Report of the chairman of the Lahore District Mission Council, 1911–12.

75. Lucas, *Rural Church in the Punjab*, 36.

76. George W. Briggs, *The Chamars, by Geo. W. Briggs, M.Sc.* (New York: Oxford University Press, 1920).

77. Ibbetson, *Panjab Castes*, 293, 297.

78. James P. Alter, *In the Doab and Rohilkhand: North Indian Christianity, 1815–1915* (Delhi: ISPCK, 1986).

79. Ludhiana, Amritsar, Ferozepore, and Jullundur.

80. Census of India 1921, *Punjab and Delhi, Part I: Report*, maps, 111.

81. Youngson, *Forty Years of the Panjab Mission*, 52.

82. Stewart, *Life and Work in India*, 118.

83. Robin Horton, "African Conversion," *Africa* 41 (1971): 85–108.

84. Susan Bayly, *Saints, Goddesses, and Kings: Muslims and Christians in South Indian Society, 1700–1900.* Cambridge South Asian Studies, 43 (Cambridge, Eng.; New York: Cambridge University Press, 1989); Webster, *The Dalit Christians: A History*, ch. 2.

85. Duncan Forrester, *Caste and Christianity: Attitudes and Policies on Caste of Anglo-Saxon Protestant Missions in India.* London Studies on South Asia no. 1 (London: Curzon Press; Atlantic Highlands, N.J.: Humanities Press, 1980), 74; Webster, *The Dalit Christians: A History*, 54–55.

86. Lucas, *Rural Church in the Punjab*, iii.

87. Ibid., 20.

88. E. P. (Edward Palmer) Thompson, *"Alien Homage": Edward Thompson and Rabindranath Tagore* (Delhi; New York: Oxford University Press, 1993), 69.

89. Sialkot Mission, *Minutes of the Annual Meeting of the Sialkot*

Mission of the United Presbyterian Church of North America (various titles) (1896–1910), 1908, 14.

90. UP, Records of the Board of Foreign Missions (RG 209, Series I), Box 7, Missionary and General Correspondence, J. G. Campbell to Dr. Anderson, Pasrur, 13 Jan. 1920.

91. George Alfred Lefroy, *The Leatherworkers of Daryaganj.* Cambridge Mission to Delhi Occasional Papers (Delhi: Cambridge Mission to Delhi, 1884), passim; H. H. Montgomery, *The Life and Letters of George Alfred Lefroy D.D., Bishop of Calcutta and Metropolitan* (London: Longmans, Green & Co., 1920), 38.

92. Pickett, *Christian Mass Movements in India: A Study with Recommendations,* 179.

93. Census of India 1911, *Punjab,* vol. 14, *Part III: Appendices to the Imperial Tables,* Pandit Harikishan Kaul (Lahore: Civil and Military Gazette, 1912), 61.

94. Census of India 1911, *Punjab,* vol. 14, *Part I: Report,* 419.

95. Eleanor Zelliot, *From Untouchable to Dalit: Essays on the Ambedkar Movement* (New Delhi: Manohar Publications, 1992); Juergensmeyer, *Religion as Social Vision,* parts II, III.

96. SPG Mission Reports, Series E, Delhi, 1891. Report of the Rev. A. Haig, Karnal, Michaelmas 1891.

97. SPG Mission Reports, Series E, Delhi, the Rev. T. Williams, 31 Mar. 1887.

98. SPG Mission Reports, Series E. A. Haig to Tucker, Delhi, 30 Dec. 1887.

99. *One Hundred Years in Delhi* (Delhi: The Brotherhood of the Ascended Christ, 1977), 7.

100. Cambridge Mission to Delhi, *Annual Report* (Delhi, 1878–1904), 1901, 45.

101. SPG Mission Reports, Series E. Report of W. Williams, Riwari, First Quarter 1891.

102. For a more extended treatment of the Delhi Mission, see Jeffrey Cox, "George Alfred Lefroy: Anglicans, Untouchables, and Imperial Institutions," in *After the Victorians: Essays in Honor of John Clive,* edited by Susan Pedersen and Peter Mandler (London: Routledge, 1994); Jeffrey Cox, "C. F. Andrews and the Failure of the Modern Missionary Movement," in *Modern Religious Rebels,* edited by Stuart Mews (London: Epworth, 1993); Cox, "Independent English Women in Delhi and Lahore."

103. Jeffrey Cox, "Religion and Imperial Power in Nineteenth Century Britain," in *Freedom and Religion in the Nineteenth Century,* edited by R. W. and R. J. Helmstadter David (Palo Alto: Stanford University Press, 1997).

104. Briggs, *The Chamars, by Geo. W. Briggs, M.Sc.;* Anath Bandhu Mukerji, *The Chamars of Uttar Pradesh: A Study in Social Geography* (Delhi: Inter-India Publications, 1980).

105. SPG Mission Reports, Series E, Delhi, R. W. Winter to Tucker, 9 May 1887.

106. SPG Mission Reports, Series E, Delhi, R. W. Winter to Tucker, 9 May 1887.

107. Cox, "Independent English Women in Delhi and Lahore," 176.

108. *Our Indian Sisters: A Quarterly Magazine of the Ladies Zenana Mission in Connection with the Baptist Missionary Society* (London: Baptist Zenana Mission, 1886–89), Apr. 1886, 91.

109. Cambridge Mission to Delhi, *Annual Report* (Delhi, 1878–1904), 1881.

110. Edward Bickersteth, *A Letter to the Rev. Canon Westcott, D. D.* Cambridge Mission to Delhi Occasional Papers (Delhi: Cambridge Mission to Delhi, 1881), 9.

111. Montgomery, *Life and Letters of Lefroy*, 106.

112. Ibid., 32.

113. Lefroy, *Leatherworkers of Daryaganj*, 5.

114. Ibid.

115. Ibid., 6.

116. Ibid.

117. Ibid., 1.

118. Ibid., 11.

119. Montgomery, *Life and Letters of Lefroy*, 38.

120. Lefroy, *Leatherworkers of Daryaganj*, 11.

121. Montgomery, *Life and Letters of Lefroy*, 38.

122. *Missionary Herald*, 1 Sept. 1890. On the cow protection movement, see Kenneth W. Jones, *Arya Dharm: Hindu Consciousness in 19th-Century Punjab* (Berkeley: University of California Press, 1976); John R. McLane, *Indian Nationalism and the Early Congress* (Princeton: Princeton University Press, 1977).

123. *Gazetteer of the Delhi District, 1883–84*, compiled and published under the authority of Punjab government, reprint, 1884 (Gurgaon [Haryana]: Vintage Books, 1998), 91, appendix vii; Mukerji, *The Chamars of Uttar Pradesh: A Study in Social Geography*, maps, 122 ff.

124. Juergensmeyer, *Religion as Social Vision*, Part I; R. S. (Ravindra S.) Khare, *The Untouchable as Himself: Ideology, Identity, and Pragmatism among the Lucknow Chamars*. Cambridge Studies in Cultural Systems, no. 8 (Cambridge, Eng.; New York: Cambridge University Press, 1984), ch. 6.

125. Alter, *In the Doab and Rohilkhand: North Indian Christianity, 1815–1915*.

126. *A Native Church for the Natives of India, Giving an Account of the Second Meeting of the Punjab CMS Native Church Council Held at Umritsar, 24–27 Dec. 1877* (Lahore, 1878); Maconachie (late I.C.S.), *Rowland Bateman*, photographs facing 77, 91.

127. CMS G2/I4/O3/188/1889: "Resolution in Regard to Giving up to

the CMS Certain Territory in Riah Tahsil. Adopted by the Sialkot Mission of the United Presbyterian Church of North America," 27 Mar. 1889, Sialkot; CMS G2/I4/O141/1890. R. Clark to W. Gray, Amritsar, 10 Mar. 1890.

128. Maconachie (late I.C.S.), *Rowland Bateman*, 104.

129. CMS G2/I4/PI/186/1889; CMS G2/I4/PI/217/1889.

130. CMS G2/I4/o/108/1916. Memorandum of the Scheme of Land Colonization suggested by the Rt. Rev. the Lord Bishop of Madras at a conference of village missionaries held at Lahore on 11 Feb. 1913.

131. CMS G2/I4/o/162/1892. T. J. L. Mayer to Gray, 14 Mar. 1892, Clarkabad.

132. Elizabeth G. K. Hewat, *Vision and Achievement 1796–1956: A History of the Foreign Missions of the Churches United in the Church of Scotland* (Edinburgh: Thomas Nelson & Sons, 1960), 118.

133. National Library of Scotland, Punjab and Murray College papers, plans, etc., acc 7548 D-17, 1917–28. Report of the Advancement Movement Committee, 28 Oct. 1926.

134. Lucas, *Rural Church in the Punjab*, 26.

135. Khushwant Singh, *Train to Pakistan*, reprint, 1956 (Delhi: Ravi Dayal, 1988), 10–11.

136. Juergensmeyer, *Religion as Social Vision*, 190.

137. Interview with Bob and Ellen Alter, 22 May 1991, Oakville Estates, Landour, Mussoorie.

138. National Library of Scotland, Punjab and Murray College papers, plans, etc., acc 7548 D-17, 1917–28. Report of the Advancement Movement Committee, 28 Oct. 1926.

139. CMS G2/I4/o/127/1912. Report of the Chairman of the Lahore District Mission Council, 1911–12.

140. Salvation Army, *Indian War Cry*, Mar. 1939.

141. SPG Committee on Women's Work, Annual Reports (manuscript), Diocese of Lahore, Miss Fiennes, 1909.

142. *After One Hundred Years: North India Mission, 1836–1936* (Bangalore: Scripture Literature Press, 1936), 88.

143. United Presbyterian Church, Sialkot Mission, Annual Report, 1884, 41.

144. Sialkot Mission, Minutes, 1896, n.p.

145. Stock, *People Movements*, 120.

146. Sialkot Mission, Minutes, 1904, 14; 1905, 39; 1906, 21.

147. Mrs. J. D. Bate, Allahabad, comp., *The North India Tune-Book, Containing Bhajans and Ghazals with Native Tunes, as Usually Sung*, hymnal (Roman Urdu) (Allahabad: North India Tract and Book Society Depot, 1886); Mrs. Emma Moore Scott, comp., *The Hindustani Tune Book, a Collection of Bhajans and Gazals, Containing the Principal Native Airs, Sung in the Missions of North India: Arranged for the Piano or Organ*, 2d ed., hymnal (Roman Urdu) (Lucknow: Methodist Publishing House, 1894);

Masihi Git Ki Kitab Sath Ragan Ke, hymnal (Roman Urdu) (London: Novello, 1916); *Zabur Aur Git Ki Kitab,* hymnal (Roman Urdu) (Allahabad: United Provinces Christian Council, 1932); *Sialkot Convention Hymn Book,* hymnal (Urdu) (Sialkot: Sialkot Convention, 1940); Salvation Army, *The Salvation Army Song Book,* hymnal (Urdu), compiled by Lieutenant Commissioner Vijri Singh (H. S. Hodgson) (Lahore: Northern India Territorial Headquarters, 1946); Uttar Pradesh Christian Council, *Kalisiyai Git Ki Kitab,* hymnal (Roman Urdu), with a preface by A. Rallia Ram (Allahabad: North Indian Christian Book and Tract Society, 1953); Karachi Masihi Convention, *Git Ki Kitab,* 3d ed., hymnal (Roman Urdu) (Karachi: Joint Christian Convention Committee, 1959); *Masihi Git Ki Kitab,* 5th ed., hymnal (Hindi) (Delhi: Indian Society for the Promotion of Christian Knowledge, 1964); *Nai Masihi Git Ki Kitab,* 7th ed., hymnal (Hindi) (Delhi: Indian Society for the Promotion of Christian Knowledge, 1987).

148. *After One Hundred Years: North India Mission, 1836–1936,* 131.

149. The Karachi Masihi Convention's *Git Ki Kitab* (1959), prepared for interdenominational singing conventions, gives the derivation of its popular Urdu hymns. Those from *Sacred Songs and Solos* include "Almost Persuaded," "Pass Me Not," "Only Trust Him," "Near the Cross," "When the Roll Is Called Up Yonder," "Precious Name," and "O Happy Day"; from the *Hindustani Git ki Kitab*: "I Will Sing of My Redeemer," "All Hail the Power of Jesus Name," "Come Thou Fount of Every Blessing," "Just as I Am," "Near the Cross," "Nearer My God to Thee," "Love Divine," "All Love Excelling," and "Guide Me, Oh Thou Great Jehovah" (also a Welsh Labour Party favorite).

150. United Presbyterian Church of North America, Records of the Board of Foreign Missions (RG 209, Series I), Box 7, Missionary and General Correspondence, J. C. Heinrich, "Dear Friends," 13 May 1939, Sheakhupura.

151. CMS G2/I4/0/217/1889; Sialkot Mission, Minutes, 1902, 41.

152. CMS G2/I4/0/228/1908.

153. Thompson, *"Alien Homage": Edward Thompson and Rabindranath Tagore,* 69.

CHAPTER 6

1. Jeffrey Cox, "Independent English Women in Delhi and Lahore," in *Religion and Irreligion in Victorian Society: Essays in Honor of R. K. Webb,* edited by R. W. Davis and R. J. Helmstadter (London: Routledge, 1992), for examples from Delhi and Lahore.

2. For an example, see Mrs. Ashley Carus-Wilson, *A Woman's Life for Kashmir: Irene Petrie, a Biography* (New York: Fleming H. Revell Company, 1901); cf. Jane Haggis, "'A Heart That Has Felt the Love of God and Longs for Others to Know It': Conventions of Gender, Tensions of Self and Constructions of Difference in Offering to Be a Lady Missionary," *Women's History Review* 7, no. 2 (1998): 171–92.

3. Dana Lee Robert, *American Women in Mission: A Social History of Their Thought and Practice. The Modern Mission Era, 1792–1992* (Macon, Ga.: Mercer University Press, 1996), on missionary wives.

4. Antoinette M. Burton, *Burdens of History: British Feminists, Indian Women, and Imperial Culture, 1865–1915* (Chapel Hill: University of North Carolina, 1994).

5. Rosemary Fitzgerald, "'Rescue and Redemption'—the Rise of Female Medical Missions in Colonial India during the Late Nineteenth and Early Twentieth Centuries," in *Nursing History and the Politics of Welfare*, edited by A. M. Rafferty, J. Robinson, and R. Elkan (London: Routledge, 1996), 64–79.

6. CMS G2/I4/P3/293/1894.

7. *Historical Sketches of the India Missions of the Presbyterian Church in the United States of America, Known as the Ludiana, the Farrukhabad, and the Kolhapur Missions: From the Beginning of the Work, in 1834, to the Time of Its Fiftieth Anniversary, in 1884* (Allahabad: Allahabad Mission Press, 1886), 76ff and passim. In 1864 there were fourteen men and fourteen women, thirteen of them married to missionaries; by 1884 there were twenty-one men and twenty-four women, eight of them unmarried.

8. Ibid., 76.

9. Sialkot Mission Minutes, 1904, 38.

10. Sialkot Mission Minutes.

11. SPG biographical file of women missionaries, cited as SPG card file. Lacking a central source of biographical information, I put together a card file on all SPG women missionaries in Delhi and Punjab, 1857–1947, from a variety of sources, including the annual reports of the Society for the Propagation of the Gospel and the Cambridge Mission to Delhi, the SPG's Committee on Women's Work manuscript reports from Delhi, the SPG's manuscript Roll of Women Missionaries, F. J. Western's *The Early History of the Cambridge Mission to Delhi* (typescript, 1950), *The Delhi Mission News*, and the memorial brasses on the wall of St. Hilda's deaconess house in Lahore. At the time I compiled this list I did not have the advantage of Ruth Roseveare's list of women who served in Delhi, found in *Delhi: Community of St. Stephen, 1886–1986* (Reepham, Norwich: privately published, 1986).

12. *Historical Sketches*, 76.

13. This society was the forerunner of the Zenana Bible and Medical Mission (ZBMM). See Henry Martyn Clark, *Robert Clark of the Punjab: Pioneer and Missionary Statesman* (London: Andrew Melrose, 1907), 256; J. C. Pollock, *Shadows Fall Apart: The Story of the Zenana Bible and Medical Mission* (London: Hodder and Stoughton, 1958), 17.

14. SPG card file.

15. Ruth Roseveare, *Delhi: Community of St. Stephen, 1886–1986* (Reepham, Norwich: privately published, 1986).

16. Zenana Bible and Medical Mission, *The Indian Female Evangelist,*

vol. 5, no. 33, Jan. 1880 (London: Indian Female Normal School and Instruction Society, 1872–1901), 7.

17. Leslie Flemming, "New Models, New Roles: U.S. Presbyterian Women Missionaries and Social Change in North India, 1870–1910," in *Women's Work for Women: Missionaries and Social Change in Asia*, edited by Leslie Flemming (Boulder, Colo.: Westview Press, 1989), 35–57.

18. Irene H. Barnes, *Behind the Pardah: The Story of C.E.Z.M.S. Work in India* (London: Marshall Brothers, 1897), 51.

19. S. S. Hewlett, *Daughters of the King* (London: James Nisbet and Co., 1886), 2.

20. Zenana Bible and Medical Mission, *Indian Female Evangelist*, vol. 12, Apr. 1892, 70.

21. Irene H Barnes, *Behind the Pardah: The Story of C.E.Z.M.S. Work in India*, 180–83.

22. Hewlett, *Daughters of the King*, 28.

23. *Report of the SPG and Cambridge Mission in Delhi and the South Punjab*, title varies (1882–1931), 1898, 20–21.

24. Ibid., 1892, 10.

25. Ibid.

26. Antoinette Burton, "Fearful Bodies into Disciplined Subjects: Pleasure, Romance and the Family Drama of Colonial Reform in Mary Carpenter's Six Months in India," *Signs* 20, no. 3 (1995): 545–74; Katherine Mayo, *Mother India*, with an introduction by Mrinalini Sinha, reprint, 1927 (Ann Arbor: University of Michigan, 2000).

27. SPG, Mission Reports, Series 3, Delhi Mission, Winter to Tucker, 24 Feb. 1885.

28. Zenana Bible and Medical Mission, *Indian Female Evangelist*, vol. 12, no. 82, Apr. 1892, 70.

29. *Our Indian Sisters: A Quarterly Magazine of the Ladies Zenana Mission in Connection with the Baptist Missionary Society* (London: Baptist Zenana Mission, 1886–89), vol. 5, Apr. 1886, 188.

30. *Report of the SPG and Cambridge Mission*, 1894, 18.

31. Ibid.

32. Hewlett, *Daughters of the King*, 1.

33. *Report of the SPG and Cambridge Mission*, 1903, 47.

34. The Manifesto was reprinted in the CMS's Punjab Mission News, and then again in Zenana Bible and Medical Mission, *The Indian Female Evangelist*, vol. 10, no. 71, July 1889 (London: Indian Female Normal School and Instruction Society, 1872–1901), 116–17.

35. Ibid., vol. 12, no. 82, Apr. 1892, 70.

36. Ibid., vol. 1, no. 8, Oct. 1873, 44.

37. SPG, Mission Reports, Series 3, Delhi Mission, Winter to Tucker, 24 Feb. 1885.

38. *Historical Sketches*, 34, 36.

39. *Directory of Christian Missions and Churches in India, Burma and Ceylon* (Nagpur: National Christian Council, 1938). On women and or-

phans, see Ruth Compton Brouwer, *New Women for God: Canadian Presbyterian Women and India Missions, 1876–1914*. Social History of Canada, no. 44 (Toronto; Buffalo: University of Toronto Press, 1990).

40. Richard O. Comfort, *The Village Church in West Pakistan* (Lahore: West Pakistan Christian Council, c. 1957), 122.

41. Baptist Zenana Missionary Society, *Annual Reports* (London, 1869–1925), 1901, 43.

42. Francesca French, *Miss Brown's Hospital: The Story of the Ludhiana Medical College and Dame Edith Brown, O.B.E., Its Founder* (London: Hodder and Stoughton, 1954), 54.

43. Irene H. Barnes, *Between Life and Death: The Story of C.E.Z.M.S. Medical Missions in India, China, and Ceylon* (London: Marshall Brothers, 1901), 129.

44. Baptist Zenana Missionary Society, *Annual Reports*, 1916.

45. Ibid., 1899, 46.

46. Ibid., 1900, 51.

47. *Historical Sketches*, 35 ff.

48. Baptist Zenana Missionary Society, *Annual Reports*, 1903, 38.

49. Pollock, *Shadows Fall Apart: The Story of the Zenana Bible and Medical Mission*, 176–77.

50. Robert Clark, *The Missions of the Church Missionary Society and the Church of England Zenana Missionary Society in the Punjab and Sindh*, edited by Robert Maconachie (London: Church Missionary Society, 1904 ed.), 105.

51. Irene H Barnes, *Behind the Pardah: The Story of C.E.Z.M.S. Work in India*, 99, 235.

52. Ibid., 99.

53. Ibid., 102.

54. Ibid., 104.

55. *Our Indian Sisters: A Quarterly Magazine of the Ladies Zenana Mission in Connection with the Baptist Missionary Society*, no. 16, Apr. 1889, 386–87.

56. CMS G2/I4/0/51/1910.

57. SPG card file.

58. At least two attended Alexandra College, Dublin (2), Alice Otley School, Worcester (2), Bedford High School (4), Cheltenham Ladies College (5), Clapham High School (3), Convent of Sacred Heart, Aberdeen (2), Godolphin School (4), Leeds Girls High School (3), Lincoln High School (2), St. Mary's, Abbott's Bromley (2).

59. These included the SPG's own deaconess house in South London, the College of the Ascension in Birmingham, and the High Church sisterhoods at Portsmouth, Truro, Warminster, and Wantage.

60. Presbyterian Historical Society, Papers of Kate Alexander Hill, Record Group 53, Folder 1, Hill to "Bessie," 8 Aug. 1897.

61. Presbyterian Historical Society, Papers of Kate Alexander Hill, Record Group 53, Folder 1, to Bessie, 27 May 1897; to Susie, 15 Aug. 1898.

62. CMS G2/I4/02/240/1884. Report to Punjab Department of Public Instruction from Miss Florie Annie Steel of Lahore Female Normal School. Number of schools/number of students = Zenana Mission, Lahore, 9/237; AP Mission, Lahore, 18/442; CMS Schools, Amritsar, 20/499; SPG Mission, Delhi, 8/166.

63. Ibid., 12.

64. Zenana Bible and Medical Mission, *Indian Female Evangelist*, vol. 5, Jan. 1873, 226.

65. The Rev. Herbert Alfred Birks, M.A., *The Life and Correspondence of Thomas Valpy French, First Bishop of Lahore*. 2 vols. (London: John Murray, 1895), vol. 1, 393–94.

66. This description is taken in part from an account in *Report of the SPG and Cambridge Mission to Delhi*, 1898, and from other sources.

67. Katherine Beynon, "Women's Work among the Eurasians in the Punjab," *East and West* 2 (1904): 42.

68. Margaret Balfour and Ruth Young, *The Work of Medical Women in India* (Oxford: Oxford University Press, 1929), 77.

69. Fitzgerald, "'Rescue and Redemption'—the Rise of Female Medical Missions in Colonial India during the Late Nineteenth and Early Twentieth Centuries," 72.

70. Frank M. Turner, *Contesting Cultural Authority: Essays in Victorian Intellectual Life* (Cambridge: Cambridge University Press, 1993).

71. R. Maconachie (late I.C.S.), *Rowland Bateman: Nineteenth Century Apostle* (London: CMS, 1917), 165.

72. National Library of Scotland, Church of Scotland. Letter Book of the Secretary of the Foreign Missions Committee, John T. Maclagan, manuscript no. 7545, 1881–90. Letter to Messrs. Duncan Flackhart & Co., North Bridge, 15 Mar. 1886.

73. Pollock, *Shadows Fall Apart: The Story of the Zenana Bible and Medical Mission*, 33, emphasis mine.

74. Ibid., 35.

75. *Historical Sketches*, 40. *SPG:* Miss Engelmann at Delhi and Miss Zeiyen at Kurnaul; *CMS:* Miss Hewlett and Miss Sharp at Amritsar; Miss Mitcheson at Peshawar; Miss Grimwood at Ujnala; and Miss Bose at Tarn Taran; *FES:* Miss Greenfield at Ludhiana; *Baptist:* Miss Thorne at Delhi, who began work in 1875; *UP:* Miss E. E. Gordon and Mrs. Johnson at Gurduspur; *AP:* Mrs. E. P. Newton at Ludhiana and Miss Thiede at Lahore. See Robert Clark's 1882 survey in CMS G2/I4/PI/170.

76. Balfour and Young, *The Work of Medical Women in India*, 22.

77. Ibid., 23–24.

78. *Historical Sketches*, 40.

79. Eugene Stock, *The History of the Church Missionary Society: Its Environment, Its Men and Its Work* (London: Church Missionary Society, 1899), vol. 2, 564.

80. CMS G2/I4/02/74/1883. Remarks by R. Clark written in church record book, Dera Ismael Khan, and Tank Medical Mission, Feb. 1883.

81. Church Missionary Society, *Register of Missionaries (Clerical, Lay, & Female) and Native Clergy from 1804 to 1904* (London: Printed for Private Circulation, 1905), 196.

82. Irene H Barnes, *Behind the Pardah: The Story of C.E.Z.M.S. Work in India*, 183.

83. CEZMS, Annual Reports of the Church of England Zenana Missionary Society, 1893–96, 1905; Barnes, 1897, 188 ff.

84. Irene H Barnes, *Behind the Pardah: The Story of C.E.Z.M.S. Work in India*, 181.

85. Irene H. Barnes, *Between Life and Death: The Story of C.E.Z.M.S. Medical Missions in India, China, and Ceylon*, 10; Balfour and Young, *The Work of Medical Women in India*, 18.

86. See *Delhi Medical Mission to Women and Children: Report and Accounts for the Year 1888*.

87. *Report of the SPG and Cambridge Mission to Delhi*, 1893, Miss Scott's report.

88. Census of 1901: England and Wales—Summary Tables. *Parliamentary Papers*, 1903, vol. 84, 187.

89. *Report of the SPG and Cambridge Mission to Delhi*, 1901, 28.

90. Taking as an index of the number of career doctors the number of unmarried women doctors over forty-five, Martha Vicinus points out that there were only twenty in 1901, only sixty in 1911. See Martha Vicinus, *Independent Women: Work and Community for Single Women, 1850–1920* (Chicago: 1985), 28–29.

91. Nineteen received an M.B. or M.D.; the rest were licensed either through the Society of Apothecaries (L.S.A.) or through the King and Queen's College of Physician and Royal College of Surgeons, Ireland; the College of Physicians and Surgeons, Edinburgh; or the Faculty of Physicians and Surgeons, Glasgow. Six received hospital training at the Royal Free Hospital, three at Guy's Hospital, and two at the London School of Medicine for Women; the rest at various hospitals.

92. BMS, Farrer Misc. Correspondence, IN/148, "The Differences between Medical Work at Home and Abroad at Pioneer Stations," written on the voyage home for BZU Annual Breakfast, Apr. 1897.

93. *Report of the SPG and Cambridge Mission to Delhi*, 1898, 25.

94. Ibid., 1897, 23, Miss Staley's report.

95. Ibid., 1898, 25.

96. Ibid., 1894, 27, 29. St. Stephen's reported 431 operations, including 103 obstetric and 45 gynecological.

97. Marie Elizabeth Hayes, *At Work: Letters of Marie Elizabeth Hayes, M.B., Missionary Doctor, Delhi, 1905–8*, edited by her mother, with an introduction by G. R. Wynne, reprint, 1909 (London: Marshall Brothers), on St. Stephen's.

98. BMS, Diaries of Dr. Ellen Farrer, Box IN/149, 1891.

99. Ibid., Jan. 5, 1902.

100. Ibid., Jan. 20, 1902.

101. Ibid., July 4, 1904.

102. Ibid., July 27, 1904.

103. Ibid., Dec. 30, 1901.

104. Ibid., Feb. 20, 1919.

105. BMS, Farrer Misc. Correspondence, IN/148. Draft of paper given to Baptist Union meetings, Manchester, 1891, "Women's Work Among the Sick Poor."

106. Ibid.

107. *Fifty Years for Bhiwani Hospital: The Farrer Jubilee* (London: Baptist Missionary Society, 1941), 3.

108. Ibid.

109. *Magazine of the London School of Medicine for Women and Royal Free Hospital* (London, 1895–1901). Only one of fifty-eight appointments listed in the latter period went directly to mission work. These are not reliable accounts, since the initial appointment was usually to a domestic hospital.

110. See her letter in the *Times of London*, Oct. 1881; 1 Nov. reply from William Muir.

111. Maneesha Lal, "The Politics of Gender and Medicine in Colonial India: The Countess of Dufferin's Fund, 1885–1888," *Bulletin of the History of Medicine* 68, no. 1 (spring 1994): 29–66; Antoinette Burton, "Contesting the Zenana: The Mission to Make 'Lady Doctors for India,' 1874–1885," *Journal of British Studies* 35 (July 1996): 368–97.

112. Balfour and Young, *The Work of Medical Women in India*, 36.

113. Zenana Bible and Medical Mission, *Indian Female Evangelist*, vol. 8, no. 57, Jan. 1886, 209.

114. "'A Five Years' Retrospect of the National Association for Supplying Female Medical Aid to the Women of India,' by Mrs. Gardner," *Magazine of the London School of Medicine for Women and Royal Free Hospital*, no. 6, Jan. 1897.

115. Ibid., no. 6, Jan. 1897, 223.

116. Cited in *The Indian Female Evangelist*, vol. 6, no. 40, Oct. 1881, 201–3.

117. CMS G2/I4/L2/1883–88. Gray to Dr. E. Neve, 27 Sept. 1886.

118. *Fifty Years for Bhiwani Hospital: The Farrer Jubilee*, 13.

119. *Our Indian Sisters: A Quarterly Magazine of the Ladies Zenana Mission in Connection with the Baptist Missionary Society*, no. 7, Jan. 1887, 156.

120. French, *Miss Brown's Hospital: The Story of the Ludhiana Medical College and Dame Edith Brown, O.B.E., Its Founder*, 5.

121. Ibid., 12.

122. Ibid., 21–22.

123. Ibid., 28.

124. CMS G2/I4/o/34/1894. Conference of Women Medical Missionaries, Ludhiana, 20–21 Dec. 1893.

125. CMS G2/I4/P3/33/1894.

126. French, *Miss Brown's Hospital: The Story of the Ludhiana Medical College and Dame Edith Brown, O.B.E., Its Founder*, 36–38.

127. Ibid., 52, 63.

128. *Directory of Christian Missions in India, Burma and Ceylon, 1932–1933* (Madras: Christian Literature Society, 1932), 246.

129. French, *Miss Brown's Hospital: The Story of the Ludhiana Medical College and Dame Edith Brown, O.B.E., Its Founder*, 62.

130. *Directory of Christian Missions in India, Burma and Ceylon, 1932–1933*, 249; Balfour and Young, *The Work of Medical Women in India*, map at end.

131. Calculated from lists in *Directory of Christian Missions in India, Burma and Ceylon, 1932–1933*, which must be considered rough estimates (probably low).

132. *Directory of Christian Missions and Churches in India, Burma and Ceylon*, 22–23.

133. BMS, Letters, IN/148. Bhiwani Hospital Circular Letter.

134. French, *Miss Brown's Hospital: The Story of the Ludhiana Medical College and Dame Edith Brown, O.B.E., Its Founder*, 42.

135. CMS G2/I4/P3/46/1900. Minutes of CMS Medical Sub-Conference, 6–7 Nov. 1899.

136. Flemming, "New Models, New Roles: U.S. Presbyterian Women Missionaries and Social Change in North India, 1870–1910."

137. Fitzgerald, "'Rescue and Redemption'—the Rise of Female Medical Missions in Colonial India during the Late Nineteenth and Early Twentieth Centuries," 76.

138. BMS, BZMS letters, Dr. Minna Bazeley (SPG) to Mr. Wells, 13 July 1941, Bangalore.

139. *Report of the SPG and Cambridge Mission to Delhi*, 1928, 21.

140. French, *Miss Brown's Hospital: The Story of the Ludhiana Medical College and Dame Edith Brown, O.B.E., Its Founder*, 78.

141. Ibid.

142. Ibid., 80.

143. Anita Desai, "The Rage for the Raj," *New Republic*, no. 3697 (25 Nov. 1985): 26–27.

144. *A Medical Jubilee*, pamphlet, n.p. (Bhiwani: Farrer Hospital, 1940).

145. *Fifty Years for Bhiwani Hospital: The Farrer Jubilee*, 6.

146. BMS, Letters, IN/148. Dr. Bissett to Miss Bowser, Bhiwani, 10 Jan. 1933.

147. French, *Miss Brown's Hospital: The Story of the Ludhiana Medical College and Dame Edith Brown, O.B.E., Its Founder*, 83–84.

148. BMS, Dr. Benzie to Dr. Chesterman, Bhiwani, 6 Apr. 1940.

149. *Fifty Years for Bhiwani Hospital: The Farrer Jubilee*, ? (lost).

150. BMS, Correspondence, IN/148, Circular letters from Bhiwani Hospital, 1942.

CHAPTER 7

1. Charles Cashdollar, *The Transformation of Theology, 1830–1890: Positivism and Protestant Thought in Britain and America* (Princeton: Princeton University Press, 1989).

2. *Lahore Civil and Military Gazette*, Supplement, 14 Nov. 1892.

3. Gauri Viswanathan, *Masks of Conquest: Literary Study and British Rule in India.* The Social Foundations of Aesthetic Forms Series (New York: Columbia University Press, 1989), on Alexander Duff in Calcutta.

4. *Report by the Panjab Provincial Committee with Evidence Taken before the Committee and Memorials Addressed to the Education Commission*, Appendix to the Report of the Indian Education Commission (Calcutta: Superintendent of Government Printing, 1884), 1.

5. Ibid., 4.

6. Ibid., 27–29.

7. Ibid., 16–17.

8. T. L. Pennell [B.Sc. M.D., F.R.C.S.], *Among the Wild Tribes of the Afghan Frontier: A Record of Sixteen Years' Close Intercourse with the Natives of the Indian Marches*, with an introduction by Field-Marshal Earl Roberts (London: Seeley & Co., 1909), 140–41.

9. J. F. Bruce, *A History of the University of the Panjab* (Lahore, 1933), 4.

10. *Report by the Panjab Provincial Committee with Evidence Taken before the Committee and Memorials Addressed to the Education Commission*, 19.

11. Ibid., 24.

12. Ibid., 45.

13. Ibid., 27–29.

14. Ibid., 53 ff.

15. National Library of Scotland, Punjab and Murray College papers, plans, etc., acc 7548 D-17, 1917–28. Memo from John A. Alexander on Murray College, Jammu, Jan. 1918.

16. Ibid., 298/13, 10 July 1906, 16 Jan. 1907.

17. Ibid., 298/13, 20 Nov. 1906; cf. Punjab University. Inspection of Affiliated College, 1906–7. Report no. 15. Scotch Mission College, Sialkot. dep. 298/14, 9 July 1907. At the time of this report there were twenty-three students on the rolls, including five living in a hostel.

18. National Library of Scotland, Punjab and Murray College papers, plans, etc., acc 7548 D-17, 1917–28. Staff of Murray College, 1918. These budget figures do not include the very large salaries paid by the mission board to the two missionaries assigned to the college, the Rev. William Scott (£469) and Professor Garret (£295).

19. *Annual Report of the SPG and Cambridge Mission to Delhi for 1885; Report of the Cambridge Mission to Delhi, 1886*.

20. *Report of the Cambridge Mission to Delhi, 1893. Report of the SPG and Cambridge Missions to Delhi, 1908, 1914.* On St. Stephen's, see: Francis Fitzhugh Monk, *A History of St. Stephen's College, Delhi: Compiled for the Cambridge Mission in Commemoration of the Fiftieth Anni-*

versary of the Founding of the College, 1931, by F. F. Monk (Calcutta: Y.M.C.A. Publishing House, 1935); Hugh Tinker, "Between Old Delhi and New Delhi: C. F. Andrews and St. Stephen's in an Era of Transition," in *Delhi through the Ages: Essays in Urban History, Culture, and Society,* edited by R. E. Frykenberg (Delhi; New York: Oxford University Press, 1986), 351–90; Aparnu Basu, "The Foundation and Early History of Delhi University," in *Delhi through the Ages: Essays in Urban History, Culture, and Society,* edited by R. E. Frykenberg (Delhi; New York: Oxford University Press, 1986), 401–30. St. Stephen's affiliated with the new Delhi University in 1922.

21. H. H. Montgomery, *The Life and Letters of George Alfred Lefroy D.D., Bishop of Calcutta and Metropolitan* (London: Longmans, Green & Co., 1920), vol. 2, 20–32.

22. John C. B. Webster, *The Christian Community and Change in Nineteenth Century North India* (Delhi: Macmillan of India, 1976), 167 ff.

23. *Directory of Christian Missions and Churches in India, Burma and Ceylon* (Nagpur: National Christian Council, 1938), 31. National Library of Scotland, Church of Scotland. Punjab Mission Council Minutes, manuscript no. ACC 7548 B7, 1940–42, Murray College Report, 31 Mar. 1940. Murray enrolled 508 students (39 female) in 1940: 202 Muslim, 185 Hindu, 64 Christian, 50 Sikh, and 7 Jain.

24. Punjab Mission Council. A reply to the committee question regarding the future of the Murray College, c. 1918. National Library of Scotland, Punjab and Murray College papers, plans, etc., acc 7548 D-17, 1917–28.

25. Pennell [M.D.], *Among the Wild Tribes of the Afghan Frontier: A Record of Sixteen Years' Close Intercourse with the Natives of the Indian Marches,* 142–43.

26. Henry Venn, *To Apply the Gospel: Selections from the Writing of Henry Venn,* Max Warren (Grand Rapids, Mich.: William B. Eerdmans, 1971), 218, citing CMS G/AZI/1, no. 8, Committee of Correspondence, 4 Dec. 1855.

27. *Report on Public Instruction in the Punjab and Its Dependencies for the Year 1890–1891,* compiled by J. Sime, DPI (Lahore, 1891), 2; Calcutta Missionary Conference, *Statistical Tables of Protestant Missions in India, Burma and Ceylon, Prepared on Information Collected at the Close of 1890, at the Request of the Calcutta Missionary Conference* (Calcutta: Baptist Mission Press, 1892), 56–61, 218. These figures must be considered estimates, calculated by juxtaposing sums from government and mission reports.

28. CMS G2/I4/0/81/1890. Examination of Mission Schools in the Diocese of Lahore by the Rev. T. R. Wade (manuscript, n.p.).

29. Ibid.

30. Zenana Bible and Medical Mission, *The Indian Female Evangelist,* vol. 5, no. 24, Apr. 1880 (London: Indian Female Normal School and Instruction Society, 1872–1901), 126.

31. Ibid., vol. 9, no. 61, Jan. 1887, 26.

32. Ibid.

33. Translation printed in ibid., vol. 7, no. 55, July 1885, 144.

34. Ibid., vol. 11, May 1891, 68.

35. Bruce, *History of the University of Panjab*, 3.

36. CMS G2/I4/02/296/1888. Sir Charles Aitchison to R. Clark, n.d., copy.

37. CMS G2/I4/02/42/1886. Tisdall to Parent Committee, Amritsar, 22 Jan. 1886.

38. CMS G2/I4/L2, William Gray to H. E. Perkins, London, 4 Feb. 1886.

39. CMS G2/I4/L2.

40. UP (RG 209, Series I), Box 7, Missionary and General Correspondence, E. E. Campbell to Dr. Anderson, Sialkot, 23 Feb. 1916.

41. The AP at Dehra Dun; the BMS at Delhi and Kharar; the CS at Sialkot; the CMS at Amritsar, Gojra, Narowal, and Clarkabad, the SPG at Delhi, the ZBMM at Lahore; the UP at Pathankot, Pasrur, and several other locations including Sangla Hill; the Methodists at Lahore; and the Salvation Army at Lahore.

42. CMS G2/I4/07/435/1891. Prospectus of the Baring High School, Batala. See Church Missionary Society, *Register of Missionaries (Clerical, Lay, & Female) and Native Clergy from 1804 to 1904* (London: Printed for Private Circulation, 1905), 159; Vinod K. Khiyalie, *Hundred Years of Baring's Mission to Batala: Christian Education and Social Change in a Punjabi Countryside* (Delhi: ISPCK, 1980).

43. CMS G2/I4/07/368/1891. R. Clark to Gray, Murree, 7 Aug. 1891.

44. Henry Martyn Clark, *Robert Clark of the Punjab: Pioneer and Missionary Statesman* (London: Andrew Melrose, 1907), 313.

45. Clark, *Robert Clark of the Punjab: Pioneer and Missionary Statesman*, 315; David Lelyveld, *Aligarh's First Generation: Muslim Solidarity in British India* (Princeton: Princeton University Press, 1978).

46. CMS G2/I4/03/152. List of girls at the Alexandra School supplied by Miss Bowles.

47. CMS G2/I4/02/152/1886.

48. Michael Millgate, *Thomas Hardy: A Biography* (New York: Random House, 1982), 55: Thomas Hardy "never forgot . . . the humiliation of sitting in Stinsford Church at his mother's side in that early summer of 1856 while the Rev Mr Shirley preached against the presumption shown by one of Hardy's class in seeking to rise, through architecture, into the ranks of professional men."

49. In 1900, twenty-five of twenty-eight candidates for examinations at various levels passed. CMS G2/I4/0/111/1901 Alexandra H.S., copy of H. I. M. Inspectress Report; G2/I4/P3/267/1903 states the reasons for Miss Edgley's resignation as headmistress.

50. CMS G2/I4/02/13/1886.

51. CMS G2/I4/0/145/1898. H. E. Perkin to PC, Sydenham, 6 Apr. 1898.

52. CMS G2/I4/0/17/1892; CMS G2/I4/0/107/1895; CMS G2/I4/P3/ 353/1899.

53. Irene H. Barnes, *Between Life and Death: The Story of C.E.Z.M.S. Medical Missions in India, China, and Ceylon* (London: Marshall Brothers, 1901), 177.

54. Ibid., 156.

55. CMS G2/I4/0/17/1892. Miss G. L. West to R. Clark, Clarkabad, 20 Nov., 1891.

56. CMS G2/I4/P7/1926. Obituary of Miss M. L. H. Warner.

57. Society for the Propagation of the Gospel, *Annual Reports* (London, 1906–35), 1934, 107.

58. See *Queen Mary's School, Delhi: Golden Jubilee, 1912–1962* (Delhi: 1962).

59. *Report of the SPG and Cambridge Mission to Delhi*, 1912, 38.

60. SPG, Committee on Women's Work. Letters received, 1918. Queen Mary's High School. Circular, by Principal H. D. Jerwood.

61. SPG, Committee on Women's Work. Letters received, 1918. H. D. Jerwood to Miss Trolloppe, 17 Sept. 1918.

62. *Report on the Progress of Education in the Punjab during the Quinquennium Ending 1926–27* (Lahore, 1927), 96.

63. SPG, Committee on Women's Work, Letters received, 1918. Queen Mary's High School. Circular, by Principal H. D. Jerwood.

64. Interview with Wilbur Thoburn, physics professor at Forman Christian College, 1937–61, Ames, Iowa, 30 Aug. 1990.

65. Bruce, *History of the University of Panjab*, 163.

66. CMS G2/I4/P5/233/1910; CMS G2/I4/P7/31/1928.

67. Bruce, *History of the University of Panjab*, 50.

68. The Rev. Herbert Alfred Birks, M.A., *The Life and Correspondence of Thomas Valpy French, First Bishop of Lahore*. 2 vols. (London: John Murray, 1895), vol. 1, 49.

69. On Gordon College, see the *Minutes of the Annual Meeting of the Sialkot Mission of the United Presbyterian Church of North America*, 1907–8; on Murray College: National Library of Scotland, Punjab and Murray College papers, plans, etc., acc 7548 D-17, 1917–28. Memo from Mr. Paterson, Murray College, Jan. 1918.

70. National Library of Scotland, Punjab and Murray College papers, plans, etc., acc 7548 D-17, 1917–28. Memo from William Scott on Murray College, Jan. 1918.

71. Michelle Maskiell, *Women between Cultures: The Lives of Kinnaird College Alumnae in British India*. Foreign and Comparative Studies. South Asian Series no. 9 (Syracuse, N.Y.: Maxwell School of Citizenship and Public Affairs, Syracuse University, 1984), 21; Kenneth W. Jones, *Arya Dharm: Hindu Consciousness in 19th-Century Punjab* (Berkeley: University of California Press, 1976), on Arya Dharm education; J. S. Grewal, *The Sikhs of the Punjab*, rev. ed., *The New Cambridge History of India*, II.3 (Cambridge: Cambridge University Press, 1999), 148.

72. Gail Minault, *Secluded Scholars: Women's Education and Muslim Social Reform in Colonial India* (New Delhi: Oxford University Press, 1998), 177.

73. *Report on Education in the Punjab for 1910–1911* (Lahore, 1911), 3.

74. *Report on the Progress of Education in the Punjab during the Quinquennium Ending 1911–1912* (Lahore, 1912), 22.

75. Ibid., 47, 124 ff.

76. Ibid., 1.

77. Maskiell, *Women between Cultures: The Lives of Kinnaird College Alumnae in British India*, 42–43, on this trend.

78. E. D. Tyndale-Biscoe, *Fifty Years against the Stream: The Story of a School in Kashmir 1880–1930* (Mysore: Wesleyan Mission Press, 1930), xv.

79. Ibid., 13.

80. C. E. Tyndale-Biscoe, "Teaching the Book," *East and West* 17 (Oct. 1919): 324.

81. E. D. Tyndale-Biscoe, *Fifty Years against the Stream: The Story of a School in Kashmir 1880–1930*, 56.

82. Ibid., 23.

83. J. C. Pollock, *Shadows Fall Apart: The Story of the Zenana Bible and Medical Mission* (London: Hodder and Stoughton, 1958), 121–24; Maskiell, *Women between Cultures: The Lives of Kinnaird College Alumnae in British India*, ch. 2.

84. Maskiell, *Women between Cultures: The Lives of Kinnaird College Alumnae in British India*, 37–38.

85. Ibid., 61.

86. Ibid., 66.

87. Ibid., 32.

88. Ibid., 64 ff.

89. Viswanathan, *Masks of Conquest: Literary Study and British Rule in India*, 7–8.

90. Ibid., 48.

91. Ibid., 55.

92. Ibid.

93. Birks, *The Life and Correspondence of Thomas Valpy French, First Bishop of Lahore*, vol. 2, 129.

94. Ibid., vol. 1, 49.

95. Cambridge Mission to Delhi, *Annual Report* (Delhi, 1878–1904), 1883, 10 ff.

96. Ibid., 1887, 9.

97. Viswanathan, *Masks of Conquest: Literary Study and British Rule in India*, 169.

98. Of the several dozen persons to whom I have put this informal question, only two answered "yes." Both were women who attended convent schools. One asserted that her training made her more sensitive to moral issues, the other that she had a better understanding of Christian imagery.

99. S. P. Sen, ed., *Dictionary of National Biography* (4 vols.) (Calcutta: Institute of Historical Studies, 1973), vol. 2, 388.

100. Ibid., vol. 2, 324.

101. *Directory of Christian Missions in India, Burma and Ceylon, 1932–1933* (Madras: Christian Literature Society, 1932); *Directory of Christian Missions and Churches in India, Burma and Ceylon.*

102. *Report on the Progress of Education in the Punjab during the Quinquennium Ending 1931–32* (Lahore, 1932), 116; *Directory of Christian Missions and Churches in India, Burma and Ceylon.* This was estimated as roughly 4 percent of the total male population. By 1932 the government claimed an enrollment of 33,196 students of depressed class background, almost all male, a number that fell back below 30,000 by the mid-1930s. The missions estimated 21,000 primary pupils in 1935 in Punjab Province, a considerable number of them Christians of depressed class background.

103. Amit Chaudhuri, "Beyond the Language of the Raj," *TLS* 4923 (8 Aug. 1997): 17–18.

104. Edward Said, "Between Worlds," *London Review of Books* 20, no. 9 (7 May 1998): 5.

105. Sara Suleri, *Meatless Days* (Chicago: University of Chicago Press, 1989), 47. "Superficially because of its dramatic societies and annual plays," Suleri adds, but "more significantly because of the histrionic terror engendered by its secret locked up space. To the city, after all, Kinnaird signified a magical arena containing a few hundred women of prime time marriageability in the architectural embrace remarkably reminiscent of the old days of the *zenana khana*, its room after room of unenterable women's rooms."

106. UP (RG 209, Series I), Box 7, Missionary and General Correspondence, Gordon College Principal's Report for 1943. The mission contribution fell from $14,500 per year in the early 1920s to $900 in 1940. Of a budget of Rs 113,642, 93,862 came from students' fees, and roughly 12,000 from a government educational grant. Salaries for three male and two female missionaries continued to come entirely from mission funds.

107. "India's Top Ten Colleges," *India Today* 25, no. 25 (19 June 2000).

108. Anita Desai, *Clear Light of Day* (New York, 1980), 125.

109. UP (RG 209, Series I), Box 7, Missionary and General Correspondence, Gordon College Principal's Report for 1943.

CHAPTER 8

1. H. H. Montgomery, *The Life and Letters of George Alfred Lefroy D.D., Bishop of Calcutta and Metropolitan* (London: Longmans, Green & Co., 1920), vol. 1, 20.

2. Lahore Missionary Conference, *Report of the Punjab Missionary Conference Held at Lahore in December and January, 1862–63* (Ludhiana: American Presbyterian Mission Press, 1863), 166–67.

3. Laura Tabili, *"We Ask for British Justice": Workers and Racial Dif-*

ference in Late Imperial Britain (Ithaca: Cornell University Press, 1994), 4.

4. Jean and John Comaroff, *Of Revelation and Revolution: Christianity, Colonialism, and Consciousness in South Africa* (Chicago: University of Chicago Press, 1991), vol. 1, p. 32.

5. Patrick Brantlinger, *Rule of Darkness: British Literature and Imperialism, 1830–1914* (Ithaca: Cornell University Press, 1988), 39.

6. CMS G2/I4/0/79/1925. Alice M. Pennell, to Dr. Cooke (secretary of Medical Department, CMs), London, 26 Apr. 1925.

7. Charles Freer Andrews, *North India*. Handbooks of English Church Expansion (Oxford: Mowbray, 1908), 177, quoting an unnamed missionary.

8. SPG. Committee on Women's Work. Letters. Beatrice Ponzoni to S. S. Allnutt, Rohtak, 20 Mar. 1910.

9. Zenana Bible and Medical Mission, *The Indian Female Evangelist*, vol. 10, no. 80, Apr. 1889 (London: Indian Female Normal School and Instruction Society, 1872–1901), 61–64.

10. SPG. Committee on Women's Work. Letters Received, cww146. H. M. Gould and F. J. Western to Miss Saunders, 13 Dec. 1923. She is listed in the annual reports as a "resignation" in 1924, but remained on the rolls anyway until 1930.

11. BMS. in/88. Agnes Miriam Young to Miss Lockhart, 13 Mar. 1921.

12. BMS. in/88. Miss Miriam Young to Miss Lockhart, Mohena (nr. Palwal), 7 July 1924.

13. BMS. in/88. Miriam Young to Miss Lockhart, 9 Nov. 1924.

14. Missionary Conference, *Report of the Punjab Missionary Conference Held at Lahore in December and January, 1862–63*, 166.

15. Church Missionary Society, *Register of Missionaries (Clerical, Lay, & Female) and Native Clergy from 1804 to 1904* (London: Printed for Private Circulation, 1905), 144; Arthur Lewis, *George Maxwell Gordon M.A., F.R.G.S., the Pilgrim Missionary of the Punjab: A History of His Life and Work 1839–1880* (London: Seeley & Co., 1889).

16. R. Maconachie (late I.C.S.), *Rowland Bateman: Nineteenth Century Apostle* (London: CMS, 1917); T. L. Pennell [B.Sc. M.D., F.R.C.S.], *Among the Wild Tribes of the Afghan Frontier: A Record of Sixteen Years' Close Intercourse with the Natives of the Indian Marches*, with an introduction by Field-Marshal Earl Roberts (London: Seeley & Co. Limited, 1909).

17. Pennell [M.D.], *Among the Wild Tribes of the Afghan Frontier: A Record of Sixteen Years' Close Intercourse with the Natives of the Indian Marches*, 53.

18. Parama Roy, *Indian Traffic: Identities in Question in Colonial and Postcolonial India* (Berkeley: University of California Press, 1998), ch. 1; Homi K. Bhabha, "Signs Taken for Wonders: Questions of Ambivalence and Authority under a Tree Outside Delhi, May 1817," *Critical Inquiry* 12 (autumn 1985): 144–65. Bhabha is interested in mimicry as an Indian response to the missionary presence.

19. Henry Martyn Clark, *Robert Clark of the Punjab: Pioneer and Missionary Statesman* (London: Andrew Melrose, 1907), 341.

20. Asha Sharma, *An American in Khadi: The Definitive Biography of Satyanand Stokes* (New Delhi: Penguin Books, 1999), 25.

21. Ibid., 35.

22. "Fakir" was properly applied to Muslim religious mendicants, but in the nineteenth century it was applied "loosely and inaccurately, to Hindu devotees and naked ascetics." See Sir Henry Yule, *Hobson-Jobson: A Glossary of Colloquial Anglo-Indian Words and Phrases, and of Kindred Terms, Etymological, Historical, Geographical and Discursive*, by Henry Yule and A. C. Burnell, 4th ed., edited by William Crooke, reprint, 1903 (Delhi: Munshiram Manoharlal, 1984), 347. The term "Sadhu," often used interchangeably by missionaries with "fakir," was more respectable because of its associations with monasticism and, especially, with pilgrimage.

23. *English Report (Translated from the Urdu) of the Fifth Annual Meeting of the Punjab and Sindh CMS Native Church Council Held at Umritsar from 26–28 December 1880* (Amritsar, 1881).

24. CMS G2/I4/02/256/1887. Clark to Gray, Simla, 23 July.

25. CMS G2/I4/02/288/1887, transcript of letter from Sant Shah.

26. BMS. Diaries of Dr. E. M. Farrer, 1890–1917. Box IN/149, 24 July, 1904.

27. Ibid., 2 Feb. 1915; 3 Jan. 1917.

28. Ibid., 1 Feb. 1917.

29. Ibid., 19 Apr. 1917.

30. Ibid., 1 July, 1917.

31. Ibid., 18 Sept., 1917.

32. Ibid., 25 Nov. 1917.

33. Friedrich Heiler, *The Gospel of Sadhu Sundar Singh*, translated by Olive Wyon, reprint, 1927 (Delhi: ISPCK, 1989); M. E. Gibbs, *The Anglican Church in India 1600–1970* (Delhi: Indian Society for the Promotion of Christian Knowledge, 1972), 366–67; Stephen Neill, *Christian Missions: The Pelican History of the Church*, vol. 6 (Harmondsworth: Penguin Books, 1964), 482–83; T. E. Riddle, *The Vision and the Call: A Life of Sadhu Sundar Singh* (Delhi: Indian Society for Promoting Christian Knowledge, 1987); T. Dayanandan Francis, *Sadhu Sundar Singh: The Lover of the Cross* (Madras: Christian Literature Society, 1989).

34. Heiler, *The Gospel of Sadhu Sundar Singh*, 43.

35. Ibid., 15, 17.

36. Ibid., 173.

37. Ibid., 10–11.

38. Daniel O'Connor, *Gospel, Raj and Swaraj: The Missionary Years of C. F. Andrews 1904–14*. Studies in the Intercultural History of Christianity, vol. 62 (Frankfurt/M.; Bern; New York; Paris: Peter Lang, 1990), 176.

39. C. F. (Charles Freer) Andrews, *What I Owe to Christ*, by C. F. An-

drews (London: Hodder & Stoughton, 1932), 170. Because of the ecclesiastical peculiarities of his position, Sundar Singh was only an "associate" of the Brotherhood.

40. O'Connor, *Gospel, Raj and Swaraj: The Missionary Years of C. F. Andrews 1904–14*, 180.

41. Heiler, *The Gospel of Sadhu Sundar Singh*, 80–85.

42. Ibid., 76–77.

43. Ibid., 77.

44. Solveig Smith, *By Love Compelled: The Salvation Army's One Hundred Years in India and Adjacent Lands* (London: Salvation Army, 1981), passim; F. A. (Frederick Arthur) Mackenzie, *Booth-Tucker, Sadhu and Saint, by F. A. Mackenzie,* with an introduction by General E. J. Higgins (London: Hodder and Stoughton, 1930).

45. Smith, *By Love Compelled: The Salvation Army's One Hundred Years in India and Adjacent Lands*, 3.

46. Ibid., 6.

47. *The Indian War Cry,* published by the Salvation Army (Poona, 1883–1947), Apr. 1920.

48. Maconachie (late I.C.S.), *Rowland Bateman: Nineteenth Century Apostle,* 116, letter from P. Ireland Jones.

49. *The Indian War Cry,* Mar. 1883.

50. Ibid., Jan. 1913.

51. Salvation Army Archives, "Promoted to Glory" (PTG) files.

52. IWC Oct. 1901.

53. *The Indian War Cry,* Jan. 1937.

54. Minutes of Decisions and Notes of Poona Council, Salvation Army, Nov. 1901. Salvation Army Archives, India, 1891–1913.

55. The Salvation Army's antiracism made their statistics opaque, although the *Salvation Army Yearbook* for 1921 identified 228 of 318 North Indian officers as Indian.

56. *The Indian War Cry,* Jan. 1899.

57. Ibid., June 1925.

58. Ibid., Sept. 1932.

59. Ibid., Feb. 1939.

60. Ibid., Feb. 1905.

61. Ibid., Feb. 1937.

62. Ibid., Apr. 1913, Mar. 1926.

63. Interview with Barkat Masih, Brigadier of Salvation Army (retired), at National Christian Council of Pakistan, 1 Mar. 1988.

64. Comaroff, *Of Revelation and Revolution: Christianity, Colonialism, and Consciousness in South Africa,* vols. 1 and 2.

65. Frederick Booth-Tucker, *Darkest India: A Supplement to General Booth's "In Darkest England and the Way Out"* (Bombay: Bombay Gazette, 1890), 1.

66. Ibid., 95.

67. *The Indian War Cry*, Sept. 1908.

68. Smith, *By Love Compelled: The Salvation Army's One Hundred Years in India and Adjacent Lands*, 6.

69. Ibid., 91.

70. *The Indian War Cry*, Aug. 1908.

71. Denzil Ibbetson, *Panjab Castes*, Chapters from the Census Report of 1881 on "The Races, Castes, and Tribes of the Panjab," reprint, 1916 (Delhi: Meeraj, 1984), 277–78.

72. *The Indian War Cry*, Aug. 1910; Rachel J. Tolan, "Colonizing and Transforming the Criminal Tribesman: The Salvation Army in British India," *American Ethnologist* 18 (Feb. 1991): 106–25; Anand A Yang, ed., *Crime and Criminality in British India* (Tucson: University of Arizona, 1985); Clark C. Spence, *The Salvation Army Farm Colonies* (Tucson: University of Arizona, 1985).

73. *The Indian War Cry*, May 1916; Imran Ali, *The Punjab under Imperialism, 1885–1947* (Princeton: Princeton University Press, 1988), 102.

74. *The Indian War Cry*, Nov. 1911.

75. Ibid., July 1912.

76. Ibid., May 1912.

77. Ibid., Apr. 1917.

78. Ibid., Sept. 1920.

79. Information from the PTG files.

80. *The Indian War Cry*, Nov. 1928.

81. Smith, *By Love Compelled: The Salvation Army's One Hundred Years in India and Adjacent Lands*.

82. See Jeffrey Cox, "Religion and Imperial Power in Nineteenth Century Britain," in *Freedom and Religion in the Nineteenth Century*, edited by R. W. and R. J. Helmstadter David (Palo Alto: Stanford University Press, 1997).

83. Richard O. Comfort, *The Village Church in West Pakistan* (Lahore: West Pakistan Christian Council, c. 1957), 126.

84. BMS. in/88. Miss Miriam Young to Miss Lockhart, Mohena (nr. Palwal), 7 July 1924.

85. BMS. in/88. Miss Miriam Young to Miss Bowser, May 1925.

86. BMS. in/88. Miss Miriam Young to Miss Lockhart, 25 Nov. 1926.

87. BMS. in/88. Miss Miriam Young to Miss Bowser, 1 Aug. 1937.

88. William R. Hutchison, *Errand to the World: American Protestant Thought and Foreign Missions* (Chicago: University of Chicago, 1987), chs. 4–7.

89. UP, Records of the Board of Foreign Missions (RG 209, Series I), Box 7, Missionary and General Correspondence, W. B. to John Heinrich, 7 Aug. 1934.

90. J. C. Heinrich, *Depressed Class Psychology*, pamphlet (Lahore: Government of Punjab, 1935).

91. UP (RG 209, Series I), Box 7, Missionary and General Correspondence, J. C. Heinrich to W. B., Martinpur, 21 1933.

92. Heinrich, *Depressed Class Psychology*, 21.

93. BMS. in/88. Miriam Young to Miss Bowser, Delhi, 24 Jan 1929, reporting on the All-Indian Women's Conference at Patna and lamenting how missionaries were out of touch with it.

94. UP (RG 209, Series I), Box 7, Missionary and General Correspondence, J. C. Heinrich, typescript, "College Extension Work at Martinpur," n.d. The request was later denied by the mission, which contained a majority hostile to Heinrich for a variety of reasons having to do with both his personality and his liberal theology.

95. UP (RG 209, Series I), Box 7, Missionary and General Correspondence, Heinrich to Dr. Caldwell, 6 July 1936.

96. UP (RG 209, Series I), Box 7, Missionary and General Correspondence, J. C. Heinrich, "Dear Friends" letter, 21 Sept. 1938.

97. UP (RG 209, Series I), Box 7, Missionary and General Correspondence, Heinrich to Dr. Caldwell, 30 May 1939, Sheikhpura. Forty-eight Christian farmers agreed to tithe their new wheat crop in return for eligibility for fee scholarships at the Sheakhpura School, which had 380 boys and girls in 1939 (only 25 percent could afford to pay fees).

98. J. C. Heinrich, *Depressed Class Psychology*.

99. Lewis Bevan Jones, *The People of the Mosque: An Introduction to the Study of Islam with Special Reference to India* (Calcutta: Association Press, 1932); John Nicol Farquhar, *The Crown of Hinduism*, reprint, 1913 (New Delhi: Oriental Books Reprint Corp., 1971); John Nicol Farquhar, *Modern Religious Movements in India*, reprint, 1915 (Delhi: Munshiram Manoharlal, 1967); on Jones, see Brian Stanley, *The History of the Baptist Missionary Society, 1792–1992* (Edinburgh: T. & T. Clark, 1992), 281; on Farquhar, see Eric J. Sharpe, *Not to Destroy but to Fulfil: The Contribution of J. N. Farquhar to Protestant Missionary Thought in India Before 1914* (Lund, Sweden: Gleerup, 1965); on Paton, see Eleanor M. Jackson, *Red Tape and the Gospel: A Study of the Significance of the Ecumenical Missionary Struggle of William Paton, 1886–1943* (Birmingham: Phlogiston, in association with the Selly Oak Colleges, 1980).

100. William A. Graham, "The Scholar's Scholar: Wilfred Cantwell Smith and a Collegial Life of the Mind," *Harvard Divinity Bulletin* 29, no. 2 (summer 2000), 6. Cantwell Smith later became director of Harvard's Center for the Study of World Religions.

101. C. F. Andrews, "The Situation in the East," *East and West* (Oct. 1907): 426.

102. Charles Freer Andrews, *North India*, 190.

103. Montgomery, *The Life and Letters of George Alfred Lefroy D.D., Bishop of Calcutta and Metropolitan*, 212.

104. C. F. Andrews, *The Testimony of C. F. Andrews*, ed. Daniel O'Connor, Madras: Christian Literature Society 1974, 102.

105. *Tribune*, 6 May 1914. I am grateful to Daniel O'Connor for calling my attention to this sermon.

106. Charles Freer Andrews, *The Testimony of C. F. Andrews*, 227.

107. See "Dialogue between Mahatma Gandhi and C. F. Andrews on Conversion (1936)," from *Harijan*, 28 Nov. 1936, reprinted in M. K. Kuriakose, ed., *History of Christianity in India: Source Materials* (Madras: Christian Literature Society, 1982), 362–33; "A Letter to Gandhi (1937)," reprinted in Andrews, *Testimony*, 118–22; also in Benarsidas Chaturvedi and Marjorie Sykes, *Charles Freer Andrews: A Narrative*, reprint, 1949 (New Delhi: Government of India Publications Division, 1971), 310; cf. David McI. Gracie, ed. and comp., *Gandhi and Charlie: The Story of a Friendship* (Cambridge, Mass.: Cowley Publications, 1989).

108. Charles Freer Andrews, *The Testimony of C. F. Andrews*, 222.

CHAPTER 9

1. *Directory of Christian Missions in India, Burma and Ceylon, 1932– 1933* (Madras: Christian Literature Society, 1932), 249 for the institutions.

2. Gail Minault, *Secluded Scholars: Women's Education and Muslim Social Reform in Colonial India* (New Delhi: Oxford University Press, 1998), 181.

3. *Report on the Progress of Education in the Punjab during the Quinquennium Ending 1931–32* (Lahore, 1932), 16; *Directory of Christian Missions and Churches in India, Burma and Ceylon* (Nagpur: National Christian Council, 1938); 33,196 were enrolled in government schools in 1932, estimated as roughly 4 percent of the total male population, which implied that only males were in school; 21,100 were reported as enrolled in mission schools in 1935. These statistics are for the Province of Punjab only.

4. J. S. Grewal, *The Sikhs of the Punjab*, rev. ed., *The New Cambridge History of India*, II.3 (Cambridge: Cambridge University Press, 1999), 130.

5. *Directory of Christian Missions and Churches in India, Burma and Ceylon*, 43; For an expansive treatment of the statistics, see Frederick and Margaret Stock, *People Movements in the Punjab, with Special Reference to the United Presbyterian Church* (South Pasadena, Calif.: William Carey Library, 1975).

6. For the CMS funding crisis, see CMS G2/I4/P7/22/1920; CMS G2/I4/P7/98/1920 Minutes of Central Missionary Council; CMS G2/I4/ P7/44/1921.

7. National Library of Scotland, Minutes of the Church of Scotland Foreign Missions Committee, 298/14, 21 Apr. 1908. The Church of Scotland began to see a decline in contributions for "general mission purposes" (as opposed to legacies and designated contributions) shortly after the turn of the century, and appointed a special committee to deal with problems of retrenchment.

8. For large-scale retrenchment in the UP mission in the 1930s, see UP (RG 209, Series I), Box 7, Missionary and General Correspondence, J. G. Campbell to Mills, Badowali, 18 Apr. 1933; E. V. Clements to Dr. White, Badomali, 27 July 1933; Dr. Mills J. Taylor to D. Emmet Alter, 14 Mar. 1934; The College Springs, Iowa, United Presbyterian Congregation had

provided full support for the D. Emmet Alter family until the Depression, when "the church was so hard hit they had to drop to partial support."

9. Stock, *People Movements*, for membership statistics.

10. Charles Freer Andrews, *The Testimony of C. F. Andrews*, edited by Daniel O'Connor (Madras: Christian Literature Society, 1974), 136–37, "Christ and Educated India," sermon preached at Agra, 1909.

11. C. M. Millington, *"Whether We Be Many or Few": A History of the Cambridge/Delhi Brotherhood* (Bangalore: Asian Trading Corporation, 1999), 122.

12. John C. B. Webster, *The Christian Community and Change in Nineteenth Century North India* (Delhi: Macmillan of India, 1976), 200ff; George Thomas, *Christians Indians and Indian Nationalism 1885–1950* (Frankfurt: Peter D. Lang, 1979); Gerald Studdert-Kennedy, *British Christians, Indian Nationalists and the Raj* (Delhi: Oxford University Press, 1991); Gerald Studdert-Kennedy, *Providence and the Raj: Imperial Mission and Missionary Imperialism* (New Delhi: Sage Publications, 1998).

13. CMS G2/I4/o/1914.

14. CMS G2/I4/o/100/1919.

15. CMS G2/I4/o/3/1920. Dixey to Wigram, Cinnemara, Assam.

16. CMS G2/I4/P6/76&83/1918.

17. CMS G2/I4/P6/no number/1916.

18. CMS G2/I4/P6/53/1918.

19. CMS G2/I4/P7/91/1919. C. M. Gough, Lahore, 28 May.

20. CMS G2/I4/o/68/1919. Report on Seditious Rioting in the Punjab. 1919.

21. Vinay Lal, "The Incident of the 'Crawling Lane': Women in the Punjab Disturbances of 1919," *Genders* 16 (spring 1993): 35–60.

22. CMS G2/I4/o/72/1920. Guilford to Wigram, Tarn Taran, 11 May; CMS Mission Report for Tarn Taran, 1921, CMS/G2/I4/o/39/1922.

23. BMS Farrer Chronicles, in/150, 26 Oct. 1920.

24. BMS in/150, 19 Jan. 1922.

25. Elizabeth G. K. Hewat, *Vision and Achievement 1796–1956: A History of the Foreign Missions of the Churches United in the Church of Scotland* (Edinburgh: Thomas Nelson & Sons, 1960), 122.

26. CMS G2/I4/P7/4/1920, Gough to PC, Lahore, 18 and 24 Dec. 1919.

27. CMS G2/I4/o/68/1919. Report on Seditious Rioting in the Punjab. 1919.

28. CMS G2/I4/P7/1926. Obituary of Miss Helen Maud Scott, 1926.

29. CMS G2/I4/o/39/1922.

30. *A Native Church for the Natives of India, Giving an Account of the Second Meeting of the Punjab CMS Native Church Council Held at Umritsar, 24–27 December 1877* (Lahore, 1878), 112.

31. Satish C. Chatterjee, "Indian Christians and National Ideals," *East and West* 12 (Apr. 1914): 214.

32. John C. B. Webster, "Presbyterian Missionaries and Gandhian Poli-

tics, 1919–1922," *Journal of Presbyterian History* 62, no. 3 (fall 1984): 246–57.

33. National Library of Scotland, Punjab and Murray College papers, plans, etc., acc 7548 D-17, 1917–28. Daska Church of Scotland Mission Compound Outline Map, 1928, with an extract from a letter from the Rev. A. Nicolson to Mr. McCachlan regarding the Cook House at Daska.

34. CMS G2/I4/0/66/1921.

35. UP (RG 209, Series I), Box 7, Missionary and General Correspondence, J. G. Campbell to Dr. Ellis, 1 Feb. 1943, Sargodha.

36. UP (RG 209, Series I), Box 7, Missionary and General Correspondence, E. V. Clements to Dr. Mills, Badomali, 30 Oct. 1945.

37. E. D. and F. Thakur Das Lucas, *The Rural Church in the Punjab: A Study of Social, Economic, Educational and Religious Conditions Prevailing amongst Certain Village Christian Communities in the Sialkot District.* Research Studies in the Economic and Social Environment of the Indian Church (Lahore, 1938), 61.

38. Imran Ali, *The Punjab under Imperialism, 1885–1947* (Princeton: Princeton University Press, 1988).

39. Lucas, *The Rural Church in Punjab*, 2–4.

40. R. Maconachie (late I.C.S.), *Rowland Bateman: Nineteenth Century Apostle* (London: CMS, 1917), 116.

41. CMS G2/I4/P7/22 and 38/1925. R. Force Jones, Lahore, 12 Mar. and 29 Apr. 1925.

42. CMS G2/I4/P7/31/1929. Survey of Needs of Central Punjab, by W. P. Hares; CMS G2/I4/P7/1930/42. Minutes of CMS/CEZMS Joint Conference, 1–4 Mar. 1930.

43. Freidrich Braun, *The Contribution of the Catholic Church Towards the Future of the People of Pakistan*, thesis for a Diploma of Theology of the Theological Faculty of the University of Bamberg, Rev. Fr. Piet de Vreede (n.d. [trans. 1987]), 12ff. By 1911 they had opened convent schools at Dalhousie, Multan, Sialkot, and Ambala, and several schools at Simla.

44. Sialkot Mission, Minutes, 1901, n.p.

45. CMS G2/I4/02/78/1883. Remarks by Reverend R. Clark written in the Church Record Book, Clarkabad, 1 Mar. 1883; CMS G2/I4/02/125/1887. F. E. Wigram, 7 Mar., S. S. *Arabia* at sea.

46. CMS G2/I4/0/206/1901. H. U. Weitbrecht. Memo on church building at Montgomerywala, Jhang Bar.

47. J. C. Heinrich, *Depressed Class Psychology*, pamphlet (Lahore: Government of Punjab, 1935), 1.

48. CMS G2/I4/0/276/1901. P. Ireland-Jones to R. Maconachie, esq.

49. CMS G2/I4/0/108/1916. Memorandum of the Scheme of Land Colonization suggested by the Rt. Rev. the Lord Bishop of Madras at a conference of village missionaries held at Lahore on 11 Feb. 1913 by H. E. Clark. The first type included Montgomerywala and Batemanabad (CMS); Youngsona-

bad (C of S); Martinpur (UP); and Khushpur (RC) with variations at Secunderabad (private) and Annfield (UP); the second type Clarkabad (CMS), Santokh Majra (AP), and Miriambad (RC); the third Hunterpur and a number of others at various times. I do not know how the Salvation Army handled land tenure at Amritnagar (Montgomery) and Shantinagar (Multan), or the American Methodists at their Jhang Bar colony.

50. H. E. Clark, in CMS G2/I4/o/108/1916.

51. UP (RG 209, Series I), Box 7, Missionary and General Correspondence, J. C. Heinrich to W. B., Martinpur, 8 Aug. 1934 and 26 Dec. 1934.

52. Sialkot Mission, *Annual Reports of the United Presbyterian Mission in India* (Sialkot, 1882–84), 1884, 4.

53. Lucas, *The Rural Church in Punjab*, 50.

54. Maconachie (late I.C.S.), *Rowland Bateman: Nineteenth Century Apostle*, 155.

55. CMS G2/I4/o/184/1914. First Visitation of the Fourth Bishop of Lahore, 2–9 Nov. 1914.

56. CMS G2/I4/o/52/1914. Asrapur, 1913. Rev. C. L. Richards.

57. CMS G2/I4/o/52/1914.

58. CMS G2/I4/o/52/1914. Annual Report of Asrapur, 1913.

59. CMS G2/I4/o/52/1914. Annual Report of Asrapur, 1913.

60. CMS G2/I4/o/71/1915.

61. CMS G2/I4/o/50/1905. Copy of entry in the Mission Record Book at Toba Tek Singh.

62. Richard G. Fox, *Lions of the Punjab: Culture in the Making* (Berkeley: University of California, 1985); Grewal, *The Sikhs of the Punjab*.

63. Census of India 1931, *Punjab Part I*, vol. 17, Khan Ahmad Hasan Khan (Lahore: Punjab Government, 1933), 20–21.

64. Mark Juergensmeyer, *Religion as Social Vision: The Movement against Untouchability in 20th-Century Punjab* (Berkeley: University of California Press, 1982).

65. Census of India 1931, *Punjab Part I*, vol. 17, iii–iv.

66. UP (RG 209, Series I), Box 7, Missionary and General Correspondence, J. G. Campbell to Dr. Taylor, Pahlgam, Kashmir, 28 July 1941.

67. UP (RG 209, Series I), Box 7, Missionary and General Correspondence, J. C. Heinrich to Dr. Caldwell, n.d., n.p., rec'd. 24 Sept. 1936.

68. T. McNair, "Problems Raised by the Indian Mass Movements," *East and West* 22 (1924): 356.

69. Pieter Streefland, *The Sweepers of Slaughterhouse: Conflict and Survival in a Karachi Neighbourhood* (Assen: Van Gorcum, 1979), 41 ff and personal communication.

70. John C. B. Webster, *The Dalit Christians: A History* (Delhi: Indian Society for Promoting Christian Knowledge, 1992); James Massey, *Dalits in India: Religion as a Source of Bondage or Liberation with Special Reference to Christians* (New Delhi: Manohar Publishers & Distributors and ISPCK, 1995).

71. Lahore Missionary Conference, *Report of the Punjab Missionary Conference Held at Lahore in December and January, 1862–63* (Ludhiana: American Presbyterian Mission Press, 1863), 159.

72. E. M. Forster, *A Passage to India*, reprint, 1924 (Harmondsworth: Penguin, 1974), 317.

Bibliography

A. Major Manuscript Collections Consulted, with Current Location
B. Primary Printed Sources Cited
C. Government Census and Education Reports Cited
D. Hymnbooks Cited
E. Secondary Books and Articles Cited
F. Theses Cited

A. MAJOR MANUSCRIPT COLLECTIONS CONSULTED, WITH CURRENT LOCATION

Baptist Missionary Society and Baptist Zenana Missionary Society. Regent's Park College, Oxford.

Baptist Missionary Society. Serampore College Library, West Bengal, India.

Church Missionary Society and Church of England Zenana Missionary Society. University of Birmingham Library.

Church of Scotland. Punjab Mission Council Minutes. Diocese of Sialkot, Church of Pakistan, Sialkot.

Church of Scotland. Records of the Church of Scotland Foreign Missions Committee and Women's Association for Foreign Missions, and Letters from Missionaries. National Library of Scotland, Edinburgh.

Diocese of Lahore. Bishop's College Archives, Calcutta.

Salvation Army. The Salvation Army, London.

Society for the Propagation of the Gospel, and the Cambridge Mission to Delhi. Rhodes House, Oxford.

United Presbyterian Church of North America. Records of the Board of Foreign Missions. Presbyterian Historical Society, Philadelphia.

B. PRIMARY PRINTED SOURCES CITED

Account of a Society for Mission to Africa and the East Instituted by Members of the Established Church. London, 1799.

After One Hundred Years: North India Mission, 1836–1936. Bangalore: Scripture Literature Press, 1936.

Andrews, Charles Freer. *North India.* Handbooks of English Church Expansion. Oxford: Mowbray, 1908.

———. "The Situation in the East." *East and West* (Oct. 1907): 419–29.

———. *The Testimony of C. F. Andrews*. Edited by Daniel O'Connor. Madras: Christian Literature Society, 1974.

———. *What I Owe to Christ, by C. F. Andrews*. London: Hodder & Stoughton, 1932.

Balfour, Margaret, and Ruth Young. *The Work of Medical Women in India*. Oxford: Oxford University Press, 1929.

Baptist Missionary Society. *Annual Reports*. Being a continuation of the Periodical Accounts relative to the Society. London, 1809–98.

Baptist Zenana Missionary Society. *Annual Reports*. London, 1869–1925.

Baptist Zenana Mission. *Jubilee 1867–1917. Fifty Years' Work among Women in the Far East*. London: Carey Press, 1917.

Barnes, Irene H. *Behind the Pardah: The Story of C.E.Z.M.S. Work in India*. London: Marshall Brothers, 1897.

———. *Between Life and Death: The Story of C.E.Z.M.S. Medical Missions in India, China, and Ceylon*. London: Marshall Brothers, 1901.

Basu, B. D. *Rise of the Christian Power in India*. Calcutta: Brahmo Press, 1923.

Bate, J. D. *A Dictionary of the Hindee Language*. Benares: Medical Hall Press, 1875.

Beynon, Katherine. "Women's Work among the Eurasians in the Punjab." *East and West* 2 (1904): 38 ff.

Bickersteth, Edward. *A Letter to the Rev. Canon Westcott, D. D.* Cambridge Mission to Delhi Occasional Papers. Delhi: Cambridge Mission to Delhi, 1881.

Birks, The Rev. Herbert Alfred, M.A. *The Life and Correspondence of Thomas Valpy French, First Bishop of Lahore*. 2 vols. London: John Murray, 1895.

Booth Tucker, Frederick. *Darkest India: A Supplement to General Booth's "In Darkest England and the Way Out."* Bombay: Bombay Gazette, 1890.

A Brief Life-Sketch of Shri Dev Guru Bhagwan (from His Birth to His Taking up the Great Mission of His Life). Lahore: Jiwan Press, 1913.

Briggs, George W. *The Chamars, by Geo. W. Briggs, M.Sc.* New York: Oxford University Press, 1920.

Bruce, J. F. *A History of the University of the Panjab*. Lahore, 1933.

Calcutta Missionary Conference. *Statistical Tables of Protestant Missions in India, Burma and Ceylon, Prepared on Information Collected at the Close of 1890, at the Request of the Calcutta Missionary Conference*. Calcutta: Baptist Mission Press, 1892.

Cambridge Mission to Delhi. *Annual Report*. Delhi, 1878–1904.

Carey, William. *An Enquiry into the Obligations of Christians, to Use Means for the Conversion of the Heathens in which the Religious State of the Different Nations of the World, the Success of Former Undertakings, and the Practicability of Further Undertakings, Are Considered*. Leicester, 1792.

Carus-Wilson, Mrs. Ashley. *A Woman's Life for Kashmir: Irene Petrie, a Biography*. New York: Fleming H. Revell Company, 1901.

Chatterjee, Satish C. "Indian Christians and National Ideals." *East and West* 12 (Apr. 1914): 209–24.

Church Missionary Intelligencer. London: Church Missionary Society, 1851.

Church Missionary Society. *Abstract of Replies to the Circular Letter of the Conference Secretaries*. London: CMS, n.d., c. 1900.

———. *Laws and Regulations of the CMS. Part IV. Organization of Native Churches*. London: CMS, 1883.

———. *Register of Missionaries (Clerical, Lay, & Female) and Native Clergy from 1804 to 1904*. London: Printed for Private Circulation, 1905.

Clark, Henry Martyn. *Robert Clark of the Punjab: Pioneer and Missionary Statesman*. London: Andrew Melrose, 1907.

Clark, Robert. *The Missions of the Church Missionary Society and the Church of England Zenana Missionary Society in the Punjab and Sindh*. Edited by Robert Maconachie. London: Church Missionary Society, 1904.

Croil, James. *The Noble Army of Martyrs and Roll of Protestant Missionary Martyrs from A.D. 1661 to 1891*. Philadelphia: Presbyterian Board of Publication, 1894.

Cust, Robert Needham. *Essay on the Prevailing Methods of the Evangelization of the Non-Christian World*. London: Luzac and Co., publishers to the India Office, 1894.

Deedes, Brooke. *An Account of the Visit of the Lord Bishop of Calcutta to the Peshawar Mission, Contributed by His Chaplain the Rev. Brooke Deedes, M.A.* Printed for private circulation. CMS G1/I4/PI/371882, 1881.

Delhi Mission News. Delhi: Cambridge Mission to Delhi, 1895–1931.

Denny, J. K. H. *Toward the Sunrising: A History of Work for the Women of India Done by Women from England, 1852–1901*. London: Marshall Brothers, 1901.

Dev Samaj. *European Sympathy with the Deva Dharma Mission*. Lahore: New Lyall Press, 1892.

———. *General Information Regarding the Dev Samaj*. Lahore: Dev Samaj Head Office, 1915.

Directory of Christian Missions and Churches in India, Burma and Ceylon. Nagpur: National Christian Council, 1938.

Directory of Christian Missions in India, Burma and Ceylon, 1932–1933. Madras: Christian Literature Society, 1932.

English Report (Translated from the Urdu) of the Fifth Annual Meeting of the Punjab and Sindh CMS Native Church Council Held at Umritsar from 26–28 December 1880. Amritsar, 1881.

Farquhar, John Nicol. *The Crown of Hinduism*. 1913. New Delhi: Oriental Books Reprint Corp., 1971.

———. *Modern Religious Movements in India.* 1915. Delhi: Munshiram Manoharlal, 1967.

Fifty Years for Bhiwani Hospital: The Farrer Jubilee. London: Baptist Missionary Society, 1941.

Forster, E. M. *A Passage to India.* 1924. Harmondsworth: Penguin, 1974.

Fox, Richard G. *Lions of the Punjab: Culture in the Making.* Berkeley: University of California, 1985.

French, Francesca. *Miss Brown's Hospital: The Story of the Ludhiana Medical College and Dame Edith Brown, O.B.E., Its Founder.* London: Hodder and Stoughton, 1954.

Gazetteer of the Delhi District, 1883–84. Compiled and published under the authority of Punjab government. 1884. Gurgaon (Haryana): Vintage Books, 1998.

Gordon, Andrew. *Our India Mission: A Thirty Years History of the India Mission of the United Presbyterian Church of North America, Together with Personal Reminiscences.* Philadelphia: Andrew Gordon, 1886.

Hayes, Marie Elizabeth. *At Work: Letters of Marie Elizabeth Hayes, M.B., Missionary Doctor, Delhi, 1905–8.* Edited by her mother. Introduction by G. R. Wynne. 1909. London: Marshall Brothers.

Heiler, Friedrich. *The Gospel of Sadhu Sundar Singh.* Translated by Olive Wyon. 1927. Delhi: I.S.P.C.K., 1989.

Heinrich, J. C. *Depressed Class Psychology.* Pamphlet. Lahore: Government of Punjab, 1935.

———. *The Psychology of a Suppressed People.* London: George Allen and Unwin, 1937.

Hewlett, S. S. *Daughters of the King.* London: James Nisbet and Co., 1886.

Historical Sketches of the India Missions of the Presbyterian Church in the United States of America, Known as the Ludiana, the Farrukhabad, and the Kolhapur Missions: From the Beginning of the Work, in 1834, to the Time of Its Fiftieth Anniversary, in 1884. Allahabad: Allahabad Mission Press, 1886.

Ibbetson, Denzil. *Panjab Castes.* Chapters from the Census Report of 1881 on "The Races, Castes, and Tribes of the Panjab." 1916. Delhi: Meeraj, 1984.

Imad-ud-din. *A Mohammedan Brought to Christ: Being the Autobiography of a Native Clergyman in India, to Which is Added His Treatise on Justification by Faith in Christ.* From the Hindustanee. London: Church Missionary Society, 1869.

———. *A Mohammedan Brought to Christ: Being the Autobiography of the Rev. Imad-Ud-Din, D.D.* Robert Clark. London: Church Missionary Society, 1884.

Imperial Gazetteer of India. Punjab. 1908. Provincial Series. New Delhi: Usha Publications, 1984.

The Indian Church Directory for the Province of India and Ceylon. Calcutta, 1890.

The Indian War Cry. Published by the Salvation Army. Poona, 1883–1947.

Janvier, L. *Dictionary of the Punjabi Language.* Ludhiana: For the Ludhiana Mission, 1854.

Jones, Lewis Bevan. *The People of the Mosque: An Introduction to the Study of Islam with Special Reference to India.* Calcutta: Association Press, 1932.

Jukes, Worthington. *Reminiscences of Missionary Work in Amritsar 1872–1873 and on the Afghan Frontier in Peshawar 1873–1890.* Typescript. Peshawar: Edwards High School, 1925.

Kabir. *The Bijak of Kabir.* Translated and edited by Linda Hess and Shukdev Singh. 1983. Delhi: Motilal Banarsidass, 1986.

Kipling, Rudyard. *Kim.* 1901. New York: Dell, 1959.

Lefroy, George Alfred. *The Leatherworkers of Daryaganj.* Cambridge Mission to Delhi Occasional Papers. Delhi: Cambridge Mission to Delhi, 1884.

———. "The Moral Tone of India." *East and West: A Quarterly Review for the Study of Missions* 1 (1903): 121–33.

Lewis, Arthur. *George Maxwell Gordon M.A., F.R.G.S., the Pilgrim Missionary of the Punjab: A History of His Life and Work 1839–1880.* London: Seeley & Co., 1889.

Lowrie, John C. *Travels in North India: Containing Notices of the Hindus; Journals of a Voyage on the Ganges and a Tour to Lahore; Notes on the Himalaya Mountains and the Hill Tribes: Including a Sketch of Missionary Undertakings.* Philadelphia: Presbyterian Board of Publications, 1842.

Lucas, E. D., and F. Thakur Das. *The Rural Church in the Punjab: A Study of Social, Economic, Educational and Religious Conditions Prevailing amongst Certain Village Christian Communities in the Sialkot District.* Research Studies in the Economic and Social Environment of the Indian Church. Lahore, 1938.

Macaulay, Thomas Babington. *Macaulay: Poetry and Prose.* Compiled by G. M. Young. Cambridge, Mass.: Harvard University Press, 1967.

Mackenzie, F. A. (Frederick Arthur). *Booth-Tucker, Sadhu and Saint, by F. A. Mackenzie* Introduction by General E. J. Higgins. London: Hodder and Stoughton, 1930.

Maconachie (late I.C.S.), R. *Rowland Bateman: Nineteenth Century Apostle.* London: CMS, 1917.

Magazine of the London School of Medicine for Women and Royal Free Hospital. London, 1895–1901.

Martin, Cecil H. *Allnutt of Delhi: A Memoir.* London: Society for Promoting Christian Knowledge, 1922.

Mayo, Katherine. *Mother India.* Introduction by Mrinalini Sinha. 1927. Ann Arbor: University of Michigan, 2000.

McNair, T. "Problems Raised by the Indian Mass Movements." *East and West* 22 (1924): 351–56.

A Medical Jubilee. Pamphlet, n.p. Bhiwani: Farrer Hospital, 1940.

Missionary Conference, Lahore. *Report of the Punjab Missionary Conference Held at Lahore in December and January, 1862–63.* Ludhiana: American Presbyterian Mission Press, 1863.

The Missionary Controversy: Discussion, Evidence and Report. London: Wesleyan Methodist Book Room, 1890.

Monk, Francis Fitzhugh. *A History of St. Stephen's College, Delhi: Compiled for the Cambridge Mission in Commemoration of the Fiftieth Anniversary of the Founding of the College, 1931, by F. F. Monk.* Calcutta: Y.M.C.A. Publishing House, 1935.

Monserrate, Antonio. *The Commentary of Father Monserrate, S.J., on His Journey to the Court of Akbar: Translated from the Original Latin by J. S. Hoyland, and Annotated by S. N. Banerjee.* London: Oxford University Press, 1922.

Montgomery, H. H. *The Life and Letters of George Alfred Lefroy D.D., Bishop of Calcutta and Metropolitan.* London: Longmans, Green & Co., 1920.

A Native Church for the Natives of India, Giving an Account of the Formation of a Native Church Council for the Punjab Mission of the Church Missionary Society, and of the Proceedings of Their First Meeting at Umritsar, 31 March–2 April 1877. Lahore, 1877.

A Native Church for the Natives of India, Giving an Account of the Second Meeting of the Punjab CMS Native Church Council Held at Umritsar, 24–27 December 1877. Lahore, 1878.

One Hundred Years in Delhi. Delhi: The Brotherhood of the Ascended Christ, 1977.

Our Indian Sisters: A Quarterly Magazine of the Ladies Zenana Mission in Connection with the Baptist Missionary Society. London: Baptist Zenana Mission, 1886–89.

Pennell, Alice M. *Pennell of the Afghan Frontier: The Life of Theodore Pennell, M.D., B.Sc., F.R.C.S.* London: Seeley, Service & Co., 1914.

Pennell, T. L. [B.Sc. M.D., F.R.C.S.]. *Among the Wild Tribes of the Afghan Frontier: A Record of Sixteen Years' Close Intercourse with the Natives of the Indian Marches.* Introduction by Field-Marshal Earl Roberts. London: Seeley & Co., 1909.

Penner, Peter. *Robert Needham Cust, 1821–1909: A Personal Biography.* Studies in British History, vol. 5. Lewiston, N.Y.: Edward Mellen Press, 1987.

Pickett, J. Waskom. *Christian Mass Movements in India: A Study with Recommendations.* New York: Abingdon Press, 1933.

Report of the 21st Annual Meeting of the Punjab CMS District Native Church Council, Amritsar, 11–13 April 1898. Lahore, 1898.

Report of the Eighteenth Meeting of the Punjab CMS District Native Church Council Held at Amritsar, 27–29 March 1895. Lahore, 1895.

Report of the General Missionary Conference Held at Allahabad, 1872–73, with a Missionary Map of India. Madras: Seeley, Jackson, and Halliday, London, 1873.

Report of the Sixth Meeting of the Punjab CMS Native Church Council Held at Umritsar, 25–27 December 1881. Amritsar, 1882.

Report of the SPG and Cambridge Mission in Delhi and the South Punjab. Title varies, 1882–1931.

Report of the Third Meeting of the Punjab C.M.S. Native Church Council Held at Umritsur from the 27th to the 30th of December 1878. London, 1879.

Rose, H. A. (Horace Arthur). *A Glossary of the Tribes and Castes of the Punjab and North-West Frontier Province: Based on the Census Report for the Punjab, 1883, by the Late Sir Denzil Ibbetson and the Census Report for the Punjab, 1892, by Sir Edward Maclagan*. [Patiala]: Languages Dept., 1970 reprint.

Sialkot Mission. *Annual Reports of the United Presbyterian Mission in India*. Sialkot, 1882–84.

———. *Minutes of the Annual Meeting of the Sialkot Mission of the United Presbyterian Church of North America*. Title varies, 1896–1910.

Smith, Sydney. "Indian Missions." *Edinburgh Review*, Apr. 1808.

Society for Promoting Female Education in the East. *Female Missionary Intelligencer*. New Series. London, 1881–99.

Society for the Propagation of the Gospel. *Annual Reports*. London, 1906–35.

Stewart, Robert. *Life and Work in India: An Account of the Conditions, Methods, Difficulties, Results, Future Prospects and Reflex Influence of Missionary Labor in India, Especially in the Punjab Mission of the United Presbyterian Church of North America*. Philadelphia: Pearl Publishing, 1899.

Stock, Eugene. *The History of the Church Missionary Society: Its Environment, Its Men and Its Work*. London: Church Missionary Society, 1899.

The Story of the Delhi Mission. London: Society for the Propagation of the Gospel, 1908.

Talks on India. An Outline of Six Missionary Instructions with Illustrations and Recitations for Young People. London: Church Missionary Society, 1908.

Taylor, H. F. Lechmere. *In the Land of the Five Rivers: A Sketch of the Work of the Church of Scotland in Panjab*. Edinburgh: R. & R. Clark, 1906.

Thompson, J. T. *A Commentary on the Gospel of Matthew in Oordoo*. Calcutta: Baptist Mission Press, 1850.

———. *A Dictionary in Hindi and English*. 1846. Calcutta: Sangbada Jnanaratnakara Press, 1870.

———. *The Psalms of David: Translated into the Hindee Language by J. T. Thompson*. Serampore, 1836.

Trumpp, Ernest, trans. and ed. *The Adi Granth, or Holy Scriptures of the Sikhs*. London: W. H. Allen, 1877.

"Trumpp, Ernst." In *Allgemeine Deutsche Biographie,* vol. 38, 687–89. Leipzig, 1894.

Tyndale-Biscoe, C. E. "Teaching the Book." *East and West* 17 (Oct. 1919).

Tyndale-Biscoe, E. D. *Fifty Years against the Stream: The Story of a School in Kashmir 1880–1930.* Mysore: Wesleyan Mission Press, 1930.

Venn, Henry. *The Missionary Life and Labours of Francis Xavier, Taken from His Own Correspondence: With a Sketch of the General Results of Roman Catholic Missions among the Heathen.* London: Longman, Green, Longman, Roberts, & Green, 1862.

———. *To Apply the Gospel: Selections from the Writing of Henry Venn.* Edited by Max Warren. Grand Rapids, Mich.: William B. Eerdmans, 1971.

Weitbrecht, H. U. *The Urdu New Testament.* Bible House Papers, no. 3 ATLA monograph preservation program and ATLA fiche 1987–2938. London: British and Foreign Bible Society, 1900.

Wenger, E. S. *Missionary Biographies in Four Volumes.* Unpublished manuscript. Serampore: Carey Library, 1936.

Westcott, B. F. *On Some Points in the Religious Office of the Universities.* London: Macmillan, 1873.

Western, F. J. *The Early History of the Cambridge Mission to Delhi.* Typescript, 1950.

Whitehead, Henry. "The Progress of Christianity in India and Mission Strategy." *East and West* 5 (Jan. 1907): 21–28.

Youngson, John F. W. *Forty Years of the Panjab Mission of the Church of Scotland, 1855–1895.* Edinburgh: R. & R. Clark, 1896.

Yule, Henry, Sir. *Hobson-Jobson: A Glossary of Colloquial Anglo-Indian Words and Phrases, and of Kindred Terms, Etymological, Historical, Geographical and Discursive, by Henry Yule and A. C. Burnell,* 4th ed. Edited by William Crooke. 1903. Delhi: Munshiram Manoharlal, 1984.

Zenana Bible and Medical Mission. *The Indian Female Evangelist.* London: Indian Female Normal School and Instruction Society, 1872–1901.

C. GOVERNMENT CENSUS AND EDUCATION
REPORTS CITED

Census of India 1911. *Punjab,* Vol. 14, *Part I: Report.* Pandit Harikishan Kaul. Lahore: Civil and Military Gazette, 1912.

Census of India 1911. *Punjab,* Vol. 14, *Part III: Appendices to the Imperial Tables.* Pandit Harikishan Kaul. Lahore: Civil and Military Gazette, 1912.

Census of India 1921. *North-West Frontier Province.* R. B. Bhai Lehna Singh. Peshawar: Government Press, 1922.

Census of India 1921. *Punjab and Delhi. Part I: Report.* L. Middleton and S. M. Jacob. Lahore: Civil and Military Gazette, 1923.

Census of India 1931. *Delhi.* Vol. 16. Khan Ahmad Hasan. Lahore: Government of India, 1933.

Census of India 1931. *North West Frontier Province.* Vol. 15. G. L. and A. D. F. Dundas Mallam. Peshawar: Government of India, 1933.

Census of India 1931. *Punjab Part I.* Vol. 17. Khan Ahmad Hasan Khan. Lahore: Punjab Government, 1933.

Census of India 1931. *Punjab Part II.* Vol. 17. Khan Ahmad Hasan Khan. Lahore: Punjab Government, 1933.

Census Report for the Punjab, 1883, by the Late Sir Denzil Ibbetson and the Census Report for the Punjab, 1892, by Sir Edward Maclagan. [Patiala]: Languages Dept., Punjab, 1970.

Report by the Panjab Provincial Committee with Evidence Taken before the Committee and Memorials Addressed to the Education Commission. Appendix to the Report of the Indian Education Commission. Calcutta: Superintendent of Government Printing, 1884.

Report on Education in the Punjab for 1910–1911. Lahore, 1911.

Report on Public Instruction in the Punjab and Its Dependencies for the Year 1890–1891. Compiled by J. Sime, DPI. Lahore, 1891.

Report on the Progress of Education in the Punjab during the Quinquennium Ending 1911–1912. Lahore, 1912.

Report on the Progress of Education in the Punjab during the Quinquennium Ending 1921–22. Lahore, 1922.

Report on the Progress of Education in the Punjab during the Quinquennium Ending 1926–27. Lahore, 1927.

Report on the Progress of Education in the Punjab during the Quinquennium Ending 1931–32. Lahore, 1932.

D. HYMNBOOKS CITED

Bate, Mrs. J. D., comp. *The North India Tune-Book, Containing Bhajans and Ghazals with Native Tunes, as Usually Sung.* Hymnal (Roman Urdu). Allahabad: North India Tract and Book Society Depot, 1886.

Karachi Masihi Convention. *Git Ki Kitab,* 3d ed. Hymnal (Roman Urdu). Karachi: Joint Christian Convention Committee, 1959.

Masihi Git Ki Kitab Sath Ragan Ke. Hymnal (Roman Urdu). London: Novello, 1916.

Nai Masihi Git Ki Kitab. 7th ed. Hymnal (Hindi). Delhi: Indian Society for the Promotion of Christian Knowledge, 1987.

Salvation Army. *The Salvation Army Song Book.* Hymnal (Urdu). Compiled by Lt. Commissioner Vijri Singh (H. S. Hodgson). Lahore: Northern India Territorial Headquarters, 1946.

Scott, Mrs. Emma Moore, comp. *The Hindustani Tune Book, a Collection of Bhajans and Gazals, Containing the Principal Native Airs, Sung in the Missions of North India: Arranged for the Piano or Organ.* 2d ed. Hymnal (Roman Urdu). Lucknow: Methodist Publishing House, 1894.

Sialkot Convention Hymn Book. Hymnal (Urdu). Sialkot: Sialkot Convention, 1940.

Uttar Pradesh Christian Council. *Kalisiyai Git Ki Kitab.* Hymnal (Roman

Urdu). Preface by A. Rallia Ram. Allahabad: North Indian Christian
  Book and Tract Society, 1953.
Zabur Aur Git Ki Kitab. Hymnal (Roman Urdu). Allahabad: United Prov-
  inces Christian Council, 1932.

E. SECONDARY BOOKS AND ARTICLES CITED

Ahmad, Aijaz. *In Theory: Classes, Nations, Literatures.* London: Verso,
  1992.
Ali, Daud. "Recognizing Europe in India: Colonial Master Narratives and
  the Writing of Indian History." In *Contesting the Master Narrative: Essays in Social History,* edited by Jeffrey Cox and Shelton Stromquist,
  95–130. Iowa City: University of Iowa, 1998.
Ali, Imran. *The Punjab under Imperialism, 1885–1947.* Princeton: Prince-
  ton University Press, 1988.
Alter, James P. *In the Doab and Rohilkhand: North Indian Christianity,
  1815–1915.* Delhi: I.S.P.C.K., 1986.
Appadurai, Arjun. *Worship and Conflict under Colonial Rule: A South
  Indian Case.* Cambridge South Asian Studies, no. 27. Cambridge, Eng.;
  New York: Cambridge University Press, 1981.
Arnold, David. *Colonizing the Body: State Medicine and Epidemic Dis-
  ease in Nineteenth-Century India.* Berkeley: University of California
  Press, 1993.
Ayandele, Emmanuel Ayankanmi. *The Missionary Impact on Modern Ni-
  geria, 1842–1914: A Political and Social Analysis.* London: Longmans,
  1966.
Bachman, E. T. "North American Doctoral Dissertations on Mission,
  1945–1981." *International Bulletin of Missionary Research* 7, no. 3
  (1983).
Barrett, David, ed. *World Christian Encyclopedia: A Comparative Survey
  of Churches and Religions in the Modern World, A.D. 1900–2000.* Nairobi; New York: Oxford University Press, 1982.
Basu, Aparnu. "The Foundation and Early History of Delhi University." In
  *Delhi through the Ages: Essays in Urban History, Culture, and Soci-
  ety,* edited by R. E. Frykenberg, 401–30. Delhi; New York: Oxford University Press, 1986.
Bayly, Susan. *Saints, Goddesses, and Kings: Muslims and Christians in
  South Indian Society, 1700–1900.* Cambridge South Asian Studies, no.
  43. Cambridge, Eng.; New York: Cambridge University Press, 1989.
Beidelman, T. O. (Thomas O.). *Colonial Evangelism: A Socio-Historical
  Study of an East African Mission at the Grassroots.* Bloomington: Indiana University Press, 1982.
Bhabha, Homi K. "Signs Taken for Wonders: Questions of Ambivalence
  and Authority under a Tree Outside Delhi, May 1817." *Critical Inquiry*
  12 (autumn 1985): 144–65.
Brantlinger, Patrick. *Rule of Darkness: British Literature and Imperialism, 1830–1914.* Ithaca: Cornell University Press, 1988.

Brouwer, Ruth Compton. *New Women for God: Canadian Presbyterian Women and India Missions, 1876–1914.* Social History of Canada, no. 44. Toronto; Buffalo: University of Toronto Press, 1990.

Brush, Stanley Elwood. "Protestants in Conflict: Policy and Early Practice in the British Punjab." *Al-Mushir* 17, no. 4–6 (June 1975).

Burns, Arthur. *The Diocesan Revival in the Church of England c. 1800–1870.* Oxford Historical Monographs. Oxford: Clarendon Press, 1999.

Burton, Antoinette M. *Burdens of History: British Feminists, Indian Women, and Imperial Culture, 1865–1915.* Chapel Hill: University of North Carolina, 1994.

———. "Contesting the Zenana: The Mission to Make 'Lady Doctors for India,' 1874–1885." *Journal of British Studies* 35 (July 1996): 368–97.

———. "Fearful Bodies into Disciplined Subjects: Pleasure, Romance and the Family Drama of Colonial Reform in Mary Carpenter's Six Months in India." *Signs* 20, no. 3 (1995): 545–74.

Campbell, James T. *Songs of Zion: The African Methodist Episcopal Church in the United States and South Africa.* New York: Oxford University Press, 1995.

Cashdollar, Charles. *The Transformation of Theology, 1830–1890: Positivism and Protestant Thought in Britain and America.* Princeton: Princeton University Press, 1989.

Chatterjee, Partha. *Nationalist Thought and the Colonial World—A Derivative Discourse.* London: Zed Books, 1986.

Chaturvedi, Benarsidas, and Marjorie Sykes. *Charles Freer Andrews: A Narrative.* 1949. New Delhi: Government of India Publications Division, 1971.

Chaudhuri, Amit. "Beyond the Language of the Raj." *TLS* 4923 (8 Aug. 1997): 17–18.

Cnattingius, Hans. *Bishops and Societies: A Study of Anglican Colonial and Missionary Expansion 1698–1850.* Published for the Church Historical Society. London: SPCK, 1952.

Cohn, Bernard. *An Anthropologist among the Historians and Other Essays.* Delhi: Oxford University Press, 1987.

———. *Colonialism and Its Forms of Knowledge: The British in India.* Princeton Studies in Culture/Power/History. Princeton: Princeton University Press, 1996.

Comaroff, Jean and John. *Of Revelation and Revolution: Christianity, Colonialism, and Consciousness in South Africa.* Chicago: University of Chicago Press, 1991.

Comfort, Richard O. *The Village Church in West Pakistan.* Lahore: West Pakistan Christian Council, n.d. (c. 1957).

Copley, Antony. *Religions in Conflict. Ideology, Cultural Contact and Conversion in Late Colonial India.* New Delhi: Oxford, 1997.

Cox, Jeffrey. "Audience and Exclusion at the Margins of Imperial History," *Women's History Review* 3, no. 4 (1994): 501–14.

———. "C. F. Andrews and the Failure of the Modern Missionary Movement." In *Modern Religious Rebels*, edited by Stuart Mews, 226–44. London: Epworth, 1993.

———. *The English Churches in a Secular Society: Lambeth 1870–1930*. Oxford University Press, 1982.

———. "George Alfred Lefroy: Anglicans, Untouchables, and Imperial Institutions." In *After the Victorians: Essays in Honor of John Clive*, edited by Susan Pedersen and Peter Mandler, 55–76. London: Routledge, 1994.

———. "Independent English Women in Delhi and Lahore." In *Religion and Irreligion in Victorian Society: Essays in Honor of R. K. Webb*, edited by R. W. Davis and R. J. Helmstadter, 166–84. London: Routledge, 1992.

———. "The Nineteenth Century Missionary Movement." In *Nineteenth Century English Religious Traditions*, edited by Dennis Paz, 197–220. Westport, Conn.: Greenwood Press, 1995.

———. "On Redefining 'Crisis': The Victorian Crisis of Faith in the Punjab, 1880–1930." In *Victorian Faith in Crisis: Essays on Continuity and Change in Nineteenth-Century Religious Belief*, edited by Richard J. Helmstadter and Bernard Lightman, 315–42. London: Macmillan, 1990.

———. "Religion and Imperial Power in Nineteenth Century Britain." In *Freedom and Religion in the Nineteenth Century*, edited by R. W. Davis and R. J. Helmstadter, 339–428. Palo Alto: Stanford University Press, 1997.

Dayanandan Francis, T. *Sadhu Sundar Singh: The Lover of the Cross*. Madras: Christian Literature Society, 1989.

Desai, Anita. *Clear Light of Day*. New York, 1980.

———. "The Rage for the Raj." *New Republic*, no. 3,697 (25 Nov. 1985): 26–27.

Dewey, Clive. *Anglo-Indian Attitudes: The Mind of the Indian Civil Service* (London: Hambledon Press, 1993).

Dirks, Nicholas B. *The Hollow Crown: Ethnohistory of an Indian Kingdom*. Cambridge, Eng.: Cambridge University Press, 1987.

———. "The Invention of Caste: Civil Society in Colonial India." *Social Analysis* 25 (1989): 42–52.

Dube, Saurabh. *Untouchable Pasts: Religion, Identity, and Power among a Central Indian Community, 1780–1950*. SUNY Series in Hindu Studies. Albany: State University of New York Press, 1998.

Embree, Ainslee T. "Christianity and the State in Victorian India: Confrontation and Collaboration." In *Religion and Irreligion in Victorian Society: Essays in Honor of R. K. Webb*, edited by R. W. and R. J. Helmstadter Davis, 151–65. London: Routledge, 1992.

Esherick, Joseph. *The Origins of the Boxer Uprising*. Berkeley: University of California Press, 1987.

Etherington, Norman. "Missionaries and the Intellectual History of Africa: A Historical Survey." *Itinerario* 7 (1983): 116–43.

Fitzgerald, Rosemary. "A 'Peculiar and Exceptional Measure': The Call for

Women Medical Missionaries for India in the Later Nineteenth Century." In *Missionary Encounters. Sources and Issues*, edited by Robert A. Bickers and Rosemary Seton, 174–96. Richmond, UK: Curzon Press, 1996.

———. "'Rescue and Redemption'—the Rise of Female Medical Missions in Colonial India during the Late Nineteenth and Early Twentieth Centuries." In *Nursing History and the Politics of Welfare*, edited by A. M. Rafferty, J. Robinson, and R. Elkan, 64–79. London: Routledge, 1996.

Flemming, Leslie. "New Models, New Roles: U.S. Presbyterian Women Missionaries and Social Change in North India, 1870–1910." In *Women's Work for Women: Missionaries and Social Change in Asia*. Edited by Leslie Flemming, 35–57. Boulder, Colo.: Westview Press, 1989.

Forrester, Duncan. *Caste and Christianity: Attitudes and Policies on Caste of Anglo-Saxon Protestant Missions in India*. London Studies on South Asia, no. 1. London: Curzon Press; Atlantic Highlands, N.J.: Humanities Press, 1980.

Frykenberg, Robert. "The Construction of Hinduism at the Nexus of History and Religion." *Journal of Interdisciplinary History* 23, no. 3 (1993): 523–50.

———. "India." In *A World History of Christianity*, edited by Adrian Hastings, 171–91. Grand Rapids, Michigan: Eerdmans, 1999.

Gagan, Rosemary R. *A Sensitive Independence: Canadian Methodist Women Missionaries in Canada and the Orient, 1881–1925*. Montreal: McGill-Queens University Press, 1992.

Gibbs, M. E. *The Anglican Church in India 1600–1970*. Delhi: Indian Society for the Promotion of Christian Knowledge, 1972.

Goel, Sita Ram. *History of Hindu-Christian Encounters*. New Delhi: Voice of India, 1989.

Gracie, David McI., ed. and comp. *Gandhi and Charlie: The Story of a Friendship*. Cambridge, Mass.: Cowley Publications, 1989.

Graham, William A. "The Scholar's Scholar: Wilfred Cantwell Smith and a Collegial Life of the Mind." *Harvard Divinity Bulletin* 29, no. 2 (summer 2000): 6–7.

Gray, R. "An Anthropologist on the Christian Kaguru." *Journal of African History* 24, no. 3 (1983).

Green, S. J. D. *Religion in the Age of Decline: Organisation and Experience in Industrial Yorkshire, 1870–1920*. Cambridge: Cambridge University Press, 1996.

Grewal, J. S. *The City of the Golden Temple*. 2d ed. Amritsar: Guru Nanak Dev University, 1996.

———. *Contesting Interpretations of the Sikh Tradition*. New Delhi: Manohar, 1998.

———. *The Sikhs of the Punjab*. Rev. ed. *The New Cambridge History of India*, II.3. Cambridge: Cambridge University Press, 1999.

Grimshaw, Patricia. *Paths of Duty: American Missionary Wives in Nineteenth-Century Hawaii*. Honolulu: University of Hawaii Press, 1989.

Haggis, Jane. "'A Heart that Has Felt the Love of God and Longs for Others to Know It': Conventions of Gender, Tensions of Self and Constructions of Difference in Offering to Be a Lady Missionary," *Women's History Review* 7, no. 2 (1998): 171–92.

Harper, Susan Billington. *In the Shadow of the Mahatma: Bishop V. S. Azariah and the Travails of Christianity in British India.* Grand Rapids, Mich.: Eerdmans, 2000.

Harrison, Mark. *Public Health in British India: Anglo-Indian Preventive Medicine 1859–1914.* Cambridge History of Medicine. Cambridge: Cambridge University Press, 1994.

Hendrickson, Kenneth E. *Making Saints: Religion and the Public Image of the British Army, 1809–1885.* Madison, N.J.: Bucknell University Press, 1998.

Hewat, Elizabeth G. K. *Vision and Achievement 1796–1956: A History of the Foreign Missions of the Churches United in the Church of Scotland.* Edinburgh: Thomas Nelson & Sons, 1960.

Horton, Robin. "African Conversion." *Africa* 41 (1971): 85–108.

Hunter, Jane. *The Gospel of Gentility: American Women Missionaries in Turn-of-the-Century China.* New Haven: Yale University Press, 1984.

Hutchins, Francis G. *The Illusion of Permanence: British Imperialism in India.* Princeton: Princeton University Press, 1967.

Hutchison, William R. *Errand to the World: American Protestant Thought and Foreign Missions.* Chicago: University of Chicago, 1987.

"India's Top Ten Colleges." *India Today* 25, no. 25 (19 June 2000).

Jackson, Eleanor M. *Red Tape and the Gospel: A Study of the Significance of the Ecumenical Missionary Struggle of William Paton, 1886–1943.* Birmingham: Phlogiston, in association with the Selly Oak Colleges, 1980.

Jones, Kenneth W. *Arya Dharm: Hindu Consciousness in 19th-Century Punjab.* Berkeley: University of California Press, 1976.

———. "Religious Identity and the Indian Census." In *The Census in British India: New Perspectives,* edited by Gerald N. Barrier, 73–101. New Delhi: Manohar, 1981.

———. *Socio-Religious Reform Movements in British India.* The New Cambridge History of India. I III. Cambridge, Eng.; New York: Cambridge University Press, 1989.

Judd, Denis. *Empire: The British Imperial Experience from 1765 to the Present.* London: HarperCollins, 1996.

Juergensmeyer, Mark. *Religion as Social Vision: The Movement against Untouchability in 20th-Century Punjab.* Berkeley: University of California Press, 1982.

Khare, R. S. (Ravindra S.). *The Untouchable as Himself: Ideology, Identity, and Pragmatism among the Lucknow Chamars.* Cambridge Studies in Cultural Systems, no. 8. Cambridge, Eng.; New York: Cambridge University Press, 1984.

Khiyalie, Vinod K. *Hundred Years of Baring's Mission to Batala: Christian Education and Social Change in a Punjabi Countryside.* Delhi: I.S.P.C.K., 1980.

Kopf, David. *British Orientalism and the Bengal Renaissance: The Dynamics of Indian Modernization, 1773–1835.* Berkeley: University of California Press, 1969.

Kuriakose, M. K., ed. *History of Christianity in India: Source Materials.* Madras: Christian Literature Society, 1982.

Labode, Modupe. "From Heathen Kraal to Christian Home: Anglican Mission Education and African Christian Girls, 1850–1900." In *Women and Missions: Past and Present: Anthropological and Historical Perceptions,* edited by Fiona Bowie, Deborah Kirkwood, and Shirley Ardener, 126–44. Providence and Oxford: Berg, 1993.

Lal, Maneesha. "The Politics of Gender and Medicine in Colonial India: The Countess of Dufferin's Fund, 1885–1888." *Bulletin of the History of Medicine* 68, no. 1 (spring 1994): 29–66.

Lal, Vinay. "The Incident of the 'Crawling Lane': Women in the Punjab Disturbances of 1919." *Genders* 16 (spring 1993): 35–60.

Latourette, Kenneth Scott. *Christianity in a Revolutionary Age.* New York: Harper, 1957–61.

———. *A History of the Expansion of Christianity.* New York: Harper, 1937–45.

Lelyveld, David. *Aligarh's First Generation: Muslim Solidarity in British India.* Princeton: Princeton University Press, 1978.

Loehlin, C. H. *The Sikhs and Their Scriptures.* Lucknow: Lucknow Publishing House, 1958.

Louis, William Roger, gen. ed. *The Oxford History of the British Empire,* vols. I–V. Oxford: Oxford University Press, 1998–99.

Macaulay, Thomas Babington. *Macaulay, Prose and Poetry, Selected by G. M. Young.* Cambridge: Harvard University Press, 1967.

MacKenzie, John M. *Orientalism: History, Theory, and the Arts.* Manchester; New York: Manchester University Press; New York: St. Martin's Press, 1995.

Mangalwadi, Vishal. *Missionary Conspiracy: Letters to a Postmodern Hindu.* 2d ed. Mussoorie, India: Nivedit Good Books Distributors, 1996.

Maskiell, Michelle. *Women between Cultures: The Lives of Kinnaird College Alumnae in British India.* Foreign and Comparative Studies. South Asian Series, no. 9. Syracuse, N.Y.: Maxwell School of Citizenship and Public Affairs, Syracuse University, 1984.

Massey, James. *Dalits in India: Religion as a Source of Bondage or Liberation with Special Reference to Christians.* New Delhi: Manohar Publishers & Distributors and I.S.P.C.K., 1995.

Maw, Martin. *Visions of India: Fulfillment Theology, the Aryan Race Theory, and the Work of British Protestant Missionaries in Victorian India.* Studies in the Intercultural History of Christianity. Frankfurt am Main: Peter Lang, 1990.

McClintock, Anne. *Imperial Leather: Race, Gender, and Sexuality in the Colonial Conquest.* New York: Routledge, 1995.

McGregor, R. S. *Outline of Hindi Grammar.* 2d ed. 1972. Oxford: Clarendon Press, 1986.

McLane, John R. *Indian Nationalism and the Early Congress.* Princeton: Princeton University Press, 1977.

Melman, Billie. *Women's Orients: English Women and the Middle East, 1718–1918: Sexuality, Religion and Work.* 2d ed. Basingstoke: Macmillan, 1995.

Millgate, Michael. *Thomas Hardy: A Biography.* New York: Random House, 1982.

Millington, C. M. *"Whether We Be Many or Few": A History of the Cambridge/Delhi Brotherhood.* Bangalore: Asian Trading Corporation, 1999.

Minault, Gail. *Secluded Scholars: Women's Education and Muslim Social Reform in Colonial India.* New Delhi: Oxford University Press, 1998.

Mukerji, Anath Bandhu. *The Chamars of Uttar Pradesh: A Study in Social Geography.* Delhi: Inter-India Publications, 1980.

Nair, Janaki. "Uncovering the Zenana: Visions of Indian Womanhood in Englishwomen's Writings, 1813–1940." *Journal of Women's History* 2, no. 1 (spring 1990): 8–34.

Namier, Sir Lewis. *The Structure of Politics at the Accession of George III.* 2d ed. 1929. London: Macmillan, 1952.

Neill, Stephen. *Christian Missions: The Pelican History of the Church,* vol. 6. Harmondsworth: Penguin Books, 1964.

———. *A History of Christianity in India, 1707–1858.* Cambridge: Cambridge University Press, 1985.

O'Connor, Daniel. *Gospel, Raj and Swaraj: The Missionary Years of C. F. Andrews 1904–14.* Studies in the Intercultural History of Christianity, vol. 62. Frankfurt/M.; Bern; New York; Paris: Peter Lang, 1990.

Peel, J. "The Colonization of Consciousness." *Journal of African History* 33, no. 2 (1992).

Pettifer, Julian, and Richard Bradley. *Missionaries.* London: BBC Books, 1990.

Piggin, F. Stuart. *Making Evangelical Missionaries, 1789–1858: The Social Background, Motives and Training of British Protestant Missionaries to India.* Evangelicals & Society from 1750, no. 2. Abingdon, Oxfordshire: Sutton Courtney Press, 1984.

Pollock, J. C. *Shadows Fall Apart: The Story of the Zenana Bible and Medical Mission.* London: Hodder and Stoughton, 1958.

Porter, Andrew. "Cambridge, Keswick, and Late Nineteenth-Century Attitudes to Africa." *Journal of Imperial and Commonwealth History* 5, no. 1 (1976): 5–34.

———. "'Commerce and Christianity': The Rise and Fall of a Nineteenth-Century Missionary Slogan." *Historical Journal* 28 (1985): 597–621.

———. "Evangelical Enthusiasm, Missionary Motivation and West Africa in the Late Nineteenth Century: The Career of G. W. Brooke." *Journal of Imperial and Commonwealth History* 6 (1977): 23–46.

———. "The Hausa Association: Sir George Goldie, the Bishop of Dover and the Niger in the 1890s." *Journal of Imperial and Commonwealth History* 7 (1979): 149–79.

———. "Late Nineteenth Century Anglican Missionary Expansion: A Consideration of Some Non-Anglican Sources." In *Studies in Church History*, edited by Keith Baker. Oxford: Blackwell, 1978.

———. "Religion and Empire: British Expansion in the Long Nineteenth Century, 1780–1914." *Journal of Imperial and Commonwealth History* 20, no. 3 (1992): 370–90.

———. "Religion, Missionary Enthusiasm, and Empire." In *The Nineteenth Century*, vol. III of *The Oxford History of the British Empire*, edited by Andrew Porter, Wm. Roger Louis, gen. ed., 222–46. Oxford: Oxford University Press, 1999.

Porter, Andrew, ed. *Atlas of British Overseas Expansion*. London: Routledge, 1991.

Porter, Bernard. *The Lion's Share: A Short History of British Imperialism, 1850–1995*. 3d ed. New York: Longman, 1996.

Powell, Avril A. *Muslims and Missionaries in Pre-Mutiny India*. London Studies on South Asia, no. 7. Richmond, UK: Curzon Press, 1993.

———. "Processes of Conversion to Christianity in Nineteenth Century North-western India." In *Religious Conversion Movements in South Asia: Continuities and Change, 1800–1900*, edited by Geoffrey A. Oddie, 24–31. Richmond, UK: Curzon, 1997.

Prakash, Gyan. "After Colonialism." In *After Colonialism: Imperial Histories and Postcolonial Displacements*, edited by Gyan Prakash. Princeton Studies in Culture/Power/History, 3–17. Princeton: Princeton University Press, 1995.

Pratt, Mary Louise. *Imperial Eyes: Travel Writing and Transculturation*. London; New York: Routledge, 1992.

Rai, Amrit. *A House Divided: The Origin and Development of Hindi*. Delhi; New York: Oxford University Press, 1984.

Ramusack, Barbara. "Cultural Missionaries, Maternal Imperialists, Feminist Allies: British Women Activists in India, 1865–1945." *Women's Studies International Forum* 13, no. 4 (1990): 309–21.

Ravindiran, V. "Discourses of Empowerment: Missionary Orientalism in the Development of Dravidian Nationalism." In *Nation Work: Asian Elites and National Identities*, edited by Timothy Brook and Andre Schmid. Ann Arbor: University of Michigan, 1999.

Riddle, T. E. *The Vision and the Call: A Life of Sadhu Sundar Singh*. Delhi: Indian Society for Promoting Christian Knowledge, 1987.

Robert, Dana Lee. *American Women in Mission: A Social History of Their Thought and Practice*. The Modern Mission Era, 1792–1992. Macon, Ga.: Mercer University Press, 1996.

Roseveare, Ruth. *Delhi: Community of St. Stephen,1886–1986.* Reepham, Norwich: Privately published, 1986.

Roy, Parama. *Indian Traffic: Identities in Question in Colonial and Post-colonial India.* Berkeley: University of California Press, 1998.

Said, Edward. "Between Worlds." *London Review of Books* 20, no. 9 (7 May 1998): 3–7.

———. *Culture and Imperialism.* New York: Vintage Books, 1993.

———. *Orientalism.* New York: Pantheon Books, 1978.

Sanneh, Lamin O. *Encountering the West: Christianity and the Global Cultural Process: The African Dimension.* World Christian Theology Series. Maryknoll, N.Y.: Orbis Books, 1993.

Sen, S. P., ed. *Dictionary of National Biography.* 4 vols. Calcutta: Institute of Historical Studies, 1973.

Sharma, Asha. *An American in Khadi: The Definitive Biography of Satyanand Stokes.* New Delhi: Penguin Books, 1999.

Sharpe, Eric J. *Not to Destroy but to Fulfil: The Contribution of J. N. Farquhar to Protestant Missionary Thought in India before 1914.* Lund, Sweden: Gleerup, 1965.

Shenk, Wilbert R. *Henry Venn, Missionary Statesman.* American Society of Missiology Series, no. 6. Maryknoll, N.Y.: Orbis Books, 1983.

———. "Rufus Anderson and Henry Venn: A Special Relationship." *International Bulletin of Missionary Research,* Oct. 1981, 168–72.

Shourie, Arun. *Missionaries in India: Continuities, Changes, Dilemmas.* New Delhi: ASA Publications, 1994.

Sidhwa, Bapsi. *Ice-Candy Man.* 1988. London: Penguin, 1989.

Singh, Khushwant. *Train to Pakistan.* 1956. Delhi: Ravi Dayal, 1988.

Sinha, Mrinalini. *Colonial Masculinity: The 'Manly Englishman' and the 'Effeminate Bengali' in the Late Nineteenth Century.* Studies in Imperialism. Manchester; New York: Manchester University Press; New York: St. Martin's Press, 1995.

Smith, Mark (Mark A.). *Religion in Industrial Society: Oldham and Saddleworth, 1740–1865.* Oxford Historical Monographs. Oxford: Clarendon Press; New York: Oxford University Press, 1994.

Smith, Solveig. *By Love Compelled: The Salvation Army's One Hundred Years in India and Adjacent Lands.* London: Salvation Army, 1981.

Spence, Clark C. *The Salvation Army Farm Colonies.* Tucson: University of Arizona, 1985.

Stanley, Brian. *The Bible and the Flag: Protestant Missions and British Imperialism in the Nineteenth and Twentieth Centuries.* Leicester, Eng.: Apollos, 1990.

———. *The History of the Baptist Missionary Society, 1792–1992.* Edinburgh: T. & T. Clark, 1992.

Stegner, Wallace Earle. *Angle of Repose.* 1971. Penguin, 1992.

Stock, Frederick and Margaret. *People Movements in the Punjab, with Special Reference to the United Presbyterian Church.* South Pasadena, Calif.: William Carey Library, 1975.

Stoler, Laura Ann. *Race and the Education of Desire: Foucault's History of Sexuality and the Colonial Order of Things.* Durham, N.C.: Duke University Press, 1995.

Streefland, Pieter. *The Sweepers of Slaughterhouse: Conflict and Survival in a Karachi Neighbourhood.* Assen: Van Gorcum, 1979.

Studdert-Kennedy, Gerald. *British Christians, Indian Nationalists and the Raj.* Delhi: Oxford University Press, 1991.

———. *Providence and the Raj: Imperial Mission and Missionary Imperialism.* New Delhi: Sage Publications, 1998.

Subaltern Studies. Delhi; New York: Oxford University Press, 1982.

Suleri, Sara. *Meatless Days.* Chicago: University of Chicago Press, 1989.

———. *The Rhetoric of English India.* Chicago: University of Chicago Press, 1992.

Tabili, Laura. *"We Are for British Justice": Workers and Racial Difference in Late Imperial Britain.* Ithaca: Cornell University Press, 1994.

Thomas, George. *Christians Indians and Indian Nationalism 1885–1950.* Frankfurt: Peter D. Lang, 1979.

Thompson, E. P. (Edward Palmer). *"Alien Homage": Edward Thompson and Rabindranath Tagore.* Delhi; New York: Oxford University Press, 1993.

Thompson, Henry Paget. *Into All Lands: The History of the Society for the Propagation of the Gospel in Foreign Parts 1701–1850.* London: SPCK, 1951.

Thorne, Susan. *Congregational Missions and the Making of an Imperial Culture in Nineteenth-Century England.* Stanford, Calif.: Stanford University Press, 1999.

Tinker, Hugh. "Between Old Delhi and New Delhi: C. F. Andrews and St. Stephen's in an Era of Transition." In *Delhi through the Ages: Essays in Urban History, Culture, and Society,* edited by R. E. Frykenberg, 351–90. Delhi; New York: Oxford University Press, 1986.

Tolan, Rachel J. "Colonizing and Transforming the Criminal Tribesman: The Salvation Army in British India." *American Ethnologist* 18 (Feb. 1991): 106–25.

Trautmann, Thomas R. *Aryans and British India.* Berkeley: University of California Press, 1997.

Turner, Frank M. *Contesting Cultural Authority: Essays in Victorian Intellectual Life.* Cambridge: Cambridge University Press, 1993.

Viswanathan, Gauri. "Coping with (Civil) Death: The Christian Convert's Rights of Passage in Colonial India." In *After Colonialism: Imperial Histories and Postcolonial Displacements,* edited by Gyan Prakash. Princeton Studies in Culture/Power/History, 183–210. Princeton: Princeton University Press, 1995.

———. *Masks of Conquest: Literary Study and British Rule in India.* The Social Foundations of Aesthetic Forms Series. New York: Columbia University Press, 1989.

———. *Outside the Fold: Conversion, Modernity, and Belief*. Princeton: Princeton University Press, 1998.

Walls, Andrew F. *The Missionary Movement in Christian History: Studies in the Transmission of Faith*. Edinburgh: T. & T. Clark, 1996.

Ward, Andrew. *Our Bones Are Scattered: The Cawnpore Massacres and the Indian Mutiny of 1857*. New York: Henry Holt and Co., 1996.

Washbrook, D. A. "India, 1818–1860: The Two Faces of Colonialism." In *The Nineteenth Century*. In *The Oxford History of the British Empire*, edited by Andrew Porter, Roger Louis, gen. ed., 395–421. New York: Oxford University Press, 1999.

Webster, John C. B. *The Christian Community and Change in Nineteenth Century North India*. Delhi: Macmillan of India, 1976.

———. *The Dalit Christians: A History*. Delhi: I.S.P.C.K., 1992.

———. "Presbyterian Missionaries and Gandhian Politics, 1919–1922." *Journal of Presbyterian History* 62, no. 3 (fall 1984): 246–57.

Williams, C. Peter. "British Religion and the Wider World: Mission and Empire, 1800–1940." In *A History of Religion in Britain: Practice and Belief from Pre-Roman Times to the Present*, edited by Sheridan Gilley and W. J. Sheils, 381–405. Oxford: Blackwell, 1994.

———. *The Ideal of the Self-Governing Church: A Study in Victorian Missionary Strategy*. Studies in Christian Mission, vol. 1. Leiden; New York: E. J. Brill, 1990.

———. "'Not Quite Gentlemen': An Examination of 'Middling Class' Protestant Missionaries from Britain, 1850–1900." *Journal of Ecclesiastical History* 31, no. 3 (July 1980).

Wiser, Charlotte Melina (Viall). *Behind Mud Walls, 1930–1960, by William H. Wiser and Charlotte Viall Wiser*. Foreword by David G. Mandelbaum. Berkeley: University of California Press, 1971.

———. *Behind Mud Walls, by Charlotte Viall Wiser and William H. Wiser*. New York: Smith, 1930.

Wurgaft, Lewis D. *The Imperial Imagination: Magic and Myth in Kipling's India*. Middletown, Conn.: Wesleyan University Press, 1983.

Yang, Anand A., ed. *Crime and Criminality in British India*. Tucson: University of Arizona, 1985.

Yates, T. E. *Venn and Victorian Bishops Abroad: The Missionary Policies of Henry Venn and Their Repercussions upon the Anglican Episcopate of the Colonial Period, 1841–1872*. Uppsala, 1978.

Zelliot, Eleanor. *From Untouchable to Dalit: Essays on the Ambedkar Movement*. New Delhi: Manohar Publications, 1992.

F. THESES CITED

Braun, Freidrich. "The Contribution of the Catholic Church Towards the Future of the People of Pakistan." Thesis for a Diploma of Theology of the Theological Faculty of the University of Bamberg. Rev. Fr. Piet de Vreede, n.d. [trans. 1987].

Brush, Stanley Elwood. "Protestants in the Punjab: Religion and Social Change in an Indian Province in the Nineteenth Century." Ph.D. diss., University of California at Berkeley, 1964.

Maughan, Steven S. "Regions Beyond and the National Church: Domestic Support for the Foreign Missions of the Church of England in the High Imperial Age, 1870–1914." Ph.D. diss., Harvard University, 1995.

Piggin, Frederic Stuart. "The Social Background, Motivation, and Training of British Protestant Missionaries to India, 1789–1858." Ph.D. diss., London (King's), 1974.

Potter, Sarah Caroline. "The Social Organization and Recruitment of English Protestant Missionaries in the Nineteenth Century." Ph.D. diss., London (econ.), 1975.

Williams, Cecil Peter. "The Recruitment and Training of Overseas Missionaries in England between 1850 and 1900." M. Litt. thesis, Bristol, 1976.

Index

In this index an "f" after a number indicates a separate reference on the next page, and an "ff" indicates separate references on the next two pages. A continuous discussion over two or more pages is indicated by a span of page numbers, e.g., "57–59." *Passim* is used for a cluster of references in close but not consecutive sequence.